Statistical Quality Control for the Six Sigma Green Belt

Statistical Quality Control for the Six Sigma Green Belt

Bhisham C. Gupta
H. Fred Walker

ASQ Quality Press
Milwaukee, Wisconsin

American Society for Quality, Quality Press, Milwaukee 53203

Printed in the United States of America
12 11 10 09 08 07 06 5 4 3 2 1

Library of Congress Cataloging-in-Publication Data

Gupta, Bhisham C., 1942–
Statistical quality control for the Six sigma green belt / Bhisham C. Gupta and H. Fred Walker.
p. cm.
Includes index.
ISBN 978-0-87389-686-3 (hard cover : alk. paper)
1. Six sigma (Quality control standard) 2. Quality control—Statistical methods. I. Walker, H. Fred, 1963– II. Title.

TS156.G8674 2007
658.5′62—dc22

2007000315

Publisher: William A. Tony
Acquisitions Editor: Matt Meinholz
Project Editor: Paul O'Mara
Production Administrator: Randall Benson

ASQ
AMERICAN SOCIETY FOR QUALITY™

Quality Press
600 N. Plankinton Avenue
Milwaukee, Wisconsin 53203
Call toll free 800-248-1946
Fax 414-272-1734
www.asq.org
http://www.asq.org/quality-press
http://standardsgroup.asq.org
E-mail: authors@asq.org

Printed on acid-free paper

In loving memory of my parents, Roshan Lal and Sodhan Devi.
—Bhisham

In loving memory of my father, Carl Ellsworth Walker.
—Fred

Contents

List of Figures . . . . *xiii*
List of Tables . . . . *xix*
Preface . . . . *xxi*
Acknowledgments . . . . *xxiii*

Chapter 1 Introduction to Statistical Quality Control **1**
1.1 Identifying the Tools of SQC 2
1.2 Relating SQC to Applied Statistics and to DOE 3
1.3 Understanding the Role of Statistics in SQC 4
1.4 Making Decisions Based on Quantitative Data 5
1.5 Practical versus Theoretical or Statistical Significance 5
1.6 Why We Cannot Measure Everything 7
1.7 A Word on the Risks Associated with Making Bad Decisions 7

Chapter 2 Elements of a Sample Survey **11**
2.1 Basic Concepts of Sampling 11
Sampling Designs 14
2.2 Simple Random Sampling 15
2.2.1 Estimation of a Population Mean and Population Total 16
2.2.2 Confidence Interval for a Population Mean and Population Total 20
2.2.3 Determination of Sample Size 20
2.3 Stratified Random Sampling 21
2.3.1 Estimation of a Population Mean and Population Total 22
2.3.2 Confidence Interval for a Population Mean and Population Total 24
2.3.3 Determination of Sample Size 26
2.4 Systematic Random Sampling 27
2.4.1 Estimation of a Population Mean and Population Total 28

2.4.2 Confidence Interval for a Population Mean and Population Total 30
2.4.3 Determination of Sample Size 30
2.5 Cluster Random Sampling 32
2.5.1 Estimation of a Population Mean and Population Total 33
2.5.2 Confidence Interval for a Population Mean and Population Total 34
2.5.3 Determination of Sample Size 37

Chapter 3 Phase I (Detecting Large Shifts)—SPC: Control Charts for Variables 39
3.1 Basic Definition of Quality and Its Benefits 40
3.2 SPC 41
Check Sheet 43
Pareto Chart 45
Cause-and-Effect (Fishbone or Ishikawa) Diagram 47
Defect Concentration Diagram 48
Run Chart 50
3.3 Control Charts for Variables 51
Process Evaluation 51
Action on Process 51
Action on Output 51
Variation 52
Common Causes or Random Causes 52
Special Causes or Assignable Causes 52
Local Actions and Actions on the System 53
Preparation for Use of Control Charts 55
Benefits of Control Charts 56
Rational Samples for a Control Chart 57
ARL 57
OC Curve 59
3.3.1 Shewhart $\bar{X}$ and R Control Charts 60
3.3.2 Shewhart $\bar{X}$ and R Control Charts When Process Mean μ and Process Standard Deviation σ Are Known 68
3.3.3 Shewhart Control Chart for Individual Observations 69
3.3.4 Shewhart $\bar{X}$ and S Control Charts 72
3.4 Process Capability 79

Chapter 4 Phase I (Detecting Large Shifts)—SPC: Control Charts for Attributes 83
4.1 Control Charts for Attributes 83
4.2 The p Chart: Control Chart for Fraction of Nonconforming Units 85
Control Limits for the p Chart 85

4.2.1 The p Chart: Control Chart for Fraction Nonconforming with Variable Samples 89
4.3 The np Chart: Control Chart for Number of Nonconforming Units 92
Control Limits for the np Control Chart 92
4.4 The c Chart (Nonconformities versus Nonconforming Units) 93
4.5 The u Chart 96

Chapter 5 Phase II (Detecting Small Shifts)—SPC: Cumulative Sum, Moving Average, and Exponentially Weighted Moving Average Control Charts 101
5.1 Basic Concepts of the CUSUM Control Chart 102
CUSUM Control Chart versus Shewhart $\bar{X}$-R Control Chart 102
5.2 Designing a CUSUM Control Chart 104
5.2.1 Two-Sided CUSUM Control Chart Using Numerical Procedure 106
5.2.2 The Fast Initial Response Feature for the CUSUM Control Chart 112
5.2.3 Combined Shewhart-CUSUM Control Chart 115
5.2.4 CUSUM Control Chart for Controlling Process Variability 116
5.3 The MA Control Chart 117
5.4 The EWMA Control Chart 120

Chapter 6 Process Capability Indices 127
6.1 Development of Process Capability Indices 127
6.2 PCI C_p 130
6.3 PCI C_{pk} 135
6.4 PCI C_{pm} 136
6.5 PCI C_{pmk} 138
6.6 PCI C_{pnst} 139
Examples Comparing C_{pnst} with PCIs C_{pk} and C_{pm} 141
6.6.1 Certain Features of the Capability Index C_{pnst} 142
6.7 PCIs P_p and P_{pk} 144

Chapter 7 Measurement Systems Analysis 147
7.1 Using SQC to Understand Variability 148
Variability in the Production or Service Delivery Process 148
Variability in the Measurement Process 148
7.2 Evaluating Measurement System Performance 149
7.2.1 MSA Based on Range 150
7.2.2 MSA Based on ANOVA 156
7.3 MCIs 162
MCI as a Percentage of Process Variation (MCI_{pv}) 162
MCI as a Percentage of Process Specification (MCI_{ps}) 163

Chapter 8 PRE-control **165**
8.1 PRE-control Background. 165
8.1.1 What Are We Trying to Accomplish with PRE-control?. 166
8.1.2 The Conditions Necessary for PRE-control to Be Valid. 166
8.2 Global Perspective on the Use of PRE-control (Understanding the Color-Coding Scheme) 167
8.3 The Mechanics of PRE-control 168
Step 1: Ensure the Process Is Sufficiently Capable 168
Step 2: Establish the PRE-control Zones 169
Step 3: Verify That the Process Is Ready to Begin PRE-control 169
Step 4: Begin Sampling 169
Step 5: Apply the PRE-control Rules.................... 169
8.4 The Statistical Basis for PRE-control 170
8.5 Advantages and Disadvantages of PRE-control 170
8.5.1 Advantages of PRE-control 171
8.5.2 Disadvantages of PRE-control 171
8.6 What Comes After PRE-control? 172

Chapter 9 Acceptance Sampling. **173**
9.1 The Intent of Acceptance Sampling 173
9.2 Sampling Inspection versus 100 Percent Inspection......... 174
9.3 Sampling Concepts 175
9.3.1 Lot-by-Lot versus Average Quality Protection...... 175
9.3.2 The OC Curve. 175
9.3.3 Plotting the OC Curve 176
9.3.4 Acceptance Sampling by Attributes 177
9.3.5 Acceptable Quality Limit...................... 178
9.3.6 Lot Tolerance Percent Defective................. 178
9.3.7 Producer's and Consumer's Risks 178
9.3.8 Average Outgoing Quality 178
9.3.9 Average Outgoing Quality Limit 179
9.3.10 Lot Size, Sample Size, and Acceptance Number 180
9.4 Types of Attribute Sampling Plans 182
9.4.1 Single Sampling Plans 182
9.4.2 Double Sampling Plans. 184
9.4.3 OC Curve for a Double Sampling Plan. 184
9.4.4 Multiple Sampling Plans. 186
9.4.5 AOQ and AOQL for Double and Multiple Plans 186
9.4.6 Average Sample Number 186
9.5 Sampling Standards and Plans. 188
9.5.1 ANSI/ASQ Z1.4-2003 188
9.5.2 Levels of Inspection 189
9.5.3 Types of Sampling 191
9.5.4 Dodge-Romig Tables 193

9.6 Variables Sampling Plans 193
9.6.1 ANSI/ASQ Z1.9-2003 194
9.7 Sequential Sampling Plans 199
9.8 Continuous Sampling Plans. 201
9.8.1 Types of Continuous Sampling Plans 201
9.9 Variables Plan When the Standard Deviation Is Known 203

Chapter 10 Computer Resources to Support SQC: MINITAB . . . 225
10.1 Using MINITAB—Version 14 225
Getting Started with MINITAB 226
Creating a New Worksheet 226
Saving a Data File 227
Retrieving a Saved MINITAB Data File 227
Saving a MINITAB Project 227
Print Options 228
10.2 The Shewhart Xbar-R Control Chart 228
10.3 The Shewhart Xbar-R Control Chart When Process Mean μ and Process Standard Deviation σ Are Known 230
10.4 The Shewhart Control Chart for Individual Observations . . . 230
10.5 The Shewhart Xbar-S Control Chart—Equal Sample Size 231
10.6 The Shewhart Xbar-S Control Chart—Sample Size Variable 233
10.7 Process Capability Analysis 235
10.8 The *p* Chart: Control Chart for Fraction Nonconforming Units 238
10.9 The *p* Chart: Control Chart for Fraction Nonconforming Units with Variable Sample Size 239
10.10 The *np* Chart: Control Chart for Nonconforming Units 239
10.11 The *c* Chart 240
10.12 The *u* Chart 241
10.13 The *u* Chart: Variable Sample Size 242
10.14 Designing a CUSUM Control Chart 243
10.15 The FIR Feature for a CUSUM Control Chart 245
10.16 The MA Control Chart 246
10.17 The EWMA Control Chart 247
10.18 Measurement System Capability Analysis 249
10.18.1 Measurement System Capability Analysis (Using Crossed Designs) 250

Chapter 11 Computer Resources to Support SQC: JMP 261
11.1 Using JMP—Version 6.0 261
Getting Started with JMP 263
Creating a New Data Table 264
Opening an Existing JMP File 265
Saving JMP Files 265
Print Options 266
Using JMP Images for Reporting 267

11.2 The Shewhart XBar and R Control Chart 268
11.3 The Shewhart XBar and S Control Chart—Equal Sample Size 270
11.4 The Shewhart XBar and S Control Chart—Sample Size Variable 272
11.5 The Shewhart Control Chart for Individual Observations 273
11.6 Process Capability Analysis.......................... 275
11.7 The *p* Chart: Control Chart for Fraction Nonconforming Units with Constant Sample Size...................... 277
11.8 The *p* Chart: Control Chart for Fraction Nonconforming Units with Sample Size Varying 281
11.9 The *np* Chart: Control Chart for Nonconforming Units 281
11.10 The *c* Chart.. 282
11.11 The *u* Chart with Constant Sample Size 284
11.12 The *u* Chart: Control Chart for Fraction Nonconforming Units with Sample Size Varying 286
11.13 The CUSUM Chart 286
11.14 The Uniformly Weighted Moving Average Chart 288
11.15 The EWMA Control Chart 290
11.16 Measurement System Capability Analysis 292
11.16.1 Measurement System Capability Analysis (Using Crossed Designs)................... 293

Appendix Statistical Factors and Tables 299

Bibliography *327*
Index *331*

List of Figures

Figure 1.1	The five tool types of SQC.	2
Figure 1.2	Relationship among applied statistics, SQC, and DOE.	3
Figure 1.3	Order of SQC topics in process or transactional Six Sigma.	4
Figure 1.4	Detecting statistical differences.	6
Figure 1.5	Detecting practical and statistical differences.	6
Figure 1.6	Sample versus population.	7
Figure 3.1	Flowchart of a process.	41
Figure 3.2	Pareto chart for data in Example 3.1.	45
Figure 3.3	Pareto chart when weighted frequencies are used.	47
Figure 3.4	An initial form of a cause and effect diagram.	48
Figure 3.5	A complete cause-and-effect diagram.	49
Figure 3.6	A rectangular prism-shaped product that has been damaged.	49
Figure 3.7	A run chart.	50
Figure 3.8	A control chart with a UCL and an LCL.	54
Figure 3.9	OC curves for the $\bar{x}$ chart with 3σ limits for different sample sizes n.	59
Figure 3.10	The $\bar{X}$ and R control charts, constructed using MINITAB, for the ball bearing data in Table 3.4.	65
Figure 3.11	The MR control chart, constructed using MINITAB, for the ball bearing data in Table 3.5.	71
Figure 3.12	The $\bar{X}$ and S control charts, constructed using MINITAB, for the ball bearing data in Table 3.4.	75
Figure 3.13	The $\bar{X}$ and S control charts for variable sample sizes, constructed using MINITAB, for the piston ring data in Table 3.6.	77
Figure 3.14	Three illustrations of the concept of process capability, where (a) shows a process that is stable but not capable, (b) shows a process that is stable and barely capable, and (c) shows a process that is stable and capable.	80
Figure 4.1	MINITAB printout of the p chart for nonconforming computer chips, using trial control limits from the data in Table 4.2.	89
Figure 4.2	MINITAB printout of the p chart for nonconforming chips with variable sample sizes, using trial control limits for the data in Table 4.3.	91

Figure 4.3	MINITAB printout of the *np* chart for nonconforming computer chips, using trial control limits for the data in Table 4.2.	93
Figure 4.4	The *c* control chart of nonconformities for the data in Table 4.4.	95
Figure 4.5	The *u* chart of nonconformities for the data in Table 4.5, constructed using MINITAB.	99
Figure 4.6	The *u* chart of nonconformities for the data in Table 4.6, constructed using MINITAB.	100
Figure 5.1	$\bar{X}$-R control chart for the data in Table 5.1.	105
Figure 5.2	CUSUM chart for the data in Table 5.1.	105
Figure 5.3	MINITAB printout of a two-sided CUSUM control chart for the data in Table 5.1.	109
Figure 5.4	MINITAB printout of the $\bar{X}$ control chart for individual values in Table 5.4.	111
Figure 5.5	MINITAB printout of the CUSUM control chart for individual values in Table 5.4.	111
Figure 5.6	MINITAB printout of the two-sided CUSUM control chart for the data in Table 5.5 using FIR.	113
Figure 5.7	MINITAB printout of the MA control chart for the data in Table 5.4.	120
Figure 5.8	MINITAB printout of the EWMA control chart for the data in Table 5.4.	125
Figure 6.1	Flowchart of a process.	128
Figure 7.1	Approximate sampling distribution of sample statistics $\bar{X}$ with sample size five.	148
Figure 7.2	Components of total variation..	149
Figure 7.3	The distinction between accurate and precise, where (a) is accurate and precise, (b) is accurate but not precise, (c) is not accurate but precise, and (d) is neither accurate nor precise..	151
Figure 7.4	The linear relationship between the actual and the observed values..	152
Figure 7.5	Percent contribution of variance components for the data in Example 7.1.	159
Figure 7.6	$\bar{X}$ and R charts for the data in Example 7.1..	160
Figure 7.7	Interaction between operators and parts for the data in Example 7.1.	161
Figure 7.8	Scatter plot for measurements versus operators.	161
Figure 7.9	Scatter plot for measurements versus parts (bolts).	162
Figure 8.1	Relationships among the SQC tools.	165
Figure 8.2	A barely capable process.	167
Figure 8.3	PRE-control zones.	168
Figure 8.4	A process with process capability equal to one...	170
Figure 9.1	An OC curve..	176
Figure 9.2	AOQ curve for $N = \infty$, $n = 50$, $c = 3$..	180
Figure 9.3	Effect on an OC curve of changing sample size (n) when acceptance number (c) is held constant.	181
Figure 9.4	Effect of changing acceptance number (c) when sample size (n) is held constant..	181
Figure 9.5	Effect of changing lot size (N) when acceptance number (c) and sample size (n) are held constant.	183

Figure 9.6	OC curves for sampling plans having the sample size equal to 10 percent of the lot size	183
Figure 9.7	OC curve for double sampling plan where $n_1 = 75$, $c_1 = 0$, $r_1 = 3$, $n_2 = 75$, $c_2 = 3$, and $r_2 = 4$.	185
Figure 9.8	AOQ curve for double sampling plan	186
Figure 9.9	ASN curve for double sampling plan	188
Figure 9.10	Switching rules for normal, tightened, and reduced inspection	190
Figure 9.11	Structure and organization of ANSI/ASQ Z1.9-2003	195
Figure 9.12	Decision areas for a sequential sampling plan	199
Figure 9.13	ANSI/ASQ Z1.4-2003 Table VIII: Limit numbers for reduced inspection	205
Figure 9.14	ANSI/ASQ Z1.4-2003 Table I: Sample size code letters	206
Figure 9.15	ANSI/ASQ Z1.4-2003 Table II-A: Single sampling plans for normal inspection	207
Figure 9.16	ANSI/ASQ Z1.4-2003 Table III-A: Double sampling plans for normal inspection	208
Figure 9.17	ANSI/ASQ Z1.4-2003 Table IV-A: Multiple sampling plans for normal inspection	209
Figure 9.18	4.20 ANSI/ASQ Z1.9-2003 Table A-2: Sample size code letters	211
Figure 9.19	ANSI/ASQ Z1.9-2003 Table C-1: Master table for normal and tightened inspection for plans based on variability unknown (single specification limit—Form 1)	212
Figure 9.20	ANSI/ASQ Z1.9-2003 Table B-5: Table for estimating the lot percent nonconforming using standard deviation method	213
Figure 9.21	ANSI/ASQ Z1.9-2003 Table B-3: Master table for normal and tightened inspection for plans based on variability unknown (double specification limit and Form 2—single specification limit)	222
Figure 10.1	The welcome screen in MINITAB	226
Figure 10.2	Showing the menu command options	227
Figure 10.3	MINITAB window showing the Xbar-R Chart dialog box	229
Figure 10.4	MINITAB window showing the Xbar-R Chart - Options dialog box	230
Figure 10.5	MINITAB window showing the Individuals-Moving Range Chart dialog box	231
Figure 10.6	MINITAB window showing the Xbar-S Chart dialog box	232
Figure 10.7	MINITAB windows showing the Xbar-S Chart and Xbar-S Chart - Options dialog boxes	234
Figure 10.8	MINITAB window showing the Capability Analysis (Normal Distribution) dialog box	237
Figure 10.9	MINITAB windows showing the process capability analysis	237
Figure 10.10	MINITAB window showing the P Chart dialog box	238
Figure 10.11	MINITAB window showing the C Chart dialog box	241
Figure 10.12	MINITAB window showing the U Chart dialog box	242
Figure 10.13	MINITAB window showing the CUSUM Chart dialog box	244

Figure 10.14 MINITAB window showing the CUSUM Chart - Options dialog box. 245
Figure 10.15 MINITAB window showing the Moving Average Chart dialog box. 246
Figure 10.16 MINITAB window showing the EWMA Chart dialog box. 248
Figure 10.17 Screen showing the selections Stat > Quality Tools > Gage Study > Gage R&R Study (Crossed). 252
Figure 10.18 Gage R&R Study (Crossed) dialog box. 252
Figure 10.19 Gage R&R Study (Crossed) - Options dialog box. 253
Figure 10.20 Percent contribution of variance components for the data in Example 10.12. 257
Figure 10.21 $\bar{X}$ and R charts for the data in Example 10.12.. 258
Figure 10.22 Interaction between operators and parts for the data in Example 10.12. 258
Figure 10.23 Scatter plot for measurements versus operators. 259
Figure 10.24 Scatter plot for measurements versus parts (bolts). 259
Figure 11.1 JMP Starter display. 262
Figure 11.2 JMP drop-down menus. 262
Figure 11.3 JMP file processing commands. 263
Figure 11.4 JMP statistical analysis commands.. 264
Figure 11.5 Creating a new data table. 264
Figure 11.6 A new data table. 265
Figure 11.7 Opening an existing JMP file. 266
Figure 11.8 Saving a newly created JMP file.. 266
Figure 11.9 Saving an existing JMP file. 267
Figure 11.10 Printing JMP output. 267
Figure 11.11 Generating an XBar and R chart.. 268
Figure 11.12 XBar chart dialog box.. 269
Figure 11.13 Generating an XBar and S chart. 271
Figure 11.14 XBar chart dialog box.. 271
Figure 11.15 XBar and S chart dialog box.. 273
Figure 11.16 Generating a control chart for individual observations.. 274
Figure 11.17 IR chart dialog box. 275
Figure 11.18 Capability analysis based on an XBar and S chart for Example 11.5. 277
Figure 11.19 Process capability analysis dialog box. 278
Figure 11.20 Process capability analysis output. 279
Figure 11.21 Generating a *p* chart. 280
Figure 11.22 *p* chart dialog box. 280
Figure 11.23 Generating a *c* chart. 282
Figure 11.24 *c* chart dialog box. 283
Figure 11.25 Generating a *u* chart. 284
Figure 11.26 *u* chart dialog box. 285
Figure 11.27 Generating a CUSUM chart. 287
Figure 11.28 CUSUM chart dialog box. 287
Figure 11.29 Specify Stats dialog box. 288
Figure 11.30 Generating a UWMA chart.. 289
Figure 11.31 UWMA chart dialog box. 290
Figure 11.32 Generating an EWMA chart. 291
Figure 11.33 EWMA chart dialog box.. 292
Figure 11.34 Initiating a Gage R&R. 295
Figure 11.35 Gage R&R dialog box. 295

Figure 11.36 Completed Gage R&R dialog box. 296
Figure 11.37 Y, Response variability charts. 296
Figure 11.38 Continuing the Gage R&R. 297
Figure 11.39 Variance components. 297
Figure 11.40 Gage R&R dialog box. 297
Figure 11.41 Gage R&R output. 298

List of Tables

Table 3.1	Check sheet summarizing the data of a study over a period of four weeks.	44
Table 3.2	Frequencies and weighted frequencies when different types of defects are not equally important.	46
Table 3.3	Percentage of nonconforming units in different shifts over a period of 30 shifts.	50
Table 3.4	Diameter measurements (in mm) of ball bearings used in the wheels of heavy construction equipment.	63
Table 3.5	Diameter measurements (in mm) of ball bearings used in the wheels of heavy construction equipment.	70
Table 3.6	The finished inside diameter measurements (in cm) of piston ring.	78
Table 4.1	The four control charts for attributes.	85
Table 4.2	Number of nonconforming computer chips out of 1000 inspected each day during the study period.	88
Table 4.3	Number of nonconforming computer chips with different size samples inspected each day during the study period.	91
Table 4.4	Total number of nonconformities in samples of five rolls of paper.	95
Table 4.5	Number of nonconformities on printed boards for laptops per sample, each sample consisting of five inspection units.	98
Table 4.6	Number of nonconformities on printed boards for laptops per sample with varying sample size.	99
Table 5.1	Data from a manufacturing process of auto parts before and after its mean experienced a shift of 1σ (sample size four).	103
Table 5.2	Values of h for a given value of k when $ARL_0 = 370$.	107
Table 5.3	Tabular CUSUM control chart for the data given in Table 5.1.	108
Table 5.4	Data from a manufacturing process of auto parts before and after its mean experienced a shift of 1σ (sample size one).	110
Table 5.5	Tabular CUSUM control chart using FIR for data in Table 5.4.	113
Table 5.6	Tabular CUSUM control chart using FIR for the process in Table 5.4, after it had experienced an upward shift of 1σ.	114

Table 5.7	MA chart (M_i's) for data in Table 5.4 with $\mu = 20$, $\sigma = 2$.	119
Table 5.8	A selection of EWMA charts with $ARL_0 \cong 500$.	123
Table 5.9	EWMA control chart (z_i's) for data in Table 5.4 with $\lambda = 0.20$, $L = 2.962$.	124
Table 6.1	Different processes with the same value of C_{pk}.	135
Table 6.2	Parts per million of nonconforming units for different values of C_{pk}.	136
Table 6.3	The values of C_{pk} and C_{pm} as μ deviates from the target.	137
Table 6.4	Values of C_p, C_{pk}, C_{pm}, C_{pmk}, and C_{pnst} for $\mu = 20, 22, 24, 26, 28$; $T = 24$; LSL = 12; and USL = 36 ($\sigma = 2$)..	143
Table 6.5	Values of C_p, C_{pk}, C_{pm}, C_{pmk}, and C_{pnst} for $\sigma = 2, 2.5, 3.0, 3.5, 4.0, 4.5$; $T = 24$, LSL = 12, and USL = 36 ($\mu = 20$).	144
Table 7.1	Data on an experiment involving three operators, 10 bolts, and three measurements (in millimeters) on each bolt by each operator..	154
Table 8.1	PRE-control rules.	169
Table 10.1	Data of 25 samples, each of size five, from a given process.	236
Table 10.2	Data on an experiment involving three operators, 10 bolts, and three measurements (in mm) on each bolt by each operator..	251
Table 11.1	Data of 25 samples, each of size five, from a given process.	276
Table 11.2	Data on an experiment involving three operators, 10 bolts, and three measurements (in mm) on each bolt by each operator..	294
Table A.1	Random numbers.	300
Table A.2	Factors helpful in constructing control charts for variables.	302
Table A.3	Values of K_1 for computing repeatability using the range method.	303
Table A.4	Values of K_2 for computing reproducibility using the range method.	304
Table A.5	Binomial probabilities.	304
Table A.6	Poisson probabilities..	309
Table A.7	Standard normal distribution.	313
Table A.8	Critical values of χ^2 with ν degrees of freedom.	314
Table A.9	Critical values of t with ν degrees of freedom.	316
Table A.10	Critical values of F with numerator and denominator degrees of freedom ν_1,ν_2, respectively ($\alpha = 0.10$)..	318

Preface

Statistical Quality Control for the Six Sigma Green Belt was written as a desk reference and instructional aid for those individuals currently involved with, or preparing for involvement with, Six Sigma project teams. As Six Sigma team members, Green Belts help select, collect data for, and assist with the interpretation of a variety of statistical or quantitative tools within the context of the Six Sigma methodology.

Composed of steps or phases titled Define, Measure, Analyze, Improve, and Control (DMAIC), the Six Sigma methodology calls for the use of many more statistical tools than is reasonable to address in one book. Accordingly, the intent of this book is to provide for Green Belts and Six Sigma team members a thorough discussion of the statistical quality control tools addressing both the underlying statistical concepts and the application. More advanced topics of a statistical or quantitative nature will be discussed in two additional books that, together with the first book in this series, *Applied Statistics for the Six Sigma Green Belt*, and this book, will comprise a four-book series.

While it is beyond the scope of this book and series to cover the DMAIC methodology specifically, this book and series focus on concepts, applications, and interpretations of the statistical tools used during, and as part of, the DMAIC methodology. Of particular interest in the books in this series is an applied approach to the topics covered while providing a detailed discussion of the underlying concepts.

In fact, one very controversial aspect of Six Sigma training is that, in many cases, this training is targeted at the Six Sigma Black Belt and is all too commonly delivered to large groups of people with the assumption that all trainees have a fluent command of the statistically based tools and techniques. In practice this commonly leads to a good deal of concern and discomfort on behalf of trainees, as it quickly becomes difficult to keep up with and successfully complete Black Belt–level training without the benefit of truly understanding these tools and techniques.

So let us take a look together at *Statistical Quality Control for the Six Sigma Green Belt*. What you will learn is that these statistically based tools and techniques aren't mysterious, they aren't scary, and they aren't overly difficult to understand. As in learning any topic, once you learn the basics, it is easy to build on that knowledge—trying to start without a knowledge of the basics, however, is generally the beginning of a difficult situation.

Acknowledgments

We would like to thank Professors John Brunette, Cheng Peng, Merle Guay, and Peggy Moore of the University of Southern Maine for reading the final draft line by line. Their comments and suggestions have proven to be invaluable. We also thank Laurie McDermott, administrative associate of the Department of Mathematics and Statistics of the University of Southern Maine, for help in typing the various drafts of the manuscript. In addition, we are grateful to the several anonymous reviewers, whose constructive suggestions greatly improved the presentations, and to our students, whose input was invaluable. We also want to thank Matt Meinholz and Paul O'Mara of ASQ Quality Press for their patience and cooperation throughout the preparation of this project.

We acknowledge MINITAB for permitting us to reprint screen shots in this book. MINITAB and the MINITAB logo are registered trademarks of MINITAB. We also thank the SAS Institute for permitting us to reprint screen shots of JMP v. 6.0 (© 2006 SAS Institute). SAS, JMP, and all other SAS Institute product or service names are registered trademarks or trademarks of the SAS Institute in the United States and other countries. We would like to thank IBM for granting us permission to reproduce excerpts from Quality Institute manual entitled, *Process Control, Capability and Improvement* (© 1984 IBM Corporation and the IBM Quality Institute).

The authors would also like to thank their families. Bhisham is indebted to his wife, Swarn; his daughters, Anita and Anjali; his son, Shiva; his sons-in-law, Prajay and Mark; and his granddaughter, Priya, for their deep love and devotion. Fred would like to acknowledge the patience and support provided by his wife, Julie, and sons, Carl and George, as he worked on this book. Without the encouragement of both their families, such projects would not be possible or meaningful.

—Bhisham C. Gupta
—H. Fred Walker

1

Introduction to Statistical Quality Control

Statistical quality control (SQC) refers to a set of interrelated tools used to monitor and improve process performance.

> **Definition 1.1** A *process*, for the purposes of this book, is a set of tasks or activities that change the form, fit, or function of one or more input(s) by adding value as is required or requested by a customer.

Defined in this manner, a process is associated with production and service delivery operations. Because Six Sigma applies to both production and service delivery/transactional operations, understanding and mastering the topics related to SQC is important to the Six Sigma Green Belt.

In this book, SQC tools are introduced and discussed from the perspective of application rather than theoretical development. From this perspective, you can consider the SQC tools as statistical "alarm bells" that send signals when there are one or more problems with a particular process. As you learn more about the application of SQC tools, it will be helpful to understand that these tools have general guidelines and rules of thumb for both design and interpretation; however, these tools are intended to be tailored to each company for use in a specific application. This means that when preparing to use SQC tools, choices must be made that impact how certain parameters within the tools are calculated, as well as how individual stakeholders involved with these tools actually interpret statistical data and results. Accordingly, choices related to the types of tools used, sample size and frequency, rules of interpretation, and acceptable levels of risk have a substantial impact on what comes out of these tools as far as usable information.

Critical to your understanding of SQC as a Six Sigma Green Belt is that SQC and statistical process control (SPC) are different. As noted earlier, SQC refers to a set of interrelated tools. SPC is but one of the tools that make up SQC. Many quality professionals continue to use the term *SPC* incorrectly by implying that SPC is used for process monitoring as a stand-alone tool. Prior to using SPC, we need to ensure that our process is set up correctly and, as much as possible, is in a state of statistical control. Likewise, once the process is in a state of statistical control, we need valid SPC data to facilitate our understanding of process capability and to enable the use of acceptance sampling.

1.1 Identifying the Tools of SQC

Figure 1.1 identifies the five basic tool types that make up SQC.

As can be seen in Figure 1.1, SQC consists of SPC (phase I and II), capability analysis (process and measurement systems), PRE-control, acceptance sampling (variables and attributes), and design of experiments (DOE). Within these five basic tool types are specific tools designed to provide information useful in a specific context or application. The remainder of this book will focus on the first four SQC tools, identified in Figure 1.1. DOE, as identified in Figure 1.1, is a component of SQC. However, DOE is also treated as a set of tools outside the context of SQC, and for this reason we will address DOE in the next two books in this series.

1.2 Relating SQC to Applied Statistics and to DOE

There is a distinct relationship among applied statistics, SQC, and DOE, as is seen in Figure 1.2.

Figure 1.2 shows that each of the SQC tools, as well as DOE, is based on applied statistics. The first book in this four-book series, *Applied Statistics for the Six Sigma Green Belt*, provides the foundational skills needed to learn the content presented here. Note that in Figure 1.2, with the possible exception of PRE-control, the level of statistical complexity increases with the use of the SQC tools moving from left to right. The level of statistical complexity is the greatest in DOE, and, in fact, there is an increasing level of statistical complexity within DOE, as you will see in the next two books in this series: *Introductory Design of Experiments for the Six Sigma Green Belt* and *Advanced Design of Experiments for the Six Sigma Green Belt.*

In understanding the relationship among applied statistics, SQC, and DOE, you should note the order in which they are presented—applied statistics, SQC, and then DOE. These topics are presented in this order in this

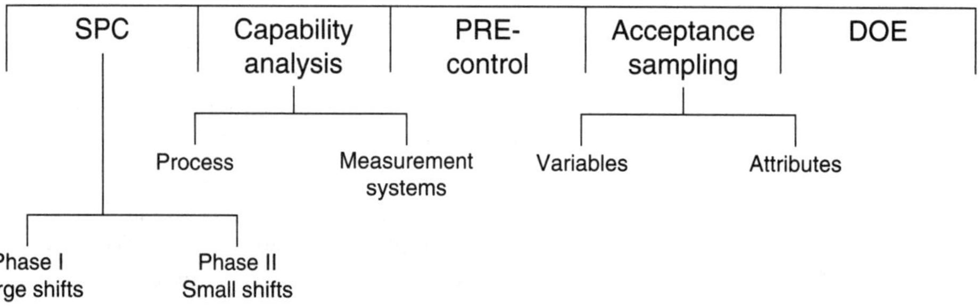

Figure 1.1 The five tool types of SQC.

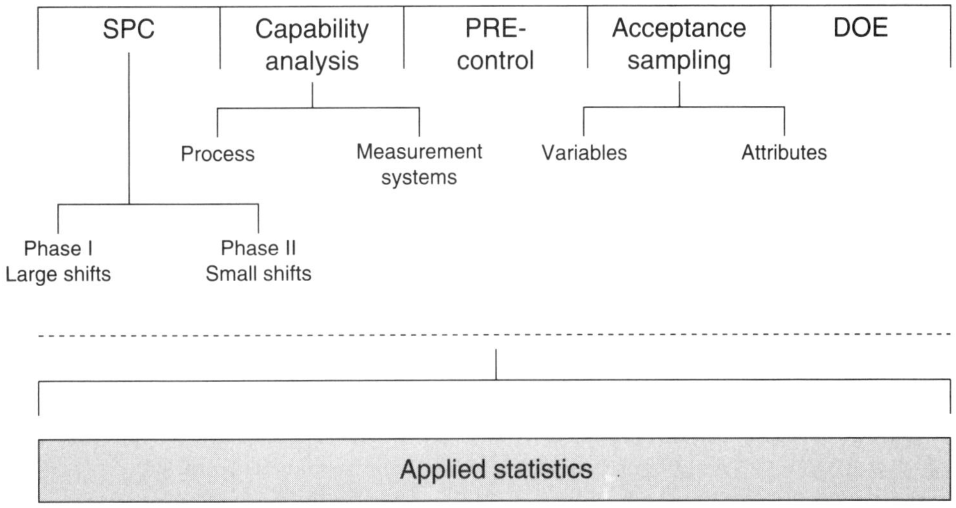

Figure 1.2 Relationship among applied statistics, SQC, and DOE.

book, and in most statistical and engineering texts and literature, to reflect the increasing level of computational difficulty. You should also know that in practice these tools would be used in a different order, which is applied statistics, DOE, and then SQC. There are three reasons, all quite logical, for changing the order of presentation: (1) moving from applied statistics to DOE is generally considered to be too rapid an increase in computational complexity for many people to easily grasp, (2) moving from applied statistics to DOE removes the opportunity for development of process knowledge, which provides the context for a study of experimental factors that come from product and process designs, and (3) it is generally necessary for us to determine which process parameters need to be monitored with DOE prior to using the process monitoring tools of SQC.

Figure 1.1 and Figure 1.2, then, represent maps of the topics addressed in SQC and provide the order of presentation of those topics in this book as well as in the greater statistical and engineering communities. Figure 1.3 represents an order in which those topics would be applied in process or transactional Six Sigma, assuming all the tools were to be applied.

The intent of Figure 1.3 is to illustrate that Six Sigma Green Belts would, where applicable, begin with DOE followed by the SQC tools. Further, Figure 1.3 illustrates that there is a cycle of iteration wherein DOE leads us to identify appropriate process parameters to monitor. We then use SQC tools to monitor those parameters, which may lead us to continue with additional experimentation and process monitoring as we refine our processes to better meet customer expectations.

Figure 1.3 also shows that once we identify with DOE the characteristics to monitor in our process, we then use SPC and capability analysis simultaneously to ensure that our process is in a state of statistical control and that our process variability and mean are consistent with our specifications. Another important point shown in Figure 1.3 is that we may or may not use a tool

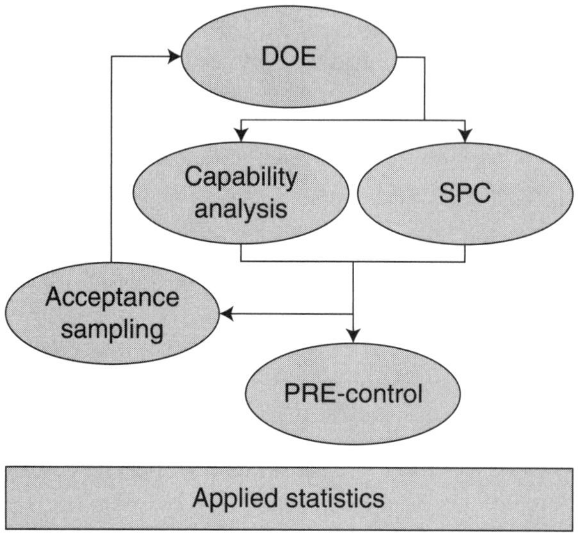

Figure 1.3 Order of SQC topics in process or transactional Six Sigma.

type called PRE-control. The very name *PRE-control* counterintuitively and incorrectly implies its use prior to SPC. If used at all, PRE-control is used after SPC, wherein processes are properly centered on target, are in a state of statistical control, are determined to be capable, and exhibit very low defect rates. Use of PRE-control as a means of reduced sampling and inspection continues to be controversial, and it is applicable only in a very small set of circumstances, as will be discussed more fully in Chapter 8. Whether or not PRE-control is used, the next tool type used, as identified in Figure 1.3, is acceptance sampling. What all these tools have in common is a statistical basis for analysis and decision making.

1.3 Understanding the Role of Statistics in SQC

As noted in section 1.2, the first book in this series focusing on the Six Sigma Green Belt is *Applied Statistics for the Six Sigma Green Belt.* Developing a working knowledge of basic statistics and how they apply to production and service delivery operations was an important step in enabling us to discuss SQC. Each SQC tool is based on statistical theory and application. The value and amount of information you are able to obtain from SQC tools are directly related to your level of understanding of basic statistical concepts. Because SQC is based on the application of statistics, much of what you read in this book assumes you have mastery of the prerequisite knowledge.

In practice, two groups of people use SQC tools:

1. Shop-floor operators and service delivery/transaction-focused people
2. Technicians, engineers, Six Sigma team members, and management team members

Each group using SQC tools has different roles and responsibilities relative to the use and implementation of the tools. For example, people in group 1 are commonly expected to collect data for, generate, and react to SQC tools. People in group 2 are commonly expected to design and implement SQC tools. They are also expected to critically analyze data from these tools and make decisions based on information gained from them.

1.4 Making Decisions Based on Quantitative Data

In practice, we are asked to make decisions based on quantitative and qualitative data on a regular basis.

> **Definition 1.2** *Quantitative data* are numerical data obtained from direct measurement or tally/count. Direct measurement uses a scale for measurement and reference, and tally/count uses direct observation as a basis for summarizing occurrences of some phenomenon.

> **Definition 1.3** *Qualitative data* are nonnumerical data obtained from direct observation, survey, personal experience, beliefs, perceptions, and perhaps historical records.

It is important to acknowledge that application of both quantitative and qualitative data has value and can be entirely appropriate in a professional work environment depending on the types of decisions we need to make. It is also important to acknowledge the difficulty in defending the use of qualitative data to make decisions in the design and process improvement efforts most commonly encountered by the Six Sigma Green Belt. Key, then, to obtaining the maximum value of information from SQC tools is realizing the power of quantitative data, because what can be directly measured can be validated and verified.

1.5 Practical versus Theoretical or Statistical Significance

As a Six Sigma Green Belt you will use applied statistics to make decisions. We emphasize the words *applied statistics* to note that applied statistics will be the basis for business decisions. When making decisions, we simply must temper our ability to detect statistical differences with our ability to act on designs and processes in a cost-effective manner. Figure 1.4 helps us visualize what we are trying to accomplish in detecting statistical differences.

In Figure 1.4 we see a normal distribution with a level of test significance (α) defined by the shaded regions in the tails of the distribution. The α identifies the region of the distribution wherein we would not expect to see evidence of process behavior if the process is behaving as intended. As a Six Sigma Green Belt you have the ability to set the level of α, which means you are actually making choices about the amount of area for the shaded region—the higher the level of α selected, the bigger the shaded region, the more discriminating the

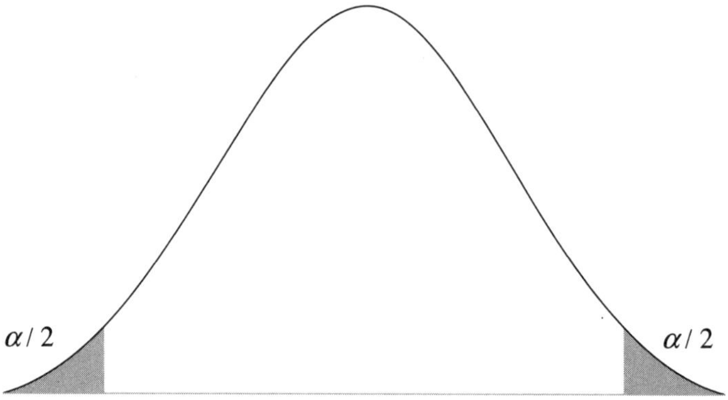

Figure 1.4 Detecting statistical differences.

test, and the more expensive it will be to make process improvement changes. While making any decisions related to α has financial implications, to understand practical differences we need to look at Figure 1.5.

In Figure 1.5 our comparison point changes from the shaded regions under the distribution tails of Figure 1.4 to the center of the distribution. Practical decisions then require that we consider how far off the intended target the observed process behavior is as compared with the statistical difference identified in Figure 1.4. It should be noted that differentiating between a practical and a statistical difference is a business or financial decision. When making a practical versus a statistical decision, we may very well be able to detect a statistical difference; however, it may not be cost effective or financially worth making the process improvements being considered.

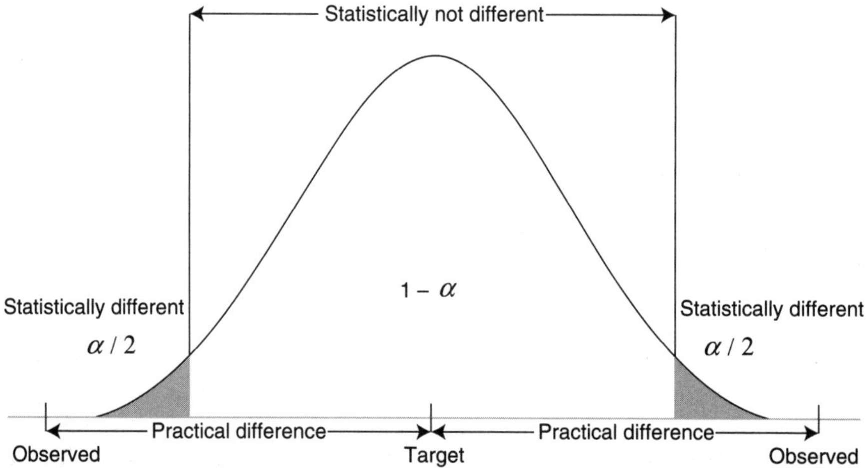

Figure 1.5 Detecting practical and statistical differences.

1.6 Why We Cannot Measure Everything

Whether in process-oriented industries such as manufacturing or in transactional-oriented industries, the volume of operations is sufficiently large to prohibit measurement of all the important characteristics in all units of production or all transactions. And even if we could measure some selected quality characteristic in all units of production or in all transactions, it is well known that we simply would not identify every discrepancy or mistake. So managing a balance between the volume of measurement and the probability of making errors during the measurement process requires us to rely on the power of statistics.

The power of statistics, in this case, refers to conclusions drawn from samples of data about a larger population, as shown in Figure 1.6.

Because we cannot afford the time or cost of measuring 100 percent of our products or transactions, sampling, along with appropriate descriptive or inferential statistics, is used to help us understand our processes. The important point contained in Figure 1.6 is that *samples*, by definition, are subsets of data drawn from a larger population. Because samples do not contain all the data from a population, there is a risk that we will draw incorrect conclusions about the larger population.

1.7 A Word on the Risks Associated with Making Bad Decisions

When relying on inferential or descriptive statistics based on samples of data, we risk making bad decisions. Bad decisions in practice lead to difficulties and problems for producers as well as consumers, and we refer to this as producer risk and consumer risk. The same bad decisions in statistical terms are referred to as Type I and Type II error, as well as alpha (α) and beta (β) risk, respectively. It is important for Six Sigma Green Belts to realize that these

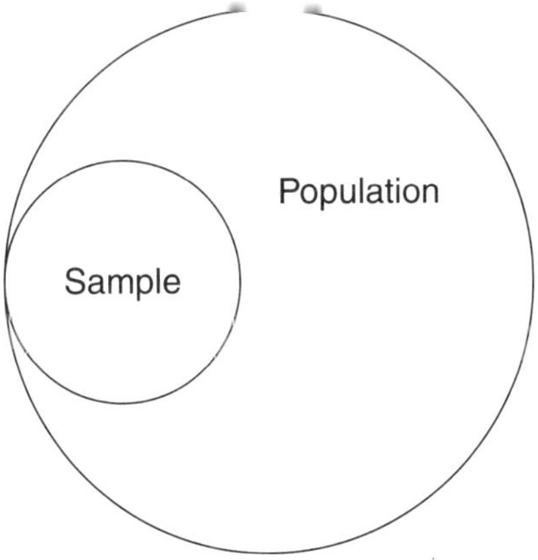

Figure 1.6 Sample versus population.

risks exist and that people from different functional areas within an organization may use different terms to describe the same thing. Lastly, we must realize that choices made during the design of SQC tools, choices related to selection of consumer and producer risk levels, quite dramatically impact performance of the tools and the subsequent information they produce for decision making.

It is not enough to simply identify the risks associated with making bad decisions; the Six Sigma Green Belt must also know the following key points:

- Sooner or later, a bad decision will be made
- The risks associated with making bad decisions are quantified in probabilistic terms
- α and β risks added together *do not* equal one
- Even though α and β go in opposite directions (that is, if α increases, β decreases), there is no direct relationship between α and β
- The values of α and β can be kept as low as we want by increasing the sample size

Definition 1.4 *Probability* is the chance that an event or outcome will or will not occur. Probability is quantified as a number between zero and one where the chance that an event or outcome will not occur in perfect certainty is zero and the chance that it will occur with perfect certainty is one. The chance that an event or outcome will not occur added to the chance that it will occur add up to one.

Definition 1.5 *Producer risk* is the risk of failing to pass a product or service delivery transaction on to a customer when, in fact, the product or service delivery transaction meets the customer quality expectations. The probability of making a producer risk error is quantified in terms of α.

Definition 1.6 *Consumer risk* is the risk of passing a product or service delivery transaction on to a customer under the assumption that the product or service delivery transaction meets customer quality expectations when, in fact, the product or service delivery is defective or unsatisfactory. The probability of making a consumer risk error is quantified in terms of β.

A critically important point, and a point that many people struggle to understand, is the difference between the probability that an event will or will not occur and the probabilities associated with consumer and producer risk—*they simply are not the same thing*. As noted earlier, probability is the percent chance that an event will or will not occur, wherein the percent chances of an event occurring or not occurring add up to one. The probability associated with making an error for the consumer, quantified as β, is a value ranging between zero and one. The probability associated with making an error for the producer, quantified as α, is also a value between zero and one. The key here is that α and β *do not add up to one.* In practice, one sets an acceptable level of α and then applies some form of test procedure (some application of an SQC tool in this case) so that the probability of committing a β error is acceptably small. So defining a level of α does not automatically set the level of β.

In closing, the chapters that follow discuss the collection of data and the design, application, and interpretation of each of the various SQC tools. You should have the following two goals while learning about SQC: (1) to master these tools at a conceptual level, and (2) to keep in perspective that the use of these tools requires tailoring them to your specific application while balancing practical and statistical differences.

2

Elements of a Sample Survey

The science of sampling is as old as our civilization. When trying new cuisine, for example, we take only a small bite to decide whether the taste is to our liking—an idea that goes back to when civilization began. However, modern advances in sampling techniques have taken place only in the twentieth century. Now, sampling is a matter of routine, and the effects of the outcomes can be felt in our daily lives. Most of the decisions regarding government policies, marketing (including trade), and manufacturing are based on the outcomes of various samplings conducted in different fields. The particular type of sampling used for a given situation depends on factors such as the composition of the population and the objectives of the sampling as well as time and budget availability. Because sampling is an integral part of SQC, this chapter focuses on the various types of sampling, estimation problems, and sources of error.

2.1 Basic Concepts of Sampling

The primary objective of sampling is to make inferences about population parameters (population mean, population total, population proportion, and population variance) using information contained in a sample taken from the population. To make such inferences, which are usually in the form of estimates of parameters and which are otherwise unknown, we collect data from the population under investigation. The aggregate of these data constitutes a sample. Each data point in the sample provides us information about the population parameter. Collecting each data point costs time and money, so it is important that some balance is kept while taking a sample. Too small a sample may not provide enough information to obtain proper estimates, and too large a sample may result in a waste of resources. This is why it is very important to remember that in any sampling procedure an appropriate sampling scheme—normally known as the *sample design*—is put in place.

The sample size is usually determined by the degree of precision desired in the estimates and the budgetary restrictions. If θ is the population parameter of interest, $\hat{\theta}$ is an estimator of θ, and E is the desired margin of error of estimation (absolute value of the difference between θ and $\hat{\theta}$), then the sample size is usually determined by specifying the value of E and the probability with which we will indeed achieve that value of E.

In this chapter we will briefly study four different sample designs: simple random sampling, stratified random sampling, systematic random sampling, and cluster random sampling from a finite population. But before we study these sample designs, some common terms used in sampling theory must be introduced.

Definition 2.1 A *population* is a collection of all conceivable individuals, elements, numbers, or entities that possess a characteristic of interest.

For example, if we are interested in the ability of employees with a specific job title or classification to perform specific job functions, the population may be defined as all employees with a specific job title working at the company of interest across all sites of the company. If, however, we are interested in the ability of employees with a specific job title or classification to perform specific job functions at a particular location, the population may be defined as all employees with the specific job title working only at the selected site or location. Populations, therefore, are shaped by the point or level of interest.

Populations can be finite or infinite. A population where all the elements are easily identifiable is considered *finite*, and a population where all the elements are not easily identifiable is considered *infinite*. For example, a batch or lot of production is normally considered a finite population, whereas all the production that may be produced from a certain manufacturing line would normally be considered infinite.

It is important to note that in statistical applications, the term *infinite* is used in the relative sense. For instance, if we are interested in studying the products produced or the service delivery iterations occurring over a given period of time, the population may be considered as finite or infinite, depending on one's frame of reference. It is important to note that the frame of reference (finite or infinite) directly impacts the selection of formulae used to calculate some statistics of interest.

In most statistical applications, studying each and every element of a population is not only time consuming and expensive but also potentially impossible. For example, if we want to study the average lifespan of a particular kind of electric bulb manufactured by a company, we cannot study the whole population without testing each and every bulb. Simply put, in almost all studies we end up studying only a small portion, called a sample, of the population.

Definition 2.2 A portion of a population selected for study is called a *sample*.

Definition 2.3 The *target population* is the population about which we want to make inferences based on the information contained in a sample.

Definition 2.4 The population from which a sample is selected is called a *sampled population.*

Normally, the sampled population and the target population coincide with each other because every effort is made to ensure that the sampled population is the same as the target population. However, situations arise when the sampled population does not cover the whole target population. In such cases, conclusions made about the sampled population are usually not applicable for the target population.

Before taking a sample, it is important that the *target population* be divided into nonoverlapping units, usually known as *sampling units.* Note that the sampling units in a given population may not always be the same. In fact, sampling units are determined by the sample design chosen. For example, in sampling voters in a metropolitan area, the sampling units might be an individual voter, the voters in a family, or all voters in a city block. Similarly, in sampling parts from a manufacturing plant, sampling units might be each individual part or a box containing several parts.

Definition 2.5 A list of all sampling units is called the *sampling frame*.

Before selecting a sample, one must decide the method of measurement. Commonly used methods in survey sampling are personal interviews, telephone interviews, physical measurements, direct observations, and mailed questionnaires. No matter what method of measurement is used, it is very important that the person taking the sample know what measurements are to be taken.

Individuals who collect samples are usually called *fieldworkers.* This is true regardless of their location—whether they are collecting the samples in a house, in a manufacturing plant, or in a city or town. All fieldworkers should be well acquainted with what measurements to take and how to take them. Good training of all fieldworkers is an important aspect of any sampling procedure. The accuracy of the measurements, which affects the final results, depends on how well the fieldworkers are trained.

It is quite common to select a small sample and examine it very carefully. This practice in sample surveying is usually called a *pretest.* The pretest allows us to make any necessary improvements in the questionnaire or method of measurement and to eliminate any difficulties in taking the measurements. It also allows a review of the quality of the measurements, or in the case of questionnaires, the quality of the returns.

Once the data are collected, the next step is to determine how to organize, summarize, and analyze them. This goal can easily be achieved by using methods of descriptive statistics discussed in Chapters 3 and 4 of *Applied Statistics for the Six Sigma Green Belt,* the first book of this series.

Brief descriptions of various sample design—simple random sampling, stratified random sampling, systematic random sampling, and cluster random sampling—are given in the following text. Later in this chapter we will see some results pertaining to these sample designs.

Sampling Designs

The most commonly used sample design is *simple random sampling*. This design consists of selecting n (sample size) sampling units in such a way that each unit has the same chance of being selected. If the population is finite of size N, however, then the simple random sampling design may be defined as selecting n (sample size) sampling units in such a way that each sample of size n, out of $\binom{N}{n}$ possible samples, has the same chance of being selected.

Example 2.1 *Suppose a Six Sigma Green Belt wants to take a sample of some machine parts manufactured during a shift at a given plant. Because the parts from which the Six Sigma Green Belt wants to take the sample are manufactured during the same shift at the same plant, it is quite safe to assume that all parts are similar. Therefore, a simple random sampling design is the most appropriate.*

The second sampling design is *stratified random sampling*, which at the same cost as simple random sampling may give improved results. However, the stratified random sampling design is most appropriate when a population can be divided into various nonoverlapping groups, called *strata*, such that the sampling units in each stratum are similar but may vary stratum to stratum. Each stratum is treated as a population by itself, and a simple random sample is taken from each of these subpopulations or strata.

In the manufacturing world, this type of situation can arise often. For instance, in Example 2.1, if the sample is taken from a population of parts that were manufactured either in different plants or in different shifts, then stratified random sampling would be more appropriate than simple random sampling across all the shifts or plants. In addition, there is the advantage of administrative convenience. For example, if the machine parts in the example are manufactured in plants located in different parts of the country, then stratified random sampling would be beneficial. Each plant may have a quality department, which can conduct the sampling within each plant. To obtain better results in this case, the quality departments in all the plants should communicate with each other before sampling to ensure that the same sampling norms will be followed. Another example of stratified random sampling in manufacturing is when samples are taken of products manufactured in different batches. In this case, products manufactured in different batches constitute different strata.

A third kind of sampling design is *systematic random sampling*. This procedure is the easiest one, and it is particularly useful in manufacturing processes where the sampling is done on line. Under this scheme, the first item is randomly selected, and thereafter every mth item manufactured is selected until we have a sample of desired size. Systematic random sampling is not only easy to select, but under certain conditions it is also more precise than simple random sampling.

The fourth and last sampling design we will consider here is *cluster random sampling*. In cluster random sampling, each sampling unit is a group or cluster of smaller units. In the manufacturing environment, this sampling scheme is particularly useful because it is not very easy to prepare a list of each part that constitutes a frame. On the other hand, it may be much easier to prepare a list of boxes, where each box contains many parts. Hence, a cluster random sample is merely a simple random sample of these boxes. Another advantage of cluster random sampling is that by selecting a simple random sample of only a few clusters, we can, in fact, have quite a large sample of smaller units, which clearly has been achieved at a minimum cost.

As mentioned earlier, the primary objective of sampling is to make inferences about population parameters using information contained in a sample taken from such a population. In the rest of this chapter, certain results pertaining to each sample design discussed earlier will be presented. However, some basic definitions, which will be useful in studying the estimation problems, will first be given.

Definition 2.6 The value assigned to a population parameter based on the information contained in a sample is called a *point estimate* or simply an *estimate* of the population parameter. The sample statistic used to calculate such an estimate is called an *estimator*.

Definition 2.7 An interval formed by a pair of values obtained by using the information contained in a sample such that the interval contains the true value of an unknown population parameter with certain probability is called a *confidence interval*. The probability with which it contains the true value of the unknown parameter is called the *confidence coefficient*.

Definition 2.8 The difference between an estimate and the true value of the estimated parameter is called the *error of estimation*. The maximum value of the error of estimation with a given probability is called the *margin of error*.

2.2 Simple Random Sampling

Simple random sampling is the most basic form of sampling design. A simple random sample can be drawn from an infinite or finite population. There are two techniques for taking a simple random sample from a finite population: sampling with replacement and sampling without replacement. Simple random sampling with replacement from a finite population and simple random sampling from an infinite population have the same statistical properties.

Definition 2.9 When sampling without replacement from a finite population, a random sample is called a *simple random sample* if each sample of size n, out of $\binom{N}{n}$ possible samples, has the same chance of being selected.

Definition 2.10 When sampling from an infinite population or sampling with replacement from a finite population, a random sample is called a *simple random sample* if each sampling unit has the same chance of being included in the sample.

A simple random sample can be taken by using tables of random numbers, which consist of digits 0, 1, 2, . . . , 9 such that each digit has the same chance of being selected. A table of random numbers, Table A.1, is given in the appendix. The first step in selecting a simple random sample using a table of random numbers is to label all the sampling units 0 to $(N - 1)$. If N is a four-digit number, for example, the labels will look like 0000, 0001, . . . , 9999. (Note that Table A.1 can be used for selecting a random sample from a population up to one million subjects.) Once all the sampling units are labeled, the second step is to select the same number of digits (columns) from the table of random numbers that matches the number of digits in N. Third, one must read down n ($\leq N$) numbers from the selected columns, starting from any arbitrary point and ignoring any repeated numbers. Note that if the sampling is done with replacement, we do not ignore the repeated numbers. The fourth and last step for taking a simple random sample of size n is to select the n sampling units with labels matching these numbers.

This method of selecting simple random samples is not as easy as it appears. In manufacturing, it may not even be possible to label all the parts. For example, suppose we want to select a simple random sample of 50 ball bearings from a big lot or a container full of such ball bearings. Now the question is whether it is economical or even possible to label all these ball bearings every time we want to select a sample. The answer is no. The method described earlier is more to develop statistical theory. In practice, to select simple random samples, we use some convenient methods so that no particular sampling unit is given any preferential treatment. For instance, to select a simple random sample of 50 units from a container, we first mix all the ball bearings and then select 50 of them from several spots in the container. This sampling technique is sometimes called *convenience sampling*.

2.2.1 Estimation of a Population Mean and Population Total

Let $y_1, y_2, \ldots, y_N$ be the sampling units of a population under consideration, and let $y_1, y_2, \ldots, y_n$ be a simple random sample from this population. Define the population parameters as follows:

μ = population mean

σ^2 = population variance

T = population total

N = population size

and the sample statistics

$\bar{y}$ = sample mean

s^2 = sample variance

n = sample size

For a simple random sample, the sample mean $\bar{y}$ and the sample variance s^2 are defined as

$$\bar{y} = \frac{y_1 + y_2 + \ldots + y_n}{n} = \frac{\sum_{i}^{n} y_i}{n}, \tag{2.1}$$

$$s^2 = \frac{1}{n-1}\left(\sum_{i}^{n}(y_i - \bar{y})^2\right) = \frac{1}{n-1}\left(\sum_{1}^{n} y_i^2 - \frac{\left(\sum y_i\right)^2}{n}\right), \tag{2.2}$$

respectively. For estimating the population mean μ we use the sample mean defined in equation (2.1), that is,

$$\hat{\mu} = \bar{y}. \tag{2.3}$$

In simple random sampling, the sample mean $\bar{y}$ is an unbiased estimator of the population mean μ, that is,

$$E\ (\bar{y}) = \mu. \tag{2.4}$$

In order to assess the accuracy of the estimator of μ, it is important to find the variance of $\bar{y}$, which will allow us to find the margin of error.

The variance of $\bar{y}$ for a simple random sampling without replacement is given by

$$V(\bar{y}) = \frac{\sigma^2}{n}\left(\frac{N-n}{N-1}\right) \cong \frac{\sigma^2}{n}\left(1 - \frac{n}{N}\right). \tag{2.5}$$

In practice we usually do not know the population variance σ^2; therefore, it becomes necessary to find an estimator of $V(\bar{y})$, which is given by

$$\hat{V}(\bar{y}) = \frac{s^2}{n}\left(1 - \frac{n}{N}\right). \tag{2.6}$$

For a simple random sample taken from either an infinite population or a finite population sampled with replacement, the variance $V(\bar{y})$ becomes

$$V(\bar{y}) = \frac{\sigma^2}{n}, \tag{2.7}$$

and its estimator is given by

$$\hat{V}(\bar{y}) = \frac{s^2}{n}. \tag{2.8}$$

If either the population is normal or the sample size is large ($n \geq 30$), then the margin of error for the estimation of the population mean with probability $(1 - \alpha)$ is given by

$$\pm z_{\alpha/2}\sqrt{V(\bar{y})}. \tag{2.9}$$

If the population variance σ^2 is unknown, then in equation (2.9) we replace $V(\bar{y})$ by its estimator $\hat{V}(\bar{y})$.

Example 2.2 *Suppose we are interested in estimating the mean yield point of steel castings produced by a large manufacturer. The following data give the yield point in units of 1000 pounds per square inch (psi) of a simple random sample of size 10.*

83.37 86.21 83.44 86.29 82.80 85.29 84.86 84.20 86.04 89.60

Solution: The sample mean for the data given in this example is

$$\bar{y}=\frac{1}{10}\left(83.37+86.21+83.44+86.29+82.80+85.29+84.86+84.20+86.04+89.60\right)$$

$$=\frac{1}{10}(852.1)=85.21.$$

The sample variance for these data is

$$s^2=\frac{1}{(10-1)}\left(83.37^2+86.21^2+\ldots+89.60^2-\frac{(83.37+86.21+\ldots+89.60)^2}{10}\right)$$

$$=\frac{1}{9}(35.595)=3.955.$$

Thus, an estimate for the population mean μ is

$$\hat{\mu}=85.21.$$

Because the population under investigation consists of all steel castings produced by the large manufacturer, it can be considered infinite. Thus, the margin of error for estimating the population mean with, say, 95 percent probability, using equations (2.8) and (2.9), is given by

$$\pm z_{0.025}\frac{s}{\sqrt{n}}=\pm 1.96\left(\frac{1.989}{\sqrt{10}}\right)=\pm 1.233.$$

An unbiased estimator of the finite population total T is given by

$$\hat{T}=N\bar{y}. \tag{2.10}$$

The variance of estimator $\hat{T}$ is given by

$$N^2V(\bar{y}). \tag{2.11}$$

The standard error of $\hat{T}$ is given by

$$N\sqrt{V(\bar{y})}. \tag{2.12}$$

If the population variance σ^2 is unknown, then in equations (2.11) and (2.12) we replace $\hat{V}(\bar{y})$ by its estimator $\hat{V}(\bar{y})$. Assuming the sample size is large ($n \geq 30$), it can be shown that the margin of error for the estimation of the population total with probability $(1-\alpha)$ is

$$\pm N\times(\text{margin of error for estimating mean})=\pm N\times z_{\alpha/2}\sqrt{\hat{V}(\bar{y})}. \tag{2.13}$$

Example 2.3 *A manufacturing company has developed a new device for the army. The company got a defense contract to supply 25,000 devices to the army. In order to meet the contractual obligations, the department of human resources wants to estimate the number of workers the company will need to hire. This can be accomplished by estimating the number of workforce hours needed to manufacture 25,000 devices. The following data show the number of hours spent by randomly selected workers to manufacture 15 devices.*

8.90 8.25 6.50 7.25 8.00 7.80 9.90 8.30
9.30 6.95 8.25 7.30 8.55 7.55 7.70

Estimate the total workforce hours needed to manufacture 25,000 devices and determine the margin of error with 95 percent probability.

Solution: In this example, we first estimate the mean workforce hours needed to manufacture one device and then determine the margin of error with 95 percent probability.

The sample mean for the data given in this example is

$$\bar{y} = \frac{1}{15}(8.90 + 8.25 + 6.50 + \ldots + 8.55 + 7.55 + 7.70)$$
$$= \frac{1}{15}(120.50) = 8.033.$$

The sample variance for these data is

$$s = \sqrt{\frac{1}{(15-1)}\left(8.90^2 + 8.25^2 + \ldots + 7.70^2 - \frac{(8.90 + 8.25 + \ldots + 7.70)^2}{15}\right)^{1/2}} = 0.900.$$

Thus, an estimate for the population mean μ is

$$\hat{\mu} = 8.033.$$

Using equation (2.9) we can see that the margin of error for estimating the population mean with 95 percent probability is

$$\pm z_{0.025}\frac{s}{\sqrt{n}} = \pm 1.96\left(\frac{0.900}{\sqrt{15}}\right) = \pm 0.455.$$

Now suppose that T is the total workforce hours needed to manufacture 25,000 devices. Using equations (2.10) and (2.13), the estimate for T is

$$\hat{T} = N \times \bar{y} = 25{,}000 \times 8.033 = 200{,}825,$$

and the margin of error for estimating the total workforce hours is

$$\pm\ 25{,}000 \times 0.455 = 11{,}375.$$

Note: If the population is normal with standard deviation σ unknown and the sample size small ($n < 30$), then in the earlier results, z is replaced by t, where the value of t is found in Student's t-table (Table A.9 in the appendix) with $(n - 1)$ degrees of freedom.

2.2.2 Confidence Interval for a Population Mean and Population Total

Once we have found estimates for the population mean, the population total, and the corresponding margins of error with probability $(1 - \alpha)$, finding a confidence interval with confidence coefficient $(1 - \alpha)$ for the population mean and population total is very simple.

A confidence interval with confidence coefficient $(1 - \alpha)$ for the population mean is

$$\hat{\mu} \pm \text{margin of error for estimating } \mu$$

or

$$\hat{\mu} \pm z_{\alpha/2}\sqrt{\hat{V}(\bar{y})}. \tag{2.14}$$

And a confidence interval with confidence coefficient $(1 - \alpha)$ for the population total is

$$\hat{T} \pm \text{ margin of error for estimating } T$$

or

$$\hat{T} \pm N \quad z_{\alpha/2}\sqrt{\hat{V}(\bar{y})}. \tag{2.15}$$

Example 2.4 *Reconsider the problem in Example 2.3 and find a 95 percent confidence interval for the population mean* μ *and the population total* T.

Solution: Using the results of Example 2.3 and equations (2.14) and (2.15), we get the following:

A 95 percent confidence for population mean μ is

$\hat{\mu} \pm$ margin of error for estimating $\mu \times 8.033 \pm 0.455 \times (7.578, 8.488)$,

and a 95 percent confidence interval for the population total T is

$\hat{T} \pm$ margin of error for estimating $T \times 200{,}825 \pm 11{,}375 \times (189{,}459, 212{,}200)$.

2.2.3 Determination of Sample Size

The sample size needed to estimate the population mean with margin of error E with probability $(1 - \alpha)$ is given by

$$n = \frac{z_{\alpha/2}^2 N\sigma^2}{(N-1)E^2 + \sigma^2 z_{\alpha/2}^2}. \tag{2.16}$$

In practice, the population variance σ^2 is usually unknown. Thus, to find the sample size n we need to find an estimate s^2 of the population variance σ^2. This can be achieved by using the data from a pilot study or previous surveys. In this case, the sample size needed to estimate the population mean with margin of error E with probability $(1 - \alpha)$ is given by

$$n = \frac{z_{\alpha/2}^2 Ns^2}{(N-1)E^2 + s^2 z_{\alpha/2}^2}. \tag{2.17}$$

If the population size N is large, then the factor $(N - 1)$ in equation (2.17) is usually replaced by N.

Note: The sample size needed to estimate the population total with margin of error E' with probability $(1 - \alpha)$ can be found by using equation (2.16) or (2.17) depending on whether the population variance σ^2 is known and replacing E with (E'/N).

Example 2.5 *Suppose in Example 2.3 we would like the margin of error for estimating the population mean to be 0.25 with probability 0.99. Determine the appropriate sample size to achieve this goal.*

Solution: From the information provided to us, we have

$$E = 0.25, \quad z_{\alpha/2} = 2.575,$$

and from Example 2.3, we have

$$N = 25{,}000 \text{ and } s = 0.900.$$

Plugging these values into equation (2.17) and replacing the factor $(N - 1)$ in the denominator by N, we get

$$\begin{aligned} n &= \frac{(2.575)^2 \times (25{,}000) \times (0.900)^2}{25{,}000(0.25)^2 + (0.900)^2(2.575)^2} \\ &\cong 86. \end{aligned}$$

Note that the sample size for estimating the population total with margin of error 6250 (= 25,000 × 0.25) is again equal to 86. To attain a sample of size 86, we take another simple random sample of size 71, which is usually known as a *supplemental sample*, and then combine this sample with the one that we had already taken, which was of size 15.

2.3 Stratified Random Sampling

It is not uncommon in a manufacturing process for a characteristic of interest to vary from country to country, region to region, plant to plant, or machine to machine. For example, a Six Sigma Green Belt might be interested in finding the longevity of parts manufactured in different regions of the United States. Clearly, the longevity of such parts may vary from region to region depending on where the parts are manufactured. This could be due to differences in raw materials, training of the workers, or differences in machines. In such cases where the population is heterogeneous, we get more precise estimates by using a sample design known as stratified random sampling. In stratified random sampling, the population is divided into different nonoverlapping groups, called *strata*, such that they constitute the whole population; the population is as homogeneous as possible within each stratum but varies between strata. Then a stratified random sample is taken by selecting a simple random sample from each stratum.

Some of the advantages of stratified random sampling over simple random sampling are as follows:

1. It provides more precise estimates for population parameters than simple random sampling would provide with the same sample size.
2. A stratified sample is more convenient to administer, which may result in a lower cost for sampling.
3. It provides a simple random sample for each subgroup or stratum, which are homogeneous. Therefore, these samples can prove to be very useful for studying each individual subgroup separately without incurring any extra cost.

Before we look into how to use the information obtained from a stratified random sample to estimate population parameters, we will briefly discuss the process of generating a stratified random sample:

- Divide the sampling population of N units into nonoverlapping subpopulations or strata of $N_1, N_2, \ldots, N_K$ units, respectively. These strata constitute the whole population of N units. That is, $N = N_1 + N_2 + \ldots + N_K$.
- Select independently from each stratum a simple random sample of size $n_1, n_2, \ldots, n_K$ so that $n = n_1 + n_2 + \ldots + n_K$ is the total sample size.
- To make full use of stratification, the strata sizes $N_1, N_2, \ldots, N_K$ must be known.

2.3.1 Estimation of a Population Mean and Population Total

Let $y_{11}, y_{12}, \ldots, y_{1N_1}; y_{21}, y_{22}, \ldots, y_{2N_2}; \ldots; y_{K1}, y_{K2}, \ldots, y_{KN_K}$ be the sampling units in $1, 2, \ldots, K$th stratum, respectively, and let $y_{11}, y_{12}, \ldots, y_{1n_1}; y_{21}, y_{22}, \ldots, y_{2n_2}; \ldots; y_{K1}, y_{K2}, \ldots, y_{Kn_K}$ be the simple random samples of sizes $n_1, n_2, \ldots, n_K$ from them, respectively. Let μ and T be the population mean and population total, respectively, and let μ_i, T_i, σ_i^2 be the population mean, total, and variance of the ith stratum, respectively. Then, we have

$$T = \sum_{i=1}^{K} T_i = \sum_{i=1}^{K} N_i \mu_i, \tag{2.18}$$

$$\mu = T/N = \frac{1}{N} \sum_{i=1}^{K} N_i \mu_i. \tag{2.19}$$

Let $\bar{y}_i$ be the sample mean of the simple random sample from the ith stratum. From the previous section we know that $\bar{y}_i$ is an unbiased estimator of the mean μ_i of the ith stratum. An unbiased estimator of the population mean μ, which we denote as $\bar{y}_{st}$, is given by

$$\hat{\mu} = \bar{y}_{st} = \frac{1}{N} \sum_{i=1}^{K} N_i \bar{y}_i, \tag{2.20}$$

where

$$\bar{y}_i = \frac{1}{n_i}\sum_{j=1}^{n_i} y_{ij}. \tag{2.21}$$

An estimator of the population total T is given by

$$\hat{T} = \sum_{i=1}^{K}\hat{T}_i = \sum_{i=1}^{K} N_i\hat{\mu}_i = \sum_{i=1}^{K} N_i\bar{y}_i = N \times \bar{y}_{st}. \tag{2.22}$$

Recall that from equation (2.5) we have

$$V(\bar{y}_i) = \frac{\sigma_i^2}{n_i}\left(\frac{N_i - n_i}{N_i - 1}\right). \tag{2.23}$$

From equations (2.20) and (2.23), it follows that the variance of the estimator $\bar{y}_{st}$ of the population mean μ is given by

$$\begin{aligned} V(\bar{y}_{st}) &= \frac{1}{N^2}\sum_{i=1}^{K} N_i^2 V(\bar{y}_i) \\ &= \frac{1}{N^2}\sum_{i=1}^{K} N_i^2 \frac{\sigma_i^2}{n_i}\left(\frac{N_i - n_i}{N_i - 1}\right). \end{aligned} \tag{2.24}$$

An estimator of the variance in equation (2.24) is given by

$$\hat{V}(\bar{y}_{st}) = \frac{1}{N^2}\sum_{i=1}^{K} N_i^2 \frac{s_i^2}{n_i}\left(1 - \frac{n_i}{N_i}\right). \tag{2.25}$$

From equations (2.22) and (2.25), it follows that the variance of the estimator of the population total T is given by

$$\begin{aligned} V(\hat{T}) &= N^2 V(\bar{y}_{st}) \\ &= \sum_{i=1}^{K} N_i^2 \frac{\sigma_i^2}{n_i}\left(\frac{N_i - n_i}{N_i - 1}\right). \end{aligned} \tag{2.26}$$

An estimator of the variance in equation (2.26) is given by

$$\begin{aligned} \hat{V}(\hat{T}) &= N^2 \hat{V}(\bar{y}_{st}) \\ &= \sum_{i=1}^{K} N_i^2 \frac{s_i^2}{n_i}\left(1 - \frac{n_i}{N_i}\right). \end{aligned} \tag{2.27}$$

If either the population is normal or the sample size is large ($n \geq 30$), then the margin of error for the estimation of the population mean with probability $(1 - \alpha)$ is given by

$$\pm z_{\alpha/2}\sqrt{V(\bar{y}_{st})} = \pm z_{\alpha/2}\frac{1}{N}\sqrt{\sum_{i=1}^{K} N_i^2 \frac{\sigma_i^2}{n_i}\left(\frac{N_i - n_i}{N_i - 1}\right)}. \tag{2.28}$$

When the strata variances are unknown, which is usually the case, the stratum variance σ_i^2 in equation (2.28) is replaced by its estimator s_i^2. Then the margin of error for the estimation of the population mean with probability $(1 - \alpha)$ is given by

$$\pm z_{\alpha/2} \frac{1}{N} \sqrt{\sum_{i=1}^{K} N_i^2 \frac{s_i^2}{n_i} \left(1 - \frac{n_i}{N_i}\right)}. \tag{2.29}$$

The margin of error for the estimation of the population total with probability $(1 - \alpha)$ is given by

$$\pm z_{\alpha/2} \sqrt{\sum_{i=1}^{K} N_i^2 \frac{\sigma_i^2}{n_i} \left(\frac{N_i - n_i}{N_i - 1}\right)}. \tag{2.30}$$

Again, when the strata variances are unknown, the stratum variance σ_i^2 in equation (2.30) is replaced by its estimator s_i^2. Then the margin of error for the estimation of the population total with probability $(1 - \alpha)$ is given by

$$\pm z_{\alpha/2} \sqrt{\sum_{i=1}^{K} N_i^2 \frac{s_i^2}{n_i} \left(1 - \frac{n_i}{N_i}\right)}. \tag{2.31}$$

2.3.2 Confidence Interval for a Population Mean and Population Total

From equations (2.29) and (2.31) we have the margins of error for estimating the population mean and population total with probability $(1 - \alpha)$. A confidence interval with confidence coefficient $(1 - \alpha)$ for the population mean and population total is given by

$$\hat{\mu} \pm z_{\alpha/2} \frac{1}{N} \sqrt{\sum_{i=1}^{K} N_i^2 \frac{s_i^2}{n_i} \left(1 - \frac{n_i}{N_i}\right)} \tag{2.32}$$

and

$$\hat{T} \pm z_{\alpha/2} \sqrt{\sum_{i=1}^{K} N_i^2 \frac{s_i^2}{n_i} \left(1 - \frac{n_i}{N_i}\right)}, \tag{2.33}$$

respectively.

Notes

1. An estimate $\bar{y}$ of the population mean obtained from a simple random sample coincides with estimate $\bar{y}_{st}$ obtained from a stratified random sample if in every stratum n_i/N_i is equal to n/N.

2. If the sample size in every stratum relative to the stratum size is small ($n_i/N_i < 5\%$), then the factor n_i/N_i in equations (2.25) through (2.33) is usually ignored.

Example 2.6 *Suppose a manufacturing company is producing parts in its facilities, which are located in three different countries, including the United States. The labor costs, raw material costs, and other overhead expenses vary tremendously from country to country. In order to meet the target value, the company is interested in estimating the average cost of a part it will produce during a certain period. The number of parts expected to be produced during that period in its three facilities is* $N_1 = 8900$, $N_2 = 10{,}600$, *and* $N_3 = 15{,}500$. *The total number of parts expected to be produced during that period in all facilities is* $N = 8900 + 10{,}600 + 15{,}500 = 35{,}000$. *To achieve its goal, the company calculated the cost of 12 randomly selected parts from facility one, 12 parts from facility two, and 16 parts from facility three, which is in the United States. These efforts produced the following data (in dollars):*

Sample from facility one

6.48, 6.69, 7.11, 6.15, 7.09, 7.27, 7.58, 6.49, 6.32, 6.47, 6.63, 6.90

Sample from facility two

10.06, 10.25, 11.03, 11.18, 10.29, 9.33, 10.42, 9.34, 11.06, 9.78, 10.54, 11.45

Sample from facility three

24.72, 24.77, 25.64, 25.65, 26.09, 24.70, 25.05, 23.21, 24.00, 26.00, 26.21, 26.00, 24.21, 26.11, 24.63, 26.38

Use these data to determine the following:

1. *An estimate of the population mean and population total*
2. *The margin of error for the estimation of the population mean and population total with probability 95 percent*
3. *A confidence interval for the population mean and population total with confidence coefficient 95 percent*

Solution: In the example, each facility constitutes a stratum. So first we determine the sample mean and the sample standard deviation for each stratum.

$$\bar{y}_1 = \frac{1}{12}(6.48 + 6.69 + 7.11 + \ldots + 6.63 + 6.90) = 6.765,$$

$$\bar{y}_2 = \frac{1}{12}(10.06 + 10.25 + 11.03 + \ldots + 10.54 + 11.45) = 10.311,$$

$$\bar{y}_3 = \frac{1}{16}(24.72 + 24.77 + 25.64 + \ldots + 24.63 + 26.38) = 25.211,$$

$$s_1^2 = \frac{1}{12-1}\left((6.48^2 + 6.69^2 + \ldots + 6.90^2) - \frac{(6.48 + 6.69 + \ldots + 6.90)^2}{12}\right) = 0.1823,$$

$$s_1 = \sqrt{0.1823} = 0.427,$$

$$s_2^2 = \frac{1}{12-1}\left((10.06^2 + 10.25^2 + ... + 11.45^2) - \frac{(10.06 + 10.25 + ... + 11.45)^2}{12}\right) = 0.4277,$$

$$s_2 = \sqrt{0.4277} = 0.654,$$

$$s_3^2 = \frac{1}{16-1}\left((24.72^2 + 24.77^2 + ... + 26.38^2) - \frac{(24.72 + 24.77 + ... + 26.38)^2}{16}\right) = 0.874$$

$$s_3 = \sqrt{0.874} = 0.935.$$

Using equations (2.20) and (2.22), the estimates of the population mean and population total are

$$\hat{\mu} = \bar{y}_{st} = \frac{1}{35{,}000}(8900 \times 6.765 + 10{,}600 \times 10.311 + 15{,}500 \times 25.211)$$

$$\cong \$16.00,$$

$$\hat{T} = N \times \bar{y}_{st} = 35{,}000 \times 16 = \$560{,}000,$$

respectively.

Using equations (2.29) and (2.31) and noting that the sample sizes relative to the stratum sizes are small, the margins of error of estimation for the population mean and population total with probability 95 percent are

$$\pm 1.96 \times \frac{1}{35{,}000}\sqrt{8900^2\frac{0.1833}{12} + 10{,}600^2\frac{0.4277}{12} + 15{,}500^2\frac{0.874}{16}} = \pm \$0.225$$

and

$$\pm 1.96\sqrt{8900^2\frac{0.1833}{12} + 10{,}600^2\frac{0.4277}{12} + 15{,}500^2\frac{0.874}{16}} = \pm \$7895.07,$$

respectively.

Using equations (2.32) and (2.33), confidence intervals for the population mean and population total with confidence coefficient 95 percent are

$$16.00 \pm 0.225 = (\$15.775, \$16.22500)$$

and

$$560{,}000 \pm 7895.07 = (\$552{,}104.93, \$567{,}895.07),$$

respectively.

2.3.3 Determination of Sample Size

The sample size needed to estimate the population mean with margin of error E with probability $(1 - \alpha)$ is given by

$$n = \frac{z_{\alpha/2}^2 \sum_{i=1}^{K} N_i^2 \sigma_i^2 / w_i}{N^2 E^2 + z_{\alpha/2}^2 \sum_{i=1}^{K} N_i \sigma_i^2}, \tag{2.34}$$

where w_i is the fraction of the total sample size allocated to the ith stratum. In the case of proportional allocation, $w_i = N_i/N$. Also, note that if the stratum population variance σ_i^2 is not known, then it is replaced with the corresponding sample variance s_i^2, which can be found from either a pilot study or historical data from a similar study.

Example 2.7 *Extending our work in Example 2.6, determine an appropriate sample size if a Six Sigma Green Belt engineer of the company is interested in attaining a margin of error of $0.10 with probability 95 percent.*

Solution: From Example 2.6, we have

$w_1 = 8900/35{,}000 = 0.254$, $w_2 = 106{,}000/35{,}000 = 0.303$, $w_3 = 15{,}500/35{,}000 = 0.443$.

Because strata variances are unknown, plugging the values of $E = 0.1$, the sample variance s_i^2, N, N_i, and w_i; $i = 1, 2, 3$ into equation (2.34), we get

$$n \cong 214.$$

In Example 2.6, in order to achieve the margin of error of 10 cents with probability 95 percent, the company must take samples of sizes 55, 65, and 95 from stratum one, two, and three, respectively (these sizes are obtained by using the formula $n_i = n \times w_i$). This means we will need supplemental samples of sizes 43, 53, and 79 from stratum one, two, and three, respectively.

Notes

1. The sample size needed to estimate the population total with margin of error E' with probability $(1 - \alpha)$ can be found by using equation (2.34) simply by replacing E with (E'/N).
2. An optimal allocation of sample size to each stratum depends on three factors: the total number of sampling units in each stratum, the variability of observations within each stratum, and the cost of taking an observation from each stratum. The details on this topic are beyond the scope of this book. For more information, see Cochran (1977), Govindarajulu (1999), Lohr (1999), and Scheaffer et al. (2006).

2.4 Systematic Random Sampling

Suppose the elements in the sampled population are numbered 1 to N. To select a systematic random sample of size n, we select an element at random from the first k ($\leq N/n$) elements and then every kth element until n elements are selected. For example, if $k = 20$ and the first element selected is number 15, then the other elements, which will be included in the sample, are 35, 55, 75, 95, and so on. Because the first element is randomly selected and then every kth element is selected, this determines a complete systematic random sample and is usually known as every kth systematic sample.

A major advantage of the systematic sample over the simple random sample is that a systematic sample design is easier to implement, particularly if the sampled population has some kind of natural ordering. Systematic sampling is very easy to implement when the sample is taken directly from the production or assembly line. Another advantage of systematic sampling is that the workers collecting the samples do not need any special training, and sampled units are evenly spread over the population of interest.

If the population is in random order, a systematic random sample provides results comparable with those of a simple random sample. Moreover, a systematic sample usually covers the whole sampled population uniformly, which may provide more information about the population than that provided by a simple random sample. However, if the sampling units of a population are in some kind of periodic or cyclical order, the systematic sample may not be a representative sample. For instance, if every fifth part produced by a machine is defective and if $k = 5$, then the systematic random sample will contain either all defective or all nondefective parts depending on whether the first part selected was defective. Therefore, a systematic sample in this case will not be a representative sample. Similarly, suppose we want to estimate a worker's productivity and we decide to take samples of his or her productivity every Friday afternoon. We might be underestimating the true productivity. On the other hand, if we pick the same day in the middle of the week, we might be overestimating the true productivity. So, to have better results using systematic sampling, we must keep in mind that it includes the days when the productivity tends to be higher as well as lower. If there is a linear trend, the systematic sample mean provides a more precise estimate of the population mean than that of a simple random sample but less precision than the stratified random sample.

2.4.1 Estimation of a Population Mean and Population Total

If our sample is an every kth systematic random sample, then clearly there are k possible systematic samples from a population of size N ($kn = N$), which we write as

$$y_{11}, y_{12}, \ldots, y_{1n}; y_{21}, y_{22}, \ldots, y_{2n}; y_{31}, y_{32}, \ldots, y_{3n}; y_{k1}, y_{k2}, \ldots, y_{kn},$$

where y_{ij} denotes the jth ($j = 1, 2, \ldots, n$) element of the ith ($i = 1, 2, \ldots, k$) systematic sample. We denote the mean of the ith sample described earlier by $\bar{y}_i$ and the mean of a randomly selected systematic sample by $\bar{y}_{sy}$, where the subscript sy means that the systematic sample was used. The $\bar{y}_{sy}$ is equal to $\bar{y}_i$ ($i = 1, 2, \ldots, k$) with probability $1/k$, where

$$\bar{y}_i = \frac{\sum_{j=1}^{n} y_{ij}}{n}.$$

It can easily be shown that

$$\hat{\mu} = \bar{y}_{sy} \tag{2.35}$$

is an unbiased estimator of the population mean μ.

Note that the mean of a systematic sample is more precise than the mean of a simple random sample if, and only if, the variance within the systematic samples is greater than the population variance as a whole, that is,

$$S_{wsy}^2 > S^2, \tag{2.36}$$

where

$$S_{wsy}^2 = \frac{1}{k(n-1)} \sum_{i=1}^{k} \sum_{j=1}^{n} (y_{ij} - \bar{y}_i), \tag{2.37}$$

$$S^2 = \frac{1}{N-1} \sum_{i=1}^{k} \sum_{j=1}^{n} (y_{ij} - \bar{Y}), \tag{2.38}$$

and

$$\bar{Y} = \frac{1}{N} \sum_{i=1}^{k} \sum_{j=1}^{n} y_{ij}. \tag{2.39}$$

Estimated variance of $\bar{y}_{sy}$ is given by

$$\hat{V}(\bar{y}_{sy}) = \frac{s_{sy}^2}{n}\left(1 - \frac{n}{N}\right), \tag{2.40}$$

where

$$s_{sy}^2 = \frac{1}{n-1} \sum_{i=1}^{n} (y_i - \bar{y}_{sy})^2. \tag{2.41}$$

An estimator of the population total T is given by

$$\hat{T} = N \times \bar{y}_{sy}, \tag{2.42}$$

and an estimated variance of $\hat{T}$ is given by

$$\hat{V}(\hat{T}) = N^2 \hat{V}(\bar{y}_{sy}) = N^2 \left(\frac{s_{sy}^2}{n}\right)\left(1 - \frac{n}{N}\right)$$

$$= N(N - n)\frac{s_{sy}^2}{n}. \tag{2.43}$$

Sometimes the manufacturing scenario may warrant first stratifying the population and then taking a systematic sample within each stratum. For example, if there are several plants and we want to collect samples on line from each of these plants, then clearly we are first stratifying the population and then taking a systematic sample within each stratum. In such cases, the formulas for estimating the population mean and total are the same as given in the previous section except that $\bar{y}_i$ is replaced by $\bar{y}_{sy}$.

The margins of error with probability $(1 - \alpha)$ for estimating the population mean and total are given by

$$\pm z_{\alpha/2}\sqrt{\hat{V}(\bar{y}_{sy})} = \pm z_{\alpha/2}\sqrt{\frac{s_{sy}^2}{n}\left(1 - \frac{n}{N}\right)} \tag{2.44}$$

and

$$\pm z_{\alpha/2}\sqrt{\hat{V}(\hat{T})} = \pm z_{\alpha/2}\sqrt{N(N-n)\frac{s_{sy}^2}{n}}, \tag{2.45}$$

respectively.

2.4.2 Confidence Interval for a Population Mean and Population Total

Using equations (2.44) and (2.45), the confidence intervals for the population mean and population total with confidence $(1 - \alpha)$ are given by

$$\hat{\mu} \pm z_{\alpha/2}\sqrt{\frac{s_{sy}^2}{n}\left(1-\frac{n}{N}\right)} \tag{2.46}$$

and

$$\hat{T} \pm z_{\alpha/2}\sqrt{N^2\frac{s_{sy}^2}{n}\left(1-\frac{n}{N}\right)}, \tag{2.47}$$

respectively.

2.4.3 Determination of Sample Size

The sample size needed to estimate the population mean with margin of error E with probability $(1 - \alpha)$ is given by

$$n = \frac{z_{\alpha/2}^2 N s_{sy}^2}{(N-1)E^2 + s_{sy}^2 z_{\alpha/2}^2}. \tag{2.48}$$

The sample size needed to estimate the population total with margin of error E' with probability $(1 - \alpha)$ can be found from equation (2.48) by replacing E with (E'/N).

Example 2.8 *A pulp and paper mill plans to buy 1000 acres of timberland for wood chips. However, before closing the deal, the company is interested in determining the mean timber volume per lot of one-fourth an acre. To achieve its goal, the company conducted an every 100th systematic random sample and obtained the data given in the following table. Estimate the mean timber volume* μ *per lot and the total timber volume* T *in one thousand acres. Determine the 95 percent margin of error of estimation for estimating the mean* μ *and the total* T *and then find 95 percent confidence intervals for the mean* μ *and the total* T.

Lot Sampled	57	157	257	357	457	557	657	757
Volume Cu. Feet	850	935	780	1150	940	898	956	865
Lot Sampled	857	957	1057	1157	1257	1357	1457	1557
Volume Cu. Feet	1180	1240	1150	980	960	1470	950	860
Lot Sampled	1657	1757	1857	1957	2057	2157	2257	2357
Volume Cu. Feet	1080	1186	1090	869	870	870	960	1058
Lot Sampled	2457	2557	2657	2757	2857	2957	3057	3157
Volume Cu. Feet	1080	980	960	880	1030	1150	1200	1070
Lot Sampled	3257	3357	3457	3557	3657	3757	3857	3957
Volume Cu. Feet	980	950	780	930	650	700	910	1300

Solution: From the given data, we have

$$\hat{\mu} = \bar{y}_{sy} = \frac{1}{40}(850 + 935 + 780 + \ldots + 1300) = \frac{1}{40}(39{,}697) = 992.425 \text{ cubic feet}$$

$$\hat{T} = N \times \bar{y}_{sy} = 4000 \times 992.425 = 3{,}969{,}700 \text{ cubic feet.}$$

To find the margin of error with 95 percent probability for the estimation of the mean μ and the total T, we need to determine the estimated variances of $\hat{\mu}$ and $\hat{T}$. We first need to find the sample variance.

$$s_{sy}^2 = \frac{1}{40-1}\left((850^2 + 935^2 + 780^2 + \ldots + 1300^2) - \frac{(850 + 935 + 780 + \ldots + 1300)^2}{40}\right)$$

$$= \frac{1}{39}(40{,}446{,}211.0 - 39{,}396{,}295.225) = \frac{1}{39}(1{,}049{,}915.775) = 26{,}920.9173$$

The estimated variances of $\hat{\mu}$ and $\hat{T}$ are given by

$$\hat{V}(\bar{y}_{sy}) = \frac{s_{sy}^2}{n}\left(1 - \frac{n}{N}\right) = \frac{26{,}920.9173}{40}\left(1 - \frac{40}{4000}\right) = 666.293,$$

$$\hat{V}(\hat{T}) = N^2\hat{V}(\bar{y}_{sy}) = 4000^2 \times 666.293 = 10{,}660{,}688{,}000.0.$$

Using equations (2.44) and (2.45), the margins of error of estimation for the population mean and population total with probability 95 percent are

$$\pm z_{\alpha/2}\sqrt{\hat{V}(\bar{y}_{sy})} = \pm 1.96\sqrt{666.293} = 50.59 \text{ cubic feet}$$

and

$$\pm z_{\alpha/2}\sqrt{\hat{V}(\hat{T})} = \pm 1.96\sqrt{10{,}660{,}688{,}000} = 202{,}360 \text{ cubic feet,}$$

respectively.

Using equations (2.32) and (2.33), confidence intervals for the population mean and population total with confidence coefficient 95 percent are

$$992.425 \pm 50.59 = (941.835, 1043.015)$$

and

$$3{,}969{,}700 \pm 202{,}360 = (4{,}172{,}060, 3{,}767{,}340),$$

respectively.

Example 2.9 *Extending our work in Example 2.8, determine an appropriate sample size if the manager of the pulp and paper company, estimating the mean timber per lot, is interested in attaining the margin of error of 25 cubic feet with probability 0.95.*

Solution: Substituting the values of s_{sy}^2, N, E, and $z_{\alpha/2}$ in equation (2.48), we get

$$n = \frac{z_{\alpha/2}^2 N s_{sy}^2}{(N-1)E^2 + s_{sy}^2 z_{\alpha/2}^2} = \frac{1.96^2 \times 4000 \times 26920.9173}{(4000-1)\times 25^2 + 26920.9173 \times 1.96^2} \cong 159.$$

Note that in Example 2.8, the sample size was 40 and the margin of error for estimating the mean timber per lot was 50.59 cubic feet with probability 95 percent. In order to attain the margin of error of 25 cubic feet, we will have to take a sample of at least size 159.

Note: In systematic sampling it is normally not possible to take only a supplemental sample to achieve a sample of full size, which in Example 2.8 is 159. However, it can be possible if we choose the values of n and k as n_1 and k_1 such that $N = n_1 k_1$ and $k = rk_1$, where r is an integer. Furthermore, we must keep the first randomly selected unit the same. For instance, in Example 2.8 we take a sample of size 160, $k_1 = 25$ and keep the first randomly selected lot as lot number 57. Our new sample will then consist of lot numbers 7, 32, 57, 82, 107, 132, 157, and so on. Obviously, the original sample is part of the new sample, which means in this case we can take only a supplemental sample of size 120 instead of taking a full sample of size 160.

2.5 Cluster Random Sampling

In all the sampling designs discussed so far, we have assumed that all the sampling units in a sampled population are such that the sampling frame can be prepared inexpensively, but this may not always be true. That is, to prepare a good frame listing is very costly, or there are not enough funds to meet that kind of cost, or all sampling units are not easily accessible. Another possible scenario is that all the sampling units are scattered, so obtaining observations on each sampling unit is not only very costly, but also very time consuming. In such cases we prepare the sampling frame consisting of larger sampling units, called *clusters,* such that each cluster consists of several original sampling units (subunits) of the sampled population. Then we take a simple random sample of the clusters and make observations on all the subunits in the selected clusters. This technique of sampling is known as the *cluster random sampling design,* or simply the *cluster sampling design.*

Cluster sampling is not only cost effective, but also a time saver because collecting data from adjoining units is cheaper, easier, and quicker than if the sampling units are far apart from each other. In manufacturing, for example, it may be much easier and cheaper to randomly select boxes that contain several parts rather than randomly selecting individual parts. However, while conducting a cluster sampling may be cost effective, it also may be less efficient in terms of precision than a simple random sampling when the sample sizes are the same. Also, the efficiency of cluster sampling may further decrease if we let the cluster sizes increase.

Cluster samplings are of two kinds: one-stage and two-stage. In *one-stage cluster sampling*, we examine all the sampling subunits within the selected clusters. In *two-stage cluster sampling*, we examine only a portion of sampling subunits, which are chosen from each selected cluster using simple random sampling. Furthermore, in cluster sampling, the cluster sizes may or may not be of the same size. Normally in field sampling it is not feasible to have clusters of equal sizes. For example, in a sample survey of a large metropolitan area, city blocks may be considered as clusters. If the sampling subunits are households or persons, then obviously it will be almost impossible to have the same number of households or persons in every block. However, in industrial sampling, one can always have clusters of equal sizes; for example, boxes containing the same number of parts may be considered as clusters.

2.5.1 Estimation of a Population Mean and Population Total

Let N be the number of clusters in the sampled population, with the ith cluster having m_i sampling subunits. We take a simple random sample of n clusters. Let y_{ij} be the observed value of the characteristic of interest of the jth subunit in the ith cluster, $j = 1, 2, \ldots, m_i$; $i = 1, 2 \ldots, n$. We have the following:

$$\text{Total of all observations in the } i\text{th cluster} = y_i = \sum_{j=1}^{m_i} y_{ij}$$

$$\text{Total number of subunits in the sample} = m = \sum_{i=1}^{n} m_i$$

$$\text{Average cluster size in the sample} = \bar{m} = \frac{1}{n}\sum_{i=1}^{n} m_i = \frac{m}{n}$$

$$\text{Total number of subunits in the population} = M = \sum_{i=1}^{N} m_i$$

$$\text{Average cluster size in the population} = \bar{M} = \frac{1}{N}\sum_{i=1}^{N} m_i = \frac{M}{N}$$

Then, an estimator of the population mean μ (average value of the characteristic of interest per subunit) is given by

$$\hat{\mu}_c = \overline{y} = \frac{\sum_{i=1}^{n} y_i}{m}, \tag{2.49}$$

and its estimated variance is given by

$$\hat{V}(\hat{\mu}_c) = \hat{V}(\overline{y}) = \left(\frac{N-n}{Nn\overline{M}^2}\right)\left(\frac{1}{n-1}\sum_{i=1}^{n}(y_i - m_i\overline{y})^2\right). \tag{2.50}$$

If $\overline{M}$ is unknown, it is replaced by $\overline{m}$, so that the estimated variance of $\hat{\mu}_c$ is

$$\hat{V}(\hat{\mu}_c) = \hat{V}(\overline{y}) = \left(\frac{N-n}{Nn\overline{m}^2}\right)\left(\frac{1}{n-1}\sum_{i=1}^{n}(y_i - m_i\overline{y})^2\right). \tag{2.51}$$

An estimator of the population total T (total value of the characteristic of interest for all subunits in the population) is given by

$$\hat{T} = M \times \overline{y} = \frac{M}{m}\sum_{i=1}^{n} y_i, \tag{2.52}$$

and its estimated variance is given by

$$\hat{V}(\hat{T}) = M^2\hat{V}(\overline{y}) = N^2\overline{M}^2\hat{V}(\overline{y}).$$

Substituting the value of $\hat{V}(\overline{y})$ from equation (2.50), we have

$$\hat{V}(\hat{T}) = N\left(\frac{N}{n} - 1\right)\left(\frac{1}{n-1}\sum_{i=1}^{n}(y_i - m_i\overline{y})^2\right). \tag{2.53}$$

The margins of error with probability $(1 - \alpha)$ for estimating the population mean and population total are given by

$$\pm z_{\alpha/2}\sqrt{\hat{V}(\overline{y})} = \pm z_{\alpha/2}\sqrt{\left(\frac{N-n}{Nn\overline{m}^2}\right)\left(\frac{1}{n-1}\sum_{i=1}^{n}(y_i - m_i\overline{y})^2\right)} \tag{2.54}$$

and

$$\pm z_{\alpha/2}\sqrt{\hat{V}(\hat{T})} = \pm z_{\alpha/2}\sqrt{N\left(\frac{N}{n} - 1\right)\left(\frac{1}{n-1}\sum_{i=1}^{n}(y_i - m_i\overline{y})^2\right)}, \tag{2.55}$$

respectively.

2.5.2 Confidence Interval for a Population Mean and Population Total

Using equations (2.54) and (2.55), the confidence intervals for the population mean and population total with confidence $(1 - \alpha)$ are given by

$$\bar{y} \pm z_{\alpha/2}\sqrt{\left(\frac{N-n}{Nn\bar{m}^2}\right)\left(\frac{1}{n-1}\sum_{i=1}^{n}(y_i - m_i\bar{y})^2\right)} \tag{2.56}$$

and

$$\frac{M}{m}\sum_{i=1}^{n} y_i \pm z_{\alpha/2}\sqrt{N\left(\frac{N}{n}-1\right)\left(\frac{1}{n-1}\sum_{i=1}^{n}(y_i - m_i\bar{y})^2\right)}, \tag{2.57}$$

respectively.

Example 2.10 *The quality manager of a company that manufactures hydraulic pumps is investigating the cost of warranty claims per year for one specific pump model. The pump model being investigated is typically installed in six applications, which include food service operations (for example, pressurized drink dispensers), dairy operations, soft-drink bottling operations, brewery operations, wastewater treatment, and light commercial sump water removal.*

The quality manager cannot determine the exact warranty repair cost for each pump; however, through company warranty claims data, she can determine the total repair cost and the number of pumps used by each industry in the six applications. In this case, the quality manager decides to use cluster sampling, using each industry as a cluster. She selects a random sample of n = *15 from the* N = *120 industries that use the pump. The data on total repair cost per industry and the number of pumps owned by each industry are provided in the following table. Estimate the average repair cost per pump and the total cost incurred by the 120 industries over a period of one year. Determine a 95 percent confidence interval for the population mean and population total.*

Sample #	Number of Pumps	Total Repair Cost During One Year of Warranty Period (in dollars)
1	5	250
2	7	338
3	8	290
4	3	160
5	9	390
6	11	460
7	5	275
8	8	358
9	9	285
10	4	215
11	6	220
12	10	310
13	9	320
14	7	275
15	5	280

Solution: To estimate the population mean μ, we proceed as follows:

m = total number of pumps in the sample = 5 + 7 + 8 + . . . + 5

$$= 103,$$

$$\bar{m} = \text{average cluster size in the sample } = \frac{1}{15}(103) = 6.867,$$

y = total repair cost for the selected clusters during one year = \$4426.00.

An estimate of the population mean μ is

$$\hat{\mu} = \bar{y} = \frac{4426.00}{103} = \$42.97.$$

Because we do not have information about the sizes of all the clusters, we need to estimate the total number of subunits in the population, that is,

$$\hat{M} = N \times \hat{\bar{M}} = N \times \bar{m} = 120 \times 6.867 = 824.$$

An estimate of the total number of pumps owned by the 120 industries is 824.

Therefore, an estimator of the population total T (total repair cost for the manufacturer during one year of warranty period [in dollars]) is given by

$$\hat{T} = \hat{M} \times \hat{\mu} = 824 \times 42.97 = \$35,407.28.$$

To determine a 95 percent confidence interval for the population mean and population total, we first need to evaluate s^2, which is given by

$$\frac{1}{n-1}\sum_{i=1}^{n}\left(y_i - m_i\bar{y}\right)^2,$$

that is,

$$s^2 = \frac{1}{15-1}\left((250 - 5 \times 42.97)^2 + (338 - 7 \times 42.97)^2 + ... + (280 - 5 \times 42.97)^2\right.$$

$$= \frac{1}{14}(38,185.3464) = 2727.5247.$$

Using equation (2.56), a 95 percent confidence interval for the population mean is

$$42.97 \mp 1.96\sqrt{\frac{120-15}{120 \times 15 \times 6.867^2}(2727.5247)}$$

$$= 42.97 \mp 3.6$$

$$= (39.37, 46.57).$$

Similarly, using equation (2.56), a 95 percent confidence interval for the population total is

$$824 \times 42.97 \mp 1.96\sqrt{120(\frac{120}{15}-1)(2727.5247)}$$

$$= 35{,}407.28 \mp 2966.74$$

$$= (32{,}440.54, 38{,}374.02).$$

2.5.3 Determination of Sample Size

The sample size needed to estimate the population mean with margin of error E with probability $(1 - \alpha)$ is given by

$$n \geq \frac{z_{\alpha/2}^2 N s^2}{N\bar{M}^2 E^2 + z_{\alpha/2}^2 s^2}, \qquad (2.58)$$

where

$$s^2 = \frac{1}{n-1}\sum_{i=1}^{n}(y_i - m_i \bar{y})^2.$$

The sample size needed to estimate the population total with margin of error E' with probability $(1 - \alpha)$ can be found from equation (2.58) by replacing E with (E'/M).

Example 2.11 *In Example 2.10, determine the sample size if the quality manager wants to estimate the repair cost per pump with a margin of error $2.00 with 95 percent probability.*

Solution: Using equation (2.58), the desired sample size is

$$n \geq \frac{(1.96)^2(120)(2727.5247)}{(120)(6.867)^2(2)^2 + (1.96)^2(2727.5247)} = 37.97.$$

The sample size should be $n = 38$. Note that in order to determine the sample size, we needed s^2 and $\bar{m}$, for which we need to have a sample and thus the sample size, which in fact we want to determine. The solution for this problem, as discussed in details in *Applied Statistics for the Six Sigma Green Belt*, is to evaluate these quantities either by using some similar data if already available or by taking a smaller sample, as we did in this example.

3

Phase I (Detecting Large Shifts)—SPC: Control Charts for Variables

The concept of quality is centuries old. However, the concept of SQC is less than a century old. SQC is merely a set of interrelated tools that includes SPC, DOE, acceptance sampling, and other tools used to monitor and improve quality. SPC consists of several tools that are useful for process monitoring. The quality control chart, which is the center of our discussion in this chapter, is one of these tools. Walter A. Shewhart, from Bell Telephone Laboratories, was the first person to apply statistical methods to quality improvement when, in 1924, he presented the first quality control chart. In 1931, Shewhart wrote a book on SQC titled *Economic Control of Quality of Manufactured Product* (D. Van Nostrand Co.). The publication of this book set the notion of SQC in full swing. In the initial stages, the acceptance of the notion of SQC in the United States was almost negligible. It was only during World War II, when the armed services adopted the statistically designed sampling inspection schemes, that the concept of SQC started to gain acceptance in American industry.

The complete adoption of modern SQC was limited from the 1950s to the late 1970s, however, because American manufacturers believed that quality and productivity couldn't go hand in hand. American manufacturers argued that producing goods of high quality would cost more because high quality would mean buying raw materials of higher grade, hiring more qualified personnel, and providing more training to workers, all of which would translate into higher costs. American manufacturers also believed that producing higher-quality goods would slow down productivity because better-qualified and better-trained workers would not compromise quality to meet their daily quotas, which would further add to the cost of their product. As a consequence, they believed they would not be able to compete in the world market and would therefore lose their market share. The industrial revolution in Japan, however, proved that American manufacturers were wrong. This revolution followed the visit of a famous American statistician, W. Edwards Deming, in 1950.

Deming (1986, 2) wrote, "Improvement of quality transfers waste of man-hours and of machine-time into the manufacture of good product and better service. The result is a chain reaction—lower costs, better competitive position, and happier people on the job, jobs and more jobs." Deming describes this chain reaction as follows:

> Improve quality → cost decreases because of less work, fewer mistakes, fewer delays or snags, better use of machine time and materials → productivity improves → capture the market with better quality and lower price → stay in business → provide jobs and more jobs. (3)

After Deming's visit in 1950, this message of a chain reaction appeared on blackboards in every meeting room of top management in the industrial world of Japan. Once the management in Japan adopted the philosophy of this chain reaction, everyone had one common goal of achieving quality.

3.1 Basic Definition of Quality and Its Benefits

Different authors have defined the concept of quality in different ways. We define it as Deming did: a product is of good quality if it meets the needs of a customer and the customer is glad that he or she bought that product. The customer may be internal or external, an individual or a corporation. If a product meets the needs of the customer, the customer is bound to buy that product again and again. On the contrary, if a product does not meet the needs of a customer, then he or she will not buy that product even if he or she is an internal customer. Consequently, that product will be deemed of bad quality, and eventually it is bound to go out of the market.

Other components of a product's quality are its reliability, how much maintenance it demands, and, when the need arises, how easily and how fast one can get it serviced. In evaluating the quality of a product, its attractability and rate of depreciation also play an important role.

As described by Deming in his telecast conferences, the benefits of better quality are numerous. First and foremost is that it enhances the overall image and reputation of the company by meeting the needs of its customers and thus making them happy. A happy customer is bound to buy the product again and again. Also, a happy customer is likely to share a good experience with the product with friends, relatives, and neighbors. Therefore, the company gets publicity without spending a dime, and this results in more sales and higher profits. Higher profits lead to higher stock prices, which means higher net worth of the company. Better quality provides workers satisfaction and pride in their workmanship. A satisfied worker goes home happy, which makes his or her family happy. A happy family boosts the morale of a worker, which means greater dedication and loyalty to the company.

Another benefit of better quality is decreased cost. This is due to the need for less rework, thus less scrap, fewer raw materials used, and fewer workforce hours and machine hours wasted. Ultimately, this means increased productivity, a better competitive position, increased sales, and a higher market share. On the other hand, losses due to poor quality are enormous. Poor quality not only affects sales and the competitive position, but it also carries with it high hidden costs that are usually not calculated and therefore not known with precision. These costs include unusable product, product sold at a discounted price, and so on. In most companies, the accounting departments provide only minimum information to quantify the actual losses incurred due to poor quality. Lack of awareness concerning the cost of poor quality could lead company managers to fail to take appropriate actions to improve quality.

3.2 SPC

What is a process? A *process* may be defined as a series of actions or operations performed in producing manufactured or nonmanufactured products. A *process* may also be defined as a combination of workforce, equipment, raw materials, methods, and environment that works together to produce output. The flowchart in Figure 3.1 shows where each component of a process fits.

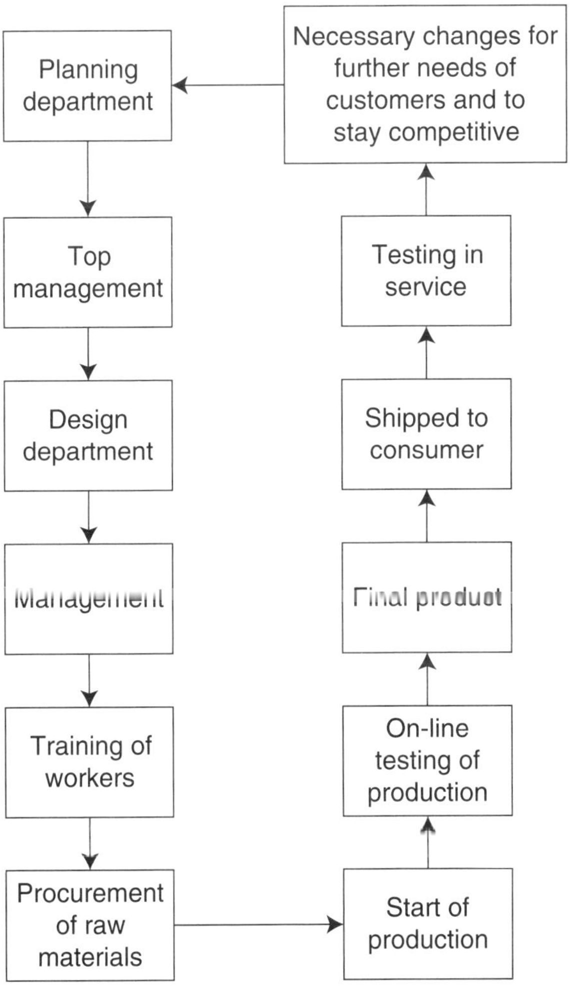

Figure 3.1 Flowchart of a process.

The quality of the final product depends on how the process is designed and executed. However, no matter how perfectly a process is designed and how well it is executed, no two items produced by the process are identical. The difference between two items is called the *variation*. Such variation occurs because of two causes:

1. Common causes or random causes
2. Special causes or assignable causes

As mentioned earlier, the first attempt to understand and remove variation in any scientific way was made by Walter A. Shewhart. Shewhart recognized that special or assignable causes are due to identifiable sources, which can be systematically identified and eliminated, whereas common or random causes are not due to identifiable sources and therefore cannot be eliminated without very expensive measures. These measures include redesigning the process, replacing old machines with new machines, and renovating part of or the whole system. A process is considered in statistical control when only common causes are present. Deming (1975, 5) states, "But a state of statistical control is not a natural state for a manufacturing process. It is instead an achievement, arrived at by elimination, one by one, by determined efforts, of special causes of excessive variation."

Because the process variation cannot be fully eliminated, controlling it is key. If process variation is controlled, the process becomes predictable. Otherwise the process is unpredictable. To achieve this goal, Shewhart introduced the quality control chart. Shewhart control charts are normally used in phase I implementation of SPC, when a process is particularly susceptible to the influence of special causes and, consequently, is experiencing excessive variation or large shifts.

Quality control charts can be divided into two major categories: control charts for variables and control charts for attributes. In this chapter we will study control charts for variables.

Definition 3.1 A quality characteristic that can be expressed numerically or measured on a numerical scale is called a *variable*.

Examples of a variable include the length of a tie-rod, the tread depth of a tire, the compressive strength of a concrete block, the tensile strength of a wire, the shearing strength of paper, the concentration of a chemical, the diameter of a ball bearing, and the amount of liquid in a 16-ounce can, and so on.

In general, in any process there are some quality characteristics that define the quality of the process. If all such characteristics are behaving in a desired manner, then the process is considered stable and it will produce products of good quality. If, however, any of these characteristics are not behaving in a desired manner, then the process is considered unstable and it is not capable of producing products of good quality. A characteristic is usually determined by two parameters: its mean and its standard deviation. In order to verify whether a characteristic is behaving in a desired manner, one needs to verify that these two parameters are in statistical control, which can be done by using quality control charts. In addition, there are several other such tools that are valuable in achieving process stability. These tools, including the control charts, constitute an integral part of SPC. SPC is very useful in any process related to manufacturing, service, or retail industries. This set of tools consists of the following:

1. Histogram
2. Stem-and-leaf diagram
3. Scatter diagram
4. Run chart (also known as a line graph or a time series graph)
5. Check sheet
6. Pareto chart
7. Cause-and-effect diagram (also known as a fishbone or Ishikawa diagram)
8. Defect concentration diagram
9. Control charts

These tools of SPC form a simple but very powerful structure for quality improvement. Once workers become fully familiar with these tools, management must get involved to implement SPC for an ongoing quality-improvement process. Management must create an environment where these tools become part of the day-to-day production or service process. The implementation of SPC without management's involvement and cooperation is bound to fail. In addition to discussing these tools, we will also explore here some of the questions that arise while implementing SPC.

Every job, whether in a manufacturing company or in a service company, involves a process. As described earlier, each process consists of a certain number of steps. No matter how well the process is planned, designed, and executed, there is always some potential for variability. In some cases this variability may be very little, while in other cases it may be very high. If the variability is very little, it is usually due to some common causes that are unavoidable and cannot be controlled. If the variability is too high, we expect that in addition to the common causes there are some other causes, usually known as assignable causes, present in the process. Any process working under only common causes or chance causes is considered to be in statistical control. If a process is working under both common and assignable causes, it is considered unstable, or not in statistical control.

The first four tools in the SPC tools list are discussed in the first volume of this series, *Applied Statistics for the Six Sigma Green Belt.* In this chapter and the two that follow, we will discuss the rest of these tools.

Check Sheet

In order to improve the quality of a product, management must try to reduce the variation of all the quality characteristics; that is, the process must be brought to a stable condition. In any SPC procedure used to stabilize a process, it is

Table 3.1 Check sheet summarizing the data of a study over a period of four weeks.

	Date	1	2	3	4	5	6	7	8	9	10	11	12	13	14	15	16	17	18	19	20	21	22	23	24	25	26	27	28
Defect type	Corrugation	1		2		1		3		1	1	1	2		1		2	1	1		1	3	2		1	2		1	1
	Streaks			1				1						1		1		1		2				1			1	1	
	Pinholes	1				1	1					1			1		1				1	1			1				
	Dirt		1		1				1					1						1							2		
	Blistering			2				2					1				2					1			2				1
	Other	1				1					1								1					1					
	Total	3	1	5	1	3	1	6	1	1	2	2	3	2	2	1	5	2	2	3	2	5	2	2	4	2	3	2	2

essential to know precisely what types of defects are affecting the quality of the final product. The check sheet is an important tool to achieve this goal. We discuss this tool using a real-life example.

Example 3.1 *In a paper mill, a high percentage of paper rolls are discarded due to various types of defects. In order to identify these defects and their frequency, a study is launched. This study is done over a period of four weeks. The data are collected daily and summarized in the following form (see Table 3.1), called the check sheet.*

The summary data not only give the total number of different types of defects but also provide a very meaningful source of trends and patterns of defects. These trends and patterns can help find possible causes for any particular defect or defects. Note that the column totals in Table 3.1 show the number of defects (rolls of paper rejected) occurring daily, whereas the row totals (not shown in Table 3.1 but shown in Figure 3.2) show the number of defects by type that occur over the total period (four weeks) of study. It is important to remark here that these types of data become more meaningful if a logbook of all changes, such as a change in raw materials, calibration of machines, or training of workers or new workers hired, is well kept.

Pareto Chart

The Pareto chart is a useful tool for learning more about attribute data quickly and visually. The Pareto chart—named after its inventor, Vilfredo Pareto, an Italian economist who died in 1923—is simply a bar graph of attribute data in a descending order of frequency by, say, defect type. For example, consider the data on defective rolls in Example 3.1 and as shown in Figure 3.2, which plots the frequency totals (row totals) of each defect, starting from highest to lowest.

The chart allows the user to quickly identify those defects that occur more frequently and those that occur less frequently. This allows the user to priori-

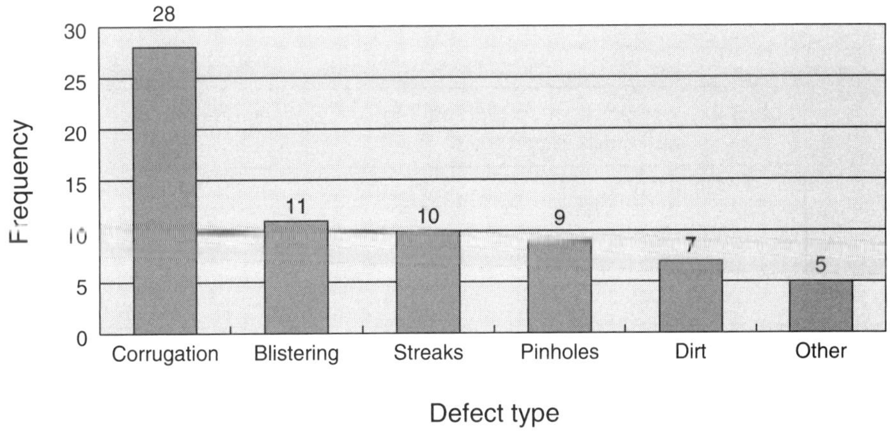

Figure 3.2 Pareto chart for data in Example 3.1.

tize his or her resources to eliminate first those defects that have the greatest effect on the quality of the product. For instance, the Pareto chart in Figure 3.2 indicates that 40 percent of the paper rolls are rejected because of corrugation. Corrugation and blistering together are responsible for 55.7 percent of the rejected paper. Corrugation, blistering, and streaks are responsible for 70 percent. To reduce the overall rejection, one should first attempt to eliminate or at least reduce the defects due to corrugation, then blistering, streaks, and so on. By eliminating these three types of defects, one would dramatically change the percentage of rejected paper and reduce the losses. It is important to note that if one can eliminate more than one defect simultaneously, then one should consider eliminating them even though some of them are occurring less frequently. Furthermore, after one or more defects are either eliminated or reduced, one should again collect the data and reconstruct the Pareto chart to determine whether the priority has changed. If another defect is now occurring more frequently, one may divert the resources to eliminate such a defect first. Note that in this example, the category "Other" may include several defects such as porosity, grainy edges, wrinkles, or brightness that are not occurring very frequently. So, if one has limited resources, one should not expend them on this category until all other defects are eliminated.

Sometimes the defects are not equally important. This is true particularly when some defects are life threatening while other defects are merely a nuisance or an inconvenience. It is quite common to allocate weights to each defect and then plot the weighted frequencies versus the defects to construct the Pareto chart. For example, suppose a product has five types of defects, which are denoted by A, B, C, D, and E, where A is life threatening, B is not life threatening but very serious, C is serious, D is somewhat serious, and E is not serious but merely a nuisance. Suppose we assign a weight of 100 to A, 75 to B, 50 to C, 20 to D, and 5 to E. The data collected over a period of study are shown in Table 3.2.

In Figure 3.3 the Pareto chart presents a completely different picture. That is, by using weighted frequencies, the order of priority of removing the defects is C, A, B, D, and E, whereas without using the weighted frequencies, this order would have been E, C, D, B, and A.

Table 3.2 Frequencies and weighted frequencies when different types of defects are not equally important.

Defect Type	Frequency	Weighted Frequency
A	5	500
B	6	450
C	15	750
D	12	240
E	25	125

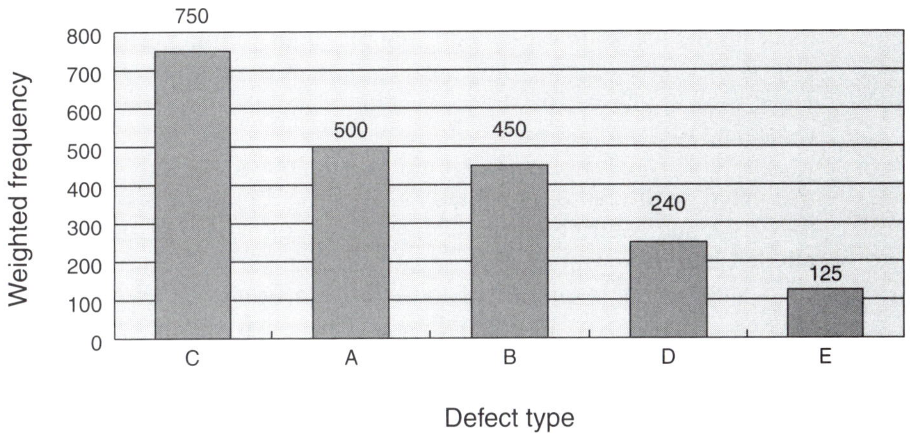

Figure 3.3 Pareto chart when weighted frequencies are used.

Cause-and-Effect (Fishbone or Ishikawa) Diagram

In an SPC-implementing scheme, identifying and isolating the causes of a particular problem or problems is very important. An effective tool for identifying such causes is the cause-and-effect diagram. This diagram is also known as a fishbone diagram because of its shape, and sometimes it is called an Ishikawa diagram after its inventor. Japanese manufacturers have widely used this diagram to improve the quality of their products. In preparing a cause-and-effect diagram, it is quite common to use a brainstorming technique. The brainstorming technique is a form of creative and collaborative thinking. This technique is used in a team setting. The team usually includes personnel from departments of production, inspection, purchasing, design, and management, along with any other members associated with the product under discussion. A brainstorming session is set up in the following manner:

1. Each team member makes a list of ideas.
2. The team members sit around a table and take turns reading one idea at a time.
3. As the ideas are read, a facilitator displays them on a board so that all team members can see them.
4. Steps 2 and 3 continue until all ideas have been exhausted and displayed.
5. Cross-questioning concerning a team member's idea is allowed only for clarification.
6. When all ideas have been read and displayed, the facilitator asks each team member if he or she has any new ideas. This procedure continues until no team member can think of any new ideas.

Once all the ideas are presented using the brainstorming technique, the next step is to analyze them. The cause-and-effect diagram is a graphical technique used to analyze these ideas. Figure 3.4 shows an initial structure of a cause-and-effect diagram.

The five spines in Figure 3.4 indicate the five major factors or categories that could be the cause, or causes, of defect(s). In most workplaces, whether they are manufacturing or nonmanufacturing, the causes of all problems usually fall into one or more of these categories.

Using a brainstorming session, the team brings up all possible causes under each category. For example, under the environment category, a cause could be the management's attitude. Management might not be willing to release any funds for research or to change suppliers; there might not be much cooperation among middle and top management; or something similar. Under the personnel category, a cause could be lack of proper training for workers, supervisors who are not helpful in solving problems, lack of communication between workers and supervisors, and workers who are afraid of asking their supervisors questions for fear of repercussions in their jobs, promotions, or raises. Once all possible causes under each major category are listed in the cause-and-effect diagram, the next step is to isolate one or more common causes and eliminate them. A complete cause-and-effect diagram may appear as shown in Figure 3.5.

Defect Concentration Diagram

A defect concentration diagram is a visual representation of the product under study that depicts all the defects. This diagram helps the workers determine if there are any patterns or particular locations where the defects occur and what kinds of defects, minor or major, are occurring. The patterns or particu-

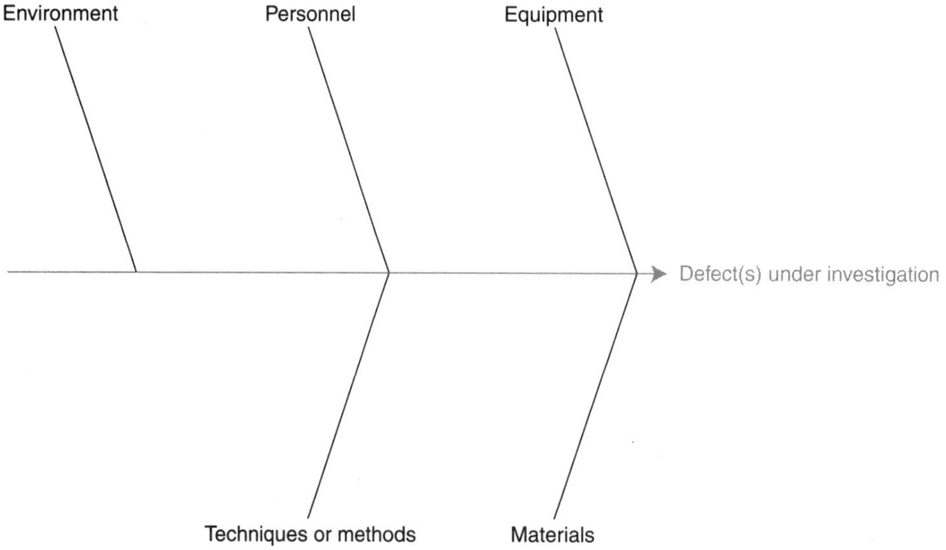

Figure 3.4 An initial form of a cause-and-effect diagram.

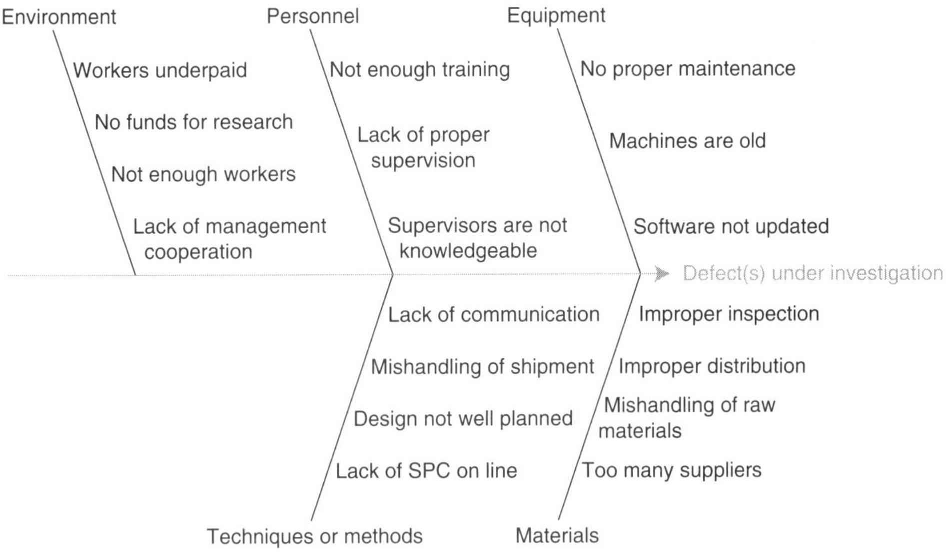

Figure 3.5 A complete cause-and-effect diagram.

lar locations may help the workers find the specific causes for such defects. It is important that the diagram show the product from different angles. For example, if the product is in the shape of a rectangular prism and defects are found on the surface, then the diagram should show all six faces, very clearly indicating the location of the defects. In Figure 3.6 the two diagonally opposite edges are damaged, which could have happened in transportation or in moving this item from the production area to the storage area.

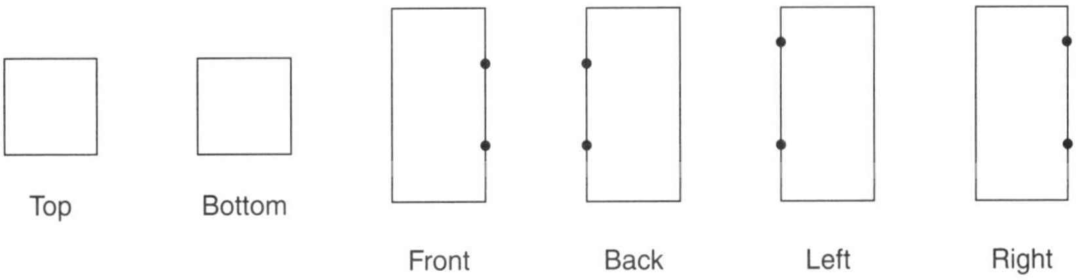

Figure 3.6 A rectangular prism-shaped product that has been damaged.

The defect concentration diagram was useful when the daughter of one of the authors made a claim with a transportation company. In 2001, the author shipped a car from Boston, Massachusetts, to his daughter in San Jose, California. After receiving the car, she found that the front bumper's paint was damaged. She filed a claim with the transportation company for the damage, but the company turned it down, simply stating that the damage was not caused by the company. Fortunately, a couple days later, she found similar damage under the back bumper, symmetrically opposite the front bumper. She again called the company and explained that this damage had clearly been done by the belts used to hold the car during transportation. This time the company could not turn down her claim, because by using a defect concentration diagram, she could prove that the damage was caused by the transportation company.

Run Chart

In any SPC procedure it is very important to detect any trends that may be present in the data. Run charts help identify such trends by plotting data over a certain period of time. For example, if the proportion of nonconforming parts produced from shift to shift is perceived to be a problem, we may plot the number of nonconforming parts against the shifts for a certain period of time to determine whether there are any trends. Trends usually help us identify the causes of nonconformities. This chart is particularly useful when the data are collected from a production process over a certain period of time.

A run chart for data in Table 3.3 is shown in Figure 3.7, in which we have plotted the percentage of nonconforming units in different shifts over a period of 10 days, starting with the morning shift.

From this run chart we can easily see that the percentage of nonconforming units is the lowest in the morning shift (shifts 1, 4, 7, . . . , 28) and the highest in the night shift (shifts 3, 6, 9, . . . , 30). There are also some problems in the evening shift, but they are not as severe as those in the night shift. Because such trends or patterns are usually created by special or assignable

Table 3.3 Percentage of nonconforming units in different shifts over a period of 30 shifts.

Shift Number	1	2	3	4	5	6	7	8	9	10
% Nonconforming	5	9	12	7	12	4	11	7	15	3
Shift Number	11	12	13	14	15	16	17	18	19	20
% Nonconforming	5	8	2	5	15	4	6	15	5	5
Shift Number	21	22	23	24	25	26	27	28	29	30
% Nonconforming	8	6	10	15	7	10	13	4	8	14

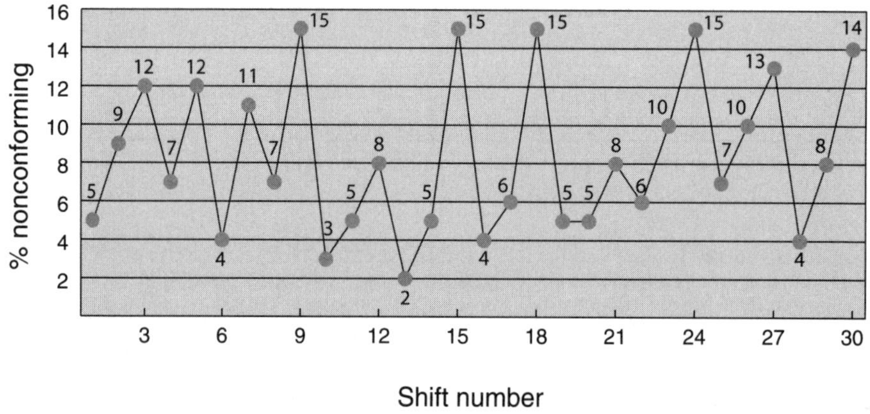

Figure 3.7 A run chart.

causes, the run chart will certainly prompt the management to explore how the various shifts differ. Does the quality of the raw materials differ from shift to shift? Is there inadequate training of workers in the later shifts? Are evening- and late-shift workers more susceptible to fatigue? Are there environmental problems that increase in severity as the day wears on?

Deming (1986, 313) points out that sometimes the frequency distribution of a set of data does not give a true picture of the data, whereas a run chart can bring out the real problems of the data. The frequency distribution gives us the overall picture of the data, but it does not show us any trends or patterns that may be present in the process on a short-term basis.

Control charts make up perhaps the most important part of SPC. We will study some of the basic concepts of control charts in the following section, and then in the rest of this chapter and the next two chapters we will study the various kinds of control charts.

3.3 Control Charts for Variables

A control chart is a simple but very powerful statistical device used to keep a process predictable. As noted by Duncan (1986), a control chart is (1) a device for describing in concrete terms what a state of statistical control is, (2) a device for attaining control, and (3) a device for judging whether control has been attained.

Before the control charts are implemented in any process, it is important to understand the process and have a concrete plan for future actions that would be needed to improve the process.

Process Evaluation

Process evaluation includes not only the study of the final product, but also the study of all the *intermediate steps* or *outputs* that describes the actual operating state of the process. For example, in the paper production process, wood chips and pulp may be considered as intermediate outputs. If the data on process evaluation are collected, analyzed, and interpreted correctly, they can show where and when a corrective action is necessary to make the whole process work more efficiently.

Action on Process

Action on process is important for any process because it prevents the production of an out-of-specification product. An action on process may include changes in raw materials, operator training, equipment, design, or other measures. The effects of such actions on a process should be monitored closely, and further action should be taken if necessary.

Action on Output

If the process evaluation indicates that no further action on the process is necessary, the last action is to ship the final product to its destination. Note that some people believe action on output consists of sampling plans and discarding the out-of-specification product, which has already been produced. Obviously, such an action on the output is futile and expensive. We are interested in correcting the output before it is produced. This goal can be achieved through the use of control charts.

Any process with a lot of variation is bad and is bound to produce products of inferior quality. Control charts can help detect variation in any process. As described earlier, in any process there are two causes of variation: common causes or random causes, and special causes or assignable causes.

Variation

No process can produce two products that are exactly alike or possess exactly the same characteristics. Any process is bound to contain some sources of variation. The difference between two products may be very large, moderate, very small, or even undetectable, depending on the source of variation, but certainly there is always some difference. For example, the moisture content in any two rolls of paper, the opacity in any two spools of paper, and the brightness of two lots of pulp will always vary. Our aim is to trace back as far as possible the sources of such variation and eliminate them. The first step is to separate the common and special causes of such sources of variation.

Common Causes or Random Causes

Common causes or *random causes* are the sources of variation within a process that is in statistical control. The causes behave like a constant system of chance. While individual measured values may all be different, as a group they tend to form a pattern that can be explained by a statistical distribution that can generally be characterized by:

1. Location parameter
2. Dispersion parameter
3. Shape (the pattern of variation, whether it is symmetrical, right skewed, left skewed, and so on)

Special Causes or Assignable Causes

Special causes or *assignable causes* refer to any source of variation that cannot be adequately explained by any single distribution of the process output, as otherwise would be the case if the process were in statistical control. Unless all the special causes of variation are identified and corrected, they will continue to affect the process output in an unpredictable way. Any process with assignable causes is considered unstable and hence not in statistical control. However, any process free of assignable causes is considered stable and therefore in statistical control. Assignable causes can be corrected by local actions, while common causes or random causes can be corrected only by actions on the system.

Local Actions and Actions on the System

Local Actions

1. Are usually required to eliminate special causes of variation
2. Can usually be taken by people close to the process
3. Can correct about 15 percent of process problems

Deming (1982) believed that as much as 6 percent of all system variations is due to special or assignable causes, while no more than 94 percent of the variations is due to common causes.

Actions on the System

1. Are usually required to reduce the variation due to common causes
2. Almost always require management action for correction
3. Are needed to correct about 85 percent of process problems

Furthermore, Deming (1951) points out that there is an important relationship between the two types of variations and the two types of actions needed to reduce such variations. We will discuss this point in more detail.

Special causes of variation can be detected by simple statistical techniques. These causes of variation are not the same in all the operations involved. Detecting special causes of variation and removing them is usually the responsibility of someone directly connected to the operation, although management is sometimes in a better position to correct them. Resolving a special cause of variation usually requires local action.

The extent of common causes of variation can be indicated by simple statistical techniques, but the causes themselves need more exploration in order to be isolated. It is usually management's responsibility to correct the common causes of variation, although personnel directly involved with the operation are sometimes in a better position to identify such causes and pass them on to management for an appropriate action. Overall, resolving common causes of variation usually requires action on the system.

As we noted earlier, about 15 percent (or according to Deming, 6 percent) of industrial process troubles are correctable by the local action taken by people directly involved with the operation, while 85 percent are correctable only by management's action on the system. Confusion about the type of action required is very costly to the organization in terms of wasted efforts, delayed resolution of trouble, and other aggravating problems. So, it would be wrong to take local action (for example, changing an operator or calibrating a machine) when, in fact, management action on the system was required (for example, selecting a supplier that can provide better and consistent raw materials).

All of this reasoning shows that strong statistical analysis of any operation in any industrial production is necessary. Control charts are perhaps the best tool to separate the special causes from the common causes.

Control Charts

1. Are used to describe in concrete terms what a state of statistical control is
2. Are used to judge whether control has been attained and thus detect whether assignable causes are present
3. Are used to attain a stable process

Suppose we take a sample of size n from a process at approximately regular intervals, and for each sample we compute a sample statistic, say X. This statistic may be the sample mean, a fraction of nonconforming product, or any other appropriate measure. Now, because X is a statistic, it is subject to some fluctuation or variation. If no special causes are present, the variation in X will have characteristics that can be described by some statistical distribution. By taking enough samples, we can estimate the desired characteristics of such a distribution. For instance, we now suppose that the statistic X is distributed as normal, and we divide the vertical scale of a graph in units of X, and the horizontal scale in units of time or any other such characteristic. Then we draw horizontal lines through the mean, called the center line (CL), and the extreme values of X, called the upper control limit (UCL) and the lower control limit (LCL). This results in the device shown in Figure 3.8, also known as a *control chart.*

The main goal of using control charts is to reduce the variation in the process and bring the process target value to the desired level. In other words, the process should be brought into a state of statistical control.

If we plot data pertaining to a process on a control chart and the data conform to a pattern of random variation that falls within the upper and lower control limits, then we say that the process is in statistical control. If, however, the data fall outside these control limits and do not conform to a pattern of random variation, then the process is considered to be out of control. In the latter case, an investigation is launched to find and correct the special causes responsible for the process being out of control.

If any special cause of variation is present, an effort is made to eliminate it. In this manner, the process can eventually be brought into a state of statistical control.

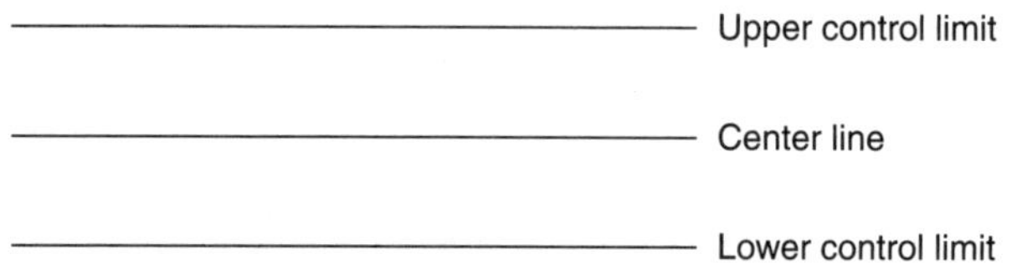

Figure 3.8 A control chart with a UCL and an LCL.

Shewhart strongly recommended that a process should not be judged to be in control unless the pattern of random variation has persisted for some time and for a sizable volume of output.

Note: If a control chart shows a process in statistical control, it does not mean that all special causes have been completely eliminated; rather, it simply means that for all practical purposes, it is reasonable to assume or adopt a hypothesis of common causes only.

Preparation for Use of Control Charts

In order for control charts to serve their intended purpose, it is important to take the following preparatory steps prior to implementing the control charts:

1. *Establish an environment suitable for action:* Any statistical method will fail unless management has prepared a responsive environment.

2. *Define the process and determine the characteristics to be studied:* The process must be understood in terms of its relationship to the other operations and users and in terms of the process elements (for example, people, equipment, materials, methods, and environment) that affect it at each stage. Some of the techniques discussed earlier, such as the Pareto chart or the fishbone diagram, can help make these relationships visible. Once the process is well understood, the next step is to determine which characteristics are affecting the process, which characteristics should be studied in depth, and which characteristics should be controlled.

3. *Determine the correlation between characteristics:* For an efficient and effective study, take advantage of the relationship between characteristics. If several characteristics of an item are positively correlated, it may be sufficient to chart only one of them. If there are some characteristics that are negatively correlated, a deeper study is required before any corrective action on such characteristics can be taken.

4. *Define the measurement system:* The characteristic must be operationally defined so that the findings can be communicated to all concerned in ways that have the same meaning today as they did yesterday. This includes specifying what information is to be gathered, where it should be gathered, how it should be gathered, and under what conditions it should be gathered. The operational definition is very important for collecting data because it can impact the control charts in many ways. Moreover, the analysis of data depends on how the data are collected. This is why it is extremely important that the data contain the pertinent information and are valid (for example, appropriate sampling

schemes are used) so that the analysis and the interpretation of the results are done appropriately. Moreover, one should always keep in mind that each measurement system has its own inherent variability. Thus, the accuracy of any measurement system is as important as the elimination of the special causes affecting the process.

5. *Minimize unnecessary variation:* Unnecessary external causes of variation should be reduced before the study begins. Methods for reducing these causes include overcontrolling the process and avoiding obvious problems that could and should be corrected even without the use of control charts. Note that in all cases a process log should be kept. It should include all relevant events (big or small) such as procedural changes, new raw materials, or change of operators. This will aid in the analysis of subsequent problems.

6. *Consider the customer's needs:* This includes any subsequent processes that use the product or service as an input and the final end-item customer. For example, a computer manufacturing company is a customer of the semiconductor industry; a car manufacturing company is a customer of tire manufacturing companies; and in a paper mill, the papermaking unit is a customer of the pulp-making unit.

Note that the most important quality characteristic is to produce what the customer wants. In other words, the company should deliver a product that meets the needs of the customer. A company may produce excellent things, but if it can't meet the needs of the customer, then the customer is not going to buy that product. So, for example, the pulp-making mill should produce the kind of pulp wanted by the papermaking mill. In this particular case, the pulp and paper mills are part of the same company, but if the pulp-making mill cannot deliver the kind of pulp the papermaking mill needs, the papermaking mill will seek another supplier. Process innovation and customer satisfaction are the most important factors in the success of any manufacturing process.

Benefits of Control Charts

Properly used control charts can:

1. Be used by operators for ongoing control of a process
2. Help the process perform consistently and predictably
3. Allow the process to achieve higher quality, higher effective capacity (because there will be either no rejection or less rejection), and hence a lower cost per unit
4. Provide a common language for discussing process performance
5. Help distinguish special causes from common causes for variability and serve as a guide for management to take local action or action on the system

Rational Samples for a Control Chart

It is important to note that the samples used to prepare a control chart should represent subgroups of output that are as homogeneous as possible. In other words, the subgroups should be such that if special causes are present, they will show up in differences between the subgroups rather than in differences between the members of a subgroup. A natural subgroup, for example, would be the output of a given shift. It is not correct to take the product of an arbitrary period of time as a subgroup, especially if the subgroup overlapped two or more shifts. This is because if a sample comes from two or more shifts, any differences between the shifts will be averaged out, and consequently, the plotted point won't indicate the presence of any special causes due to shifts. As another example, if the process used six machines, it would be better to take a sample from the output of each machine than to have a sample that consists of items from all six machines. This is because the difference between the machines may be the special cause of variation. It will be easier to detect this special cause if a sample is taken from each machine. Thus, it is true that careful selection of a subgroup or sample is perhaps the most important item in setting up a control chart.

The next step in selecting a sample is to determine the sample size. Factors usually considered in determining the sample size and the frequency of the samples are the average run length (ARL) and the operating characteristic curve, also known as an OC curve. We will discuss both the ARL and the OC curve.

ARL

Definition 3.2 A *run* is a number of successive points plotted in a control chart.

Definition 3.3 An *average run length* is the average number of points plotted before a point falls outside the control limits, indicating the process is out of control.

In Shewhart control charts, the ARL can be determined by using the formula

$$\text{ARL} = \frac{1}{p}, \tag{3.1}$$

where p is the probability that any point will fall outside the control limits. It is quite common to use ARL as a benchmark for checking the performance of a control chart.

To illustrate, consider a process quality characteristic that is normally distributed. For an $\bar{X}$ control chart with 3σ control limits, the probability that a point will fall outside the control limits when the process is stable is $p = 0.0027$, which is the probability that a normal random variable deviates from the mean μ by at least 3σ. The ARL for the $\bar{X}$ control chart when the process is stable is

$$ARL_0 = \frac{1}{0.0027} = 370.$$

In other words, when the process is stable, we should expect that, on the average, an out-of-control signal or false alarm will occur once in every 370 samples. The ARL can also be used to determine how often a false alarm will occur, simply by multiplying the ARL_0 by the time t between the samples. For example, if samples are taken every 30 minutes, a false alarm will occur on the average once every 185 hours. On the other hand, ARL can be used in the same manner to find out how long it will take before a given shift in the process mean is detected. This concept, which we are going to discuss in depth in section 3.3, is illustrated in the following example using an $\bar{X}$ control chart.

Example 3.2 *Suppose a process quality characteristic that is normally distributed is plotted in a Shewhart* $\bar{X}$ *control chart with* 3σ *control limits. Suppose that the process mean* μ_0 *experiences an upward shift of* 1.5σ*. Determine how long, on the average, it will take to detect this shift if a sample of size four is taken every hour.*

Solution: Because the process mean has experienced an upward shift of 1.5σ, the new process mean will be $\mu_0 + 1.5\sigma$. Furthermore, because the sample size is four, the UCL in this case is also $\mu_0 + 3\sigma_{\bar{x}} = \mu_0 + 3\frac{\sigma}{\sqrt{4}} = \mu_0 + 1.5\sigma.$ In other words, the CL of the control chart will coincide with the UCL. The probability p that a point will fall beyond the control limits is

$$\begin{aligned} p &= P(z \leq -6) + P(z \geq 0) \\ &\cong 0.00000 + 0.5 \\ &= 0.5. \end{aligned}$$

Consequently, the ARL is given by

$$ARL = \frac{1}{0.5} = 2.$$

Therefore, it will take an average of two hours to detect a shift of 1.5σ in the process mean.

In practice, the decision of how large the samples should be and how frequently they should be taken is based on the cost of taking samples and how quickly one would like to detect the shift. Large samples taken more frequently would certainly give better protection against shifts because it will take less time to detect any given shift. For instance, in Example 3.2, if the samples are taken every half hour instead of every hour, then it will take only one hour instead of two to detect the shift of 1.5σ, and the process will produce fewer nonconforming units. So, when calculating the cost of taking samples, one must consider how much money will be saved by detecting the shift more quickly and producing fewer nonconforming units.

OC Curve

Definition 3.4 The *operating characteristic curve* is a graph of the probability (β) of a point falling within the control limits versus the process shift.

A set of OC curves for the $\bar{X}$ chart with 3σ limits for different sample sizes n is shown in Figure 3.9. Note that the scale on the horizontal axis is in process standard deviation σ.

By carefully studying the OC curves in Figure 3.9, we see that:

1. For a given sample size n and α, where α is the probability of a point exceeding the control limits when the process is stable, a larger shift corresponds to a smaller probability β.

2. With a larger sample size, there is a smaller probability (β) for a given process shift.

For a detailed discussion of the construction of the OC curve, refer to the first volume of this series, *Applied Statistics for the Six Sigma Green Belt.*

As mentioned earlier, OC curves are very helpful in determining the sample size needed to detect a shift of size $d\sigma$ with a given probability $(1 - \beta)$. For example, if we want to determine the sample size required to detect a shift of

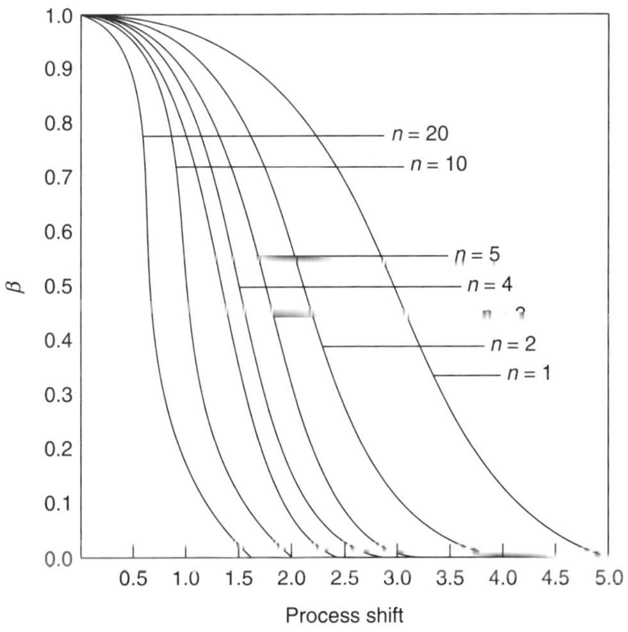

Figure 3.9 OC curves for the $\bar{x}$ chart with 3σ limits for different sample sizes n.

1σ with probability 95 percent, from Figure 3.9, with $d = 1$ and $\beta = 0.05$, we find the size n will be slightly higher than 20.

Having studied some basic concepts of control charts, we now discuss some special control charts that are very popular and useful in any industry, manufacturing or nonmanufacturing.

3.3.1 Shewhart $\bar{X}$ and R Control Charts

Certain rules are widely followed in preparing Shewhart $\bar{X}$ and R control charts:

1. Take a series of samples from the process under investigation. Samples consisting of four or five items taken frequently are usually good, for the following reasons:
   a. Samples of size four or five are more cost effective.
   b. If samples are larger than 10, the estimate of process standard deviation obtained using the range is not very efficient. Moreover, the R chart is also not very effective.
   c. With samples of size four or five, there are fewer chances for any special causes occurring during the collection of a sample. It is commonly known that if the type of variation is changing (special cause vs. common cause variation), the sample size should be as small as possible so that the average of samples does not mask the changes.
2. Enough samples should be collected so that the major source of variation has an opportunity to occur. Generally, at least 25 samples of size four or five is considered sufficient to give a good test for process stability.
3. During the collection of data, a complete log of any changes in the process, such as changes in raw materials, operators, or tools or any calibration of tools, machines, and so on, must be maintained. Keeping a log is important for finding the special causes in a process.

Calculation of Sample Statistics

The sample statistics that need to be determined in order to prepare Shewhart $\bar{X}$ and R control charts are the sample mean ($\bar{x}$) and the sample range (R). For example, let $x_1, x_2, \ldots, x_n$ be a random sample from a process that is under investigation. We have

$$\bar{x} = \frac{x_1 + x_2 + \ldots + x_n}{n}, \tag{3.2}$$

$$R = \max(x_i) - \min(x_i). \tag{3.3}$$

Example 3.3 *Let 5, 6, 9, 7, 8, 6, 9, 7, 6, and 5 be a random sample from a process under investigation. Find the sample mean and the sample range.*

Solution: Using these data, we have

$$\bar{x} = \frac{5+6+9+7+8+6+9+7+6+5}{10} = 6.8,$$

$$R = \max\ (x_i) - \min\ (x_i) = 9 - 5 = 4.$$

Calculation of Control Limits

Step 1. First, calculate $\bar{x}_i$ and R_i for the ith sample, for $i = 1, 2, 3, \ldots, m$, where m is the number of samples collected during the study period.

Step 2. Calculate

$$\bar{R} = \frac{R_1 + R_2 + \ldots + R_m}{m}, \tag{3.4}$$

$$\bar{\bar{x}} = \frac{\bar{x}_1 + \bar{x}_2 + \ldots + \bar{x}_m}{m}. \tag{3.5}$$

Step 3. Calculate the 3σ control limits for the $\bar{X}$ control chart

$$\begin{aligned} \text{UCL} &= \bar{\bar{x}} + 3\hat{\sigma}_{\bar{x}} \\ &= \bar{\bar{x}} + 3\frac{\hat{\sigma}}{\sqrt{n}} \\ &= \bar{\bar{x}} + 3\frac{\bar{R}}{d_2\sqrt{n}} \\ &= \bar{\bar{x}} + A_2\bar{R}, \end{aligned} \tag{3.6}$$

$$\text{CL} = \bar{\bar{x}}, \tag{3.7}$$

$$\begin{aligned} \text{LCL} &= \bar{\bar{x}} - 3\hat{\sigma}_{\bar{x}} \\ &= \bar{\bar{x}} - 3\frac{\hat{\sigma}}{\sqrt{n}} \\ &= \bar{\bar{x}} - 3\frac{\bar{R}}{d_2\sqrt{n}} \\ &= \bar{\bar{x}} - A_2\bar{R}, \end{aligned} \tag{3.8}$$

where the values of A_2 and d_2 for various sample sizes are given in Table A.2.

Note: Instead of calculating 3σ limits (common in the United States), we can also calculate the probability limits (common in Europe) at the desired level of significance α simply by replacing 3 with $z_{\alpha/2}$ in equations (3.6) and (3.8). Thus, the control limits will be

$$\begin{aligned} \text{UCL} &= \bar{\bar{x}} + z_{\alpha/2}\frac{\hat{\sigma}}{\sqrt{n}} \\ &= \bar{\bar{x}} + z_{\alpha/2}\frac{\bar{R}}{d_2\sqrt{n}}, \end{aligned} \tag{3.9}$$

$$\begin{aligned} \text{LCL} &= \bar{\bar{x}} - z_{\alpha/2}\frac{\hat{\sigma}}{\sqrt{n}} \\ &= \bar{\bar{x}} - z_{\alpha/2}\frac{\bar{R}}{d_2\sqrt{n}}. \end{aligned} \tag{3.10}$$

Step 4. Calculate the control limits for the R control chart

$$\begin{aligned} \text{UCL} &= \bar{R} + 3\hat{\sigma}_R \\ &= \bar{R} + 3d_3\frac{\bar{R}}{d_2} \\ &= (1 + 3\frac{d_3}{d_2})\bar{R} \\ &= D_4\bar{R}, \end{aligned} \tag{3.11}$$

$$\text{CL} = \bar{R}, \tag{3.12}$$

$$\begin{aligned} \text{LCL} &= \bar{R} - 3\hat{\sigma}_R \\ &= \bar{R} - 3d_3\frac{\bar{R}}{d_2} \\ &= (1 - 3\frac{d_3}{d_2})\bar{R} \\ &= D_3\bar{R}, \end{aligned} \tag{3.13}$$

where the values of D_3 and D_4 for various sample sizes are given in Table A.2. The first implementation of control charts is referred to as *phase I*. In phase I it is important that we calculate the preliminary control limits, which allows us to find the extent of variation in sample means and sample ranges if the process is stable. In other words, at this point only common causes would affect the process. If all the plotted points fall within the control limits and there is no evidence of any pattern, then the control limits are suitable for a current or future process. However, if some points exceed the control limits, then such points are ignored and every effort is made to eliminate any evident special causes present in the process. Fresh control limits are then calculated by using the remaining data, and the whole process is repeated again. Remember that ignoring the points that exceed the control limits without eliminating the special causes may result in unnecessarily narrow control limits, which may lead to putting the points beyond the control limits when, in fact, they should not be. Furthermore, it is highly recommended that for preliminary control limits, 25 samples of size four or five should be used. Otherwise, the control limits may not be suitable for the current and future process.

Example 3.4 *Table 3.4 provides data on the diameter measurements of ball bearings used in the wheels of heavy construction equipment. Twenty-five samples, each of size four, are taken directly from the production line. Samples come from all three shifts, and no sample contains data from more than one shift. Use these data to construct* $\bar{X}$ *and* R *charts and to verify that the process is stable.*

Table 3.4 Diameter measurements (in mm) of ball bearings used in the wheels of heavy construction equipment.

Sample	Observations				$\bar{x}_i$	R_i
1	15.155	15.195	15.145	15.125	15.155	0.070
2	15.095	15.162	15.168	15.163	15.147	0.073
3	15.115	15.126	15.176	15.183	15.150	0.068
4	15.122	15.135	15.148	15.155	15.140	0.033
5	15.148	15.152	15.192	15.148	15.160	0.044
6	15.169	15.159	15.173	15.175	15.169	0.016
7	15.163	15.147	15.137	15.145	15.148	0.026
8	15.150	15.164	15.156	15.170	15.160	0.020
9	15.148	15.162	15.163	15.147	15.155	0.016
10	15.152	15.138	15.167	15.155	15.153	0.029
11	15.147	15.158	15.175	15.160	15.160	0.028
12	15.158	15.172	15.142	15.120	15.148	0.052
13	15.133	15.177	15.145	15.165	15.155	0.044
14	15.148	15.174	15.155	15.175	15.155	0.027
15	15.143	15.137	15.164	15.156	15.150	0.027
16	15.142	15.150	15.168	15.152	15.153	0.026
17	15.132	15.168	15.154	15.146	15.150	0.036
18	15.172	15.188	15.178	15.194	15.183	0.022
19	15.174	15.166	15.186	15.194	15.180	0.028
20	15.166	15.178	15.192	15.184	15.180	0.026
21	15.172	15.187	15.193	15.180	15.183	0.021
22	15.182	15.198	15.185	15.195	15.190	0.016
23	15.170	15.150	15.192	15.180	15.173	0.042
24	15.186	15.194	15.175	15.185	15.185	0.019
25	15.178	15.192	15.168	15.182	15.180	0.024
					$\bar{\bar{x}} = 15.1628$	$\bar{R} = 0.03479$

Solution: From Table A.2 for a sample of size $n = 4$, we have $D_3 = 0$ and $D_4 = 2.282$. Thus, the control limits for the R chart are

$$LCL = D_3\bar{R} = 0 \times 0.03479 = 0,$$

$$UCL = D_4\bar{R} = 2.282 \times 0.03479 = 0.07936.$$

It is customary to prepare the R chart first and verify that all the plotted points fall within the control limits, and only then proceed to construct the $\bar{X}$ chart. In fact, the concept of bringing the process variability under control first and then proceeding to control the average does make a lot of sense. This is because it is almost impossible to bring the process average under control without controlling the process variability.

The R chart for the preceding data is given in Figure 3.10, which shows that all the plotted points fall within the control limits and that there is no evidence of any special pattern. Therefore, we may conclude that the only variation present in the process is due to common causes. In this case, we can proceed to calculate the control limits for the $\bar{X}$ chart. From Table A.2 for a sample of size $n = 4$, we get $A_2 = 0.729$. We have

$$LCL = \bar{\bar{x}} - A_2\bar{R} = 15.1628 - 0.729 \times 0.03479 = 15.13746,$$

$$UCL = \bar{\bar{x}} + A_2\bar{R} = 15.1628 + 0.729 \times 0.03479 = 15.18814.$$

The $\bar{X}$ chart for these data is given in Figure 3.10, which shows that point 22 exceeds the UCL. Moreover, there are too many consecutive points that fall below the CL. This indicates that the process is not under control and that there are some special causes present that are affecting the process average. A thorough investigation should be launched to find the special causes, and appropriate action should be taken to eliminate them before recalculating the control limits for an ongoing process.

A process is considered out of control not only when the points exceed the control limits, but also when the points show patterns of nonrandomness. The Western Electric *Statistical Quality Control Handbook* (1956, 27) gives a set of decision rules for determining nonrandom patterns on control charts. In particular, it suggests the patterns are nonrandom if:

1. Two out of three successive points exceed the 2σ warning limits
2. Four out of five successive points fall at a distance of 1σ or beyond from the CL
3. Eight successive points fall on one side of the CL
4. Seven successive points run either upward or downward

3.3.1.1 Interpretation of Shewhart $\bar{X}$ and R Control Charts

We should investigate any out-of-control points—that is, points on or beyond the 3σ control limits—or any patterns of nonrandomness on the R chart before interpreting the $\bar{X}$ chart. As discussed earlier, the reason for doing this is simple. It is not possible to bring the average under control without first bringing

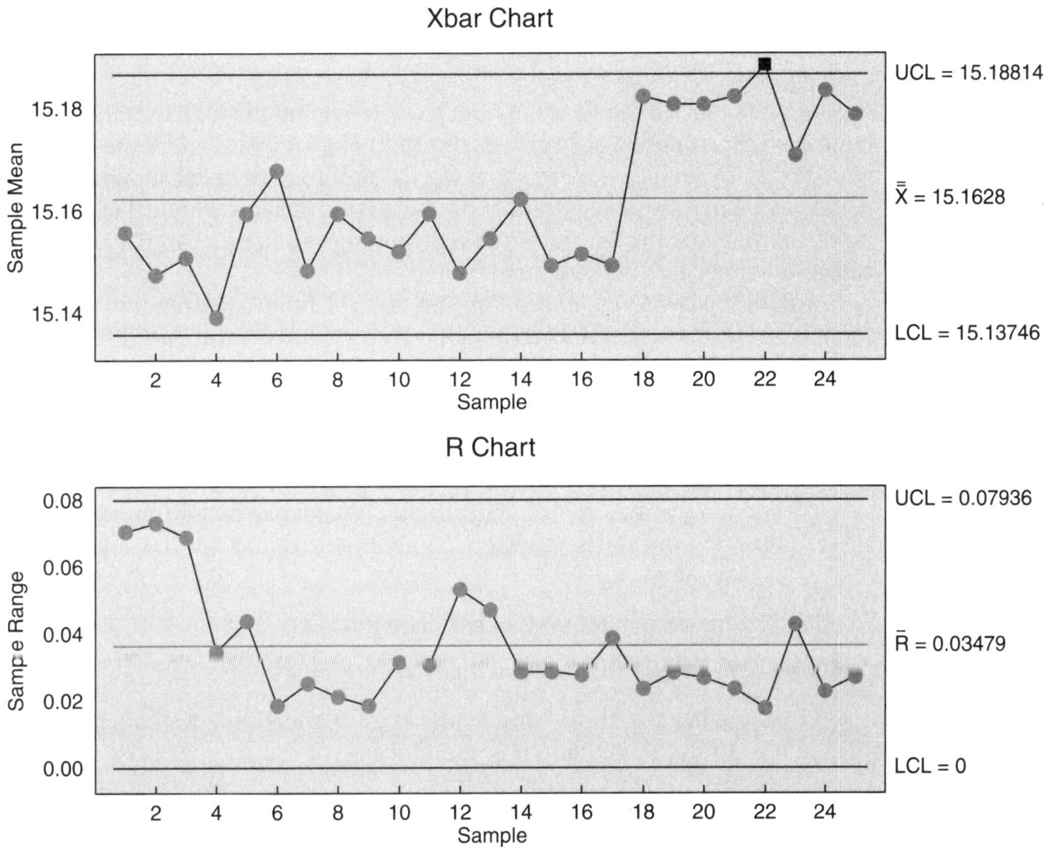

Figure 3.10 The $\bar{X}$ and R control charts, constructed using MINITAB, for the ball bearing data in Table 3.4.

the variability under control. Normally the $\bar{X}$ chart is placed above the R chart, and they are aligned with each other in such a manner that the average and the range for any sample are plotted on the same vertical line. Examine whether one, both, or neither chart indicates that the process is out of control for any given sample. If any point exceeds the control limits in either or both charts, then the sample did not come from a stable process. In other words, there are some special or assignable causes present in the system. More precisely, if the plotted point exceeds the control limits in the R chart, it is evident that the variability of the process has changed. But before a full-blown investigation is launched, some preliminary checks should be made:

1. Check that all calculations are correct or that the data are entered in the computer correctly.

2. Check whether there is any change in workers, machines, or the supplier of raw materials.

If the points exceed the control limits in the $\bar{X}$ chart, then the process mean has changed. Again, follow the preliminary checks before launching an investigation.

If points exceed the limits in both the $\bar{X}$ chart and the R chart, this usually indicates that a sudden shift has occurred in the lot from which the samples were taken. In such cases, after making the preliminary checks, there should be an investigation concentrating on the period during which that lot was produced. Depending on the process, stopping production until the special causes are detected should be considered.

In addition to points exceeding the control limits, nonrandom patterns such as a run of seven points moving upward or downward, or a run of eight successive points falling above or below the CL should be checked.

An upward run or a run above the CL in an R chart indicates:

1. A greater variability or a tendency of perpetuating a greater variability in the output of the process is occurring. This may be due to new material of undesirable low quality or a difference between the shifts. Immediate attention to detect special causes is warranted.
2. The measurement system has changed.

A downward run or a run below the CL in an R chart indicates:

1. A smaller variability or a tendency of perpetuating a smaller variability in the output of the process is occurring. This is usually a good sign for the process. A thorough investigation should be made so that similar conditions are maintained as long as possible. Similar conditions should be implemented elsewhere in the process.
2. The measurement system has changed.

A run relative to an $\bar{X}$ chart indicates:

1. The process average has changed or is still changing.
2. The measurement system has changed.

3.3.1.2 Extending the Current Control Limits for Future Control

If current data from at least 25 sample periods are contained within the current control limits, we may use these limits to cover future periods. However, these limits are used for future periods on the condition that immediate action will be taken if any out-of-control indication appears or if the points consistently fall very close to the CL. The latter case indicates that the process has improved and that new control limits should be recalculated. Again, note that in any case, control limits for future use should be extended for only 25 to 30 sample periods at a time.

It is pertinent to note that a change in sample size will affect the control limits for both the $\bar{X}$ chart and the R chart; therefore, whenever there is a change in sample size, new control limits should be recalculated. This situation may arise if it is decided to take smaller samples more frequently, which usually is the case when one wants to catch larger shifts (larger than 1.5σ) without increasing the total number of parts sampled over the whole sampling period. Another scenario is when it is decided to increase the sample size but sample less frequently, which usually is the case when one wants to catch smaller shifts (shifts of 1.5σ or smaller). To recalculate the new control limits, proceed as follows:

1. Estimate the process standard deviation using the existing sample size

$$\hat{\sigma} = \frac{\bar{R}}{d_2}, \tag{3.14}$$

where $\bar{R}$ is the sample range average for the period with ranges in control, and the value of d_2 is found in Table A.2 for the existing sample size.

2. Using the values for d_2, D_3, D_4, and A_2 from Table A.2 for the new sample size, calculate the new range and control limits as follows:

Estimate the new sample range average, that is,

$$\bar{R}_{\text{new}} = d_2 \times \hat{\sigma}. \tag{3.15}$$

Then the new control limits for the $\bar{X}$ control chart are

$$\begin{aligned} \text{LCL} &= \bar{\bar{x}} - A_2 \times \bar{R}_{\text{new}}, \\ \text{CL} &= \bar{\bar{x}}, \\ \text{UCL} &= \bar{\bar{x}} + A_2 \times \bar{R}_{\text{new}}, \end{aligned} \tag{3.16}$$

and the new control limits for the R control chart are

$$\begin{aligned} \text{LCL} &= D_3 \times \bar{R}_{\text{new}}, \\ \text{CL} &= \bar{R}_{\text{new}}, \\ \text{UCL} &= D_4 \times \bar{R}_{\text{new}}. \end{aligned} \tag{3.17}$$

Example 3.5 *To illustrate the technique of calculating the new control limits, consider the* $\bar{\text{X}}$ *and* R *control charts developed for the ball bearing data in Example 3.4. The charts in Figure 3.10 are based on a sample size of four. Because one point in the* $\bar{\text{X}}$ *chart exceeded the control limit, there may be a small shift in the process mean. Thus, the Six Sigma Green Belt wants to increase the sample size to six. Determine the control limits required for the new samples of size six for both the* $\bar{\text{X}}$ *chart and the* R *chart.*

Solution: From Table A.2 for $n = 4$, $d_2 = 2.059$. From Example 3.4 and using equation (3.14), we have

$$\hat{\sigma} = \frac{\bar{R}}{d_2} = \frac{0.03479}{2.059} = 0.0169.$$

Again, from Table A.2 for $n = 6$, $d_2 = 2.534$. Using equation (3.15), we have

$$\bar{R}_{\text{new}} = 2.534 \times 0.0169 = 0.0428246.$$

The new control limits for the $\bar{X}$ control chart for samples of size six are

$$\text{LCL} = 15.1628 - 0.483 \times 0.0428246 = 15.1421,$$

$$\text{CL} = 15.1628,$$

$$\text{UCL} = 15.1628 + 0.483 \times 0.0428246 = 15.18348.$$

The new control limits for the R control chart for samples of size six are

$$\text{LCL} = 0 \times 0.0428246 = 0,$$

$$\text{CL} = 0.0428246,$$

$$\text{UCL} = 2.004 \times 0.0428246 = 0.08582.$$

Note that the net result of increasing the sample size is to narrow the control limits for the $\bar{X}$ chart and to move the CL and the control limits for the R chart higher. This is because the expected range value for the larger sample increases. In this example, however, the LCL for the R chart remains the same because the value of D_3 for sample sizes four and six is zero.

3.3.2 Shewhart $\bar{X}$ and R Control Charts When Process Mean μ and Process Standard Deviation σ Are Known

If the process mean μ and the process standard deviation σ are known, then the $\bar{X}$ chart and the R chart are developed as follows:

Step 1. Calculate $\bar{x}_i$ and R_i for the ith sample for $i = 1, 2, 3, \ldots, m$, where m is the number of samples collected during the study period.

Step 2. Calculate the control limits for the $\bar{X}$ control chart

$$\text{UCL} = \mu + 3\frac{\sigma}{\sqrt{n}}, \tag{3.18}$$

$$\text{CL} = \mu, \tag{3.19}$$

$$\text{LCL} = \mu - 3\frac{\sigma}{\sqrt{n}}. \tag{3.20}$$

Note: Instead of calculating 3σ limits, we can also calculate the probability limits at the desired level of significance α simply by replacing 3 with $z_{\alpha/2}$ in equations (3.18) and (3.20).

Step 3. Calculate the control limits for the *R* control chart.

Recalling that $\sigma = R/d_2$ and $\sigma_R = d_3\sigma$, we have

$$\begin{aligned} \text{UCL} &= d_2\sigma + 3\sigma_R \\ &= d_2\sigma + 3d_3\sigma \\ &= (d_2 + 3d_3)\sigma \\ &= D_2\sigma, \end{aligned} \tag{3.21}$$

$$\text{CL} = \sigma, \tag{3.22}$$

$$\begin{aligned} \text{LCL} &= d_2\sigma - 3\sigma_R \\ &= d_2\sigma - 3d_3\sigma \\ &= (d_2 - 3d_3)\sigma \\ &= D_1\sigma, \end{aligned} \tag{3.23}$$

where the values of D_1 and D_2 for various sample sizes are given in Table A.2.

3.3.3 Shewhart Control Chart for Individual Observations

Sometimes it is necessary to study SPC using individual observations only because it may not be feasible to form rational subgroups of size greater than one. This scenario, for example, would arise when:

1. Sampling is very expensive and it is not economical to take samples of size greater than one.
2. Observations are collected through experimentation and it may take several days or weeks to take one observation.
3. The circumstances warrant that each unit must be inspected or the process is completely automated, so that the measurement on each observation can be taken without much extra expense.
4. Only a few units are produced each day and the difference is between the units and not within the units, so one observation from each unit is sufficient.
5. Sampling is destructive and the units are very expensive. For example, certain bulbs for projectors are very expensive. If we want to study the life of such bulbs, then collecting the data will cause the bulbs to be destroyed.

The control charts for individual observations are very similar to $\bar{X}$ and R control charts. However, in the case of individual observations, because the sample contains only one observation, it is not possible to find the sample range in the usual manner. Instead, we find the sample range as the absolute difference between the two successive observations. This type of sample range is usually known as the *moving range* (MR), that is,

$$MR_k = |x_k - x_{k-1}|, \tag{3.24}$$

where $k = 2, 3, \ldots, n$; n is the total number of observations. Instead of using the sample means $\bar{x}_i$, the individual observations x_i are used. Note that sometimes the control chart for individual observations is also known as an *individual moving range control chart*, or simply an *IMR control chart*. To illustrate construction of an IMR control chart, we reproduce observations of column 1 of Table 3.4 in Table 3.5.

Example 3.6 *Use the ball bearing data in Table 3.5 to construct the* X *(individual) and* R *control charts.*

Table 3.5 Diameter measurements (in mm) of ball bearings used in the wheels of heavy construction equipment.

Sample	Observation	MR_k
1	15.155	
2	15.095	0.060
3	15.115	0.020
4	15.122	0.007
5	15.148	0.026
6	15.169	0.021
7	15.163	0.006
8	15.150	0.013
9	15.148	0.002
10	15.152	0.004
11	15.147	0.005
12	15.158	0.011
13	15.133	0.025
14	15.148	0.015
15	15.143	0.005
16	15.142	0.001
17	15.132	0.010
18	15.172	0.040
19	15.174	0.002
20	15.166	0.008
21	15.172	0.006
22	15.182	0.010
23	15.170	0.012
24	15.186	0.016
25	15.178	0.008
	$\bar{X} = 15.1528$	$\bar{R} = 0.01387$

Solution: Because the sample range is determined from two successive observations, the sample size for estimating the process standard deviation and for constructing the R chart is considered to be equal to two. From Table A.2 for $n = 2$, we have $D_3 = 0$ and $D_4 = 3.269$. The control limits for the R chart are

$$\text{LCL} = D_3\bar{R} = \times 0.01387 = 0,$$

$$\text{UCL} = D_4\bar{R} = 3.269 \times 0.01387 = 0.0453.$$

As in the case of the $\bar{X}$ and R charts, it is customary to prepare the R chart first and verify that all the plotted points fall within the control limits, and only then proceed to construct the X chart.

The R chart for the preceding data is given in Figure 3.11, which shows that process variability is not under control, because the first point exceeds the UCL, and point 16 is almost on the LCL. As a matter of principle, we should investigate the special causes of this variability and eliminate such causes before we construct the X chart. We assume here, for illustration, that these special causes have been detected and eliminated, and therefore we proceed to calculate the control limits for the X chart. Note that in practice, these

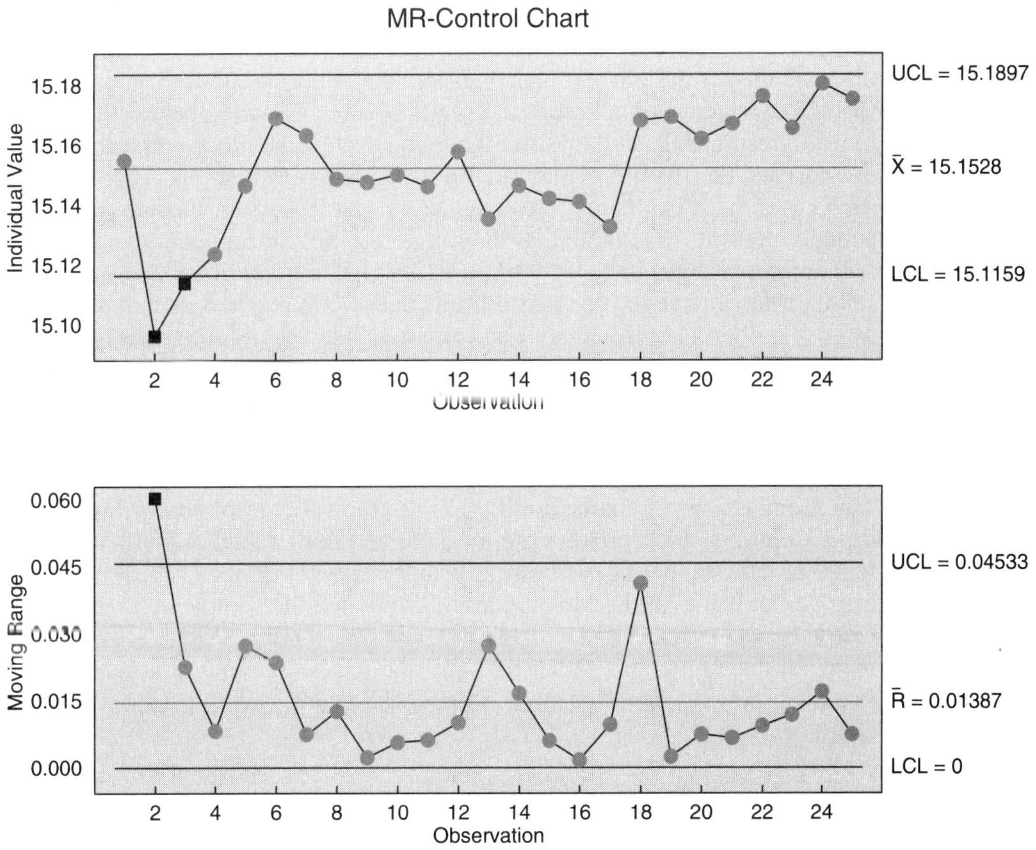

Figure 3.11 The MR control chart, constructed using MINITAB, for the ball bearing data in Table 3.5.

observations should be ignored after detecting and eliminating the special causes, and the control limits should be recalculated. Again, from Table A.2 for a sample of size $n = 2$, we get $d_2 = 1.128$. Thus, we have

$$\text{LCL} = \bar{x} - 3\hat{\sigma} = \bar{x} - 3\frac{\bar{R}}{d_2} = 15.1528 - 3\frac{0.01387}{1.128} = 15.1159,$$

$$\text{UCL} = \bar{x} + 3\hat{\sigma} = \bar{x} + 3\frac{\bar{R}}{d_2} = 15.1528 + 3\frac{0.01387}{1.128} = 15.1897.$$

Notice, however, there is little difference in how we compute the control limits for the $\bar{X}$ chart and the X chart. For calculating the control limits of the X chart, we always use sample size $n = 1$. In other words, we do not use the sample size $n = 2$ or the control limits as $\bar{x} \pm 3\hat{\sigma}/\sqrt{2}$; rather, we simply use the control limits as $\bar{x} \pm 3\hat{\sigma}$ because $n = 2$ is used only for determining the control limits of the R chart and for estimating σ. The X chart for the preceding data is given in Figure 3.11, which shows that points 2 and 3 fall below the LCL. Moreover, there are too many consecutive points that fall above the CL. This indicates that the process is not under control and that there are some special causes present that are affecting the process average. Therefore, a thorough investigation should be launched to find the special causes, and appropriate action should be taken to eliminate them.

Note: There are some limitations of using Shewhart charts for individual observations. If the process characteristic is nonnormal, the rules applicable to the $\bar{X}$ chart may not hold for the X chart, because $\bar{x}$ usually behaves like normal as a result of the central limit theorem, even if the process distribution is not normal. This would not be true for individual observations. Therefore, in such cases the X charts may give signals of special causes when they are not actually present. Also, note that the ranges are not independent, because the two adjacent ranges have a common point. Hence a run of successive points falling near or beyond the control limits does not have the same significance as in an ordinary control chart. For more detailed discussion on this topic, we recommend Montgomery (2005b), an excellent source.

3.3.4 Shewhart $\bar{X}$ and S Control Charts

The $\bar{X}$ and S control charts, similar to the $\bar{X}$ and R control charts, are developed from measured process output data, and both $\bar{X}$ and S charts are used together. The standard deviation s is usually a more efficient indicator of process variability than the range, particularly when the sample sizes are large (10 or greater). The sample standard deviation s for the S chart is calculated using all the data points rather than just the maximum and minimum values in a data set, as is done for the R chart. S charts are usually preferred over R charts when:

- The sample is of size 10 or larger
- The sample size is variable
- The process is automated so the s for each sample can be easily calculated

The sample standard deviation s is determined using the formula

$$s = \sqrt{\frac{1}{n-1}\left(\sum_{i=1}^{n} x_i^2 - \frac{1}{n}\left(\sum_{i=1}^{n} x_i\right)^2\right)}. \tag{3.25}$$

The control limits for the $\bar{X}$ and S control charts are determined as shown in the following section.

Calculation of Control Limits

Step 1. First, calculate $\bar{x}_i$ and s_i for the ith sample, for $i = 1, 2, 3, \ldots, m$, where m is the number of samples collected during the study period.

Step 2. Calculate

$$\bar{s} = \frac{s_1 + s_2 + \ldots + s_m}{m}, \tag{3.26}$$

$$\bar{\bar{x}} = \frac{\bar{x}_1 + \bar{x}_2 + \ldots + \bar{x}_m}{m}. \tag{3.27}$$

Step 3. Calculate the control limits for the $\bar{X}$ chart

$$\begin{aligned} \text{UCL} &= \bar{\bar{x}} + 3\frac{\hat{\sigma}}{\sqrt{n}} \\ &= \bar{\bar{x}} + 3\frac{\bar{s}}{c_4\sqrt{n}} \\ &= \bar{\bar{x}} + A_3\bar{s}, \end{aligned} \tag{3.28}$$

$$\text{CL} = \bar{\bar{x}}, \tag{3.29}$$

$$\begin{aligned} \text{LCL} &= \bar{\bar{x}} - 3\frac{\hat{\sigma}}{\sqrt{n}} \\ &= \bar{\bar{x}} - 3\frac{\bar{s}}{c_4\sqrt{n}} \\ &= \bar{\bar{x}} - A_3\bar{s}, \end{aligned} \tag{3.30}$$

where the values of A_3 and c_4 for various sample sizes are given in Table A.2.

Note: Instead of calculating 3σ limits, we can also calculate the probability limits at the desired level of significance α simply by replacing 3 with $z_{\alpha/2}$ in equations (3.24) and (3.25). Thus, the control limits will be

$$\begin{aligned} \text{UCL} &= \bar{\bar{x}} + z_{\alpha/2}\frac{\hat{\sigma}}{\sqrt{n}} \\ &= \bar{\bar{x}} + z_{\alpha/2}\frac{\bar{s}}{c_4\sqrt{n}}, \end{aligned} \tag{3.31}$$

$$\text{CL} = \bar{\bar{x}}, \tag{3.32}$$

$$\begin{aligned}\text{LCL} &= \bar{\bar{x}} - z_{\alpha/2}\frac{\hat{\sigma}}{\sqrt{n}} \\ &= \bar{\bar{x}} - z_{\alpha/2}\frac{\bar{s}}{c_4\sqrt{n}}.\end{aligned} \tag{3.33}$$

Step 4. Calculate the control limits for the S chart

$$\begin{aligned}\text{UCL} &= \bar{s} + 3\hat{\sigma}_s \\ &= \bar{s} + 3\frac{\bar{s}}{c_4}\sqrt{1-c_4^2} \\ &= \left(1 + 3\frac{1}{c_4}\sqrt{1-c_4^2}\right)\bar{s} \\ &= B_4\bar{s},\end{aligned} \tag{3.34}$$

$$\text{CL} = \bar{s}, \tag{3.35}$$

$$\begin{aligned}\text{LCL} &= \bar{s} - 3\hat{\sigma}_s \\ &= \bar{s} - 3\frac{\bar{s}}{c_4}\sqrt{1-c_4^2} \\ &= \left(1 - 3\frac{1}{c_4}\sqrt{1-c_4^2}\right)\bar{s} \\ &= B_3\bar{s}.\end{aligned} \tag{3.36}$$

The development of the $\bar{X}$ and S control charts is illustrated in the following example.

Example 3.7 *Use the ball bearing data in Table 3.4 to construct the* $\bar{X}$ *and S control charts.*

Solution: From Table A.2 for a sample of size $n = 4$, we have $B_3 = 0$ and $B_4 = 2.266$. Thus, the control limits for the S control chart are

$$\text{LCL} = B_3\bar{s} = 0 \times 0.01557 = 0,$$

$$\text{UCL} = B_4\bar{s} = 2.266 \times 0.01557 = 0.03527.$$

It is customary to prepare the S control chart first and verify that all the plotted points fall within the control limits, and only then do we construct the $\bar{X}$ control chart. As described earlier, the concept of first bringing the process variability under control and then proceeding to control the average does make a lot of sense because without controlling the process variability, it is impossible to bring the process average under control.

The S chart for the preceding data is given in Figure 3.12, which shows that points 2 and 3 almost coincide with the UCL. Moreover, point 17 is

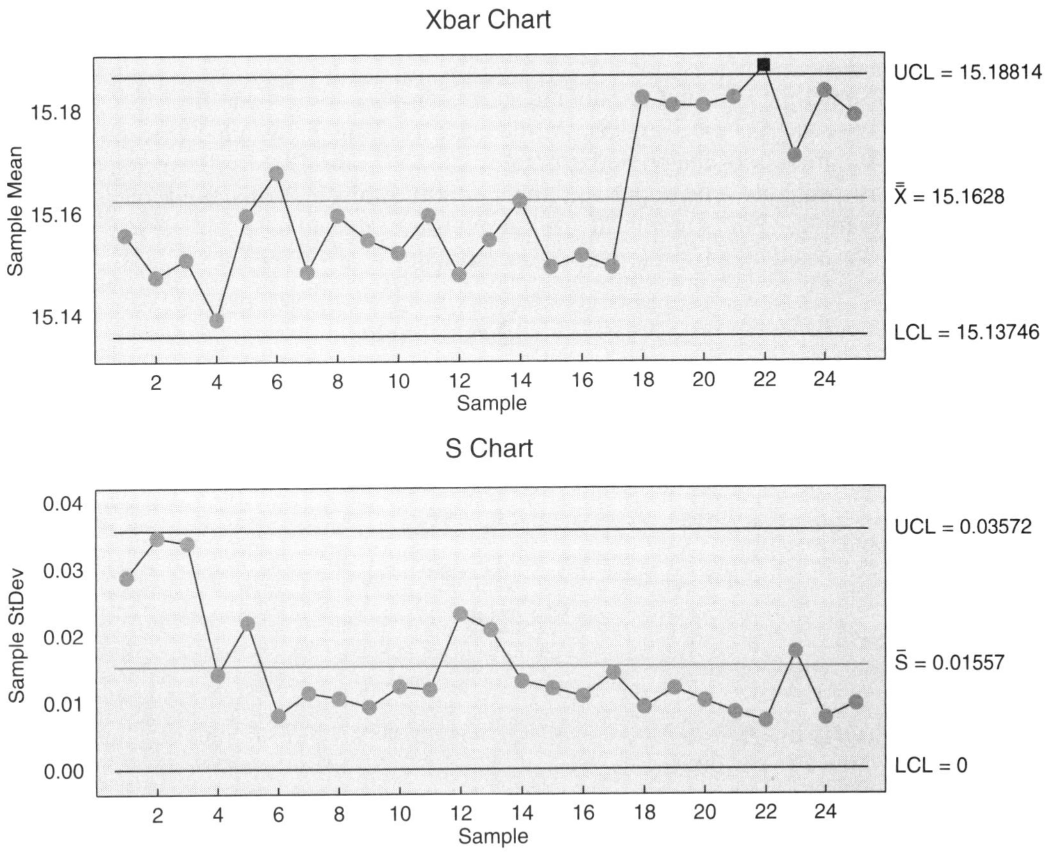

Figure 3.12 The $\bar{X}$ and S control charts, constructed using MINITAB, for the ball bearing data in Table 3.4.

almost on the CL. If this point were clearly below the CL, we would have had a run of nine points below the CL. These observations indicate that the process variability is marginally under control, and therefore, the process should be carefully monitored. Because the process variability is under control, albeit marginally, we can proceed to calculate the control limits for the $\bar{X}$ chart. From Table A.2 for a sample of size $n = 4$, we get $A_3 = 1.628$. Thus, we have

$$LCL = \bar{\bar{x}} - A_3\bar{s} = 15.1628 - 1.628 \times 0.01557 = 15.13746,$$

$$UCL = \bar{\bar{x}} + A_3\bar{s} = 15.1628 + 1.628 \times 0.01557 = 15.13746.$$

The $\bar{X}$ chart for the data in Table 3.4 is given in Figure 3.12, which shows that point 22 exceeds the UCL. Moreover, there are too many consecutive points that fall below the CL. This indicates that the process is not under control and that there are some special causes present that are affecting the process average. Thus, a thorough investigation should be launched to find the special causes, and appropriate action should be taken to eliminate them before we proceed to recalculate the control limits for an ongoing process.

3.3.4.1 Shewhart $\bar{X}$ and S Control Charts When Sample Size Is Variable

Sometimes it is not possible to select samples of the same size. In such cases we construct the $\bar{X}$ and S control charts by using the weighted mean $\bar{\bar{x}}$ and the square root of the pooled estimator s^2 of σ^2 as the CLs for the $\bar{X}$ and S charts, respectively. The upper and lower control limits are calculated for individual samples. For example, if the sample sizes are $n_1, n_2, n_3, \ldots, n_m$, then the weighted mean $\bar{\bar{x}}$ and the pooled estimator s^2 are given by

$$\bar{\bar{x}} = \frac{\sum_{i=1}^{m} n_i \bar{x}_i}{\sum_{i=1}^{m} n_i} = \frac{\sum_{i=1}^{m} n_i \bar{x}_i}{N}, \tag{3.37}$$

$$\bar{s} = \sqrt{s^2} = \sqrt{\frac{\sum_{i=1}^{m} (n_i - 1)s_i^2}{\sum_{i=1}^{m} (n_i - 1)}} = \sqrt{\frac{\sum_{i=1}^{m} (n_i - 1)s_i^2}{N - m}}, \tag{3.38}$$

where $N = n_1 + n_2 + n_3 + \ldots + n_m$; m is the number of samples selected during the study period.

The control limits for the $\bar{X}$ and S charts are given by

$$\text{UCL}_{\bar{x}} = \bar{\bar{x}} + A_3 s_i, \tag{3.39}$$

$$\text{LCL}_{\bar{x}} = \bar{\bar{x}} - A_3 s_i, \tag{3.40}$$

and

$$\text{UCL}_s = \bar{s} + B_4 s_i, \tag{3.41}$$

$$\text{LCL}_s = \bar{s} - B_3 s_i, \tag{3.42}$$

respectively. The values A_3, B_3, and B_4 depend on the individual sample sizes. To illustrate the development of these charts, we use the data presented in Example 3.8.

Example 3.8 *A manufacturing process produces piston rings with a finished inside diameter of 9 centimeters and a standard deviation of 0.03 centimeter. From this process, 30 samples of variable sizes are carefully selected so that no sample comes from two machines or two shifts. In other words, every effort is made to ensure that no sample masks any special causes. The data are shown in Table 3.6. Construct* $\bar{X}$ *and* S *control charts for these data* *and plot all the points in the* X̄ *and* S *charts to determine whether the process is stable.*

Solution: Using equations (3.37) and (3.38) and the data given in Table 3.6, we get

$$\bar{\bar{x}} = 9.0002, \; \bar{s} = 0.02812.$$

Now using equations (3.39)–(3.42), the control limits for both $\bar{X}$ and S control charts, shown in Figure 3.13, are calculated. From Figure 3.13 we see that process variability is under control; however, point 19 in the $\bar{X}$ chart falls below the LCL, which implies that some special causes affecting the process mean are present in the process.

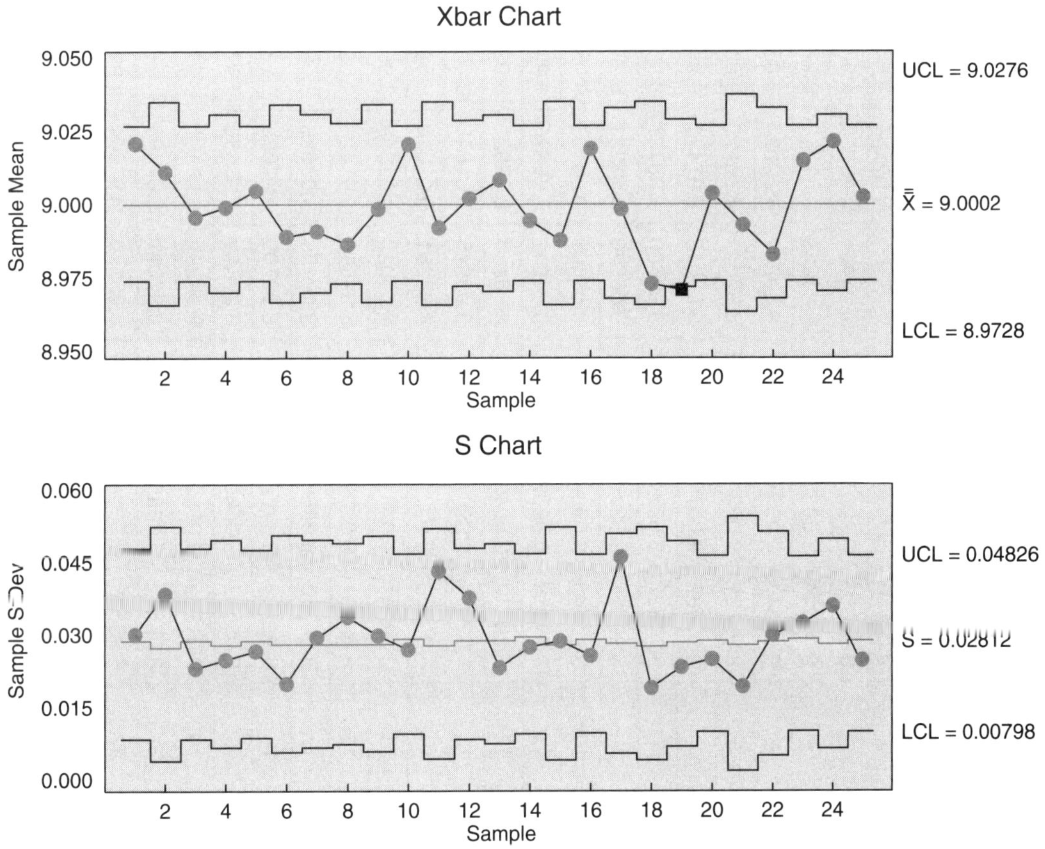

Figure 3.13 The $\bar{X}$ and S control charts for variable sample sizes, constructed using MINITAB, for the piston ring data in Table 3.6.

Table 3.6 The finished inside diameter measurements (in cm) of piston rings.

Sample #	Observations									
1	9.01759	8.97730	9.02472	9.03616	9.05257	9.00121	9.00361	8.98826	9.05866	9.05982
2	9.00974	8.95902	9.02650	8.97163	9.04754	9.05096	—	—	—	—
3	8.97809	8.98972	8.97877	9.01464	9.00623	8.98055	9.00877	9.03749	8.96140	9.00595
4	9.04504	8.99329	8.99112	9.01239	8.97850	8.97543	8.97958	9.02115	—	—
5	9.04544	8.95615	9.00747	8.99861	8.99077	9.03892	8.98887	8.98418	9.01795	9.01016
6	8.98229	9.02346	8.98103	8.97341	8.96475	9.00518	8.99561	—	—	—
7	9.02982	9.00707	9.00735	8.96042	8.97471	8.94890	8.99009	9.02050	—	—
8	9.01322	8.99716	8.98482	8.92890	9.03727	8.96801	9.02173	8.98401	8.95438	—
9	8.99775	9.02773	8.99505	9.00820	9.03221	8.94485	8.98242	—	—	—
10	8.98140	8.99443	8.99374	9.05063	9.00155	9.03501	9.04670	9.03164	9.04678	9.00865
11	8.94018	9.06380	8.97868	9.01246	8.96870	8.99593	—	—	—	—
12	8.96117	9.00420	9.02410	9.06514	8.97921	9.02223	8.98201	9.02577	8.94999	—
13	9.02374	8.99673	8.96257	8.99945	9.01848	9.02770	9.02901	9.00383	—	—
14	8.94363	9.00214	8.97526	8.98661	9.02040	9.02238	8.96735	8.99283	9.02029	9.01754
15	8.99341	9.02318	8.96106	9.00023	9.01309	8.95582	—	—	—	—
16	9.02781	9.02093	8.97963	8.98019	9.01428	9.03871	9.03058	9.01304	9.06247	9.00215
17	8.96783	8.94662	9.02595	9.07156	9.02688	8.96584	8.99007	—	—	—
18	8.98993	8.97726	8.97231	8.93709	8.97035	8.96499	—	—	—	—
19	8.95677	9.00000	8.98083	8.97502	8.93080	8.94690	8.98951	8.96032	—	—
20	9.01965	9.00524	9.02506	8.99299	8.95167	8.98578	9.03979	9.00742	8.99202	9.01492
21	8.97892	8.98553	9.01042	8.97291	9.01599	—	—	—	—	—
22	8.99523	9.00044	9.02239	8.93990	8.96644	8.99666	8.96103	—	—	—
23	9.05596	9.02182	8.94953	9.03914	8.97235	9.00869	9.01031	9.01371	8.99326	9.03646
24	9.03412	8.97335	9.00136	9.08037	9.04301	8.97701	9.02727	9.03449	—	—
25	9.00277	9.00651	9.02906	8.97863	8.99956	8.99291	8.97211	9.02725	8.97847	9.03710

Note: If the sample sizes do not vary too much, then it is quite common to use the average sample size $\bar{n}$ ($\bar{n} = (n_1 + n_2 + n_3 + ... + n_m) / m$) instead of using the variable sample sizes. As a rule of thumb, if all the samples are within 20 percent of the average sample size $\bar{n}$, then it is quite reasonable to use the average sample size instead of variable sample sizes. However, if any point(s) in the $\bar{X}$ or S charts fall on or very close to the control limits, then it is prudent to recalculate the control limits, at least for that sample using the actual sample size, and determine whether that point falls within the control limits. If the point falls on or exceeds the recalculated control limits using the actual sample size, then the process is deemed unstable; otherwise, the process is considered stable.

3.4 Process Capability

In this section we will briefly study the concept of process capability, and in Chapter 6 we will study how to quantify it. So far, our emphasis has been on how to build a quality characteristic in a given product, and we have measured everything in terms of the control limits. But it is a well-known fact that a quality characteristic of a product is usually evaluated in terms of the specification limits, which are often determined by the customer. It is of paramount importance to understand, however, that the control limits and the specification limits are two entirely different entities. The control limits, as we saw earlier in this chapter, are determined by the natural variability of the process, whereas specification limits are determined by the customer, by management, or by the design department. Specification limits are usually defined in terms of the expectations of how a product should perform, whereas control limits are the means to achieve these expectations. A process that produces a product that meets the expectations is called a *capable process*.

The expected value of a quality characteristic is called the *target value*. The largest and smallest acceptable values of a quality characteristic are known as the *upper specification limit* (USL) and the *lower specification limit* (LSL), respectively. The upper and lower control limits used in $\bar{X}$ and R charts for individual values are usually known as the *upper natural tolerance limit* (UNTL) and the *lower natural tolerance limit* (LNTL), respectively. It is important to note that there is no direct relationship between the control limits and the specification limits.

It is very common to examine the capability of a process only after it is stable. However, it is also important to note that a stable process is not necessarily a capable process. A visual presentation of this scenario is given in Figure 3.14.

To further illustrate the concept of process capability, we use the following example.

Example 3.9 *Consider a quality characteristic of a process that is normally distributed, and suppose that the process is stable with respect to the 3σ control limits. Furthermore, suppose that 30 samples of size five from this process provide the following summary statistics:*

$$\bar{\bar{x}} = 0.740, \ \bar{R} = 0.175, \ n = 5.$$

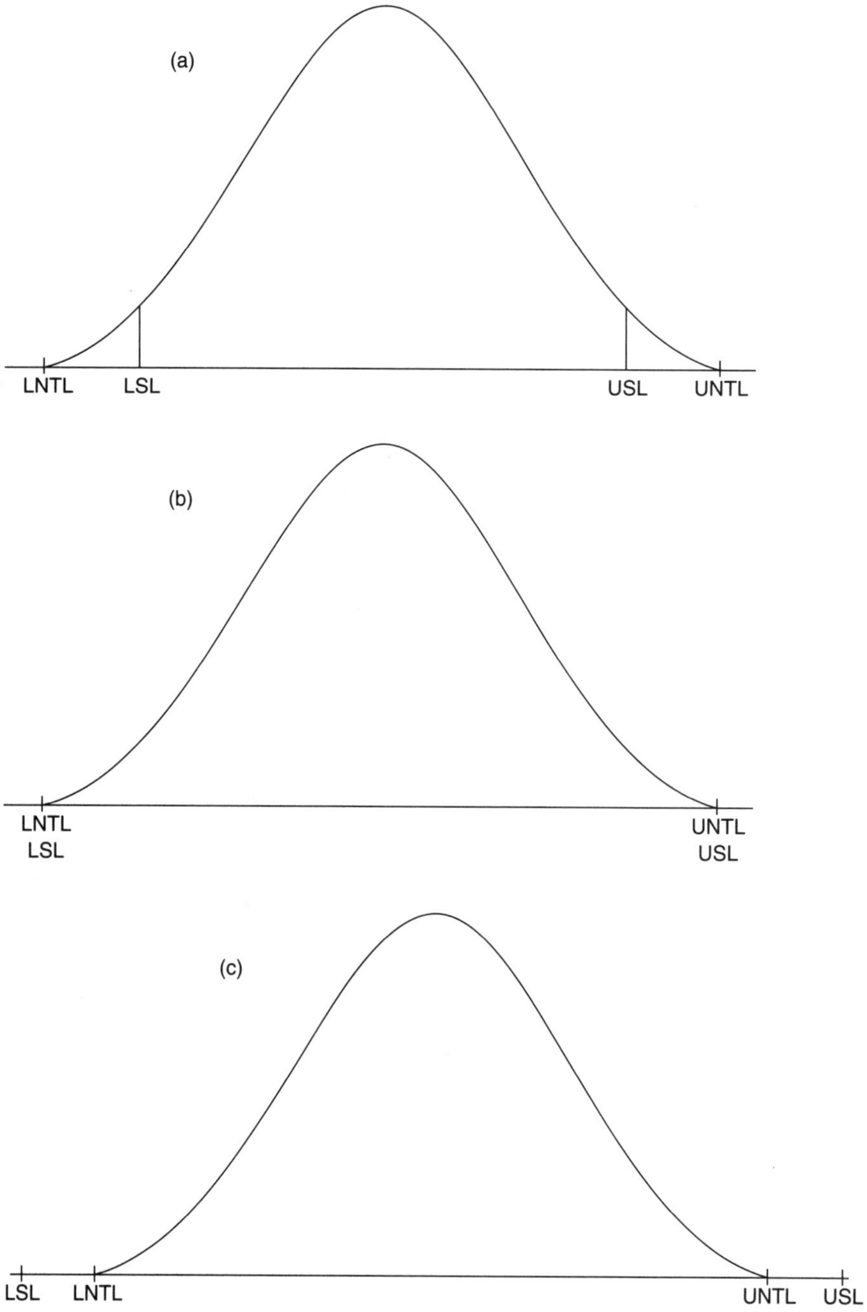

Figure 3.14 Three illustrations of the concept of process capability, where (a) shows a process that is stable but not capable, (b) shows a process that is stable and barely capable, and (c) shows a process that is stable and capable.

Also, we are given that LSL = 0.520 and USL = 0.950. Determine whether the process is capable.

Solution: From the given information, we have

$$\hat{\sigma} = \frac{\bar{R}}{d_2} = \frac{0.175}{2.326} = 0.075,$$

$$z_{\text{LSL}} = \frac{0.520 - 0.740}{0.075} = -2.93,$$

$$z_{\text{USL}} = \frac{0.950 - 0.740}{0.075} = 2.80.$$

Therefore, the percentage of nonconforming is

$$\begin{aligned} P(z \le -2.93) + P(z \ge 2.80) &= 0.0017 + 0.0026 \\ &= 0.0043. \end{aligned}$$

That is, less than 0.5 percent of the product is outside the specification limits. In other words, the process is almost capable.

From Example 3.9, it can be seen that if the specification limits are narrower, then the percentage of nonconforming will increase. On the other hand, if the specification limits remain the same but the process standard deviation becomes smaller, then the percentage of nonconforming will further reduce; that is, the percentage of a conforming product will be higher. So, to make the process more capable and continuously improve it, one should not only eliminate the special causes but also make full effort to eliminate the common causes and consequently reduce the process standard deviation. In order to eliminate the common causes, one must make use of the statistical techniques available in DOE, which we will discuss in our next volume.

4

Phase I (Detecting Large Shifts)—SPC: Control Charts for Attributes

As noted in the previous chapter, quality characteristics are usually of two types: variables and attributes. In Chapter 3, we studied control charts for variables for detecting large shifts. However, not all quality characteristics can be numerically measured. For example, we may be interested in finding out whether the new-car paint meets the specifications in terms of shine, uniformity, and scratches. In this example we cannot quantify the shine, the blemishes, or the scratches. In other words, we cannot numerically measure the shine, the uniformity, or the scratches; consequently, to study the quality of paint on new cars, we cannot use control charts for variables. This type of situation sometimes arises when a quality characteristic is measurable, but because of cost, time, or both, we do not want to take the measurements. Rather, we may prefer to use a more economical method, such as a go or no-go gauge. Therefore, it is important that we study control charts appropriate for quality characteristics that cannot be numerically measured. Such control charts are called *control charts for attributes*. In this chapter, we will study various control charts for attributes for detecting large shifts, which usually occur in phase I implementation of SPC.

4.1 Control Charts for Attributes

When a quality characteristic cannot be numerically measured, we classify such product as defective or nondefective. In SPC it has become more common to use the terminology *conforming* or *nonconforming* instead of *nondefective* or *defective*. Throughout this book, we shall use *conforming* or *nonconforming*.

Definition 4.1 A quality characteristic that classifies any product as conforming or nonconforming is called an *attribute*.

For instance, quality characteristics such as the determination that a soda can is not leaking, a stud has regular edges, a rod fits into a slot, a 100-watt lightbulb meets the desired standard, and a steel rivet meets the manufacturer's quality specifications are examples of attributes. Note that the data collected on a quality characteristic that is an attribute are simply count data. Moreover, the sample sizes when using control charts for attributes are normally much larger (usually in the hundreds) than a sample of size four or five that we usually use in control charts for variables.

In general, variable control charts are more informative than attribute control charts. They are very effective in detecting a defect even before it occurs, whereas attribute control charts are used only after the defects have occurred. There are cases, however, when variable control charts have limitations. For example, consider a product that is nonconforming due to any one of 10 quality characteristics that do not conform to specifications. In this case we cannot control all 10 quality characteristics by using one variable control chart, because one variable control chart can control only one quality characteristic at a time. Therefore, to control all 10 quality characteristics, we will have to use 10 different variable control charts. On the other hand, one attribute control chart can study all the quality characteristics because a nonconforming unit is nonconforming irrespective of the number of quality characteristics that do not conform to specifications. We can conclude that both variable and attribute control charts have pros and cons.

In some cases the quality characteristic is such that instead of classifying a unit as conforming or nonconforming, it records the number of nonconformities per manufactured unit—for example, the number of holes in a roll of paper, the number of irregularities per unit area of a spool of cloth, the number of blemishes on a painted surface, the number of loose ends in a circuit board, the number of nonconformities per unit length of a cable, the number of nonconformities of all types in an assembled unit, and so on. In such cases, we use control charts that fall under the category of control charts for attributes. These control charts are used to reduce the number of nonconformities per unit length, area, or volume of a single manufactured unit, or to reduce the number of nonconformities per manufactured or assembled unit.

The control charts for attributes are quite similar to the control charts for variables; that is, the CL and the control limits are set in the same manner as in the control charts for variables. However, it is important to note that the reasons for using control charts for variables and control charts for attributes are quite distinct. As noted in Chapter 3, the purpose of using control charts for variables in any process is to reduce the variability due to special or assignable causes, whereas control charts for attributes are used to monitor the number of nonconforming units, the number of nonconformities per manufactured or assembled unit, or simply the number of nonconformities per unit length, area, or volume of a single manufactured unit.

In this chapter, we will study four types of control charts for attributes: the p chart, the np chart, the c chart, and the u chart. Table 4.1 gives a very brief description of these charts, which can help determine the appropriate type of control chart for the quality characteristic under investigation.

Table 4.1 The four control charts for attributes.

Control Chart	Quality Characteristic under Investigation	Sample Size
p chart	Percentage or fraction of nonconforming units in a subgroup or a sample, where sample size can be variable	Varying or constant
np chart	Number of nonconforming units in a sample	Constant
c chart	Number of nonconformities in a sample or in one or more inspection units	Constant
u chart	Number of nonconformities per unit, where sample size can be variable	Varying or constant

4.2 The *p* Chart: Control Chart for Fraction of Nonconforming Units

The most frequently used attribute control chart is the p chart. It is used whenever we want to find the fraction or percentage of units that do not conform to the specifications in a situation where the observed quality characteristic is an attribute or a variable measured by a go or no-go gauge. A p chart can be used to study one or more quality characteristics simultaneously. Because each inspected unit is classified as conforming or nonconforming and it is assumed that the conformity or nonconformity of each unit is defined independently, which is true only if the process is stable, the probability of occurrence of a nonconforming unit at any given time is the same. Then the basic rules of the p chart are governed by the binomial probability distribution with parameters n and p, where n is the sample size and p is the fraction of nonconforming units produced by the process under investigation.

The binomial probability distribution function of a random variable X with parameters n and p is defined by

$$P(X = x) = \binom{n}{x} p^x (1-p)^{n-x} \qquad x = 0, 1, \ldots, n. \tag{4.1}$$

The mean and the standard deviation of the random variable X are given by np and $\sqrt{np(1-p)}$, respectively. For more details on binomial distribution, refer to *Applied Statistics for the Six Sigma Green Belt.*

Control Limits for the *p* Chart

The following steps detail how to develop a p control chart:

1. Select m ($m \geq 25$) samples of size n ($n \geq 50$) units from the process under investigation. Note, however, that if we have some prior information or any clue that the process is producing a very small fraction of nonconforming units, then the sample size should be large enough so that the probability that it contains some nonconforming units is relatively high.

2. Find the number of nonconforming units in each sample.
3. Find the fraction p_i of nonconforming units for each sample, that is,

$$p_i = \frac{x}{n}, \tag{4.2}$$

where x is the number of nonconforming units in the ith ($i = 1, 2, \ldots, m$) sample.
4. Find the average nonconforming $\bar{p}$ over the m samples, that is,

$$\bar{p} = \frac{p_1 + p_2 + \ldots + p_m}{m}. \tag{4.3}$$

The value of $\bar{p}$ determines the CL for the p chart and is an estimate of p, the process fraction of nonconforming units.
5. Using the well-known result that the binomial distribution with parameters n and p for large n can be approximated by the normal distribution with mean np and variance $np(1-p)$, it can be seen that $\bar{p}$ will be approximately normally distributed with mean p and standard deviation $\sqrt{\frac{p(1-p)}{n}}$. Hence the upper and lower 3σ control limits and the CL for the p chart are

$$UCL = \bar{p} + 3\sqrt{\frac{\bar{p}(1-\bar{p})}{n}}, \tag{4.4}$$

$$CL = \bar{p}, \tag{4.5}$$

$$LCL = \bar{p} - 3\sqrt{\frac{\bar{p}(1-\bar{p})}{n}}. \tag{4.6}$$

In equations (4.4) and (4.5), $\sqrt{\frac{\bar{p}(1-\bar{p})}{n}}$ is an estimator of $\sqrt{\frac{p(1-p)}{n}}$, the standard deviation of $\hat{p}$. Furthermore, if the control charts are being implemented for the first time, then the control limits given by equations (4.4)–(4.6) should be treated as the trial limits. In other words, before using these control limits any further, the points corresponding to all the samples used to determine these limits should be plotted and verified, and it should be established that all the points fall within these control limits and that there is no evident pattern present. If any sample points exceed the control limits or if there is any pattern, then the possible special causes should be detected and eliminated before recalculating the control limits for future use. When recalculating the control limits, points that exceeded the trial control limits should be ignored, provided any special causes related to such points have been detected and eliminated.

Note: Sometimes for small values of $\bar{p}$, n, or both, the value of the LCL may be negative. In such cases, we always set the LCL at zero because the fraction of nonconforming units can never go below zero.

Interpreting the Control Chart for Fraction Nonconforming

1. If any point or points exceed the upper or lower control limit, we conclude that the process is not stable and that some special causes are present in the process.
2. The presence of special causes, which may be favorable or unfavorable, must be investigated, and appropriate action(s) should be taken.
3. A point above the UCL is generally an indication that:
   - The control limit or the plotted point is in error.
   - The process performance has deteriorated or is deteriorating.
   - The measurement system has changed.
4. A point below the LCL is generally an indication that:
   - The control limit or the plotted point is in error.
   - The process performance has improved or is improving. This condition of the process should be investigated very carefully so that such conditions of improvement are implemented on a permanent basis at this location and elsewhere in the industry.
   - The measurement system has changed.
5. As in the case of $\bar{X}$ and R charts, or $\bar{X}$ and S charts, the presence of any unusual patterns or trends is either an indication of an unstable process or an advance warning of conditions that, if left unattended or without any appropriate action, could make the process unstable.
6. If $\bar{p}$ is moderately high ($n\bar{p} \geq 5$), then an approximately equal number of points should fall on either side of the CL. Therefore, either of the following conditions could indicate that the process has shifted or a trend of a shift has started:
   - A run of seven or more points going up or going down.
   - A run of seven or more points falling below or above the CL.
7. A run above the CL or a run going up generally indicates that:
   - The process performance has deteriorated and may still be deteriorating.
   - The measurement system has changed.
8. A run below the CL or a run going down generally indicates that:

- The process performance has improved and may still be improving.
- The measurement system has changed.

To illustrate the construction of the p chart, we consider the data in Example 4.1, shown in Table 4.2.

Example 4.1 *A semiconductor industry tracks the number of nonconforming computer chips produced each day. A team of Six Sigma Green Belts wants to improve the overall quality by reducing the fraction of nonconforming computer chips. To achieve this goal, the team decided to set up a p chart based on daily inspections of 1000 chips over a period of 30 days. Table 4.2 gives the number of nonconforming chips out of 1000 inspected chips each day during the study period.*

Solution: Using the data in Table 4.2, we develop the trial control limits of the p chart.

First we calculate the sample fraction nonconforming values (p_i), which are listed in columns 3 and 6 of Table 4.2. Substituting the sample fraction nonconforming values in equation (4.3), we get

$$\bar{p} = 0.00837.$$

Plugging the values of $\bar{p} = 0.00837$ and $n = 1000$ into equations (4.4) and (4.6), we get the control limits for the p chart:

Table 4.2 Number of nonconforming computer chips out of 1000 inspected each day during the study period.

Day	Number of Nonconforming x	Sample Fraction Nonconforming p_i	Day	Number of Nonconforming x	Sample Fraction Nonconforming p_i
1	9	0.009	16	12	0.012
2	5	0.005	17	5	0.005
3	6	0.006	18	6	0.006
4	11	0.011	19	12	0.012
5	11	0.011	20	10	0.010
6	12	0.012	21	6	0.006
7	7	0.007	22	7	0.007
8	11	0.011	23	11	0.011
9	6	0.006	24	11	0.011
10	6	0.006	24	11	0.011
11	8	0.008	26	5	0.005
12	5	0.005	27	12	0.012
13	8	0.008	28	11	0.011
14	5	0.005	29	7	0.007
15	8	0.008	30	9	0.009

$$UCL = 0.01701,$$
$$CL = 0.00837,$$
$$LCL = 0.0.$$

The p control chart for the data in Table 4.2 is shown in Figure 4.1.

From the p control chart in Figure 4.1 we observe that all the points are well within the control limits. We should note, however, that starting from point number 9, seven successive points fall below the CL. This indicates that from day 9 through 15, the number of nonconforming chips was relatively low. An investigation to determine the process conditions on these days should be made so that similar conditions could be implemented for future use. Otherwise, because all the points of the current data fall within the control limits and no patterns exist, the trial control limits can be extended for use over the next 30 days, when the control chart should again be reevaluated.

4.2.1 The *p* Chart: Control Chart for Fraction Nonconforming with Variable Samples

There are times when, for various reasons, it is not possible to select samples of equal sizes. This is particularly true when the samples consist of 100 percent inspection during a fixed period of time on each day of the study. The procedure to develop a p chart with variable sample sizes is very similar to the procedure for a p chart with constant sample size.

For example, suppose we have m samples of sizes $n_1, n_2, n_3, \ldots, n_m$. To develop a p chart for variable sample sizes, we proceed as follows:

1. From the process under investigation, select m ($m \geq 25$) samples of sizes $n_1, n_2, n_3, \ldots, n_m$ ($n_i \geq 50$) units.
2. Find the number of nonconforming units in each sample.
3. Find the fraction p_i of nonconforming units for each sample

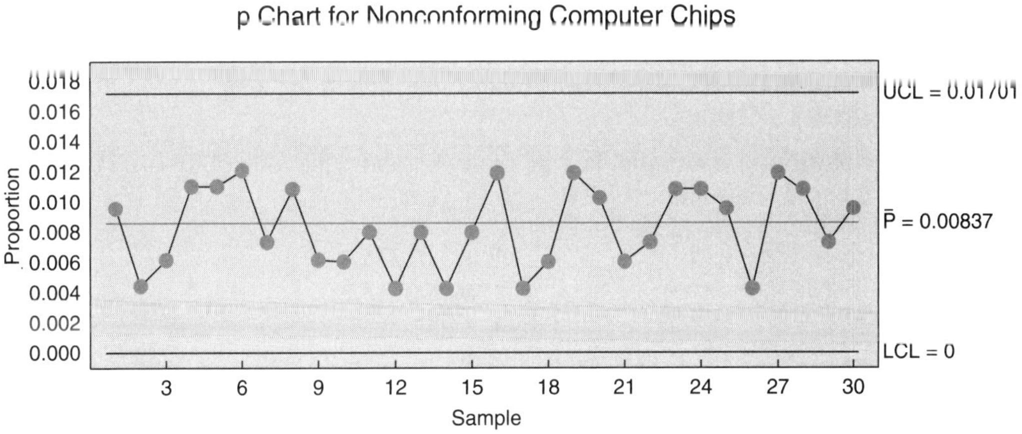

Figure 4.1 MINITAB printout of the p chart for nonconforming computer chips, using trial control limits from the data in Table 4.2.

$$p_i = \frac{x}{n_i}, \tag{4.7}$$

where x is the number of nonconforming units in the ith ($i = 1, 2, \ldots, m$) sample.

4. Find the average fraction $\bar{p}$ of nonconforming units over the m samples, that is,

$$\bar{p} = \frac{n_1 p_1 + n_2 p_2 + \ldots + n_m p_m}{n_1 + n_2 + n_3 + \ldots + n_m}. \tag{4.8}$$

The value of $\bar{p}$ determines the CL for the p chart and is an estimate of p, the process fraction of nonconforming units.

5. The control limits for p with variable sample sizes are determined for each sample separately. The upper and lower 3σ control limits for the ith sample are

$$\text{UCL} = \bar{p} + 3\sqrt{\frac{\bar{p}(1-\bar{p})}{n_i}}, \tag{4.9}$$

$$\text{CL} = \bar{p}, \tag{4.10}$$

$$\text{LCL} = \bar{p} - 3\sqrt{\frac{\bar{p}(1-\bar{p})}{n_i}}. \tag{4.11}$$

Note that the CL is the same for all samples, whereas the control limits will be different.

To illustrate construction of a p chart with variable sample size, we consider the data in Table 4.3 of Example 4.2.

Example 4.2 *Suppose in Example 4.1 that all the chips manufactured during a fixed period of time are inspected each day. However, the number of computer chips manufactured varies during that fixed period on each day. The data collected for the study period of 30 days are shown in Table 4.3. Construct a* p *chart for these data and determine whether the process is stable.*

Solution: Using the data in Table 4.3 and equations (4.8)–(4.11), we get the trial control limits as

$$\text{UCL} = 0.01675,$$
$$\text{CL} = 0.00813,$$
$$\text{LCL} = 0.0.$$

The p chart for the data in Table 4.3 is as shown in Figure 4.2.

From Figure 4.2 we see that all the points are well within the control limits and that there is no apparent pattern or trend in the chart, which means the process is stable. Also, recall that in Figure 4.1 we had a run of seven points that fell below the CL. In Figure 4.2 there is no such run, even though we are dealing with the same process. Such differences are normal when samples are taken at different times.

Table 4.3 Number of nonconforming computer chips with different size samples inspected each day during the study period.

Day	Number of Nonconforming x	Sample Size n_i	Day	Number of Nonconforming x	Sample Size n_i
1	7	908	16	7	962
2	11	986	17	11	926
3	8	976	18	7	917
4	7	991	19	9	978
5	7	944	20	7	961
6	5	906	21	6	970
7	11	928	22	9	905
8	5	948	23	9	962
9	10	994	24	8	900
10	8	960	25	11	998
11	7	982	26	5	935
12	6	921	29	6	970
13	7	938	28	6	967
14	10	1000	29	9	983
15	6	982	30	8	976

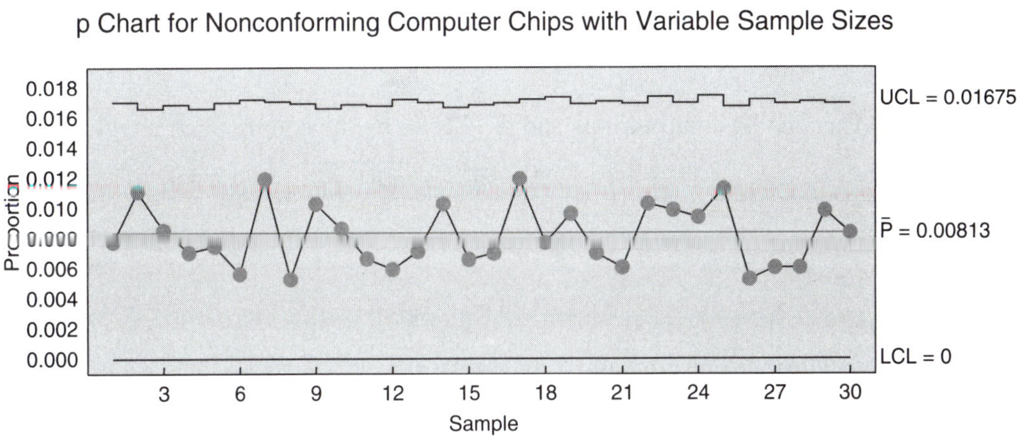

Figure 4.2 MINITAB printout of the p chart for nonconforming chips with variable sample sizes, using trial control limits for the data in Table 4.3.

4.3 The *np* Chart: Control Chart for Number of Nonconforming Units

In an *np* chart, we plot the number of nonconforming units in an inspected sample instead of the fraction of nonconforming units in the inspected sample. Other than this difference, the *np* chart is very similar to the *p* chart. However, note that in the *p* chart the sample sizes could be equal or unequal, whereas in the *np* chart the sample sizes are equal. Otherwise, both the *p* chart and the *np* chart can be implemented under the same circumstances. Following are specific points pertinent to the *np* chart:

- The inspection sample sizes should be equal
- The sample size should be large enough to include some nonconforming units

Record the sample size and the number of observed nonconforming units in each sample, and plot the number of nonconforming units on the control chart.

Control Limits for the *np* Control Chart

Select m samples, each of size n, from the process under investigation, and determine the number of nonconforming units that exist in each sample. Let the number of nonconforming units found be denoted by $x_1, x_2, x_3, \ldots, x_m$, respectively. Then the control limits are found.

First, calculate $n\bar{p}$, the average number of nonconforming units per sample, that is,

$$n\bar{p} = \frac{x_1 + x_2 + x_3 + \ldots + x_m}{m}. \tag{4.12}$$

Then the 3σ control limits and the CL for the *np* control chart are given by

$$\text{UCL} = n\bar{p} + 3\sqrt{n\bar{p}(1-\bar{p})}, \tag{4.13}$$

$$\text{CL} = n\bar{p}, \tag{4.14}$$

$$\text{LCL} = n\bar{p} - 3\sqrt{n\bar{p}(1-\bar{p})}. \tag{4.15}$$

To illustrate construction of the *np* chart, we consider the data in Table 4.2 of Example 4.1.

Example 4.3 *Consider the data on computer chips in Table 4.2, Example 4.1. Construct an np chart for these data and verify whether the process is stable.*

From the *np* control chart in Figure 4.3 we observe that all the points are well within the control limits. However, as in Figure 4.1, starting from point 9, seven successive points fall below the CL. This indicates that from day 9 through 15, the number of nonconforming units was relatively low. An investigation to determine the process conditions on these days should be made so

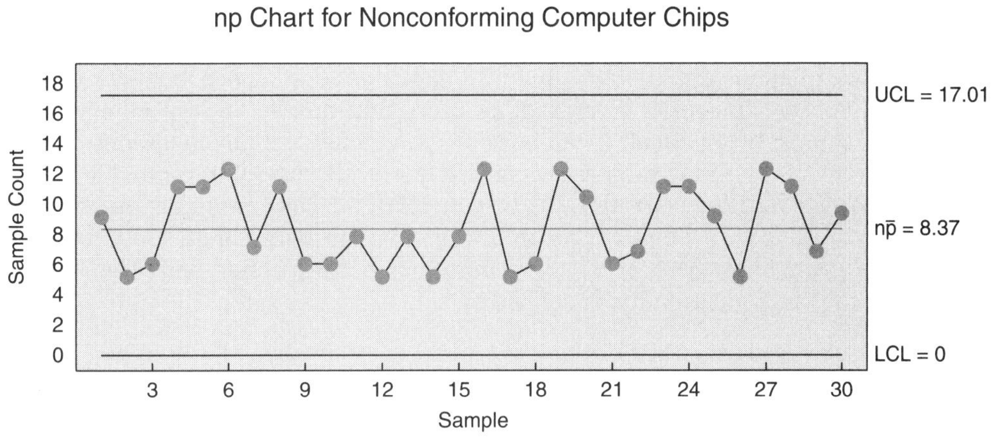

Figure 4.3 MINITAB printout of the *np* chart for nonconforming computer chips, using trial control limits for the data in Table 4.2.

that similar conditions could be extended for future use. Otherwise, because all the points of the current data fall within the control limits and no patterns are present, the trial control limits can be extended for use over the next 30 days, when the control chart should again be reevaluated.

4.4 The *c* Chart (Nonconformities versus Nonconforming Units)

In many situations we are interested in studying the number of nonconformities in a sample, which is also known as an inspection unit, rather than studying the fraction or total number of nonconforming units in a sample. This is particularly true when a unit is nonconforming due to various types of nonconformities. For example, we may want to study the quality of electric motors that could be nonconforming due to defective bearings, a defective gear, a defective seal, or a defective terminal connection of the winding. As another example, suppose we are interested in studying the quality of printed circuit boards for laptops that could be nonconforming due to a shorted trace, an open via, a cold solder joint, or a solder short. In these cases we may be more likely to study the nonconformities rather than the nonconforming units. The control chart that is most commonly used to study nonconformities is the *c* control chart. Whereas the *p* control chart studies the fraction of nonconforming units and the *np* control chart studies the total number of nonconforming units in each sample, the *c* control chart studies the total number of nonconformities in each sample. The letter *c* in *c* control chart denotes the total number of nonconformities, which may be of one kind or of various kinds, in an inspection unit.

To illustrate, suppose that to develop trial control limits for a *c* control chart for electric motors, we select samples of size 100 motors each, where each sample would be considered as one inspection unit or several inspection units, depending on how the inspection units are defined. Note that the size of an inspection unit is purely a matter of convenience, but the *c* control charts are constructed with sample sizes or the number of inspection units in a sample being equal. It can be shown that under certain conditions (conditions of a Poisson process, which are briefly discussed in *Applied Statistics for the Six Sigma Green Belt*), the number of nonconformities *c* is distributed according to a Poisson probability distribution with parameter λ, where λ is the average number of nonconformities per inspection unit. The Poisson probability distribution is defined as

$$p(x)=\frac{e^{-\lambda}\lambda^{x}}{x!} \qquad x=0,1,2,3,\ldots, \tag{4.16}$$

where the mean and the variance of the Poisson distribution are given by λ. Now suppose that we select *m* samples, with each sample being one inspection unit, and let the number of nonconformities in these samples be c_1, c_2, c_3, . . . , c_m, respectively. Then the parameter λ, which is usually unknown, is estimated by

$$\hat{\lambda}=\bar{c}=\frac{c_1+c_2+c_3+\ldots+c_m}{m}. \tag{4.17}$$

The 3σ control limits for the *c* control chart are defined as follows:

$$\text{UCL}=\bar{c}+3\sqrt{\bar{c}}, \tag{4.18}$$

$$\text{CL}=\bar{c}, \tag{4.19}$$

$$\text{LCL}=\bar{c}-3\sqrt{\bar{c}}. \tag{4.20}$$

Note that for small values of $\bar{c}$ (≤ 5), the Poisson distribution is asymmetric: the value of a Type I error (α) above the UCL and below the LCL is usually not the same. For small values of $\bar{c}$ it may be more prudent to use probability control limits rather than the 3σ control limits. The probability control limits can be found by using Poisson distribution tables.

To illustrate construction of a *c* control chart using 3σ control limits, we consider the data in Table 4.4 of Example 4.4.

Example 4.4 *A paper mill has detected that almost 90 percent of rejected paper rolls is due to nonconformities of two types: holes and wrinkles in the paper. The Six Sigma Green Belt team in the mill decides to set up control charts to reduce or eliminate the number of these nonconformities. To set up the control charts, the team collected data by taking random samples of five rolls each day for 30 days and counting the number of nonconformities (holes and wrinkles) in each sample. The data are shown in Table 4.4. Set up a c control chart using these data.*

Solution: Using the data in Table 4.4, the estimate of the population parameter is given by

$$\hat{\lambda} = \bar{c} = \frac{\sum_{i=1}^{30} c_i}{30} = \frac{222}{30} = 7.4.$$

Therefore, using equations (4.18)–(4.20), the 3σ control limits of the phase I c control chart are given by

$$\text{UCL} = 7.4 + 3\sqrt{7.4} = 15.56,$$

$$\text{CL} = 7.4,$$

$$\text{LCL} = 7.4 - 3\sqrt{7.4} = -0.76 = 0.$$

Note that if the LCL turns out to be negative, as in this example, then we set the LCL at zero because the number of nonconformities cannot be negative. The c control chart for the data in Table 4.4 is as shown in Figure 4.4.

Table 4.4 Total number of nonconformities in samples of five rolls of paper.

Day	Total Number of Nonconformities	Day	Total Number of Nonconformities	Day	Total Number of Nonconformities
1	8	11	7	21	9
2	6	12	6	22	6
3	7	13	6	23	8
4	7	14	8	24	7
5	8	15	6	25	6
6	7	16	6	26	9
7	8	17	8	27	9
8	7	18	9	28	7
9	6	19	8	29	7
10	9	20	9	30	8

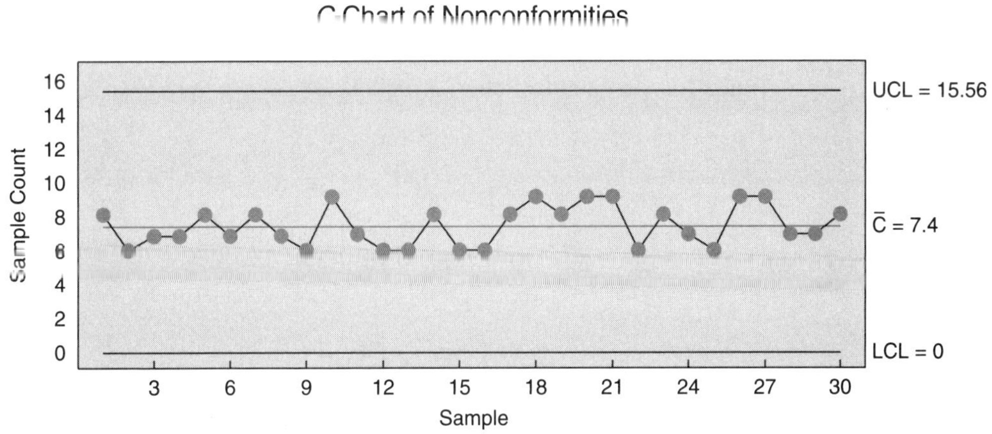

Figure 4.4 The c control chart of nonconformities for the data in Table 4.4.

From Figure 4.4, we can see that the process is stable. In other words, there are no special causes present, and the only causes that are affecting the process are the common causes. To eliminate the imperfections in the paper, the management must take action on the system, such as examining the quality of the wood chips and pulp, replacing old equipment, and providing more training for the workers. Also, to further enhance the process and eliminate the nonconformities, the quality engineers should use the techniques available in DOE, which we will discuss in our next volume, *Design of Experiments for the Six Sigma Green Belt.*

Notes

1. If the economic factors and time allow, one should take samples or inspection units large enough so that the LCL is positive. The LCL can be positive only if $\bar{c} > 9$. This means that the sample size should be such that it can catch nine or more nonconformities with high probability. An advantage of having a positive LCL is that it will allow us to see the conditions under which the nonconformities are very low, and consequently it will give us the opportunity to perpetuate these conditions on-site and implement them elsewhere in the industry.

2. As noted earlier, the size of the inspection unit is usually determined based on what is convenient. However, to determine the actual inspection unit size, one should also take into consideration the statistical characteristics of the process, such as the ARL, the state of the process (that is, whether the process has deteriorated or improved), and other factors that may require us to increase or decrease the sample size. So, while using control charts for nonconformities, particularly in phase I, situations may arise when the sample size may vary. In these situations, we use the *u* control chart instead of the *c* control chart. We will discuss the *u* control chart in the following section.

   If the samples consist of *n* inspection units, then the control limits for the *c* control chart are given by

$$\text{UCL} = n\bar{c} + 3\sqrt{n\bar{c}}, \tag{4.21}$$

$$\text{CL} = n\bar{c}, \tag{4.22}$$

$$\text{LCL} = n\bar{c} - 3\sqrt{n\bar{c}}. \tag{4.23}$$

4.5 The *u* Chart

The *u* control chart is essentially the *c* control chart except that the *u* control chart is always based on the number of nonconformities per inspection unit. In other words, the actual sample size may not be equal to one, or may vary, but the control limits of the u chart are always determined based on one inspection unit. If n is constant, one can use either a c chart or a u chart. For a u chart the CL is determined by $\bar{u} = \bar{c}/n$, and the 3σ control limit is given by

$$\text{UCL} = \bar{u} + 3\sqrt{\bar{u}/n}, \tag{4.24}$$

$$\text{LCL} = \bar{u} - 3\sqrt{\bar{u}/n}. \tag{4.25}$$

If the sample size varies, then we define $\bar{u}$ as

$$\bar{u} = \frac{c_1 + c_2 + \ldots + c_m}{n_1 + n_2 + \ldots + n_m} = \frac{\bar{c}}{\bar{n}}, \tag{4.26}$$

where m is the number of samples selected during the study period; c_1, c_2, $c_3, \ldots, c_m$ are the number of nonconformities in the m samples; and $\bar{n}$ is the average sample size, which is given by

$$\bar{n} = \frac{n_1 + n_2 + \ldots + n_m}{m}. \tag{4.27}$$

In this case the CL is fixed, but the control limits are different; that is, the CL and the 3σ control limits for the ith sample are given by

$$\text{UCL} = \bar{u} + 3\sqrt{\bar{u}/n_i}, \tag{4.28}$$

$$\text{CL} = \bar{u}, \tag{4.29}$$

$$\text{LCL} = \bar{u} - 3\sqrt{\bar{u}/n_i}. \tag{4.30}$$

Sometimes, if the samples do not vary too much, the n_i's in equations (4.28) and (4.30) are replaced by $\bar{n}$ so that the control limits are

$$\text{UCL} = \bar{u} + 3\sqrt{\bar{u}/\bar{n}}, \tag{4.31}$$

$$\text{CL} = \bar{u}, \tag{4.32}$$

$$\text{LCL} = \bar{u} - 3\sqrt{\bar{u}/\bar{n}}. \tag{4.33}$$

To illustrate construction of a u chart, we consider the data in Table 4.5 of Example 4.5.

Example 4.5 *A Six Sigma Green Belt team in a semiconductor industry found that the printed boards for laptops have nonconformities of several types, such as shorted trace, cold solder joint, and solder short, and the number of nonconformities is unacceptable. In order to reduce the number of nonconformities in the printed boards for laptops, the Six Sigma Green Belt team wants to set up a u chart. They collect data by selecting samples of five inspection units, where each inspection unit consists of 30 boards. The data, which are shown in Table 4.5, were collected over a period of 30 days.*

Table 4.5 Number of nonconformities on printed boards for laptops per sample, each sample consisting of five inspection units.

Day	Number of Nonconformities per Sample	Day	Number of Nonconformities per Sample
1	48	16	42
2	49	17	34
3	38	18	30
4	49	19	49
5	43	20	44
6	37	21	47
7	45	22	33
8	48	23	37
9	39	24	33
10	46	25	34
11	40	26	49
12	44	27	50
13	43	28	49
14	35	29	35
15	31	30	39

Solution: Using the data in Table 4.5, we have

$$\bar{c} = 41.333.$$

Therefore,

$$\bar{u} = \frac{\bar{c}}{5} = \frac{41.333}{5} = 8.2667.$$

Hence, the control limits are given by

$$\text{UCL} = \bar{u} + 3\sqrt{\bar{u}/n} = 8.2666 + 3\sqrt{8.2666/5} = 12.124,$$

$$\text{CL} = \bar{u} = 8.2667,$$

$$\text{UCL} = \bar{u} - 3\sqrt{\bar{u}/n} = 8.2666 - 3\sqrt{8.2666/5} = 4.409.$$

The *u* chart for the data in Table 4.5 is as shown in Figure 4.5. The *u* chart in Figure 4.5 shows that there are no assignable causes present in the process. In other words, only common causes are affecting the process. Therefore, management needs to take action on the system.

To illustrate construction of the *u* chart when the sample sizes vary, we consider the following example.

Example 4.6 *Suppose in Example 4.5, due to some administrative reasons, it was not possible to examine five inspection units every day. In other words, the sample size varied. The data obtained are as shown in Table 4.5. Construct and interpret a u chart for the data in Table 4.6.*

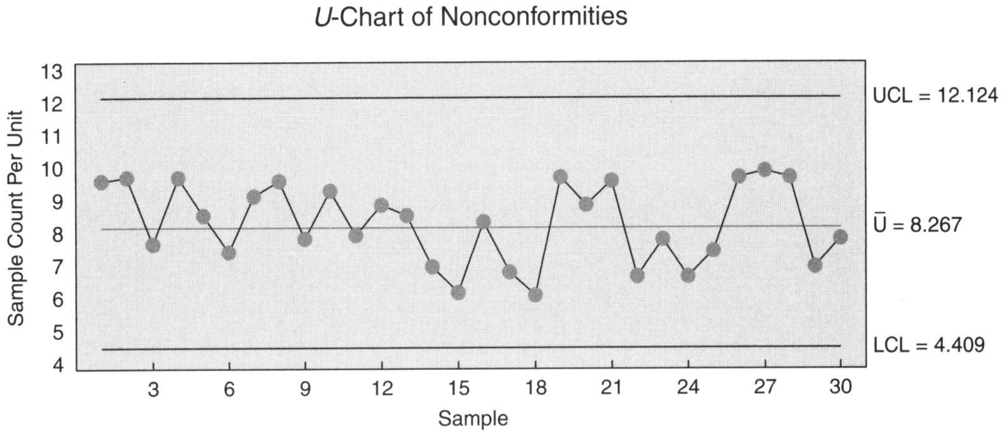

Figure 4.5 The *u* chart of nonconformities for the data in Table 4.5, constructed using MINITAB.

Table 4.6 Number of nonconformities on printed boards for laptops per sample with varying sample size.

Day	Sample Size	Number of Nonconformities per Sample	Day	Sample Size	Number of Nonconformities per Sample
1	3	33	5	16	40
2	5	40	4	17	40
3	3	38	5	18	37
4	5	43	4	19	40
5	5	45	5	20	37
6	5	35	4	21	39
7	5	35	5	22	48
8	3	41	5	23	39
9	3	40	5	24	36
10	5	30	3	25	39
11	5	36	3	26	36
12	5	40	5	27	43
13	3	33	3	28	36
14	4	36	4	29	49
15	4	38	3	30	40

Solution: Using the data in Table 4.6, we have

$$\bar{u} = \frac{c_1 + c_2 + \ldots + c_m}{n_1 + n_2 + \ldots + n_m}$$

$$= \frac{33 + 40 + 38 + \ldots + 40}{3 + 5 + 3 + \ldots + 3} = \frac{1162}{126} = 9.22.$$

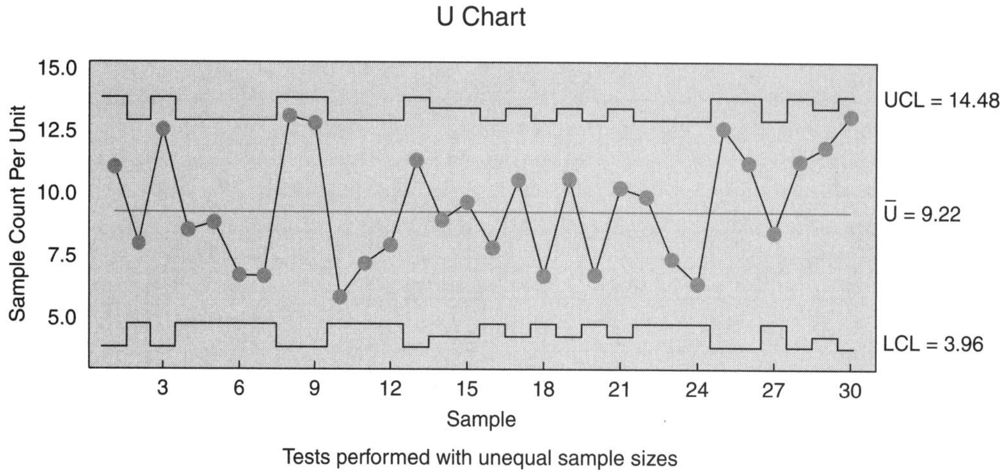

Figure 4.6 The *u* chart of nonconformities for the data in Table 4.6, constructed using MINITAB.

The control limits are calculated for each individual sample. For example, the control limits for sample one are given by

$$\text{UCL} = \bar{u} + 3\sqrt{\bar{u} / n_1} = 9.22 + 3\sqrt{9.22 / 3} = 14.48,$$

$$\text{CL} = \bar{u} = 9.22,$$

$$\text{UCL} = \bar{u} - 3\sqrt{\bar{u} / n_1} = 9.22 - 3\sqrt{9.22 / 3} = 3.96.$$

The control limits for the rest of the samples are calculated in the same manner. The CL, however, remains the same. The *u* chart for the data in Table 4.6 is as shown in Figure 4.6.

The *u* chart in Figure 4.6 shows that all the points are within the control limits. However, there are several points that fall beyond the warning control limits. Moreover, points 8 and 9 in particular fall very close to the UCLs. All these observations about the process indicate that there may be some special causes present in the process. In other words, the process may be on the verge of being unstable. Therefore, precautions should be taken to avoid the process becoming unstable, but certainly without overcontrolling it.

5

Phase II (Detecting Small Shifts)—SPC: Cumulative Sum, Moving Average, and Exponentially Weighted Moving Average Control Charts

In Chapters 3 and 4 we studied Shewhart control charts for detecting large shifts in any process. In this chapter we will study the next generation of control charts: cumulative sum (CUSUM), moving average (MA), and exponentially weighted moving average (EWMA) control charts. As noted earlier, the large shifts usually occur in phase I of implementing SPC, when a process has a strong influence of special causes and, consequently, large shifts are occurring in the process. By the time phase I implementation of SPC is over, most of the special causes are eliminated or at least reduced, and as a result, the occurrence of large shifts becomes a rare event. In other words, after phase I implementation of SPC is complete and phase II implementation commences, the process is usually under control; as a result, it may be having only small shifts. Shewhart control charts are known to be not very effective in detecting small shifts that are less than 1.5σ. One possibility when the shifts are small is to increase the sensitivity of the Shewhart control charts by using the following criteria from Western Electric (1956, 27):

a. Two out of three consecutive points fall outside the 2σ warning limits

b. Four out of five consecutive points fall at a distance of 1σ or more from the CL

c. Eight consecutive points fall above or below the CL

If one point falls outside the 3σ control limits or if any conditions from this list occur, the process is considered to be out of control. Subsequently, an appropriate action is taken, such as increasing the sampling frequency, increasing the sample size, or both. However, even though these actions do increase the sensitivity, as Champ and Woodall (1987) point out, using these rules, the in-control ARL is only 91.75. Under normality, the false-alarm rate is little more than four times the false-alarm rate of a Shewhart chart when the criteria from Western Electric are not used. Moreover, the advantage of the simplicity of Shewhart charts, which is an important feature, is lost. Keeping all this in mind, it is fair to say that when the shifts are small, the Shewhart chart with these modifications is not a viable alternative to the CUSUM control chart. Also, the CUSUM control chart has another major advantage over the Shewhart control chart. In the CUSUM control chart, the ith point uses the information contained in all the samples collected at time i and before, whereas the Shewhart control chart uses only the information contained in the ith sample. In other words, the Shewhart control chart ignores all information provided by the samples collected before the ith sample. But at the same time, we must note that this feature of the CUSUM control chart makes the plotted points dependent, and therefore it is difficult to interpret any pattern other than when the point exceeds the decision interval for an upward or downward shift.

Other control charts that are very effective in detecting small shifts are the MA and EWMA control charts. CUSUM, MA, and EWMA control charts are excellent alternatives to the Shewhart control chart for controlling processes in phase II. Relatively speaking, the MA chart is not as effective as CUSUM and EWMA charts. The CUSUM and EWMA control charts can be used to monitor not only the process mean but also the process variance and the fraction nonconforming and nonconformities. However, our major focus of discussion of these control charts is on the process mean. An excellent reference for a detailed study of CUSUM control charts is Hawkins and Olwell (1998).

5.1 Basic Concepts of the CUSUM Control Chart

CUSUM Control Chart versus Shewhart $\bar{X}$-R Control Chart

The basic assumptions of a CUSUM control chart are:

1. The observations are independently and identically normally distributed with mean μ and standard deviation σ.

2. The mean μ and standard deviation σ are known.

Note that in practice the parameters μ and σ are never known. Hence, we always end up estimating them. It is very important to remember that while estimating these parameters, precision is essential. Even a small error, particularly in estimating μ, will have an accumulative effect, which will cause false alarms. One way to avoid such problems is to take very large samples when estimating these parameters.

Before we begin our formal discussion of designing the CUSUM control chart, we first use a small set of data to show how the CUSUM chart is more effective than the Shewhart control chart in detecting small shifts in the process mean. Note that the CUSUM chart we will discuss in this section has no decision interval. In other words, it is not a formal CUSUM control chart.

Example 5.1 *Consider a manufacturing process of auto parts. We are interested in studying a quality characteristic of the parts manufactured by the process. Let the quality characteristic when the process is under control be normally distributed with mean 20 and standard deviation 2. The data shown in Table 5.1 give the first 10 random samples of size four, which are taken when the process is stable and producing the parts with mean value 20 and standard deviation 2. The last 10 random samples, again of size four, were taken from that process after its mean experienced an upward shift of one standard deviation, resulting in a new process with mean 22. Construct the Shewhart* $\bar{X}$*-R control chart and the CUSUM control chart for the data in Table 5.1. Then comment on the outcomes of the* $\bar{X}$*-R control chart and the CUSUM chart.*

Table 5.1 Data from a manufacturing process of auto parts before and after its mean experienced a shift of 1σ (sample size four).

Sample (i)	Sample				$\bar{X}_i$	$\bar{Z}_i = \dfrac{\bar{X}_i - 20}{\sigma/\sqrt{n}}$	$S_i = \bar{Z}_i + S_{i-1}$
1	19.35	20.05	18.92	15.70	18.5050	−1.4950	−1.4950
2	17.50	19.37	17.03	19.35	18.3125	−1.6875	−3.1825
3	22.99	18.61	18.35	17.77	19.4300	−0.5700	−3.7525
4	22.83	19.56	21.14	23.50	21.7575	1.7575	−1.9950
5	18.70	21.26	19.71	19.07	19.6850	−0.3150	−2.3100
6	20.70	17.90	22.05	20.62	20.3175	0.3175	−1.9925
7	22.80	19.80	20.15	21.01	20.9400	0.9400	−1.0525
8	20.28	17.15	24.81	19.68	20.4800	0.4800	−0.5725
9	16.87	22.37	18.91	18.43	19.1450	−0.8550	−1.4275
10	18.96	21.16	19.74	20.56	20.1050	0.1050	−1.3225
11	23.96	18.75	22.48	25.85	22.7600	2.7600	1.4375
12	19.20	23.18	24.17	20.77	21.8300	1.8300	3.2675
13	21.18	24.33	19.78	26.46	22.9375	2.9375	6.2050
14	20.42	20.74	24.66	21.70	21.8800	1.8800	8.0850
15	22.76	21.47	20.36	22.84	21.8575	1.8575	9.9425
16	23.01	21.48	21.86	17.99	21.0850	1.0850	11.0275
17	23.12	23.82	21.42	21.96	22.5800	2.5800	13.6075
18	21.37	22.05	25.24	22.70	22.8400	2.8400	16.4474
19	21.84	23.89	15.97	22.67	21.0925	1.0925	17.5400
20	18.49	21.65	22.88	24.67	21.9225	1.9225	19.4625

Solution: As described earlier, the basic principle of the CUSUM chart is to detect small shifts in the process mean at time i by calculating the accumulated sum S_i of deviations of the sample means $\bar{X}_1, \bar{X}_2, \ldots, \bar{X}_i$ from the target value (μ_0) measured in standard deviation units. That is,

$$S_i = \sum_{j=1}^{i} \frac{(\bar{X}_j - \mu_0)}{\sigma/\sqrt{n}} = \frac{(\bar{X}_i - \mu_0)}{\sigma/\sqrt{n}} + S_{i-1} \qquad (5.1)$$

$$= \bar{Z}_i + S_{i-1},$$

where $\bar{Z}_1, \bar{Z}_2, \ldots, \bar{Z}_i$ are the standardized values of $\bar{X}_1, \bar{X}_2, \ldots, \bar{X}_i$, respectively. In Example 5.1, the target value is 20 and the accumulated sum of deviations of the sample means from the target value at time i, when measured in standard deviation units, is given in column 5 of Table 5.1. From equation (5.1) one can see that if the samples come from a stable process with mean μ_1, the points (i, S_i) when plotted on a chart will:

a. Randomly scatter around the zero line

b. Clearly show an upward trend

c. Clearly show a downward trend

The result depends on whether $\mu_1 = \mu_0$, $\mu_1 > \mu_0$, or $\mu_1 < \mu_0$.

The $\bar{X}$-R control chart and the CUSUM chart are as shown in Figures 5.1 and 5.2. The $\bar{X}$-R control chart shows that the process is clearly stable and showing no abnormality other than sample number 13, which comes close to the UCL. In other words, the chart is not detecting that the samples starting with the 11th sample came from the process after it had experienced an upward shift of one standard deviation. However, the CUSUM chart shows an upward trend, which started at the 11th sample. Furthermore, as noted by Lucas (1982), CUSUM control charts give tighter process control than classical control charts such as Shewhart control charts. With the tighter control provided by CUSUM control charts, more emphasis is placed on keeping the process on target rather than allowing it to drift within the limits. Moreover, the sensitivity of the CUSUM control chart would not be seriously affected if we took samples of size $n = 1$ instead of $n > 1$. In fact, CUSUM control charts more frequently use $n = 1$ or individual values. In CUSUM control charts for individual values, the quantities $\bar{X}_i$, $\bar{Z}_i$, and $\sigma/\sqrt{n}$ in Table 5.1 are replaced by X_i, Z_i, and σ, respectively. We will look at developing the CUSUM control chart in the next section.

5.2 Designing a CUSUM Control Chart

In section 5.1 we saw that CUSUM charts are very effective in detecting small shifts. Unlike the $\bar{X}$ Shewhart control charts, CUSUM control charts can be designed to detect one-sided or two-sided shifts. These charts are defined by two parameters, k and h, called the reference value and the decision interval, which are defined in section 5.2.1. The two-sided process control using the CUSUM control chart is achieved by concurrently using two

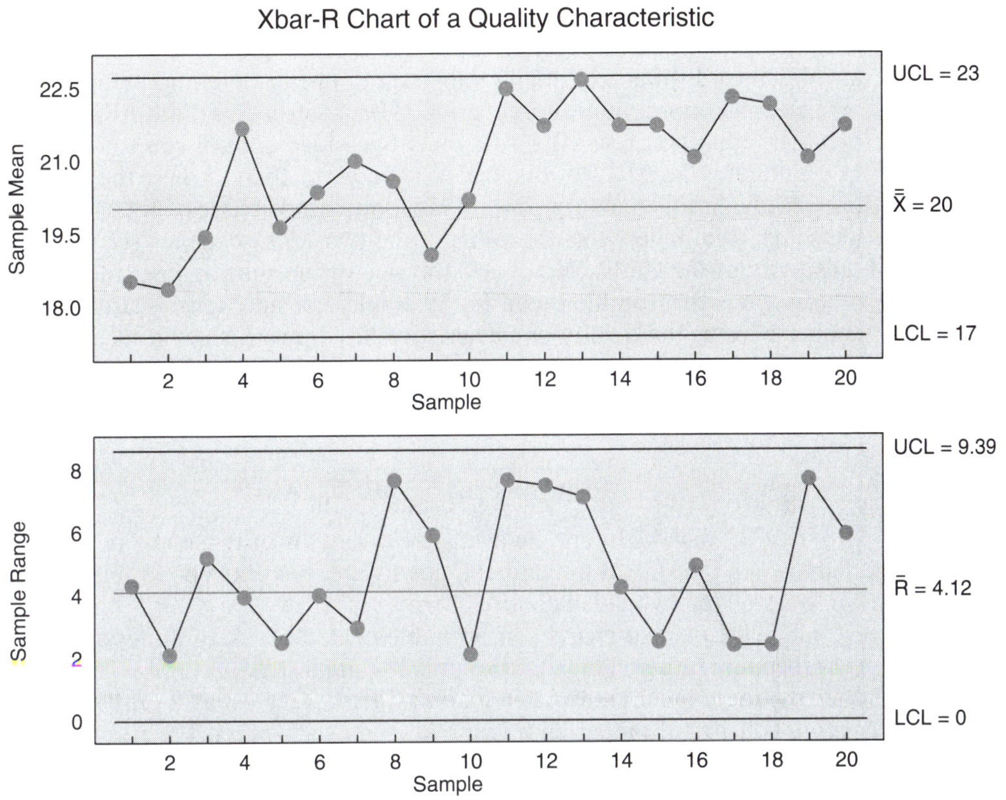

Figure 5.1 $\bar{X}$-R control chart for the data in Table 5.1.

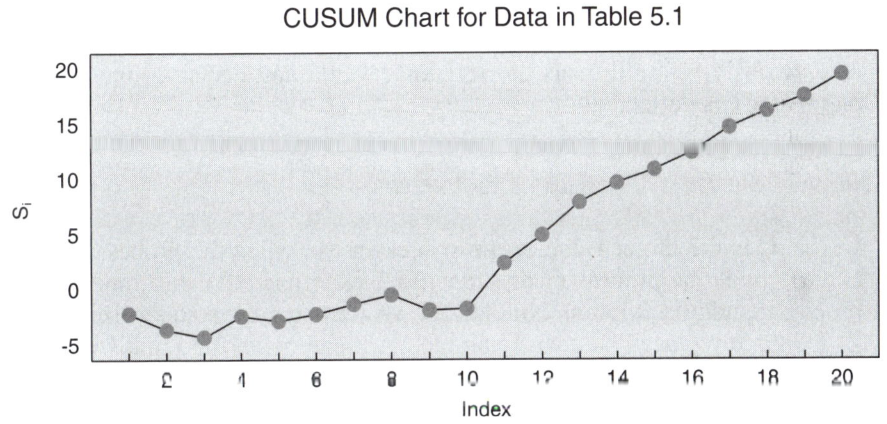

Figure 5.2 CUSUM chart for the data in Table 5.1.

one-sided CUSUM control charts. In both one-sided CUSUM charts, one can use the same or different reference values, depending on whether the upward and downward shifts are equally important or one is more important than the other. Furthermore, in designing a CUSUM control chart, the ARL usually plays an important role. The ARL of a two-sided control chart is obtained by combining the ARLs of two one-sided control charts, where the ARLs of one-sided control charts for upward and downward shifts are not necessarily the same. Again, note that the value of the two ARLs depends solely on the sensitivity of the shifts. Sometimes the size of the shift on one side may be more serious than on the other. For example, consider tensile strength of a copper wire as the quality characteristic. Any upward shift in mean tensile strength may not be as serious as a downward shift. It can be seen from Van Dobben de Bruyn (1968) that

$$\frac{1}{\text{ARL(two-sided)}} = \frac{1}{\text{ARL}^{+}} + \frac{1}{\text{ARL}^{-}}, \tag{5.2}$$

where ARL^{+} and ARL^{-} are the average run lengths of two one-sided control charts when the shift is upward and downward, respectively. In this section, we focus on the two-sided control chart.

CUSUM control charts can be implemented by using either a numerical procedure or a graphical procedure. The *numerical procedure* consists of constructing a table known as a *tabular CUSUM*, whereas a *graphical procedure* consists of preparing a graph known as a *V-mask*. Practitioners usually prefer to use numerical procedure. For visual observation, however, the tabular CUSUM can be plotted in a graph. The tabular CUSUM in Table 5.3 is plotted in Figure 5.3. In this book we will discuss only the construction of a tabular CUSUM.

5.2.1 Two-Sided CUSUM Control Chart Using Numerical Procedure

The tabular CUSUM control charts are defined by the two parameters k and h, previously referred to as the reference value and decision interval. The parameter k is defined as

$$k = \frac{|\mu_1 - \mu_0|}{2\sigma}, \tag{5.3}$$

where μ_0 is the target value or the process mean when the process is under control, μ_1 is the process mean after it has experienced a shift, and σ is the process standard deviation. Note that if we are using the standardized values Z_i, then σ is replaced by 1. In Example 5.1 it can be verified that $k = 0.5$. As a rule of thumb, the parameter h is usually equal to 4 or 5 (if the observations are not standardized, then h is equal to 4σ or 5σ, where σ is the process standard deviation). In practice, however, h should be chosen so that the value of the ARL is neither too small nor too large. This is because small values of ARL cause too many false alarms, whereas large values of ARL allow the process to continue running even when it has experienced a shift and is producing nonconforming products. Preferably, h should be such that when

Table 5.2 Values of h for a given value of k when $ARL_0 = 370$.

k	0.25	0.50	0.75	1.00	1.25	1.50
h	8.01	4.77	3.34	2.52	1.99	1.61

$\mu_1 = \mu_0$, that is, when the process has experienced no shift, the value of ARL, which we denote by ARL_0, is approximately equal to 370. The value 370 of ARL_0 is purposely chosen because it matches the ARL_0 of the Shewhart control chart under normal distribution with control limits equal to 3σ. Hawkins (1993) gives a table of k values and the corresponding values of h such that ARL_0 for a two-sided CUSUM control chart is equal to 370. Table 5.2 provides certain values of h and k so that $ARL_0 = 370$. Clearly, $h = 5$ with $k = 0.5$ will produce ARL_0, which will be slightly higher than 370.

Hawkins and Olwell (1998, 48–49) have given very extensive tables for ARL as a function of k and h, and for h as a function of k and ARL, for a one-sided CUSUM for mean shift of standardized normal data. Hawkins and Olwell also provide some computer programs that can be used to generate values of ARL and h that are not encountered in these tables. Having defined the parameters k and h, we are now ready to define the statistics needed to implement one-sided CUSUM control charts using a numerical procedure. Thus, we define here

$$S_i^+ = \max\,[0, z_i - k + S_{i-1}^+], \tag{5.4}$$

$$S_i^- = \min\,[0, z_i + k + S_{i-1}^-], \tag{5.5}$$

where the initial values of S_0^+ and S_0^- are zero. The statistics S_i^+ and S_i^-, respectively, are used to implement one-sided CUSUM control charts when the shifts are upward and downward. For a two-sided CUSUM control chart, the statistics S_i^+ and S_i^- are used simultaneously. We illustrate the implementation of the numerical procedure for the CUSUM control chart by using the data in Example 5.1.

Example 5.2 *Columns 1, 3, and 4 of Table 5.1 have been reproduced in Table 5.3, and two new columns have been appended, one for S_i^+ and another for S_i^-, where S_i^+ and S_i^- are defined in equations (5.4) and (5.5), respectively, and with $k = 0.5$ and $h = 5$.*

Solution: Using column 3 of Table 5.3, we have

$$\begin{aligned} S_1^+ &= \max\,[0, \bar{Z}_1 - k + S_0^+] \\ &= \max\,[0, -1.4950 - 0.50 + 0] = 0.00, \end{aligned}$$

$$\begin{aligned} S_1^- &= \min\,[0, \bar{Z}_1 + k + S_0^-] \\ &= \min\,[0, -1.4950 + 0.50 + 0] = -0.9950, \end{aligned}$$

$$S_2^+ = \max\,[0, \bar{Z}_2 - k + S_1^+]$$
$$= \max\,[0, -1.6875 - 0.50 + 0] = 0.00,$$
$$S_2^- = \min\,[0, \bar{Z}_2 + k + S_1^-]$$
$$= \min\,[0, -1.6875 + 0.50 - 0.9950] = -2.1825.$$

Similarly, we can calculate S_i^+ and S_i^- for i = 3, 4, . . . , 20. All these values are listed in columns 4 and 5 of Table 5.3. Table 5.3 gives us a complete summary of a two-sided CUSUM control chart for the data in Example 5.1. From column 4 we see that the value of S_i^+ at i = 13 is 6.0275, which is greater than the decision interval h = 5; therefore, we conclude that at this point the process is out of control due to an upward mean shift. Also, note that in column 5, no value of S_i^- has gone below the decision interval h = –5, which implies that no downward mean shift has occurred. Moreover, the first nonzero value of S_i^+ occurred at sample number 11, which implies that the process mean shifted between the time when samples 10 and 11 were

Table 5.3 Tabular CUSUM control chart for the data given in Table 5.1.

Sample (i)	$\bar{X}_i$	$\bar{Z}_i = \dfrac{\bar{X}_i - 20}{\sigma/\sqrt{n}}$	$S_i^+ = \max(0, Z_i - k + S_{i-1}^+)$	$S_i^- = \min(0, Z_i + k + S_{i-1}^-)$
1	18.5050	–1.4950	0.0000	–0.9950
2	18.3125	–1.6875	0.0000	–2.1825
3	19.4300	–0.5700	0.0000	–2.2525
4	21.7575	1.7575	1.2575	0.0000
5	19.6850	–0.3150	0.4425	0.0000
6	20.3175	0.3175	0.2600	0.0000
7	20.9400	0.9400	0.7000	0.0000
8	20.4800	0.4800	0.6800	0.0000
9	19.1450	–0.8550	0.0000	–0.3550
10	20.1050	0.1050	0.0000	0.0000
11	22.7600	2.7600	2.2600	0.0000
12	21.8300	1.8300	3.5900	0.0000
13	22.9375	2.9375	6.0275	0.0000
14	21.8800	1.8800	7.4075	0.0000
15	21.8575	1.8575	8.7650	0.0000
16	21.0850	1.0850	9.3500	0.0000
17	22.5800	2.5800	11.4300	0.0000
18	22.8400	2.8400	13.7700	0.0000
19	21.0925	1.0925	14.3625	0.0000
20	21.9225	1.9225	15.7850	0.0000

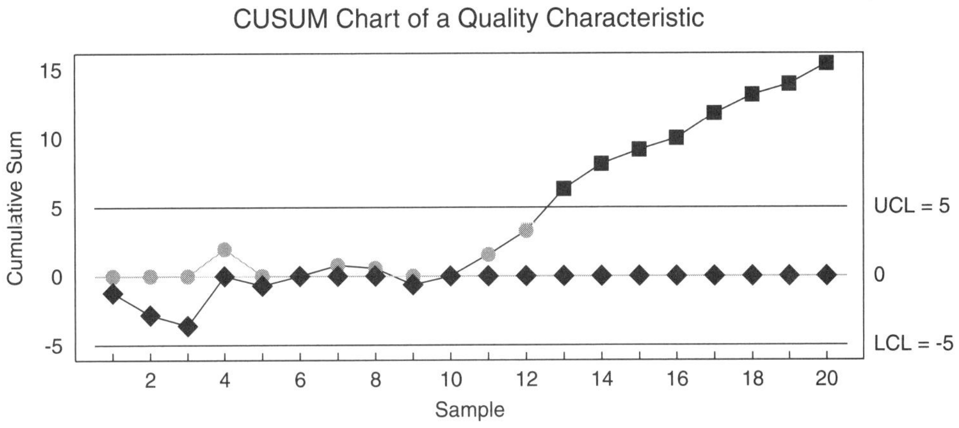

Figure 5.3 MINITAB printout of a two-sided CUSUM control chart for the data in Table 5.1.

taken. These conclusions are also confirmed by the CUSUM control chart shown in Figure 5.3.

Once we conclude that the process is out of control, it is pertinent to estimate the new process mean, or the shifted mean μ_1. Without having found such an estimate, it is difficult to make any appropriate changes or adjustments in the process to bring it back to its target value μ_0. This estimate can be found simply by determining the average of the observations taken during the periods when the shift occurred and when it was concluded that the process was out of control. In this example, because the sample size n is greater than 1, we have

$$\hat{\mu}_1 = \bar{\bar{X}} = \sum \bar{X}_i / m = (22.76 + 21.83 + 22.94)/3 = 22.51,$$

where m is the number of periods between the time when the shift occurred and when it was concluded that the process was out of control.

Example 5.3 *Reconsider the data presented in Example 5.1. Now we will take random samples of size one to see if our conclusions change significantly. These data are given in Table 5.4. The first 10 observations were taken when the process was stable and manufacturing products with mean value 20 and standard deviation 2. The last 10 observations were taken from the same process after its mean experienced an upward shift of one standard deviation, resulting in a new process with mean 22.*

Solution: In this example, we construct both the $\bar{X}$ Shewhart control chart for individual values and the CUSUM control chart. The MINITAB printouts of the $\bar{X}$ control chart and the CUSUM control chart are shown in Figures 5.4 and 5.5. The $\bar{X}$ control chart again shows no abnormalities in the process. In other words, it has not detected the one standard deviation shift in the process mean, whereas the CUSUM control chart, as we can see from Figure 5.5, has detected this shift. We will first discuss the construction of the CUSUM control chart for individual values.

Following the same steps as shown in Example 5.2 and using the data in Table 5.4, the entries in the other columns of Table 5.4 are obtained as follows:

$$S_1^+ = \max\,[0, Z_1 - k + S_0^+]$$
$$= \max\,[0, -0.33 - 0.50 + 0] = 0.00,$$

$$S_1^- = \min\,[0, Z_1 + k + S_0^-]$$
$$= \min\,[0, -0.33 + 0.50 + 0] = 0.00,$$

$$S_2^+ = \max\,[0, Z_2 - k + S_1^+]$$
$$= \max\,[0, -0.33 - 0.50 + 0] = 0.00,$$

$$S_2^- = \min\,[0, Z_2 + k + S_1^-]$$
$$= \min\,[0, 0.33 + 0.50 + 0] = 0.00.$$

Table 5.4 Data from a manufacturing process of auto parts before and after its mean experienced a shift of 1σ (sample size one).

Sample #	X_i	$Z_i = (X_i - \mu)/\sigma$	$S_i^+ = \max(0, Z_i - k + S_{i-1}^+)$	$S_i^- = \min(0, Z_i + k + S_{i-1}^-)$
1	19.35	–0.33	0.00	0.00
2	20.05	0.03	0.00	0.00
3	18.92	–0.54	0.00	–0.04
4	15.70	–2.15	0.00	–1.69
5	17.50	–1.25	0.00	–2.44
6	19.37	–0.32	0.00	–2.26
7	17.03	–1.48	0.00	–3.24
8	19.35	–0.33	0.00	–3.07
9	22.99	1.50	1.00	–1.07
10	18.61	–0.70	0.00	–1.27
11	23.92	1.96	1.46	0.00
12	18.75	–1.13	0.00	–0.63
13	*22.48*	1.24	0.74	0.00
14	*25.85*	2.93	3.17	0.00
15	*19.20*	–0.60	2.07	–0.10
16	*23.18*	1.59	3.16	0.00
17	*24.17*	2.09	4.75	0.00
18	*20.77*	0.39	4.64	0.00
19	*21.18*	1.09	5.23	0.00
20	24.33	2.17	6.90	0.00

We can calculate the other values of S_i^+ and S_i^- for i = 3, 4, . . . , 20 in the same manner. These values are listed in columns 4 and 5 of Table 5.4, which gives us a complete summary of a two-sided CUSUM chart for the data in this example. From column 4 of Table 5.4 we see that the value of S_i^+ at point 19 is 5.23, which is clearly greater than the decision interval of $h = 5$. Therefore, we conclude that at this point the process is out of control due to an upward mean shift. Also, note that in column 5, no value of S_i^- has gone below the decision interval of $h = -5$, which implies that no downward mean shift has occurred. Again, the first nonzero value of S_i^+ (before it crossed the decision interval h) occurred at sample number 13, which implies that the process mean shifted during the period when samples 12 and 13 were taken. These conclusions are also confirmed by the CUSUM control chart shown in Figure 5.5.

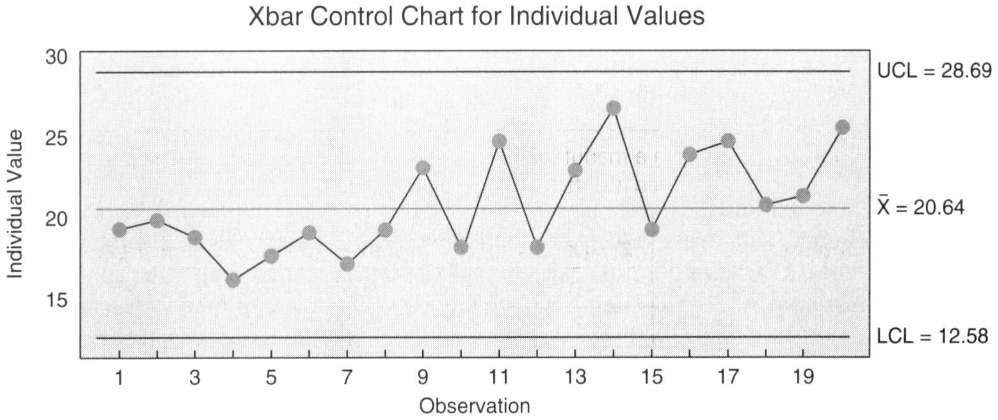

Figure 5.4 MINITAB printout of the $\bar{X}$ control chart for individual values in Table 5.4.

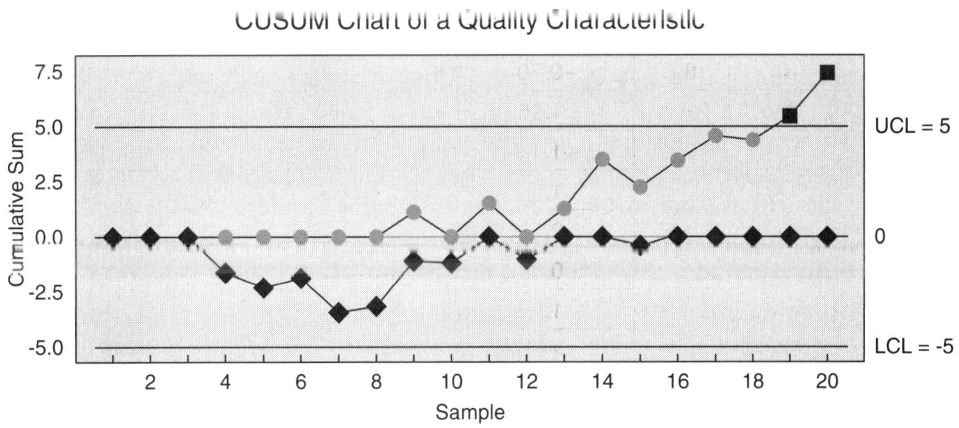

Figure 5.5 MINITAB printout of the CUSUM control chart for individual values in Table 5.4.

Once again, we have concluded that the process is out of control. Therefore, we should now find the estimate of the new process mean μ_1, which is given by $\hat{\mu}_1 = \bar{X} = \sum X_i/m = (22.48 + 25.85 + 19.20 + 23.18 + 24.17 + 20.77 + 21.18)/7 = 22.404$, where m is the number of periods between the time when the shift occurred and when it was concluded that the process is out of control.

Summarizing the results of Examples 5.2 and 5.3, we have the following:

a. In both cases, the regular Shewhart $\bar{X}$-R control chart in Example 5.2 and the $\bar{X}$ control chart for individual values in Example 5.3 did not detect the one standard deviation shift in the process mean.

b. In Example 5.2 the CUSUM control chart indicated that the process was out of control at period $i = 13$, which means the third sample taken after the actual shift occurred. Twelve parts were selected before we knew that the process was out of control.

c. In Example 5.3 the CUSUM control chart indicated that the process was out of control at period $i = 19$, which means the ninth sample taken after the actual shift occurred. Nine parts were selected before we knew that the process was out of control.

Note that in Examples 5.2 and 5.3, if the parts were selected at the same frequency, say, every half hour, then it would be quicker to determine that the process is out of control with samples of size one rather than size four, a result that may be true in general. In fact, CUSUM charts are often constructed using samples of size one. Finally, it is recommended that in order to avoid any confusion of using different values of σ, and for the sake of simplicity, one should use the standardized values (z_i) rather than the actual values (x_i).

5.2.2 The Fast Initial Response Feature for the CUSUM Control Chart

Lucas and Crosier (1982) introduced the fast initial response (FIR) feature, which improves the sensitivity either at process start-up or immediately after any control action has been taken. In standard CUSUM control charts, we use the initial value $S_0 = 0$, but in a CUSUM control chart with the FIR feature the starting value of S_0 is set up at some value greater than zero. Lucas and Crosier point out that control of the process is less certain following a possibly ineffective control action, and therefore extra sensitivity is warranted. The FIR feature in CUSUM control charts provides this extra sensitivity. Furthermore, Lucas and Crosier recommend setting up the starting CUSUM value at $h/2$. For illustration of FIR, we rework Example 5.3.

Example 5.4 *Reconsider the data in Example 5.3, where the observations represent quality characteristics of auto parts manufactured by a given process. These data are reproduced in Table 5.5. Construct the tabular CUSUM control chart for these data using the FIR feature.*

Solution: Table 5.5 gives the complete tabular CUSUM using FIR for the data in Example 5.3, and the graph is shown in Figure 5.6.

Table 5.5 Tabular CUSUM control chart using FIR for data in Table 5.4.

Sample #	X_i	$Z_i = (X_i - \mu)/\sigma$	$S_i^+ = \max(0, Z_i - k + S_{i-1}^+)$	$S_i^- = \min(0, Z_i + k + S_{i-1}^-)$
1	19.35	–0.33	1.67	–2.33
2	20.05	0.03	1.20	–1.80
3	18.92	–0.54	0.16	–1.84
4	15.70	–2.15	0.00	–3.49
5	17.50	–1.25	0.00	–4.24
6	19.37	–0.32	0.00	–4.06
7	17.03	–1.48	0.00	–5.04
8	19.35	–0.33	0.00	–4.87
9	22.99	1.50	1.00	–2.87
10	18.61	–0.70	0.00	–3.07
11	23.92	1.96	1.46	–0.61
12	18.75	–1.13	0.00	–1.24
13	*22.48*	1.24	0.74	0.00
14	*25.85*	2.93	3.17	0.00
15	*19.20*	–0.60	2.07	–0.10
16	*23.18*	1.59	3.16	0.00
17	*24.17*	2.09	4.75	0.00
18	*20.77*	0.39	4.64	0.00
19	*21.18*	1.09	5.23	0.00
20	24.33	2.17	6.90	0.00

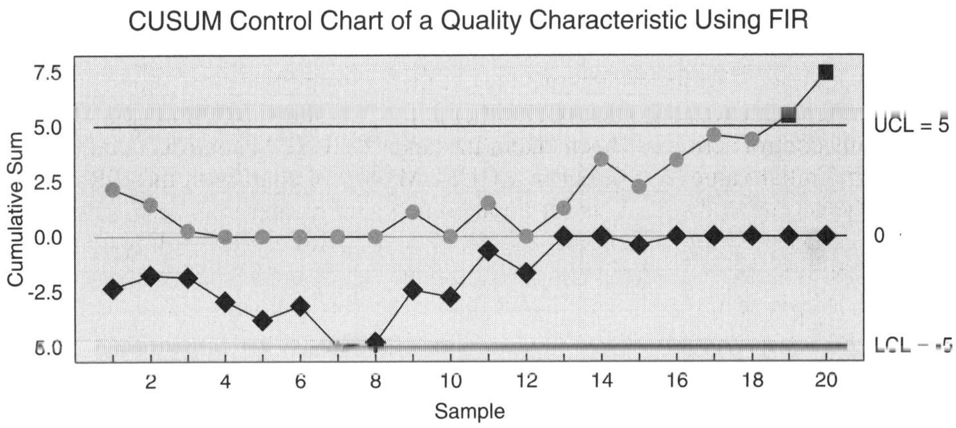

Figure 5.6 MINITAB printout of the two-sided CUSUM control chart for the data in Table 5.5 using FIR.

In Example 5.3, the CUSUM chart parameters were $k = 0.5$ and $h = 5$, and the starting CUSUM value was $S_0^+ = S_0^- = 0$. In this example, we used $S_0^+ = h/2 = 2.5$ $S_0^- = -h/2 = -2.5$. Note that by using FIR, the CUSUM for downward shift in column 5 showed that at period $i = 7$, there was a downward shift. However, before an upward shift occurred, the CUSUM for the upward shift in column 4 had very little effect. The CUSUM values quickly changed to zero, and after the zero value, the starting value of 2.5 had no effect. This happened because these observations came from the process that had not experienced any upward shift. However, if these observations had come from a process that had experienced an upward shift, then perhaps the result would have been altogether different.

To see the effect of FIR when the process is out of control, we construct a CUSUM chart for the previous process after it experienced an upward shift of 1σ. For comparative purposes, we use the observations starting from the 11th observation in Table 5.4, as they were taken after the process experienced an upward shift of 1σ. These observations and the corresponding CUSUM with $S_0^+ = h/2 = 2.5$ $S_0^- = -h/2 = -2.5$ are shown in Table 5.6.

Example 5.5 *Reproduce observations 11 through 20 from Table 5.4 in Table 5.6 and construct the tabular CUSUM control chart for these data using the FIR feature. Compare the effects of the FIR feature in this example with the effects of the FIR feature in Example 5.4.*

Solution: Table 5.6 gives the complete tabular CUSUM control chart for the data in Table 5.4. Note that in this example, these data come from a process after it had experienced an upward shift of 1σ. Clearly, the FIR feature has quite a significant effect on the CUSUM chart. In this case, the 14th sample identifies that the process is out of control, whereas in Example 5.4 we had made this conclusion only after the 19th sample. However, because the shift was only upward, the CUSUM chart for the downward shift had no effect. In summary, we can say that the FIR feature for the CUSUM chart is

Table 5.6 Tabular CUSUM control chart using FIR for the process in Table 5.4, after it had experienced an upward shift of 1σ.

Sample #	X_i	$Z_i = (X_i - \mu)/\sigma$	$S_i^+ = \max(0, Z_i - k + S_{i-1}^+)$	$S_i^- = \min(0, Z_i + k + S_{i-1}^-)$
11	23.92	1.96	3.96	–0.64
12	18.75	–1.13	2.33	–0.67
13	*22.48*	1.24	3.07	0.00
14	*25.85*	2.93	5.50	0.00
15	*19.20*	–0.60	4.40	–0.10
16	*23.18*	1.59	5.49	0.00
17	*24.17*	2.09	7.08	0.00
18	*20.77*	0.39	6.97	0.00
19	*21.18*	1.09	7.56	0.00
20	24.33	2.17	9.23	0.00

very valuable whenever there is some change in the process; otherwise, the FIR feature has no significant effect.

One-Sided CUSUM Control Chart

In our previous discussion we noted that a situation can arise where one may be interested in detecting a shift in one direction only, that is, in either the upward or downward direction instead of both directions simultaneously. In applications, situations do arise where the shift in one direction is more serious than a shift in the other direction, as, for example, in the case of tensile strength of a copper wire. In such cases, to construct the CUSUM control chart, one needs to calculate only S^+ or S^- depending on whether we are interested in detecting an upward or downward shift. However, to construct a one-sided CUSUM, one must note that the values of k and h are not the same as for a two-sided CUSUM control chart with the same value of ARL. In other words, if we keep the same values of k and h for a one-sided CUSUM as for a two-sided CUSUM, then the value of ARL will be much higher. For more discussion on this topic, see Hawkins and Olwell (1998).

5.2.3 Combined Shewhart-CUSUM Control Chart

As Hawkins and Olwell (1998, 71) put it, "CUSUMs are excellent diagnostics for detecting and diagnosing step changes in process parameters. However, these are not the only changes that can occur. Transient special causes are also an important reality, and an important source of quality problems. They cannot be ignored, and relying solely on CUSUM charts for SPC is shortsighted. Just as Shewhart charts are not particularly effective in detecting less-than-massive persistent changes in a process parameter, the CUSUM charts are not particularly effective in detecting massive transient changes in process parameters. In fact, the CUSUMs are meant to detect persistent but small changes in process parameters. Proper SPC requires the use of both types of controls: CUSUMs for persistent but small changes and Shewhart charts for large transient problems."

Lucas (1982) introduced a combined Shewhart-CUSUM quality control scheme. The combined Shewhart-CUSUM control chart gives an out-of-control signal if the most recent sample is either outside the Shewhart control limits or beyond the CUSUM decision interval value. Lucas recommends using the standardized values z_i for the combined Shewhart-CUSUM control chart, which is

$$z_i = \frac{(x_i - \mu_0)}{\sigma},$$

where μ_0 is the target mean value and σ is the process standard deviation. Note that if rational subgroups of size $n > 1$ are used, then z_i, x_i, and σ are replaced by $\bar{z}_i$, $\bar{x}_i$, and $\sigma/\sqrt{n}$, respectively.

In the combined Shewhart-CUSUM control chart, an out-of-control signal at time i is given not only when S_i^+ or S_i^- exceeds the decision interval value h, but also when the z_i or $\bar{z}_i$ falls outside the Shewhart control limits.

It can be seen from Lucas (1982) that ARL_0 for the combined Shewhart-CUSUM chart with $h = 5$, $k = 0.5$, and Shewhart control limits ± 3 is 223.9 without the FIR feature and 206.5 with the FIR feature ($S_0 = 2.5$). Both these values are much smaller than 370, the ARL_0 for an in-control Shewhart control chart. This would cause the process to have more frequent false alarms. For example, if samples are taken every hour, the Shewhart control chart would cause a false alarm every 15.4 days, whereas combined, a Shewhart-CUSUM chart without the FIR feature would cause a false alarm every 9.3 days, and with the FIR feature every 8.5 days. In order to avoid this scenario, Lucas recommends taking Shewhart control limits ± 3.5, which results in ARL_0 being approximately equal to 392.7 without the FIR feature and 359.7 with the FIR feature, again with $S_0 = 2.5$. These values of ARL_0 are certainly more comparable to 370. Thus, the combined Shewhart-CUSUM chart can be implemented just by using the basic CUSUM chart so that an out-of-control signal occurs whenever either the CUSUM value exceeds the decision interval value or the absolute value of z_i or $\bar{z}_i$ becomes greater than 3.5.

5.2.4 CUSUM Control Chart for Controlling Process Variability

No process is immune to changes in variability. Consequently, any unnoticed changes in process variability can adversely affect the conclusion made about the process mean using CUSUM charts. Hence, while using CUSUM charts, controlling process variability is as important as controlling the process mean.

Consider a process with its quality characteristic X_i distributed as normal with mean μ and variance σ^2. Then the standardized random variable

$$Z_i = \frac{X_i - \mu}{\sigma}$$

is distributed as standard normal. Hawkins (1981) showed that the random variable $\sqrt{|Z_i|}$ is approximately distributed as normal with mean 0.822 and standard deviation 0.349; that is, the random variable

$$V_i = \frac{\sqrt{|Z_i|} - 0.822}{0.349}$$

is distributed as standard normal. Furthermore, when the variance of X_i increases, the mean of V_i will increase. However, any change in the mean of V_i can be detected by designing a two-sided CUSUM chart, as follows:

$$V_i^+ = \max\,[0, v_i - k + V_{i-1}^+], \tag{5.6}$$

$$V_i^- = \min\,[0, v_i + k + V_{i-1}^-], \tag{5.7}$$

where $V_0^+ = V_0^- = 0$ and k and h are the reference value and the decision interval. As Hawkins and Olwell (1998) point out, we can use the FIR feature in the same manner as in the basic CUSUM chart, that is, by taking $V_0^+ = V_0^- = h/2$. The interpretation of this CUSUM chart is very much parallel to the CUSUM chart in section 5.2.1. Thus, if either of the CUSUM values V_i^+ or V_i^- exceeds the decision interval, an out-of-control signal for the variance occurs.

5.3 The MA Control Chart

Consider the process of manufacturing auto parts discussed earlier in this chapter. Let $x_1, x_2, x_3, \ldots, x_n$ be the observation on the quality characteristics under investigation. Then the moving average M_i of span m at time i is defined as

$$M_i = \frac{x_1 + x_2 + \ldots + x_i}{i}, \qquad i = 1, 2, \ldots, m-1 \tag{5.8}$$

$$M_i = \frac{x_{i-m+1} + x_{i-m+2} + \ldots + x_i}{m}, \qquad i = m, m+1, \ldots, n \tag{5.9}$$

Example 5.6 *Suppose in the manufacturing process of auto parts we collect five observations on the quality characteristic under investigation. Find the moving averages* M_i, $i = 1, 2, \ldots, 5$ *of span 3.*

Solution: Because $n = 5$ and $m = 3$, we have

$$M_1 = x_1,\ M_2 = \frac{x_1 + x_2}{2},\ M_3 = \frac{x_1 + x_2 + x_3}{3},\ M_4 = \frac{x_2 + x_3 + x_4}{3},\ \text{and } M_5 = \frac{x_3 + x_4 + x_5}{3}$$

The variance of the moving average M_i is given by

$$\text{For } i < m \qquad V(M_i) = \left(\frac{x_1 + x_2 + \ldots + x_i}{i}\right) = \frac{1}{i^2}\sum_{j=1}^{i} V(x_j) = \frac{\sigma^2}{i}, \qquad j > 0 \tag{5.10}$$

$$\text{For } i \geq m \qquad V(M_i) = \left(\frac{x_{i-m+1} + x_{i-m+2} + \ldots + x_i}{m}\right) = \frac{1}{m^2}\sum_{j=i-m+1}^{i} V(x_j) = \frac{\sigma^2}{m}, \tag{5.11}$$

where σ^2 is the process variance. The variance of the moving averages in Example 5.6 is

$$V(M_1) = \sigma^2,\ V(M_2) = \frac{\sigma^2}{2},\ V(M_3) = \frac{\sigma^2}{3},\ V(M_4) = \frac{\sigma^2}{3} \text{ and, } V(M_5) = \frac{\sigma^2}{3}.$$

Now consider a quality characteristic of a process that is normally distributed with target mean value μ_0 and variance σ^2. The probability control limits for M_i with Type I error α for $i < m$ are

$$\text{UCL} = \mu_0 + z_{\alpha/2}\frac{\sigma}{\sqrt{i}}, \tag{5.12}$$

$$\text{LCL} = \mu_0 - z_{\alpha/2}\frac{\sigma}{\sqrt{i}}, \tag{5.13}$$

and for $i \geq m$ the control limits are

$$\text{UCL} = \mu_0 + z_{\alpha/2}\frac{\sigma}{\sqrt{m}}, \tag{5.14}$$

$$\text{LCL} = \mu_0 - z_{\alpha/2}\frac{\sigma}{\sqrt{m}}. \tag{5.15}$$

In order to have 3σ control limits, replace $z_{\alpha/2}$ in equations (5.12)–(5.15) with 3. The process is considered out of control as soon as M_i falls outside the control limit. Because the plotted points (i, M_i) are not independent, no reasonable interpretation can be made about the patterns in the graph. For detecting smaller shifts, m should be large. However, note that a large value of m would mean a longer time in detecting bigger shifts. To illustrate, we consider the data in Table 5.4.

Note: In the preceding discussion we considered the MA chart for individual values. Sometimes the process allows us to take samples of size $n > 1$. In such situations, the individual values in Table 5.7 are replaced by the sample means. Furthermore, the probability control limits in equations (5.12)–(5.15) are defined as follows:

for $i < m$

$$\text{UCL} = \mu_0 + z_{\alpha/2}\frac{\sigma}{\sqrt{in}}, \tag{5.16}$$

$$\text{LCL} = \mu_0 - z_{\alpha/2}\frac{\sigma}{\sqrt{in}}, \tag{5.17}$$

and for $i \geq m$

$$\text{UCL} = \mu_0 + z_{\alpha/2}\frac{\sigma}{\sqrt{mn}} \tag{5.18}$$

$$\text{LCL} = \mu_0 - z_{\alpha/2}\frac{\sigma}{\sqrt{mn}} \tag{5.19}$$

Example 5.7 *Consider the data in Table 5.4, the manufacturing process of auto parts from Example 5.1. Design an MA control chart for these data with span $m = 4$ and interpret the results.*

Table 5.7 MA chart (M_i's) for data in Table 5.4 with $\mu = 20$, $\sigma = 2$.

Sample #	**1**	**2**	**3**	**4**	**5**	**6**	**7**	**8**	**9**	**10**
X_i	19.35	20.05	18.92	15.70	17.50	19.37	17.03	19.35	22.99	18.61
M_i	19.35	19.70	19.44	18.51	18.04	17.87	17.40	18.31	19.69	19.50
Sample #	**11**	**12**	**13**	**14**	**15**	**16**	**17**	**18**	**19**	**20**
X_i	23.92	18.75	22.48	25.85	19.20	23.18	24.17	20.77	21.18	24.33
M_i	21.22	21.07	20.94	22.75	21.57	22.68	23.10	21.83	22.33	22.61

Solution: The data from Table 5.4 are reproduced in Table 5.7. The M_i values are determined as shown in the following equations, and these values are then entered in Table 5.7.

$M_1 = X_1 = 19.35,$

$M_2 = (X_1 + X_2)/2 = (19.35 + 20.05)/2 = 19.70,$

$M_3 = (X_1 + X_2 + X_3)/3 = (19.35 + 20.05 + 18.92)/3 = 19.44,$

$M_4 = (X_1 + X_2 + X_3 + X_4)/4 = (19.35 + 20.05 + 18.92 + 15.70)/4 = 18.51,$

$M_5 = (X_2 + X_3 + X_4 + X_5)/4 = (20.05 + 18.92 + 15.70 + 17.50)/4 = 18.04,$

.

.

.

$M_{20} = (X_{17} + X_{18} + X_{19} + X_{20})/4 = (24.17 + 20.77 + 21.18 + 24.33)/4 = 22.61.$

Now the points (i, M_i) from Table 5.7 are plotted in the MA control chart. The MA control chart for the data in Table 5.4 is as shown in Figure 5.7. The 17th point falls outside the control limits. The process is out of control at time $i = 17$. Note that the control limits for $i < m$ are wider and varying, but from $i = m$ onward the control limits become narrower and steady. The 3σ control limits in Figure 5.7 are determined using equations (5.12) and (5.13), as shown here.

For time period $i = 1$, these limits are

$$\text{UCL} = 20 + 3\frac{2}{\sqrt{1}} = 26,$$

$$\text{LCL} = 20 - 3\frac{2}{\sqrt{1}} = 14.$$

For time period $i = 2$, these limits are

$$\text{UCL} = 20 + 3\frac{2}{\sqrt{2}} = 24.24,$$

$$\text{LCL} = 20 - 3\frac{2}{\sqrt{2}} = 15.76.$$

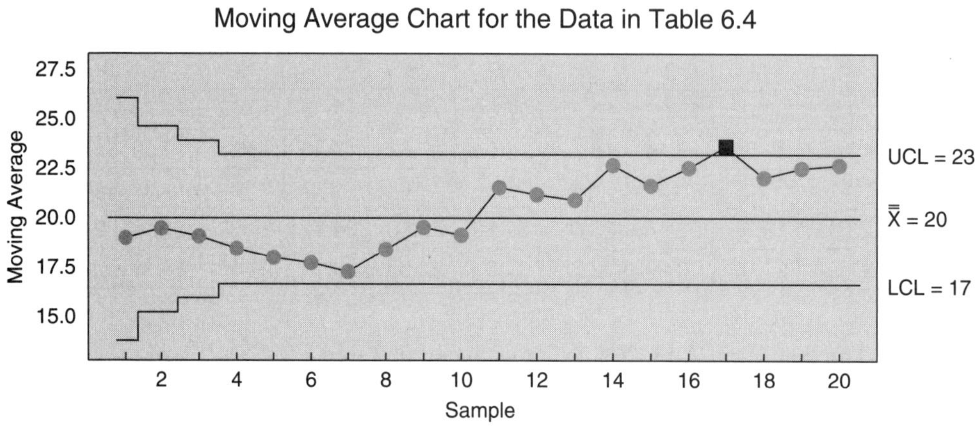

Figure 5.7 MINITAB printout of the MA control chart for the data in Table 5.4.

Similarly, for time period $i = 20$, these limits are

$$\text{UCL} = 20 + 3\frac{2}{\sqrt{20}} = 21.34,$$

$$\text{LCL} = 20 - 3\frac{2}{\sqrt{20}} = 18.66.$$

5.4 The EWMA Control Chart

The EWMA control chart is very useful for processes in which only one observation per period is available. Like the CUSUM control chart, the EWMA chart has the capability of detecting small shifts in the process mean. The EWMA control chart was introduced by S. W. Roberts (1959), who called it a geometric moving average chart. In recent years, however, the chart has come to be known as an exponentially weighted moving average chart, and in the rest of this chapter and in subsequent chapters, we shall use this terminology. The EWMA chart uses information on all the observations, not only the last observation.

The basic concept is to plot a statistic, which is defined as

$$z_i = \lambda x_i + (1-\lambda) z_{i-1}, \tag{5.20}$$

where $0 < \lambda \leq 1$ is a constant, the initial value z_0 is set at the process target mean value μ_0 (if μ_0 is not given, then we set z_0 at $\bar{x}$), and λ is the weight. The statistics z_i, z_{i-1} in equation (5.20) are the exponentially weighted moving averages at time i, $i - 1$, respectively, and x_i is the value of the observation at time i. Furthermore, note that z_i is the weighted average of all the previous observations. This can easily be shown by using iterative method, as follows:

$$\begin{aligned} z_i &= \lambda x_i + (1-\lambda) z_{i-1} \\ &= \lambda x_i + (1-\lambda)[\lambda x_{i-1} + (1-\lambda) z_{i-2}] \\ &= \lambda x_i + \lambda(1-\lambda) x_{i-1} + (1-\lambda)^2 z_{i-2} \\ &\;\cdot \\ &\;\cdot \\ &\;\cdot \\ &= \lambda \sum_{j=0}^{i-1} (1-\lambda)^j x_{i-j} + (1-\lambda)^i z_0 . \end{aligned} \tag{5.21}$$

At any time i, the most recent observation x_i is assigned the weight λ, while at any earlier time $(i-j), j = 1, 2, \ldots, i-1$, the corresponding observation x_{i-j} is assigned the weight $\lambda(1-\lambda)^j$, which decreases geometrically as j increases. For example, if $\lambda = 0.3$, then the current observation is assigned the weight of 0.3, and the preceding observations are assigned the weights of 0.21, 0.147, 0.1029, 0.072, 0.0504, and so on. We can see that the older observations carry a lesser weight. This makes a lot of sense, particularly when the process mean is changing slowly but continuously. Moreover, it is also interesting to note that because EWMA uses the weighted *average* of all past and present observations, it is not very sensitive to the normality assumption.

If we assume the observations x_i are independent with process mean μ and variance σ^2, then from equation (5.21) the mean of the statistic z_i is given by

$$\begin{aligned} E(z_i) &= \lambda \sum_{j=0}^{i-1} (1-\lambda)^j \mu + (1-\lambda)^i E(z_0) \\ &= \lambda[1 + (1-\lambda) + (1-\lambda)^2 + \ldots + (1-\lambda)^{i-1}]\mu + (1-\lambda)^i E(z_0). \end{aligned}$$

The quantity inside the brackets is a geometric series with the ratio equal to $(1-\lambda)$. Recall that the sum of a finite geometric series is $[1 + r + r^2 + \ldots + r^{n-1} = (1-r^n)/(1-r)]$. The quantity in the bracket equals $\dfrac{1-(1-\lambda)^i}{\lambda}$.

Therefore, we have

$$E(z_i) = \mu + (1-\lambda)^i (\mu_0 - \mu). \tag{5.22}$$

Note that if z_0 is set at $\bar{x}$, then the equation (5.22) reduces to

$$E(z_i) = \mu \tag{5.23}$$

because $E(\bar{x}) = \mu$. It is customary to set the target value μ_0 at μ. In any case, in all applications we set the expected value of z_i at μ as defined in equation (5.23). If μ is not known or the target value is not given, then the EWMA control chart uses the value of $\bar{x}$. The variance of the statistic z_i is given by

$$V(z_i)=(\lambda^2+\lambda^2(1-\lambda)^2+\lambda^2(1-\lambda)^4+...+\lambda^2(1-\lambda)^{2i})\sigma^2$$
$$=\lambda^2[1+(1-\lambda)^2+(1-\lambda)^4+...+(1-\lambda)^{2i}]\sigma^2.$$

Again, the quantity inside the brackets is a geometric series with the ratio equal to $(1-\lambda)^2$. We have

$$\begin{aligned} V(z_i) &= \lambda^2\frac{[1-(1-\lambda)^{2i}]}{[1-(1-\lambda)^2]}\sigma^2 \\ &= \lambda^2\frac{[1-(1-\lambda)^{2i}]}{[2\lambda-\lambda^2]}\sigma^2 \\ &= \left(\frac{\lambda}{2-\lambda}\right)[1-(1-\lambda)^{2i}]\sigma^2. \end{aligned} \tag{5.24}$$

From equations (5.23) and (5.24) it follows that the CL and the control limits for the EWMA control charts are given by

$$\text{UCL}=\mu_0+3\sigma\sqrt{\left(\frac{\lambda}{2-\lambda}\right)[1-(1-\lambda)^{2i}]}, \tag{5.25}$$

$$\text{CL}=\mu_{0,} \tag{5.26}$$

$$\text{LCL}=\mu_0-3\sigma\sqrt{\left(\frac{\lambda}{2-\lambda}\right)[1-(1-\lambda)^{2i}]}. \tag{5.27}$$

Note that the control limits in equations (5.25) and (5.27) are variable. However, when i becomes very large, the quantity $[1-(1-\lambda)^{2i}]$ approaches unity, and consequently, the EWMA control limits become constant, which are given by

$$\text{UCL}=\mu_0+3\sigma\sqrt{\left(\frac{\lambda}{2-\lambda}\right)}, \tag{5.28}$$

$$\text{CL}=\mu_{0,} \tag{5.29}$$

$$\text{LCL}=\mu_0-3\sigma\sqrt{\left(\frac{\lambda}{2-\lambda}\right)}. \tag{5.30}$$

In both cases, the value of λ has to be determined, which we discuss in the following text. The general form of the EWMA control chart is given by

$$\text{UCL}=\mu_0+L\sigma\sqrt{\left(\frac{\lambda}{2-\lambda}\right)[1-(1-\lambda)^{2i}]}, \tag{5.31}$$

$$\mathrm{CL} = \mu_{0,} \tag{5.32}$$

$$\mathrm{LCL} = \mu_0 - L\sigma\sqrt{\left(\frac{\lambda}{2-\lambda}\right)[1-(1-\lambda)^{2i}]}, \tag{5.33}$$

and if i is very large, these equations reduce to

$$\mathrm{UCL} = \mu_0 + L\sigma\sqrt{\left(\frac{\lambda}{2-\lambda}\right)}, \tag{5.34}$$

$$\mathrm{CL} = \mu_{0,} \tag{5.35}$$

$$\mathrm{LCL} = \mu_0 - L\sigma\sqrt{\left(\frac{\lambda}{2-\lambda}\right)}. \tag{5.36}$$

Several authors, including Crowder (1987, 1989) and Lucas and Saccucci (1990), have studied the problem of determining the ARL for different values of the parameters λ and L. Quesenberry (1997) has discussed in detail some of their results. Lucas and Saccucci (1990) have provided tables of ARL as a function of λ, L, and δ, where δ is a shift in the process mean, measured in units of the process standard deviation. Some of their results are shown in Table 5.8.

Example 5.8 *Consider the data in Table 5.4 on the manufacturing process of auto parts in Example 5.1. Design an EWMA control chart for these data with* $\lambda = 0.20$, L = 2.962, $\mu_0 = 20$, *and* $\sigma = 2$ *and interpret the results.*

Solution: The data from Table 5.4 are reproduced in Table 5.9. The z_i values are determined as shown in the following equations, which are then entered in Table 5.9. Thus, using equation (5.20), we have

Table 5.8 A selection of EWMA charts with $ARL_0 \cong 500$.

δ	$\lambda = 0.05$ $L = 2.615$	$\lambda = 0.10$ $L = 2.814$	$\lambda = 0.20$ $L = 2.962$	$\lambda = 0.25$ $L = 2.998$	$\lambda = 0.40$ $L = 3.054$
0.25	84.1	106	150	170	224
0.50	28.8	31.3	41.8	48.8	71.2
0.75	16.4	15.9	18.2	20.1	28.4
1.00	11.4	10.3	10.5	11.1	14.3
1.50	7.1	6.1	5.5	5.5	5.9
2.00	5.2	4.4	3.7	3.6	3.5
2.50	4.2	3.4	2.9	2.7	2.5
3.00	3.5	2.9	2.4	2.3	2.0
4.00	2.7	2.2	1.9	1.7	1.4

Table 5.9 EWMA control chart (z_i's) for data in Table 5.4 with $\lambda = 0.20$, $L = 2.962$.

Sample #	**1**	**2**	**3**	**4**	**5**	**6**	**7**	**8**	**9**	**10**
x_i	19.35	20.05	18.92	15.70	17.50	19.37	17.03	19.35	22.99	18.61
z_i	19.87	19.91	19.71	18.91	18.63	18.78	18.43	18.61	19.49	19.31
Sample #	**11**	**12**	**13**	**14**	**15**	**16**	**17**	**18**	**19**	**20**
x_i	23.92	18.75	22.48	25.85	19.20	23.18	24.17	20.77	21.18	24.33
z_i	20.23	19.93	20.44	21.52	21.06	21.48	22.02	21.77	21.65	22.19

$$\begin{aligned} z_1 &= \lambda x_1 + (1-\lambda) z_0 \\ &= 0.20 \times 19.35 + (1-0.20) \times 20 \\ &= 19.87, \end{aligned}$$

$$\begin{aligned} z_2 &= \lambda x_2 + (1-\lambda) z_1 \\ &= 0.20 \times 20.05 + (1-0.20) \times 19.87 \\ &= 19.91, \end{aligned}$$

$$\begin{aligned} z_3 &= \lambda x_3 + (1-\lambda) z_2 \\ &= 0.20 \times 18.92 + (1-0.20) \times 19.91 \\ &= 19.71. \end{aligned}$$

.

.

.

$$\begin{aligned} z_{20} &= \lambda x_{20} + (1-\lambda) z_{19} \\ &= 0.20 \times 24.33 + (1-0.20) \times 21.65 \\ &= 22.19. \end{aligned}$$

The control limits in Figure 5.6 with $\lambda = 0.20$, $L = 2.962$, $\mu_0 = 20$, and $\sigma = 2$ are determined using equations (5.31)–(5.36).

For time period $i = 1$, these limits are

$$\begin{aligned} \text{UCL} &= 20 + 2.962 \times 2\sqrt{\left(\frac{0.2}{2-0.2}\right)[1-(1-0.2)^2]} \\ &= 21.1848, \end{aligned}$$

$$\begin{aligned} \text{LCL} &= 20 - 2.962 \times 2\sqrt{\left(\frac{0.2}{2-0.2}\right)[1-(1-0.2)^2]} \\ &= 18.8152. \end{aligned}$$

For time period $i = 2$, these limits are

$$UCL = 20 + 2.962 \times 2\sqrt{\left(\frac{0.2}{2-0.2}\right)[1-(1-0.2)^4]}$$
$$= 21.5173,$$
$$LCL = 20 - 2.962 \times 2\sqrt{\left(\frac{0.2}{2-0.2}\right)[1-(1-0.2)^4]}$$
$$= 18.4827.$$

.
.
.

Similarly, for period $i = 20$ (because i is fairly large) these limits are

$$UCL = 20 + 2.962 \times 2\sqrt{\left(\frac{0.2}{2-0.2}\right)}$$
$$= 21.9746,$$
$$LCL = 20 - 2.962 \times 2\sqrt{\left(\frac{0.2}{2-0.2}\right)}$$
$$= 18.0254.$$

Now the points (i, z_i) from Table 5.9 are plotted in the EWMA control chart. The EWMA control chart for the data in Table 5.4 is as shown in Figure 5.8. The 17th point falls outside the control limits. This means the process is out of control at time $i = 17$.

Note that in this example, both the MA chart and the EWMA chart showed that the process was out of control at time $i = 17$, whereas the CUSUM control chart indicated that the process was out of control at period $i = 19$.

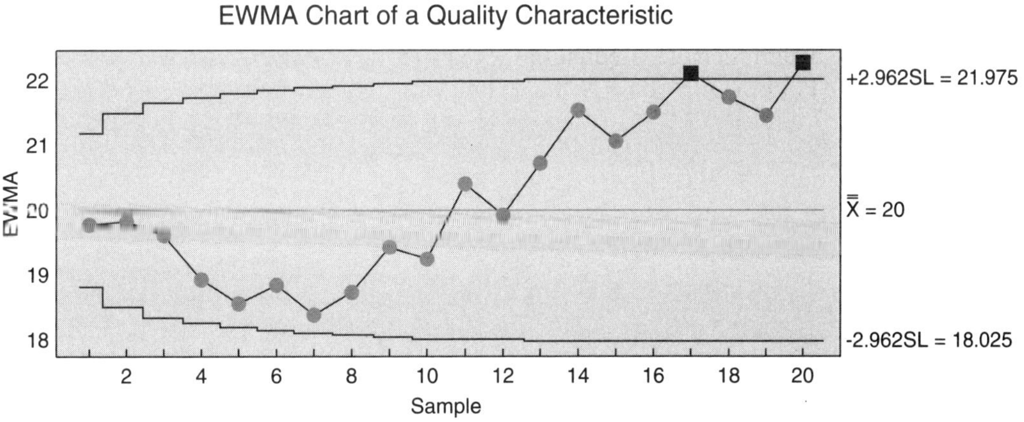

Figure 5.8 MINITAB printout of the EWMA control chart for the data in Table 5.4.

6

Process Capability Indices

In Chapter 3 we defined a process as a series of actions or operations performed in producing manufactured or nonmanufactured products. A process may also be defined as a combination of workforce, equipment, raw materials, methods, and environment that works together to produce output. Figure 6.1, which was presented earlier as Figure 3.1, shows where each component of a process fits.

The quality of the final product depends on how the process is designed and executed. However, no matter how perfectly a process is designed or how well it is executed, no two items produced by the process are identical. The difference between two items is called the *variation*. Such variation occurs because of two causes:

1. Common causes or random causes
2. Special causes or assignable causes

Shewhart was the first to attempt to understand and remove variation in a very systematic way, in 1924 when he presented the graph of a control chart. In Chapters 3, 4, and 5 we studied various types of control charts, including Shewhart control charts, and noted that they help bring the process into control. Recall that a process is brought into control by eliminating special or assignable causes so that the process contains only common or random causes, and consequently, the process is stable and thus predictable. To study process capability, it is essential that the process is stable; otherwise, studying process capability is simply a futile exercise.

6.1 Development of Process Capability Indices

Once the process is under statistical control and thus predictable, the next concern of a manufacturer is to ensure that he or she can deliver the product the consumer wants. In other words, the manufacturer wants to determine whether the process is capable of delivering the desired product. One way to

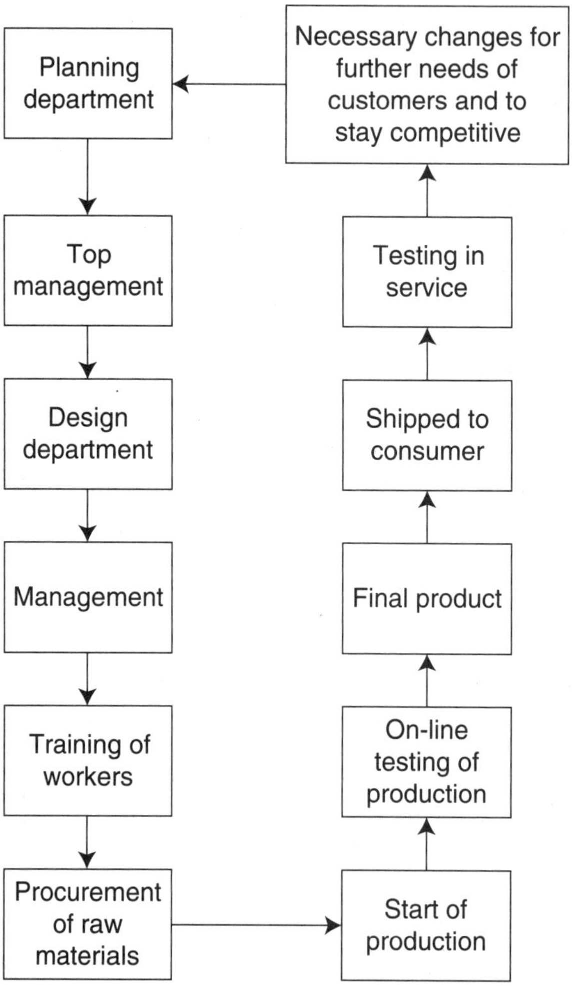

Figure 6.1 Flowchart of a process.

address such a concern is to quantify the capability. A *process capability index* (PCI) is a unitless measure that quantifies the process capability, specifically the relationship between the process output and the designed tolerances. This measure has become an important tool in process capability analysis. Moreover, because the PCI is a unitless measure of capability, it has become an easy tool for communication between the manufacturer and the supplier. More and more manufacturers and suppliers are using PCI as an important part of their contract to ensure quality.

A *process capability analysis* is simply a comparison of the distribution of a process output with the product tolerances. As noted by Kotz and Lovelace (1998), results of process capability analysis have proven very valuable in many ways. Deleryd (1996) and Kotz and Lovelace (1998, 3) developed a list of the 13 most common ways of using the results of process capability analysis:

1. As a basis in the improvement process.
2. As an alarm clock.
3. As specifications for investments. By giving specifications for levels of PCIs expected to be reached by new machines, the purchasing process is facilitated.
4. As a certificate for customers. The supplier is able to attach with the delivery the results from the process capability studies conducted when the actual products were produced.
5. As a basis for new constructions. By knowing the capability of the production processes, the designer knows how to set reasonable specifications in order to make the product manufacturable.
6. For control of maintenance efforts. By continuously conducting process capability studies, it is possible to see if some machines are gradually deteriorating.
7. As specifications for introducing new products.
8. For assessing reasonableness of customer demands.
9. For motivation of coworkers.
10. For deciding priorities in the improvement process.
11. As a base for inspection activities.
12. As a receipt for improvement.
13. For formulating quality improvement programs.

To implement a process capability analysis, one needs to consider the following:

1. The target value specification, which is usually defined by the customer.
2. The specification limits, which should be defined by the customer or the customer's technical staff and agreed upon by the manufacturer. Furthermore, the specification limits should be such that they allow manufacturing variability without jeopardizing proper function of the product.
3. An analysis of the process that would allow the manufacturer to determine whether the product can meet the customer's specifications.

Once production starts, the manufacturer conducts capability studies to compare the measures of the quality characteristic of the manufactured product with the specification limits. This is where PCIs are used.

The first-generation PCIs were established by Japanese manufacturers in the 1970s. They used the following indices:

C_p—Inherent capability of a process

k—Position of the process in relation to the target value

C_{pk}—Position of the 6σ process in relation to the target value

C_{pl}—Position of the 6σ process in relation to the LSL

C_{pu}—Position of the 6σ process in relation to the USL

In this chapter we will study these and various other capability indices frequently used in process capability analysis. This book does not cover every aspect of these indices. However, an excellent reference for a more detailed study is Kotz and Lovelace (1998).

Throughout the study of these indices, we are going to assume that the process producing the desired quality characteristic is under control and thus predictable.

6.2 PCI C_p

Let X be the process quality characteristic we want to monitor. Let USL and LSL be the upper specification limit and lower specification limit, respectively. The performance of the process with respect to these limits is defined as follows:

$$\text{Percentage of nonconforming produced by the process at the upper end} = P(X > \text{USL}),$$

$$\text{Percentage of nonconforming produced by the process at the lower end} = P(X < \text{LSL}).$$

The total percentage of nonconforming products produced by the process is defined as

$$P(X < \text{LSL or } X > \text{USL}) = 1 - P(\text{LSL} < X < \text{USL}).$$

In the preceding paragraph we saw the performance of the process with respect to the specification limits. Now we will look at the performance of the process with respect to the natural tolerance limits (NTLs), that is, the UNTL and the LNTL.

The performance of the process with respect to the NTLs is the percentage of the product produced by the process with its quality characteristic falling within the interval $(\mu - 3\sigma, \mu + 3\sigma)$, where μ and σ, respectively, are the mean and the standard deviation of the process quality characteristic. Assuming that the process quality characteristic is normally distributed and that the process is under control, the percentage of the product produced by the process with its quality characteristic falling within the interval $(\mu - 3\sigma, \mu + 3\sigma)$ is approximately 99.74 percent. As noted earlier, a PCI is the comparison between what a process is expected to produce and what it is actually producing. We now define the PCI C_p, one of the first five indices used in Japan and proposed by Juran et al. (1974) as follows:

$$C_p = \frac{\text{USL} - \text{LSL}}{\text{UNTL} - \text{LNTL}}$$
$$= \frac{\text{USL} - \text{LSL}}{(\mu + 3\sigma) - (\mu - 3\sigma)} \tag{6.1}$$
$$= \frac{\text{USL} - \text{LSL}}{6\sigma}.$$

Note that the numerator in equation (6.1) is the desired range of the process quality characteristic, whereas the denominator is the actual range of the process quality characteristic. From this definition, we see that a process can produce a product of desired quality and that the process is capable only if the range in the numerator is at least as large as that in the denominator. In other words, the process is capable only if $C_p \geq 1$ and larger values of C_p are indicative of a process. For a 6σ process (3.4 defects per million opportunities [DPMO]), $C_p = 2$. A predictable process—which is normally distributed with $C_p = 1$ and its mean located at the center of the specification limits, usually known as the target value of the process characteristic—is expected to produce 0.27 percent nonconforming units. Montgomery (2005b) gives a comprehensive list of values of the PCI C_p and associated process nonconforming for one-sided specifications and two-sided specifications.

Because C_p is very easy to calculate, it is widely used in the industry. However, the fact that it does not take into consideration the position of the process mean is a major drawback. A process could be incapable even if the value of C_p is large (>1). For example, a process could produce 100 percent defectives if the process mean falls outside the specification limits and is far from the target value. Furthermore, the value of C_p will become even larger if the value of the process standard deviation σ decreases, while the process mean moves away from the target value.

Note that the numerator in equation (6.1) is always known, but the denominator is usually unknown. This is because in almost all practical applications, the process standard deviation σ is unknown. To calculate C_p we must replace σ in equation (6.1) by its estimator $\hat{\sigma}$. From Chapter 4 we know that σ can be estimated either by the sample standard deviation S or by $\bar{R}/d_2$. However, remember that the estimate $\bar{R}/d_2$ is normally used only when the process is under control and the sample size is fewer than 10. An estimated value of C_p is given by

$$\hat{C}_p = \frac{\text{USL} - \text{LSL}}{6\hat{\sigma}}. \tag{6.2}$$

We illustrate the computation of $\hat{C}_p$ with the following example.

Example 6.1 *The following table gives the summary statistics on* $\bar{\text{X}}$ *and* R *for 25 samples of size* n = 5 *collected from a process producing tie rods for certain types of cars. The measurement data are the lengths of the tie rods, and the measurement scale is in millimeters.*

Sample Number	$\bar{X}$	R	Sample Number	$\bar{X}$	R
1	274	6	14	268	8
2	265	8	15	271	6
3	269	6	16	275	5
4	273	5	17	274	7
5	270	8	18	272	4
6	275	7	19	270	6
7	271	5	20	274	7
8	275	4	21	273	5
9	272	6	22	270	4
10	273	8	23	274	6
11	269	6	24	273	5
12	273	5	25	273	6
13	274	7			

The target value and the specification limits for the lengths of the rods are 272 and 272 ± 8, respectively. Calculate the value of $\hat{C}_p$ *assuming that the tie rod lengths are normally distributed, and find the percentage of nonconforming tie rods produced by the process.*

Solution: To find the value of $\hat{C}_p$ and the percentage of nonconforming tie rods produced by the process, we first need to estimate the process mean μ and the process standard deviation σ. These estimates may be found by using $\bar{\bar{X}}$ and $\bar{R}/d_2$, respectively. We get

$$\hat{\mu} = \bar{\bar{X}} = \frac{1}{m}\sum_{i=1}^{m} \bar{X}_i$$

$$= \frac{1}{25}(274 + 265 + 269 + \ldots + 273)$$

$$= 272,$$

$$\hat{\sigma} = \bar{R}/d_2 = \frac{1}{m}\sum_{i=1}^{m} R_i / d_2$$

$$= \frac{1}{25}(6 + 8 + \ldots + 5 + 6)/2.326$$

$$= 6/2.326 = 2.58,$$

where the value of d_2 for different samples of size five is found from Table A.2. Substituting the values of USL, LSL, and $\hat{\sigma}$ in equation (6.2), we get

$$\hat{C}_p = \frac{280 - 284}{6(2.58)} = 1.03,$$

which indicates that the process is capable. To find the percentage of nonconforming tie rods produced by the process, we proceed as follows:

$$\begin{aligned}\text{Percentage of nonconforming} &= (1 - P(264 \le X \le 280))\ 100\% \\ &= (1 - P(-3.1 \le Z \le 3.1))\ 100\% \\ &= (1 - 0.9980)\ 100\% = 0.2\%.\end{aligned}$$

In this example, the percentage of nonconforming tie rods is as expected when we consider the value of $\hat{C}_p$. But as noted earlier, this may not always be the case, because C_p does not take into consideration where the process mean is located. To better explain this, we use the following example.

Example 6.2 *Suppose that the process in Example 6.1 had a special cause variation, and as a result, the process had an upward shift. Furthermore, suppose that after the process experienced this shift, we took another set of 25 random samples of size* n = 5 *and these samples produced* $\bar{\bar{X}} = 276$ *and* $\bar{R} = 6$. *In this example the value of* $\bar{\bar{X}}$ *changed from 272 to 276 while* $\bar{R}$ *remained the same.*

Solution: From the given values of $\bar{\bar{X}}$ and $\bar{R}$, we obtain

$$\hat{\mu} = 276 \text{ and } \hat{\sigma} = 2.58.$$

Because the process standard deviation did not change, the value of $\hat{C}_p$ remained the same, that is, $\hat{C}_p = 1.03$. However, the percentage of nonconforming tie rods produced by the process will be

$$\begin{aligned}\text{Percentage of nonconforming} &= (1 - P(264 \le X \le 280))100\% \\ &= (1 - P(\frac{264-276}{2.58} \le \frac{X-276}{2.58} \le \frac{280-276}{2.58}))100\% \\ &= (1 - P(-4.65 \le Z \le 1.55))100\% \\ &\cong 6.06\%.\end{aligned}$$

Even though the value of C_p did not change after the process mean experienced a shift, the process is producing nonconforming units, which are 30 times more nonconforming than in the previous example. In other words, C_p did not measure the effect that the upward or downward shift had on the ability of the process to produce products within the specification limits. This major drawback of C_p makes it less reliable than many other PCIs. We will study several of these indices here, but first we will look at an alternative but equivalent interpretation of C_p, which is given by finding the percentage of specification band used, that is,

$$\text{Percentage of specification band used} = \frac{1}{C_p} \times 100\,.$$

A smaller percentage of specification band used indicates a better process. Again, for reasons discussed earlier, this interpretation can sometimes be misleading.

The other two PCIs first used by Japanese manufacturers are C_{pl} and C_{pu}. These indices are related to the LSL and the USL, respectively, and are defined as follows:

$$C_{pl} = \frac{\mu - \text{LSL}}{3\sigma}, \tag{6.3}$$

$$C_{pu} = \frac{\text{USL} - \mu}{3\sigma}. \tag{6.4}$$

The estimates of C_{pl} and C_{pu} are given by

$$\hat{C}_{pl} = \frac{\bar{\bar{X}} - \text{LSL}}{3\hat{\sigma}}, \tag{6.5}$$

$$\hat{C}_{pu} = \frac{\text{USL} - \bar{\bar{X}}}{3\hat{\sigma}}. \tag{6.6}$$

To illustrate the computation of $\hat{C}_{pl}$ and $\hat{C}_{pu}$, we use the information in Examples 6.1 and 6.2.

Example 6.3 *Using the information given in Example 6.1, compute* $\hat{C}_{pl}$ *and* $\hat{C}_{pu}$.

Solution:

$$\hat{C}_{pl} = \frac{\bar{\bar{X}} - \text{LSL}}{3\hat{\sigma}} = \frac{272 - 264}{3(2.58)} = 1.03$$

$$\hat{C}_{pu} = \frac{\text{USL} - \bar{\bar{X}}}{3\hat{\sigma}} = \frac{280 - 272}{3(2.58)} = 1.03$$

Note that both $\hat{C}_{pl}$ and $\hat{C}_{pu}$ are equal to $\hat{C}_p$, which is always the case when the process mean is centered between the specification limits. Moreover, when both $\hat{C}_{pl}$ and $\hat{C}_{pu}$ are equal, the percentage of nonconforming units below the LSL and the percentage of nonconforming units above the USL are the same.

Example 6.4 *Using the information in Example 6.2, compute* $\hat{C}_{pl}$ *and* $\hat{C}_{pu}$.

Solution:

$$\hat{C}_{pl} = \frac{\bar{\bar{X}} - LSL}{3\hat{\sigma}} = \frac{276 - 264}{3(2.58)} = 1.55$$

$$\hat{C}_{pu} = \frac{USL - \bar{\bar{X}}}{3\hat{\sigma}} = \frac{280 - 276}{3(2.58)} = 0.52$$

In this case, the value of $\hat{C}_{pl}$ is much larger than 1, whereas the value of $\hat{C}_{pu}$ is much smaller than 1, which indicates that most of the nonconforming units produced by the process are falling above the USL. Finally, note that both C_{pl} and C_{pu} are sensitive to where the process mean is located.

6.3 PCI C_{pk}

To overcome the centering problem in C_p discussed in the preceding section, the PCI C_{pk} was introduced. The PCI C_{pk}, which is again one of the first five used in Japan, is defined as

$$C_{pk} = \min(C_{pl}, C_{pu}). \tag{6.7}$$

The index C_{pk} is related to the index C_p as

$$C_{pk} = (1-k)C_p, \tag{6.8}$$

where

$$k = \frac{|(\text{USL} + \text{LSL})/2 - \mu|}{(\text{USL} - \text{LSL})/2}. \tag{6.9}$$

Furthermore, it can be seen that $0 \leq k \leq 1$, so C_{pk} is always less than or equal to C_p. Also note that when the process mean μ coincides with the midpoint between the specification limits, $k = 0$, and therefore C_{pk} equals C_p.

C_{pk} takes care of the centering problem only if the process standard deviation remains the same. If the process standard deviation changes, then the value of C_{pk} may not change even when the process mean moves away from the center. It can be seen that this will always be the scenario when the distance of the process mean from the nearest specification limit in terms of σ remains the same. For example, in Table 6.1 we consider four processes with the same specification limits but different process means (μ) and different standard deviations (σ) such that the value of C_{pk} in each case remains the same.

The value of C_{pk} for each process remains the same even though the process mean has been moving away from the center, because in each case, the distance between the process mean and the nearest specification limit (in this example, the LSL) is three times the process standard deviation. So, we can say that in some ways C_{pk} is not an adequate measure of centering. Table 6.2 gives the parts per million (ppm) of nonconforming units for different values of C_{pk} when it is assumed that the process characteristic is normally distributed.

From Table 6.2, we can see that each process in Table 6.1 will produce 1350 nonconforming ppm. This is possible only if the process standard deviation is shrinking while the process mean is shifting and the NTLs remain within the specification limits. In fact, by definition, the process with standard

Table 6.1 Different processes with the same value of C_{pk}.

Process	LSL	USL	Center	μ	σ	C_{pk}
1	12	36	24	24	4	1.00
2	12	36	24	22	3.33	1.00
3	12	36	24	20	2.67	1.00
4	12	36	24	18	2.00	1.00

Table 6.2 Parts per million of nonconforming units for different values of C_{pk}.

C_{pk}	1.00	1.33	1.67	2.00
ppm	1350	30	1	.001

deviation $\sigma = 2$ would be of Six Sigma quality if the process mean were at the center point. In this case, however, the process is producing 1350 nonconforming ppm because the process mean is off center by 3σ, a shift larger than 1.5σ, which would be tolerable only in a Six Sigma quality process.

Boyles (1991) gave the upper and lower bounds on percentage of conforming units associated with values of C_{pk} as

$$100 \times ((2P(Z \leq 3C_{pk}) - 1) \leq (\text{percentage of conforming units}) \leq 100 \times P(Z \leq 3C_{pk})). \quad (6.10)$$

For example, bounds on percentage of conforming units associated with $C_{pk} = 1$ are

$$100 \times ((2P(Z \leq 3) - 1) \leq (\text{percentage of conforming units}) \leq 100 \times P(Z \leq 3))$$

or

$$99.73 \leq (\text{percentage of conforming units}) \leq 99.865.$$

From this inequality we can easily determine that the bounds on percentage of nonconforming units associated with $C_{pk} = 1$ are

$$0.135 \leq (\text{percentage of nonconforming units}) \leq 0.27$$

or

$$1350 \leq (\text{nonconforming ppm}) \leq 2700.$$

6.4 PCI C_{pm}

The PCI C_{pk} was introduced because the capability index C_p did not consider the position of the process mean relative to the target value, which usually coincides with the center of the specification limits. However, from our discussion in section 6.3, it should be quite clear that even C_{pk} does not adequately serve the intended purpose when the process standard deviation is changing. To meet this challenge, a new capability index, C_{pm}, was introduced.

Taguchi (1985, 1986) applied the loss function to quality improvement, where the characteristics of Taguchi's loss function are:

- Quality is best when on target
- Quality decreases as products deviate
- Customer dissatisfaction grows with deviation

- Dissatisfaction can be expressed as dollar loss to customer and society
- Dollar loss can often be approximated by a simple quadric function

Taguchi (1986), focusing on the reduction of variation from the target value, defined the capability index C_p as

$$C_p = \frac{\text{USL} - \text{LSL}}{6\tau}, \tag{6.11}$$

where

$$\tau^2 = E(X - T)^2 = \sigma^2 + (\mu - T)^2. \tag{6.12}$$

Chan et al. (1988) independently introduced Taguchi's index C_p and called it C_{pm}. They noted that C_{pm} reacts to changes in the process in much the same manner as C_{pk}.

However, the changes in C_{pm} are more severe than in C_{pk}. This can be seen by comparing the values of C_{pk} and C_{pm} presented in Table 6.3.

Consider, for example, USL = 22, LSL = 10, $T = 16$, $\sigma = 1$, and let μ vary. Then the changes in the values of C_{pk} and C_{pm} as μ deviates from the target are as shown in Table 6.3.

Because in practice μ and σ are not known, to measure the capability of a process it becomes necessary to estimate μ and σ. Thus, using the estimates of μ and σ, the estimator for C_{pm} most commonly used is

$$\hat{C}_{pm} = \frac{\text{USL} - \text{LSL}}{6\sqrt{s^2 + (\bar{x} - T)^2}}, \tag{6.13}$$

where

$$s^2 = \frac{1}{n-1}\sum_{i=1}^{n}(x_i - \bar{x})^2 \tag{6.14}$$

Taguchi (1985) proposed a slightly different estimator for C_{pm}, that is,

$$C'_{pm} = \frac{d}{3\sqrt{[fs^2 + n(\bar{x} - T)^2]/(f+1)}} \tag{6.15}$$

$$f = n-1,\ d = (\text{USL}-\text{LSL})/2.$$

Kotz and Lovelace (1998) prefer this estimator over the one given in equation (6.13) due to some statistical properties.

Table 6.3 The values of C_{pk} and C_{pm} as μ deviates from the target.

μ	16	15	14	13	12
C_{pk}	2.00	1.67	1.33	1.00	0.67
C_{pm}	2.00	1.41	0.89	0.63	0.49

Example 6.5 *Consider a stable process that has lower and upper specification limits of 24 and 44, respectively, and the target value at* T = *34. Suppose a random sample of size 25 from this process produced a sample mean of* $\bar{x}$ = *36 and standard deviation of* s = *2.5. Determine the point estimates for* C_p, C_{pk}, *and* C_{pm}.

Solution: Using the information given in this example and the formulas presented earlier, we obtain the following point estimates:

$$\hat{C}_p = \frac{\text{USL} - \text{LSL}}{6s} = \frac{44-24}{6 \times 2.5} = 1.33,$$

$$\hat{C}_{pk} = \min\left(\frac{\bar{x} - \text{LSL}}{3s}, \frac{\text{USL} - \bar{x}}{3s}\right) = \min(1.6,\ 1.06) = 1.06,$$

$$\hat{C}_{pm} = \frac{\text{USL} - \text{LSL}}{6\sqrt{s^2 + (\bar{x} - T)^2}} = \frac{44-24}{6\sqrt{(2.5)^2 + (36-34)^2}} = 1.04,$$

$$\hat{C}'_{pm} = \frac{d}{3\sqrt{[fs^2 + n(\bar{x} - T)^2]/(f+1)}}$$

$$= \frac{(44-24)/2}{3\sqrt{[24(2.5)^2 + 25(36-34)^2]/25}} = 1.054.$$

6.5 PCI C_{pmk}

The PCI C_{pmk} was introduced as a further improvement over C_{pm} by Pearn et al. (1992). The index C_{pmk} is usually known as a third-generation capability index and is defined as

$$C_{pmk} = \min\left(\frac{\mu - \text{LSL}}{3\tau}, \frac{\text{USL} - \mu}{3\tau}\right), \tag{6.16}$$

where τ is as defined in equation (6.10). Thus, C_{pmk} can also be defined as

$$C_{pmk} = \min\left(\frac{\mu - \text{LSL}}{3\sqrt{\sigma^2 + (\bar{x} - T)^2}}, \frac{\text{USL} - \mu}{3\sqrt{\sigma^2 + (\bar{x} - T)^2}}\right). \tag{6.17}$$

The relationship between C_{pmk} and C_{pm} is similar to that between C_{pk} and C_p. In other words,

$$C_{pmk} = (1-k)C_{pm}, \tag{6.18}$$

where k is as defined in equation (6.9).

A point estimator for C_{pmk} is given by

$$\hat{C}_{pmk} = \frac{(\text{USL} - \text{LSL})/2 + |\bar{x} - T|}{3\hat{\tau}}, \tag{6.19}$$

where

$$\hat{\tau} = \sqrt{s^2 + (\bar{x} - T)^2}. \tag{6.20}$$

Example 6.6 *Find an estimator* $\hat{C}_{pmk}$ *of* C_{pmk} *for the process in Example 6.5.*

Solution: Substituting the values of LSL, USL, T, s, and $\bar{x}$ in equation (6.19) we get

$$\hat{C}_{pmk} = \frac{(44-24)/2 + |36-34|}{3\sqrt{2.5^2 + (36-34)^2}}$$

$$= \frac{12}{3\sqrt{10.25}} = 1.25.$$

Chen and Hsu (1995) show that the preceding estimator is asymptotically normal. Wallgren (1996) emphasizes that C_{pmk} is more sensitive than C_{pk} or C_{pm} to the deviation of the process mean from the target value. Later in this chapter we will use numerical data to see this characteristic of C_{pmk}, C_{pm}, C_{pk}, and some other indices. Pearn and Kotz (1994) and Vännman (1995) rank the four indices in terms of their sensitivity to differences between the process mean and the target value as (1) C_{pmk}, (2) C_{pm}, (3) C_{pk}, and (4) C_p.

6.6 PCI C_{pnst}

Gupta (2005) recently introduced the capability index C_{pnst}. Before we formally define this index, we will give some background and rationale.

Deming (1986) points out that "there is no process, no capability and no meaningful specifications, except in statistical control. When a process has been brought into a statistical control it has a definable capability, expressible as the economic level of quality of the process." Thus, NTLs should play a very important role in defining the PCI. Some indices—the ones we have discussed so far, for example—have successfully solved the problem of process variation (σ) and process centering (that is, the distance $\mu - T$ between the process mean μ and the target value T). Particularly, these indices are second- and third-generation indices—namely, C_{pk}, C_{pm}, and C_{pmk}—which are defined as we saw earlier in terms of process variation (σ) and process centering $\mu - T$ and the distance between the process mean and the specification limits, that is, $\mu - LSL$ and $USL - \mu$. However, none of these indices consider the distance between the NTLs and the specification limits. A process becomes barely capable or incapable as the NTLs coincide or cross the specification limits. A process should be deemed incapable before the process mean coincides or crosses the specification limits. Once the position of the NTLs is determined by the position of the mean μ, it is the distance between the NTLs and the specification limits that is more important than the distance between μ and the specification limits.

The capability index C_{pnst} is defined as

$$C_{pnst} = \min\left(\frac{\text{LNTL} - \text{LSL}}{3\tau}, \frac{\text{USL} - \text{UNTL}}{3\tau}\right), \tag{6.21}$$

where LNTL and UNTL are the lower and the upper natural tolerance limits and τ is as defined in equation (6.12). Furthermore, using the customary definition of LNTL and UNTL, that is,

$$\text{LNTL} = \mu - 3\sigma,\ \text{UNTL} = \mu + 3\sigma,$$

C_{pnst} can be expressed as

$$\begin{aligned} C_{pnst} &= \min\left(\frac{\mu - 3\sigma - \text{LSL}}{3\sqrt{\sigma^2 + (\mu - T)^2}}, \frac{\text{USL} - \mu - 3\sigma}{3\sqrt{\sigma^2 + (\mu - T)^2}}\right) \\ &= \min\left(\frac{\frac{\mu - \text{LSL}}{3\sigma} - 1}{\sqrt{1 + \left(\frac{\mu - T}{\sigma}\right)^2}}, \frac{\frac{\text{USL} - \mu}{3\sigma} - 1}{\sqrt{1 + \left(\frac{\mu - T}{\sigma}\right)^2}}\right) \\ &= \frac{1}{\sqrt{1 + \left(\frac{\mu - T}{\sigma}\right)^2}} \min\left(\frac{\mu - \text{LSL}}{3\sigma} - 1, \frac{\text{USL} - \mu}{3\sigma} - 1\right). \end{aligned} \tag{6.22}$$

Using the notation of Montgomery (2005b, 342), we can express C_{pnst} as

$$\begin{aligned} C_{pnst} &= \frac{1}{\sqrt{1 + \xi^2}} \min\left(\frac{\mu - LSL}{3\sigma} - 1, \frac{USL - \mu}{3\sigma} - 1\right) \\ &= \frac{1}{\sqrt{1 + \xi^2}} (C_{pk} - 1), \end{aligned} \tag{6.23}$$

where

$$\xi = \frac{\mu - T}{\sigma}.$$

A point estimator of C_{pnst} is given by

$$\hat{C}_{pnst} = \frac{1}{\sqrt{1 + v^2}} (\hat{C}_{pk} - 1), \tag{6.24}$$

where

$$\nu = \hat{\xi} = \frac{\hat{\mu} - T}{\hat{\sigma}} \tag{6.25}$$

and

$$\hat{\mu} = \bar{x}, \ \hat{\sigma} = s = \sqrt{\frac{1}{n-1}\left(\sum_{i=1}^{n} x_i^2 - \frac{\left(\sum_{i=1}^{n} x_i\right)^2}{n}\right)} \tag{6.26}$$

or

$$\hat{\mu} = \bar{\bar{x}}, \ \hat{\sigma} = \frac{\bar{R}}{d_2} \ \text{or} \ \frac{\bar{s}}{c_4}. \tag{6.27}$$

Values of d_2 and c_4 for various sample sizes are given in Table A.2. Note that the second set of estimates is used only if the process is in a state of control and the estimate based on the sample range is used for sample sizes fewer than 10. Also, note that $\hat{C}_{pnst}$ has an asymptotic normal distribution.

Examples Comparing C_{pnst} with PCIs C_{pk} and C_{pm}

Example 6.7 *(Bothe 2002) Consider two processes, A and B, with the following summary statistics:*

$$\mu_A = 3.0 \qquad \mu_B = 0.0$$
$$\sigma_A = 1.143 \qquad \sigma_B = 2.66.$$

Further, it is given that LSL = –5, USL = 5, and $T \neq M$.
Plugging these values into equation (6.7), we get

$$C_{pk}(A) = 0.58 \qquad C_{pk}(B) = 0.63.$$

Process A has a smaller C_{pk} value than process B. However, process A is producing a higher percentage of conforming parts than process B, which is clearly a contradiction. Now if we choose $T = 1.5$ ($T \neq M$), so that T is equidistant from the two means, then substituting all the values in equation (6.21), we get

$$C_{pnst} = -0.2545 \text{ for process A}$$
$$= 0.3222 \text{ for process B},$$

which indicates that process A is better than process B. Moreover, both values of C_{pnst} are negative, which indicates that both processes are producing nonconforming parts and therefore are not capable.

Example: 6.8 *(Bothe 2002) Consider two processes, A and B, with the following summary statistics:*

$$\mu_A = 12 \qquad \mu_B = 15$$
$$\sigma_A = 2 \qquad \sigma_B = 0.667.$$

Also, it is given that LSL = 6, USL = 18, and T = 12. Furthermore, it is known that process A is inferior to process B—inferior in the sense that it is more likely to produce a higher percentage of nonconforming parts.

From Bothe (2002), we have C_{pm} for processes A and B equal to 1.0 and 0.65, respectively, which is again not indicative of the actual capability.

Now, using the summary statistics and the values of LSL, USL, and T in equation (6.21), we get

$$C_{pnst} = 0.0 \text{ for process A}$$
$$= 0.1085 \text{ for process B,}$$

which are consistent and indicate that process A is inferior to process B. Moreover, both values of C_{pnst} are positive, which indicates that both processes are capable. However, process A is just barely capable. In other words, process A is more likely than process B to produce nonconforming parts.

Example 6.9 *(Pearn et al. 1992) Consider two processes, A and B, with the following summary statistics:*

$$\mu_A = T - \frac{d}{2}, \ \mu_B = T + \frac{d}{2}, \ \sigma_A = \sigma_B = \frac{d}{3}, \ T = \frac{1}{4}(3(\text{USL}) + \text{LSL}),$$

where d = 1/2(USL – LSL). Furthermore, under these conditions, processes A and B are expected to produce 0.27 percent and 50 percent, respectively, nonconforming parts.

However, from Pearn et al. (1992) it is known that for both processes, C_{pm} = 0.555, which, again, is clearly a contradiction. Substituting the values provided to us in equation (6.21), we get

$$C_{pnst} = 0.0 \text{ for process A}$$
$$= -0.55 \text{ for process B,}$$

which are again consistent with what we would expect. Furthermore, the values of C_{pnst} indicate that process A is barely capable and process B is not capable at all.

These examples show that the capability index C_{pnst} generally presents a clearer picture than the indices C_{pk} and C_{pm}.

6.6.1 Certain Features of the Capability Index C_{pnst}

1. The index C_{pnst} can take any real value: negative, zero, or positive.
2. $C_{pnst} < 0$ implies that at least one of the NTLs does not fall within the specification limits, which indicates that the process is no longer capable.

3. $C_{pnst} = 0$ implies that at least one of the NTLs has coincided with the specification limits, and hence the process is barely capable. Under the normality assumptions, the process is producing either 1350 ppm or 2700 ppm nonconforming parts, depending on whether one or both NTLs have coincided with the specification limits. Furthermore, any change in the process—that is, a change in process mean, process variation, or both—can make the process incapable.

4. $0 < C_{pnst} < 1$ implies that the process is capable. The higher the value of the index, the better the process. As C_{pnst} approaches 1, the process mean is approaching the target value and the NTLs are moving away from the specification limits toward the target value.

5. $C_{pnst} \geq 1$ implies a very desirable situation. The process standard deviation σ has become very small, and the distance between the specification limits and the NTLs is at least 3σ; that is, the distance between the target value T and the specification limits is at least 6σ, which means the process is performing at a Six Sigma quality level or better. The process mean may shift as much as 1.5σ off the target value without causing any problems. This is because a shift in the mean of 1.5σ on either side of the target would lead to a rate of at most 3.4 ppm nonconforming. This is, in fact, another way of looking at a process performing at a Six Sigma quality level.

6. It can easily be seen that as the process mean moves away from the target value, the value of the process standard deviation remains fixed (say at $\sigma = 2$), whereas the distance between the NTLs and the specification limits and the value of C_{pnst} are changing (for example, see Table 6.4). The change in C_{pnst} occurs much faster than in any other of the indices (C_p, C_{pk}, C_{pm}, or C_{pmk}).

7. Similarly, it can be seen that the process variation is increasing while the value of the process mean μ is fixed (say, $\mu = 20$), and the distance between the NTLs and the specification limits

Table 6.4 Values of C_p, C_{pk}, C_{pm}, C_{pmk}, and C_{pnst} for μ = 20, 22, 24, 26, 28; T = 24; LSL = 12; and USL = 36 (σ = 2).

M	C_p	C_{pk}	C_{pm}	C_{pmk}	C_{pnst}
20	2	1.333	0.894	0.590	0.149
22	2	1.667	1.414	1.179	0.471
24*	2	2.000	2.000	2.000	1.000
26	2	1.667	1.414	1.179	0.471
28	2	1.333	0.894	0.596	0.149

*Target value

Table 6.5 Values of C_p, C_{pk}, C_{pm}, C_{pmk}, and C_{pnst} for σ = 2, 2.5, 3.0, 3.5, 4.0, 4.5; T = 24, LSL = 12, and USL = 36 (μ = 20).

σ	C_p	C_{pk}	C_{pm}	C_{pmk}	C_{pnst}
2	2.000	1.333	0.894	0.596	0.149
2.5	1.600	1.067	0.848	0.565	0.035
3.0	1.333	0.889	0.800	0.533	–0.067
3.5	1.143	0.762	0.753	0.502	–0.157
4.0	1.000	0.663	0.707	0.471	–0.236
4.5	0.889	0.593	0.664	0.443	–0.305

and the value of the index C_{pnst} are changing (for example, see Table 6.5)—again, at a much faster rate than the values of any other indices.

6.7 PCIs P_p and P_{pk}

The capability indices we have studied so far have one characteristic in common: each one is used when the process is stable. In 1991 the American Automotive Industry Group (AAIG), consisting of representatives from Ford Motor Company, General Motors Corporation, American Daimler/Chrysler Corporation, and the American Society for Quality, was founded. This group of individuals standardized the supplier quality reporting procedure for the industry. It also advocated for the use of two sets of PCIs—one consisting of C_p and C_{pk}, and the other consisting of P_p and P_{pk}. Furthermore, the group advised using C_p and C_{pk} when the process is stable and P_p and P_{pk} when the process is not in control, where the two sets of indices—P_p and P_{pk}, and C_p and C_{pk}—are defined in exactly the same manner and differ only in their estimates. We have

$$\hat{P}_p = \frac{\text{USL} - \text{LSL}}{6\hat{\sigma}_s}, \tag{6.28}$$

$$\hat{C}_p = \frac{\text{USL} - \text{LSL}}{6\hat{\sigma}_{\bar{R}/d_2}}. \tag{6.29}$$

and

$$\hat{P}_{pk} = \min\left(\frac{\text{USL} - \bar{\bar{X}}}{3\hat{\sigma}_s}, \frac{\bar{\bar{X}} - \text{LSL}}{3\hat{\sigma}_s}\right), \tag{6.30}$$

$$\hat{C}_{pk} = \min\left(\frac{USL - \bar{\bar{X}}}{3\hat{\sigma}_{\bar{R}/d_2}}, \frac{\bar{\bar{X}} - LSL}{3\hat{\sigma}_{\bar{R}/d_2}}\right). \tag{6.31}$$

In other words, they differ only in the method in which one estimates the standard deviation. The estimate $\hat{\sigma}_s$ is the usual standard deviation $s=\sqrt{\sum_{i=1}^{n}\sum_{j=1}^{m}(x_{ij}-\overline{\overline{x}})^2/(mn-1)}$, and $\hat{\sigma}_{\overline{R}/d_2}=\overline{R}/d_2$ is an estimate obtained using the subgroup ranges R_i, $i = 1, 2, \ldots, m$ and the corresponding value of d_2. Note that the estimate $\hat{\sigma}_s$ measures the process variability by using the variability within and between subgroups, whereas $\hat{\sigma}_{\overline{R}/d_2}$ uses only the variability within the subgroups. When the process is stable, there is very little variability between the subgroups; the two sets of indices are essentially the same because the estimates $\hat{\sigma}_s$ and $\hat{\sigma}_{\overline{R}/d_2}$ are approximately equal. But if the process is not stable, there is potentially a very large variability between the subgroups. This would mean that $\hat{\sigma}_{\overline{R}/d_2}$ underestimates the process standard deviation, and consequently C_{pk} would overestimate the process capability. Fortunately, this situation will not arise, because the use of C_{pk} is recommended only when the process is stable.

Kotz and Lovelace (1998, 253) strongly argue against the use of P_p and P_{pk}: "We highly recommend against using these indices when the process is not in statistical control. Under these conditions, the P-numbers are meaningless with regard to process capability, have no tractable statistical properties, and infer nothing about long-term capability of the process. Worse still, they provide no motivation to the user companies to get their process in control. The P-numbers are a step backwards in the efforts to properly quantify process capability, and a step towards statistical terrorism in its undiluted form." Montgomery (2005b, 349) agrees with Kotz and Lovelace: "The process performance indices P_p and P_{pk} are more than a step backwards. They are a waste of engineering and management effort—they tell you nothing." The authors wholeheartedly agree with Kotz and Lovelace and Montgomery. No one can judge a process when its future behavior is so unpredictable.

7

Measurement Systems Analysis

Measurement Systems Analysis (MSA) is used to understand and quantify the variability associated with measurements and measurement systems. In the *Measurement Systems Analysis Reference Manual,* the Automotive Industry Action Group (AIAG) and MSA Work Group (2002, 64) define measurement and measurement systems as follows:

> **Definition 7.1** *Measurement:* "the assignment of numbers [or values] to material things to represent the relations among them with respect to particular properties."

> **Definition 7.2** *Measurement system:* "the collection of instruments or gauges, standards, operations, methods, fixtures, software, personnel, environment and assumptions used to quantify a unit of measure or fix assessment to the feature characteristic being measured; the complete process used to obtain measurements."

These definitions will serve as the basis of our discussion. However, we must first provide a clarification. The term *MSA* is commonly used interchangeably with the term *Gage repeatability and reproducibility* (Gage R&R). MSA is a more comprehensive analysis quantifying variability components from gage stability, gage bias, gage linearity, and gage repeatability and reproducibility (that is, variability from operator measurements). Gage R&R is, in fact, a subset or component of MSA. The underlying reason for mistaken interchange of the two terms is that many, if not most, problems with measurement systems are detected and corrected with the Gage R&R procedure without having to continue with a more comprehensive MSA. For a detailed discussion of analysis techniques for gage stability, gage bias, and gage linearity, see AIAG and MSA Work Group (2002).

7.1 Using SQC to Understand Variability

In each of the preceding chapters of this book, and in the previous book, *Applied Statistics for the Six Sigma Green Belt*, we have discussed the concept of variability in both manufacturing and service delivery processes. The fact that variability exists in virtually any and all processes cannot be overemphasized. In many of our previous discussions and related references, the point has been made that variability in processes can be quantified by a probability distribution. Further, we made the point that a probability distribution of statistics (sample mean) from repeated samples would form the normal distribution through a concept called the central limit theorem (CLT). Figure 7.1 graphically describes the CLT.

As we can see in Figure 7.1, regardless of the distribution shape in a production or service delivery process, a plot of statistics from repeated samples forms the normal distribution.

Variability in the Production or Service Delivery Process

An interesting point is that variability is present in production or service delivery processes. We make the point that common cause variation, the type of variation expected in natural process behavior, can be reduced but not completely eliminated. And we continue to make the point that special cause variation, the type of variation not expected in natural process behavior, can and must be eliminated.

Variability in the Measurement Process

It is critically important that we understand that the methods, procedures, tools, and equipment we use to make measurements constitute an independent process that creates, and is susceptible to, its own variation. This means

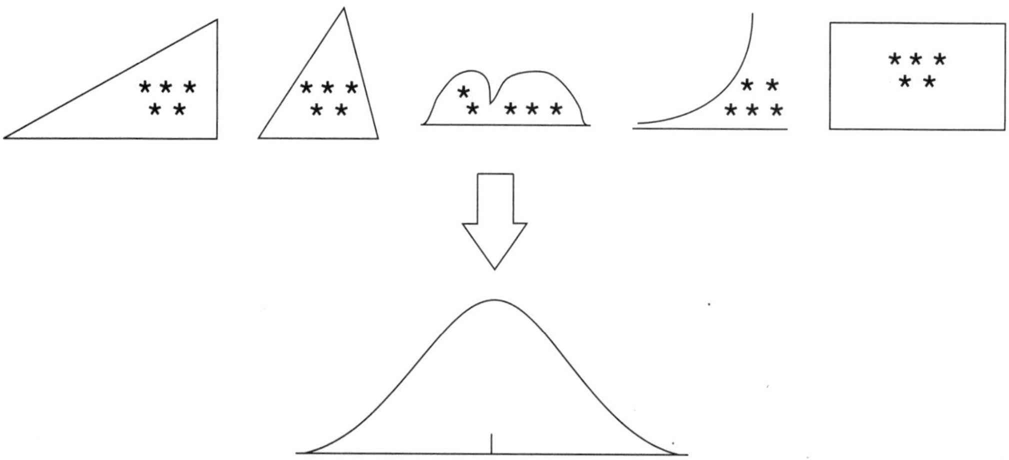

Figure 7.1 Approximate sampling distribution of sample statistics $\bar{X}$ with sample size five.

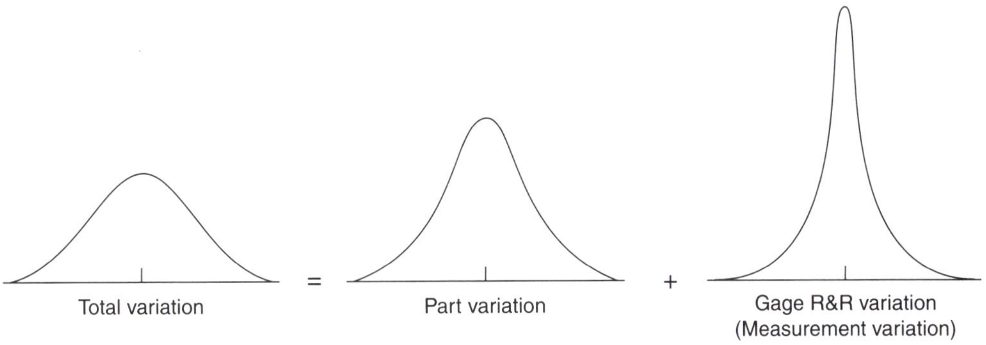

Figure 7.2 Components of total variation.

there are two sources or components of variation present in each measurement we take, as is shown in Figure 7.2.

It is important to ensure that the component of variability associated with the measurement system does not consume an excessive amount of variability as is allowed in the process specification. The purpose of MSA, then, is to quantify measurement system variability.

7.2 Evaluating Measurement System Performance

So far we have focused on bringing a process under statistical control, or, in other words, reducing the overall variation in the process. In this chapter, we focus on the MSA, which constitutes an important part of the total process variation. The total process variation can be divided into three major categories: variation due to parts, variation due to measurement instruments or equipment (gage), and variation due to operators. Part-to-part variation may be due to environment, methods, materials, machines, or some combination thereof, and other factors. Variation caused by the measurement instrument and variation caused by the operators who use the instrument are two of the components that constitute the variation from the measurement system. In the industrial world, these components are usually referred to as repeatability and reproducibility, respectively. Thus, repeatability and reproducibility may be considered as the major indicators of measurement system performance. In addition, sometimes there is a third component: the variation caused by the interaction between the operators and the instrument.

Because repeatability refers to the variation generated by the instrument (that is, measurement equipment or gage), it is referred to as instrument or equipment variation (EV). Reproducibility refers to variation generated by operators using measurement instruments, and it is referred to as operator or appraiser variation (AV). The study of Gage R&R is usually referred to as a *Gage R&R* study.

The *Measurement Systems Analysis Reference Manual* gives several methods for conducting Gage R&R. In this book we will study MSA using two methods, one based on range and the other based on the analysis of variance (ANOVA).

Because ANOVA is an advanced statistical technique that is not covered in our first volume, *Applied Statistics for the Six Sigma Green Belt,* or in this book, details will be kept to a minimum. We will focus our attention on explaining and interpreting the results of an example that we will work out using computer software.

7.2.1 MSA Based on Range

Various authors, including IBM (1986) and Barrentine (2003), have presented a form of what is known as the range method. Before we discuss the details of this method, we will define certain terms, namely, measurement capability index, K_1-Factor, and K_2-Factor. In addition, we will define some other terms that are very useful in understanding the MSA.

An *MSA* is a technique for collecting and analyzing data to evaluate the effectiveness of the measurement process. To collect data, we randomly select some parts and then select a certain number of operators (usually three or more, but as a general rule, the more the better). Each operator takes multiple measurements (at least two) on each part, and all the parts are measured in random order. These measurements are also known as trials. Using the terminology of the control charts discussed in earlier chapters, the measurements on each part (or the number of trials) constitute a rational subgroup, and the number of parts times the number of operators constitutes the number of subgroups or samples. Then $\bar{R}$ is defined as the average of the ranges of trials within the same operator, and $\bar{\bar{R}}$ is defined as the average of the $\bar{R}$'s between the operators.

> **Definition 7.3** The *measurement capability index* (MCI) is a measurement that quantifies our belief that the gage is reliable enough to support decisions made under the existing circumstances.

The MCI relates to four characteristics of a measurement system, which are the key to any measurement system. These characteristics are:

1. Precision
2. Accuracy
3. Stability
4. Linearity

The characteristic precision is further subdivided into two categories: repeatability and reproducibility.

> **Definition 7.4** *Repeatability* measures the preciseness (consistency) of the observations taken under the same conditions, which is achieved by computing the variance of such observations.

For example, we say a gage possesses the characteristic of repeatability if an operator obtains similar observations when measuring the same part again and again.

> **Definition 7.5** *Reproducibility* measures the preciseness (consistency) of the observations taken by different operators when measuring the same part.

For example, we say a gage possesses the characteristic of reproducibility if various operators obtain similar observations when measuring the same part again and again.

> **Definition 7.6** *Accuracy of a measurement system* is the closeness of the average of measurements taken to the true value.

The distinction between precision and accuracy is explained in the diagram in Figure 7.3.

> **Definition 7.7** *Stability* is defined by the total variation in measurements obtained with a measurement system on the same master or same parts when measuring a single characteristic over an extended period of time.

The smaller the total variation, the more stable the measurement system.

> **Definition 7.8** The difference between the true value (master measurement) and the average of the observed measurements of the same part has the same distribution over the entire measurement range. *Linearity* is best explained by the diagram in Figure 7.4.

In any manufacturing process, the total variability consists of two components—one due to the variability among the parts and the other due to the variability in the measurement system. The MCI of a measurement system, which is directly related to the variability due to the measurement system, is

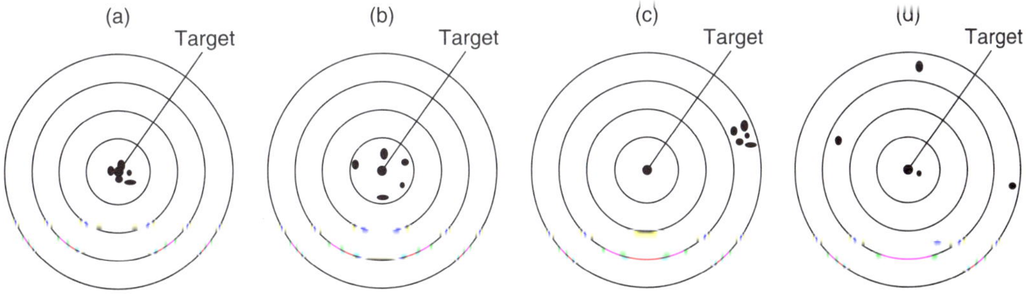

Figure 7.3 The distinction between accurate and precise, where (a) is accurate and precise, (b) is accurate but not precise, (c) is not accurate but precise, and (d) is neither accurate nor precise.

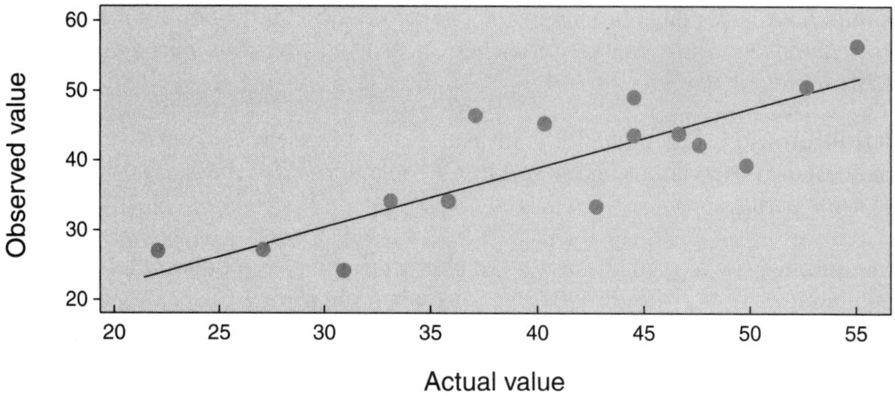

Figure 7.4 The linear relationship between the actual and the observed values.

a very pertinent factor in improving any process. The total variability due to the measurement system itself consists of three components: variability due to operators, variability due to the measurement instrument, and variability due to the interaction between the operators and the measurement instrument. Statistically, these relationships can be expressed as follows:

$$\sigma^2_{\text{total}} = \sigma^2_{\text{parts}} + \sigma^2_{\text{meas.}}, \tag{7.1}$$

$$\sigma^2_{\text{meas.}} = \sigma^2_{\text{inst.}} + \sigma^2_{\text{operator}} + \sigma^2_{\text{parts} \times \text{operator}}. \tag{7.2}$$

The total variability due to the measurement ($\sigma^2_{\text{meas.}}$) is also known as the total Gage R&R variability. The instrument variability is represented by the variability in the repeated measurements by the same operator, and for this reason it is also known as repeatability. In the ANOVA method, the repeatability variance component is the error variance (that is, $\sigma^2_{\text{inst.}} = \sigma^2_{\text{EV}} = \sigma^2$). The remainder of the variability in the measurement system comes from various operators who use the instrument and from the interaction between the instruments and the operators. Note that the interaction appears when any operator can measure one type of part better than another. This total variability from the operators and from the interaction between the operators and the instruments is also known as reproducibility. Equation (7.2) can also be expressed as

$$\sigma^2_{\text{meas.}} = \sigma^2_{\text{repeatability}} + \sigma^2_{\text{reproducibility}}. \tag{7.3}$$

Using Barrentine's approach, repeatability is defined as

$$\text{Repeatability} = \text{EV} = 5.15\,\hat{\sigma}_{\text{repeatability}} = 5.15\frac{\overline{\overline{R}}}{d_2} = K_1\overline{\overline{R}}, \qquad \text{where } K_1 = \frac{5.15}{d_2} \tag{7.4}$$

and where the factor 5.15 represents the 99 percent range of the standard normal distribution, which follows from the fact that

$$P(-2.575 \leq Z \leq 2.575) = 0.99. \tag{7.5}$$

Note that the AIAG recommends using the factor 6 instead of 5.15 because it covers almost 100 percent—or to be exact, 99.74 percent—of the range. Values of K_1 for various sample sizes (that is, the number of trials or the number of measurements taken on the same part by the same operator) are given in Table A.3. Duncan (1986) points out that this estimation procedure should be slightly modified if $N = r \times n$ = (# operators) × (# parts) is less than 16. If N is less than 16, then K_1 is defined as

$$K_1 = \frac{5.15}{d_2^*}. \tag{7.6}$$

The values of d_2^* are listed in Duncan (1986), Table D3. The values of K_1 listed in Table A.3 are determined according to the value of N. Again, using Barrentine's notation (2003, 57), the *Reproducibility* = AV, *ignoring the interaction term*, is defined as

$$\text{Reproducibility} = \text{AV} = \sqrt{(K_2 R_{\bar{x}})^2 - \frac{(\text{EV})^2}{(r \times n)}}, \tag{7.7}$$

where r is the number of trials, n is the number of parts or samples, EV is as given in equation (7.4), $R_{\bar{x}}$ is the range of the operator's means, and the factor K_2 is defined as

$$K_2 = \frac{5.15}{d_2^*}. \tag{7.8}$$

The value of d_2^* can be found from Duncan's Table D3 by selecting $g = 1$ and $m = n$ (# operators). For example, if we have five operators, then from Duncan's Table D3 for $g = 1$, $m = 5$, we have

$$K_2 = \frac{5.15}{2.48} = 2.077$$

We now illustrate the range-based method and then the ANOVA method with the following example.

Example 7.1 *A manufacturer of bolts (parts) used in automotive applications has installed a new measuring gage. In order to perform the MSA on the new gage, the quality manager randomly selects three Six Sigma Green Belts from the quality control department, who decide to conduct the MSA by taking a random sample of 10 bolts. Each Six Sigma Green Belt takes three measurements on each bolt, which is randomly selected. The data obtained are as shown in Table 7.1.*

Table 7.1 Data on an experiment involving three operators, 10 bolts, and three measurements (in millimeters) on each bolt by each operator.

Bolt (Part) Number	Operator 1			Operator 2			Operator 3		
	Trial 1	Trial 2	Trial 3	Trial 1	Trial 2	Trial 3	Trial 1	Trial 2	Trial 3
1	26	22	26	21	23	21	24	22	26
2	28	26	28	24	29	26	24	25	24
3	28	31	28	28	27	28	32	30	27
4	35	33	31	35	31	30	34	35	31
5	37	35	38	36	38	35	35	34	35
6	40	38	40	40	38	40	36	37	38
7	39	42	41	40	39	43	43	41	43
8	42	43	46	42	46	42	43	44	45
9	50	52	50	53	52	53	49	53	49
10	28	3	28	28	27	28	32	30	27
	$\bar{R}_1 = 3.0,\ \bar{x}_1 = 35.33$			$\bar{R}_2 = 2.5,\ \bar{x}_2 = 34.67$			$\bar{R}_3 = 3.0,\ \bar{x}_3 = 34.93$		

Solution: We first discuss Gage R&R using the range-based method (Barrentine 2003, IBM 1984).

Step 1: Verify gage calibration is current.

Step 2: Identify operators. Three operators are typically used in gage studies; however, the more operators, the better.

Step 3: Select a random sample of parts and have each operator measure all parts. One operator measures all parts, taking several measurements on each part, then the second operator takes measurements, then the third operator takes measurement, and so on. All parts are measured in random order.

Step 4: Calculate the sample mean, the intertrial range for each sample, and the average range for each operator. The sample means and average ranges are provided in Table 7.1.

Step 5: Calculate the range of sample means ($R_{\bar{x}}$), that is,

$$R_{\bar{x}} = \max(\bar{x}_i) - \min(\bar{x}_i)$$
$$= 35.33 - 34.67 = 0.66.$$

Step 6: Calculate the average range ($\bar{\bar{R}}$) for operators:

$$\bar{\bar{R}} = \frac{\bar{R}_1 + \bar{R}_2 + \bar{R}_3}{3}$$

$$= \frac{3.00 + 2.50 + 3.00}{3} = 2.83.$$

Step 7: Calculate repeatability (this value is also referred to as equipment variation [EV]) and the estimate of the standard deviation of repeatability ($\sigma_{\text{repeatability}}$):

$$\text{Repeatability (EV)} = \bar{\bar{R}} \times K_1 = 2.83 \times 3.05 = 8.63,$$

where from Table A.3, $K_1 = 3.05$

$$\hat{\sigma}_{\text{repeatability}} = \frac{\text{EV}}{5.15} = \frac{8.63}{5.15} = 1.67.$$

Step 8: Calculate reproducibility (this value is also referred to as operator or appraiser variation [AV]) and the estimate of the standard deviation of repeatability ($\sigma_{\text{repeatability}}$)

$$\text{Reproducibility (AV)} = \sqrt{(R_{\bar{x}} \times K_2)^2 - [(\text{EV})^2 / n \times r]},$$

where from Table A.4, $K_2 = 2.70$, n = # of parts or samples, and r = # of trials. We have

$$\text{Reproducibility (AV)} = \sqrt{(0.66 \times 2.70)^2 - [(8.63)^2 / 10 \times 3]}$$

$$= 0.83.$$

Note that if the number under the radical is negative, then AV is zero. The estimate of the standard deviation of reproducibility is

$$\hat{\sigma}_{\text{reproducibility}} = \frac{0.83}{5.15} = 0.16.$$

Using this method, the reproducibility is calculated by ignoring the interaction term, and the standard deviation of reproducibility may merely be looked upon as the operator standard deviation.

Step 9: Calculate Gage R&R (that is, repeatability and reproducibility) and the estimate of Gage R&R standard deviation.

$$\text{Gage R\&R} = \sqrt{(\text{repeatability})^2 + (\text{reproducibility})^2}$$

$$= \sqrt{(8.63)^2 + (.83)^2}$$

$$= 8.67$$

The estimate of Gage R&R standard deviation is given by

$$\hat{\sigma}_{\text{gage}} = \frac{8.67}{5.15} = 1.68.$$

7.2.2 MSA Based on ANOVA

MSA using the ANOVA method is done by using two types of experimental designs: crossed and nested, or hierarchical, designs. Crossed designs are used when each operator measures the same parts, whereas nested, or hierarchical, designs are used when each operator measures different parts—in which case we say that the parts are nested within operators. In this chapter we will discuss crossed designs. Nested, or hierarchical, designs are beyond the scope of this book.

Gage R&R Study—ANOVA Method (Based on Data in Table 7.1)

Two-Way ANOVA Table with Interaction

Source	DF	SS	MS	F	P
Part Numbers	9	6135.73	681.748	165.532	0.000
Operators	2	6.76	3.378	0.820	0.456
Part Numbers*Operators	18	74.13	4.119	1.477	0.131
Repeatability	60	167.33	2.789		
Total	89	6383.95			

Alpha to remove interaction term = 0.25

In the Two-Way ANOVA Table with Interaction, we test three hypotheses:

- H_0: All parts are similar versus H_1: All parts are not similar
- H_0: All operators are equally good versus H_1: All operators are not equally good
- H_0: Interactions between parts and operators are negligible versus H_1: Interactions between parts and operators are not negligible

The decision whether to reject any of these hypotheses depends on the *p* value (shown in the last column of the Two-Way ANOVA Table with Interaction) and the corresponding value of the level of significance. If the *p* value is less than or equal to the level of significance (σ), we reject the null hypothesis. Otherwise, we do not reject the null hypothesis. For example, the *p* value for parts is zero, which means we reject the null hypothesis that the parts are similar at any level of significance. In other words, the measurement system is capable of distinguishing the different parts. The *p* value for operators is 0.456. Therefore, at any level of significance less than 0.456, we do not reject the null hypothesis that the operators are equally good (in most applications, an acceptable value of the level of significance is 0.05). Finally, the interactions are not negligible at a significance level greater than 0.131. Because the chosen value of alpha is 0.25, the interaction term is not removed from the ANOVA.

Two-Way ANOVA Table without Interaction

Source	DF	SS	MS	F	P
Part Numbers	9	6135.73	681.748	220.222	0.000
Operators	2	6.76	3.378	1.091	0.341
Repeatability	78	241.46	3.096		
Total	89	6383.95			

Alpha to remove interaction term = 0.1

Because in this case the value of alpha is less than 0.131, the interaction term is removed from the Two-Way ANOVA Table without Interaction. In this case, the SS (sum of squares) and DF (degrees of freedom) are merged with corresponding terms of repeatability, which act as an error due to uncontrollable factors. The interpretation for parts and operators is the same as in the Two-Way ANOVA Table with Interaction. However, it is important to note that the *p* values can change from one ANOVA table to another. For example, the *p* values for operators are different in the two tables. We will not discuss here the reason for these changes in the *p* values, as it is beyond the scope of this book.

Gage R&R

		%Contribution
Source	VarComp	(of VarComp)
Total Gage R&R	3.2321	4.12
Repeatability	2.7889	3.55
Reproducibility	0.4432	0.56
Operators	0.0000	0.00
Operators*Part Numbers	0.4432	0.56
Part-to-Part	75.2922	95.88
Total Variation	78.5243	100.00

Process tolerance = 60

The first column in the Gage R&R MINITAB printout provides the breakdown of the variance components (estimates of variances). The second column provides percent contribution of the variance components, which becomes the basis of a Gage R&R study using the ANOVA method. For example, the total variation due to gage is 4.12 percent, of which 3.55 percent variation is contributed by the repeatability and the remaining 0.56 percent is contributed by the reproducibility. The variation due to parts is 95.88 percent of the total variation. This implies that the measurement system is very capable.

Note that the percent contributions are calculated simply by dividing the variance components by the total variation and then multiplying by 100. The percent contribution due to repeatability, for example, is given by

$$\frac{2.7889}{78.5243} \times 100 = 3.55\%.$$

Source	StdDev (SD)	Study Var (6 * SD)	%Study Var (%SV)	%Tolerance (SV/Toler)
Total Gage R&R	1.79780	10.7868	20.29	17.98
Repeatability	1.67000	10.0200	18.85	16.70
Reproducibility	0.66574	3.9944	7.51	6.66
Operators	0.00000	0.0000	0.00	0.00
Operators*Part Numbers	0.66574	3.9944	7.51	6.66
Part-to-Part	8.67711	52.0626	97.92	86.77
Total Variation	8.86139	53.1684	100.00	88.61

Number of distinct categories = 6

This part of the MINITAB printout provides various percent contributions using estimates of standard deviations, which are obtained by taking the square root of the variance components. The comparison with standard deviation does make more sense because the standard deviation uses the same units as those of the measurements. The study variation (that is, measurement system variation, which is equivalent to the process variation in the study of process control) is obtained by multiplying the standard deviation by 6. The percent study variations are calculated by dividing the standard deviation by the total variation and then multiplying by 100. The percent contribution due to part-to-part, for example, is given by

$$\frac{8.67711}{8.86139} \times 100 = 97.92\%.$$

The percent tolerance is obtained by dividing the (6*SD) by the process tolerance and then multiplying by 100. The process tolerance of total Gage R&R, for example, is given by

$$\frac{10.7868}{60} \times 100 = 17.98\%.$$

Note that the total percent tolerances in this example do not add up to 100. Rather, the total sum is 88.61, which means the total variation is using 88.61 percent of the specification band.

The last entry in the MINITAB printout is the number of distinct categories, which in this case is 6. The number of distinct categories can be determined as follows:

$$\text{Number of distinct categories} = \text{Integral part of}\left(\frac{\text{part-to-part SD}}{\text{total Gage R\&R SD}}\times 1.4142\right)$$

$$= \text{Integral part of}\left(\frac{8.67711}{1.79780}\times 1.4142\right)$$

$$= 6.$$

Under AIAG's recommendations, a measurement system is capable if the number of categories is greater than or equal to five. In this example, the measurement system is capable of separating the parts into the different categories in which they belong. This quantity is equivalent to the one defined in Montgomery (2005b) and is referred to as signal-to-noise ratio (SNR), that is,

$$\text{SNR} = \sqrt{\frac{2\rho_p}{1-\rho_p}}, \tag{7.9}$$

where

$$\rho_p = \frac{\sigma_p^2}{1-\rho_p^2}. \tag{7.10}$$

7.2.2.1 Graphical Representation of Gage R&R Study

Figure 7.5 shows the various percent contributions of Gage R&R, repeatability, reproducibility, and part-to-part variations, which we discussed in the previous section.

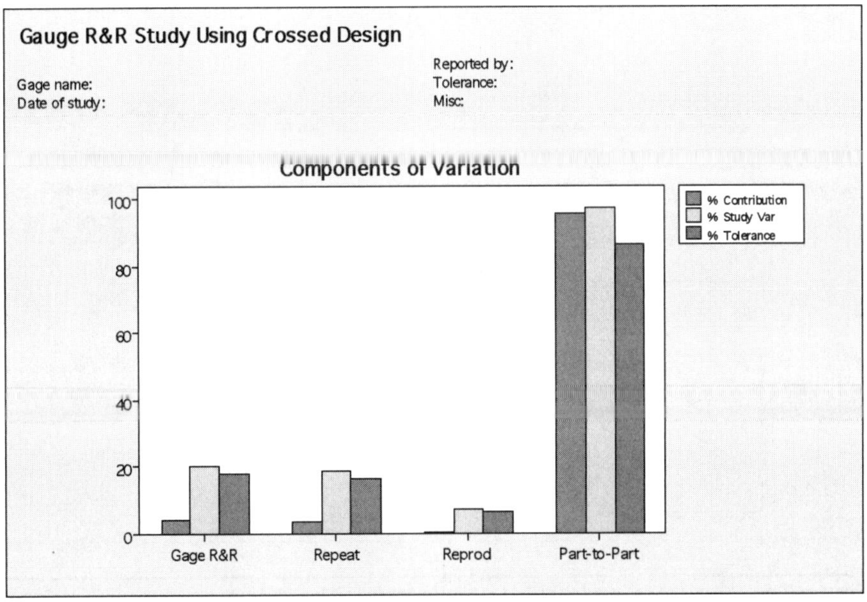

Figure 7.5 Percent contribution of variance components for the data in Example 7.1.

As usual, in Figure 7.6 we first interpret the R chart. All the data points are within the control limits, which indicates that the operators are measuring consistently. The $\bar{X}$ chart shows many points beyond the control limits, but this does not mean the measurement system is out of control. Rather, this indicates the narrower control limits because the variation due to repeatability is small and the measurement system is capable of distinguishing the different parts.

Figure 7.7 plots the average of each part by any single operator. In this graph we have three lines because we have three operators. These lines intersect one another, but they are also very close to one another. This implies that there is some interaction between the operators and the parts, which is significant only at significance level 0.131 or greater.

In Figure 7.8, the clear circles represent the measurements by each operator, and the dark circles represent the means. The spread of measurements for each operator is almost the same. The means fall on a horizontal line, which indicates that the average measurement for each operator is also the same. In this example, the operators are measuring the parts consistently. In other words, the variation due to reproducibility is low.

In Figure 7.9, the clear circles represent the measurements on each part, and the dark circles represent the mean for each part. In this case, the spread of measurements for each part is not exactly the same, but is nonetheless very small. This means that each part is measured with the same precision and accuracy. Greater variability among the means indicates that the measurement system is quite capable of distinguishing the parts belonging to different categories. Combining the outcomes of Figures 7.8 and 7.9, we can say that, overall, the Gage R&R variability is not very significant.

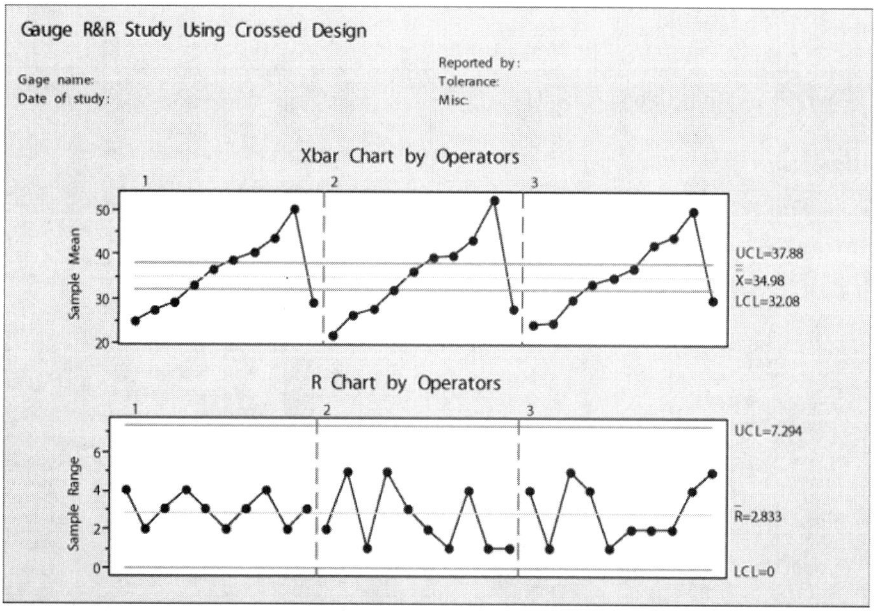

Figure 7.6 $\bar{X}$ and R charts for the data in Example 7.1.

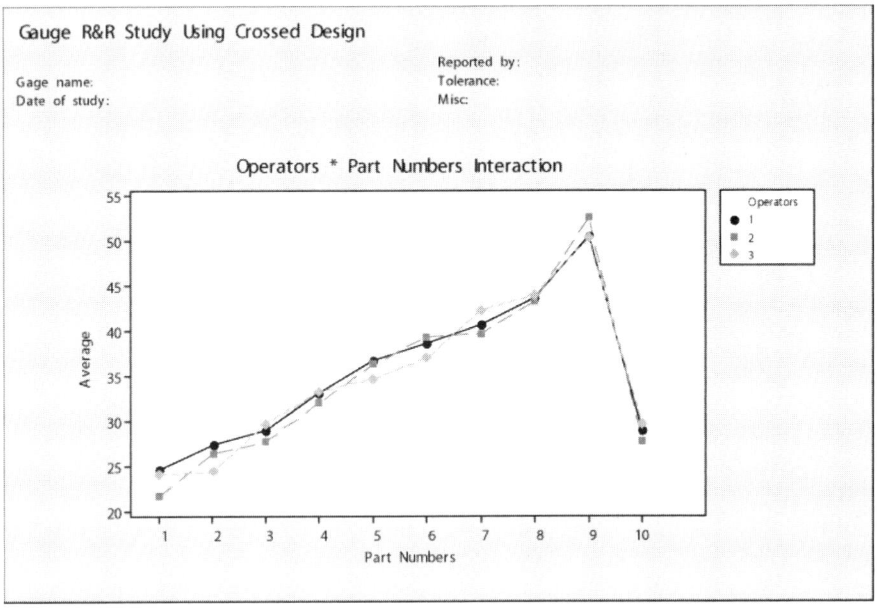

Figure 7.7 Interaction between operators and parts for the data in Example 7.1.

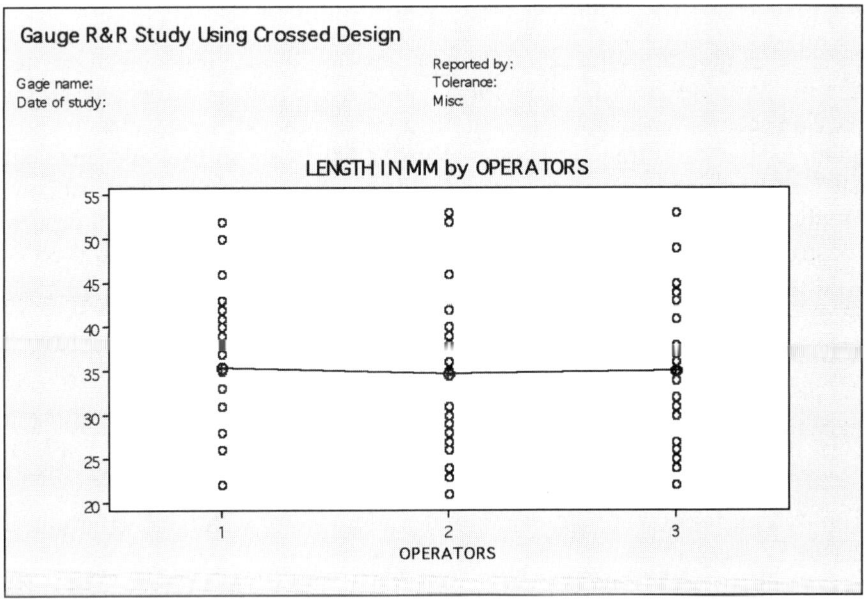

Figure 7.8 Scatter plot for measurements versus operators.

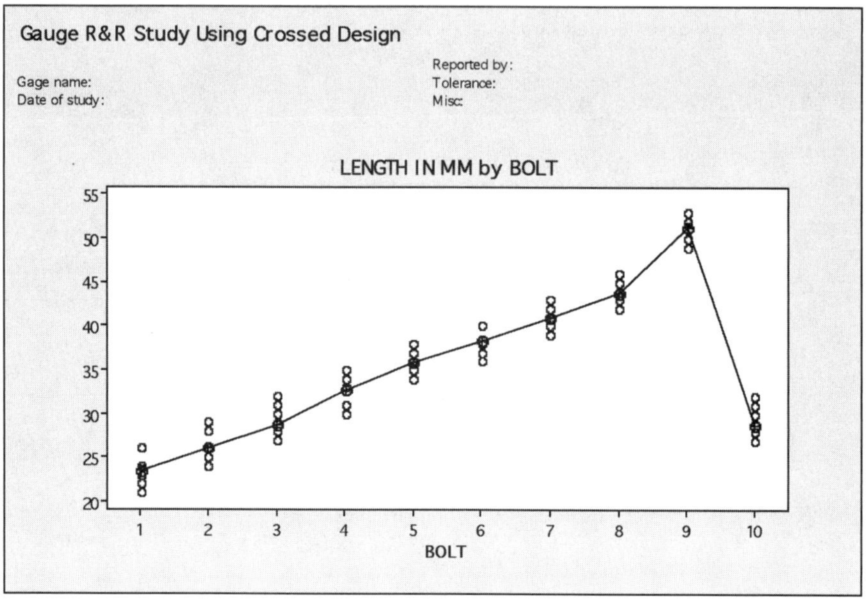

Figure 7.9 Scatter plot for measurements versus parts (bolts).

7.3 MCIs

As the PCI quantifies the ability of a process to produce products of desired quality, likewise the MCI quantifies the ability of a measurement system to provide accurate measurements. In other words, the MCI evaluates the adequacy of the measurement system. Various MCIs are in use, and one such MCI was defined in equation (7.9). We discuss here the other two most commonly used MCIs: percentage of process variation and percentage of process specification. The MCI should always be used in conjunction with the PCI (Barrentine 2003).

MCI as a Percentage of Process Variation (MCI_{pv})

$$MCI_{pv} = 100 \times \frac{\hat{\sigma}_{\text{Gage R\&R}}}{\hat{\sigma}_{\text{total}}} \tag{7.11}$$

The criteria for assessment of this index are usually as follows (Barrentine 2003):

≤ 20 percent: good

> 20 percent, ≤ 30 percent: marginal

> 30 percent: unacceptable

Using the preceding ANOVA table for the data in Example 7.1, we have

$$MCI_{pv} = 100 \times \frac{1.79780}{8.86139} = 20\%.$$

This MCI indicates that the measurement system is good.

MCI as a Percentage of Process Specification (MCI_{ps})

$$MCI_{ps} = \frac{6 \times \hat{\sigma}_{\text{Gage R\&R}}}{\text{USL} - \text{LSL}} \tag{7.12}$$

The criteria for assessment of this index are the same as MCI_{pv} (Barrentine 2003):

≤ 20 percent: good

> 20 percent, ≤ 30 percent: marginal

> 30 percent: unacceptable

Again, using the preceding ANOVA table for the data in Example 7.1 and with process tolerance 60, we have

$$MCI_{ps} = 100 \times \frac{6 \times 1.79780}{60} = 18\%.$$

Thus, this MCI indicates that the measurement system is good.

8

PRE-control

In Chapter 1, Figure 1.1 clarified how the SQC tools are related primarily to applied statistics and DOE. Figure 1.1 has been revised and is given here as Figure 8.1 to clarify relationships among the SQC tools.

As can be seen in Figure 8.1, PRE-control, if it is used at all, is used *after* a process is determined to be capable and operating in a state of statistical control.

8.1 PRE-control Background

Dorian Shainin developed the term *PRE-control* and the supporting concepts in the early 1980s. While PRE-control is not a formal trademark, this SQC tool is most commonly identified in professional literature as *PRE-control*, wherein the first three letters remain capitalized. In the years following the

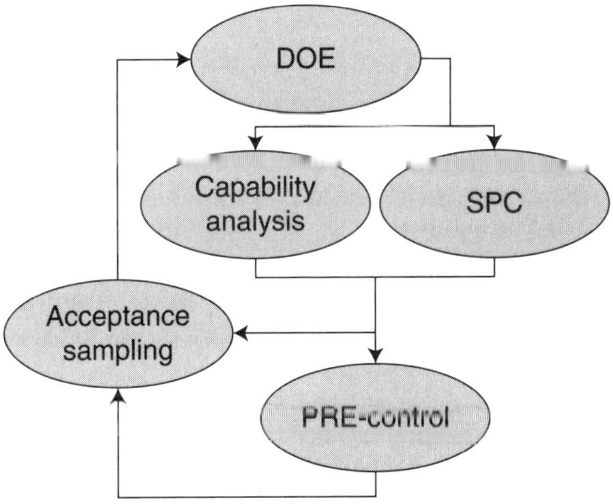

Figure 8.1 Relationships among the SQC tools.

development and introduction of PRE-control, many papers have been written in support of it, and many have been written criticizing this SQC technique. For more about the development and implementation of PRE-control, see the references in the bibliography.

8.1.1 What Are We Trying to Accomplish with PRE-control?

PRE-control is used as a mechanism to reduce the amount of sampling and inspection required to validate that a process is producing products and services consistent with customer expectations, as defined by tolerances or specifications. In many, if not most, applications, SPC (and process capability analysis) is used to validate process performance by monitoring statistically significant signals that indicate the presence or absence of variation due to assignable causes. SPC, however, does require regular sampling of rational subgroups (typically, sample sizes of five or more), and sampling, measurement, and inspection can become expensive, particularly when production volume is high. As noted in Figure 8.1, PRE-control follows the use of SPC (and process capability analysis), and it requires much less sampling, inspection, and measurement than does SPC. PRE-control, therefore, is intended to indicate process performance that is less expensive than SPC once a process has achieved long-term statistical control. However, PRE-control is not intended to be a substitute for SPC (Ledolter and Swersey 1997).

8.1.2 The Conditions Necessary for PRE-control to Be Valid

For PRE-control to be valid, a process must satisfy the following conditions:

- Be in a state of statistical control
- Be capable, as determined by a process capability analysis
- Exhibit a low defect rate

These conditions are commonly cited in professional literature. However, for PRE-control to be valid, it is necessary to further define what it means to be in statistical control, to be capable, and to have a low defect rate.

> **Definition 8.1** *Statistical control* means there are no assignable causes of variation working on the process. Note that being in a state of statistical control does *not* necessarily mean that any given process is producing products or services that meet customer expectations, as defined with a specification. In fact, it is entirely possible that a process could be in a state of statistical control (that is, have no assignable causes of variation) and not meet customer expectations, as was discussed in Chapter 6, "Process Capability Indices."

Also, as was discussed in Chapter 6, there are several PCIs, of which C_p and C_{pk} are the most commonly used. In the case where the C_p and C_{pk} ratios are one, the process variability equals the tolerance, as can be seen in Figure 8.2. Figure 8.2 illustrates what is commonly referred to as the worst case, where, as described in Chapter 6, the process is barely capable of acceptable process performance.

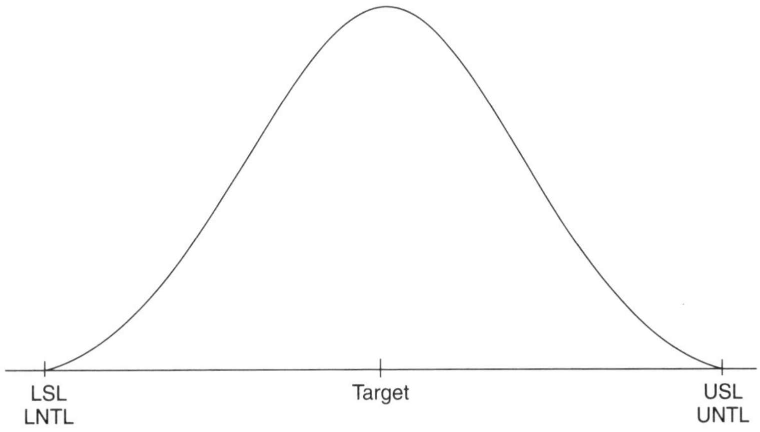

Figure 8.2 A barely capable process.

We see in Figure 8.2 that any process drift or shift will result in the production of products or services outside customer specifications or tolerances. So for PRE-control to be a valid SQC tool, the process capability ratio must be something greater than one, which means there is some room for the process to vary and yet still produce products or services that meet customer expectations. How high the PCI C_{pk} should be to make PRE-control valid is commonly defined in professional literature as 1.5, which equates to six standard deviations of variability consuming only 0.88 of the tolerance. Process capability ratios at or above two are commonly considered to be economically unjustified. And because PRE-control is valid only on processes with capability ratios at or above 1.5, and processes with capability ratios above 2 are not particularly common, PRE-control has a fairly limited range of use.

Lastly, what constitutes a low defect rate as a condition validating the use of PRE-control is a matter of debate. There are no guidelines, heuristics, or rules of thumb to qualify a process as having a low defect rate. Several publications cited in the bibliography identify the term *"near zero" defect rate* to describe the conditions necessary to validate the use of PRE-control. It is clear that whatever value is selected for a low defect rate standard, the process must be inherently stable and capable, and it must have been through enough iterations of process improvement that defects are extremely unlikely to occur.

8.2 Global Perspective on the Use of PRE-control (Understanding the Color-Coding Scheme)

PRE-control uses a color-coding scheme associated with each of six zones consistent with Figure 8.3.

Figure 8.3 shows two green zones (some authors consider there to be only one large green zone), two yellow zones, and two red zones. Because PRE-control is based on the standard normal distribution, which is a symmetrical distribution, there is one green, one yellow, and one red zone on each side of the process target (center). Whether or not intended by the originator of

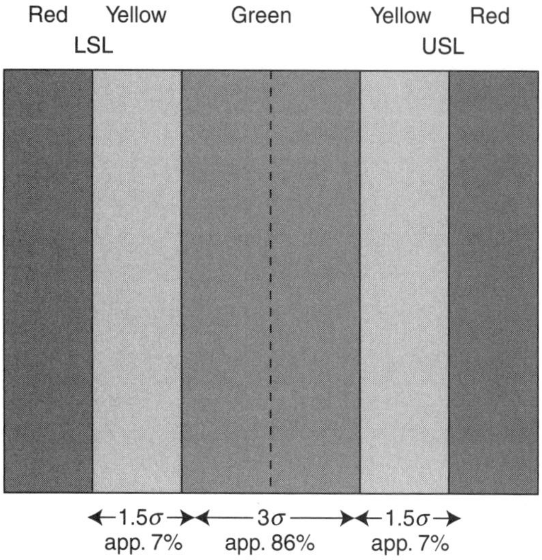

Figure 8.3 PRE-control zones.

PRE-control, these zones apply a color-coding scheme used throughout the world, as reflected in traffic-control systems.

In virtually all countries, green, yellow, and red signify for vehicular and pedestrian traffic the operational conditions of "go," "caution," and "stop," respectively. As will be discussed in the next section, green indicates that the process is performing as expected and warrants continued production. Yellow indicates a low probability of observing process behavior if the process is performing as expected; caution, along with additional sampling and testing, is warranted. Red indicates that the product or service does not conform to customer expectations, specifications, or tolerance and that the process should be stopped. This color-coding scheme is embedded in the mechanics of how we actually use PRE-control.

8.3 The Mechanics of PRE-control

Use of PRE-control is accomplished with the following steps.

Step 1: Ensure the Process Is Sufficiently Capable

Several authors advocate that for PRE-control to be valid in a worst-case situation, process capability must be equal to one. When process capability is equal to one, the process variability is exactly equal to the specification or tolerance—in this case there is no room for process drift without producing products or services that are defective. Remember from the discussion in section 8.1.2 that the process capability must be at least 1.5 (that is, process variability consumes 0.88 of the specification or tolerance) in order for the process to be a candidate for PRE-control.

Step 2: Establish the PRE-control Zones

Zones for PRE-control are established by dividing the specification or tolerance by four. Having defined four zones within the specification or tolerance, two of the zones are green and two of the zones are yellow, consistent with Figure 8.3.

Step 3: Verify That the Process Is Ready to Begin PRE-control

A process is considered ready to begin PRE-control when five consecutive pieces or service delivery iterations produce output that, when measured, fall within the green zone established in step 2. If the process is determined to be capable, as defined in step 1, and yet does not produce five consecutive pieces in the green zone established in step 2, the process is not yet a candidate for PRE-control and additional process improvements must be completed.

Step 4: Begin Sampling

Sampling for PRE-control involves pulling samples of two consecutive pieces. Frequency of sampling is based on the amount of production completed without having to adjust the process. If 25 samples are taken without having to adjust the process, sampling frequency is considered to be adequate. If the process requires adjustment prior to taking 25 samples, sampling should be conducted more frequently. Likewise, if more than 25 samples are taken before a process adjustment is required, sampling frequency can be decreased to let the process run longer before sampling.

Step 5: Apply the PRE-control Rules

Rules for the use of PRE-control are provided in Table 8.1.

Table 8.1 PRE-control rules.

Each Sample (Two Consecutive Pieces)	PRE-control Zone	Measurement Requirement	PRE-control Step to Follow
1	Green	Piece 2 not needed	Run process, step 4
1 2	Yellow Green	Measure piece 2	Run process, step 4
1 2	Yellow Yellow	Measure piece 2 Reset process Pieces 1 and 2 in same yellow zone Pieces 1 and 2 in opposite yellow zones	Step 3
1	Red	Reset process	Step 1

8.4 The Statistical Basis for PRE-control

The statistical basis for PRE-control is related to probability and the standard normal distribution (mean = 0 and standard deviation = 1). For further explanation of the standard normal distribution, refer to Chapter 7 in *Applied Statistics for the Six Sigma Green Belt.*

The statistical basis for PRE-control begins in a worst-case situation with a process capability equal to one, in which case the process variability is exactly equal to the specification or tolerance. Dividing the specification/tolerance by four establishes the boundaries for four zones, the reasons for which will be described in more detail in the next section. For now, two of the zones contained within the specification will be referred to as green zones and two will be referred to as yellow zones. Dividing the specification/tolerance, or in this case the process variability, by four creates the probability that 86 percent of the observations will fall within the green zones and 7 percent of the observations will fall within each of the yellow zones, as shown in Figure 8.3. With 7 percent of the process output falling in a single yellow zone, we have (1/14) chance of actually observing process output in a single yellow zone. With 7 percent of the process falling in each of two yellow zones (one zone on each side of the process target), we have (1/14)(1/14) = 1/196 chance of actually observing process output from the same sample falling in *both* yellow zones.

We can see in Figure 8.4 that, with a process capability equal to one, we expect to see a very small number of observations beyond the specifications/ tolerance.

8.5 Advantages and Disadvantages of PRE-control

Use of PRE-control involves balancing advantages and disadvantages. As noted earlier, PRE-control, if it is used at all, is used *after* a process is deter-

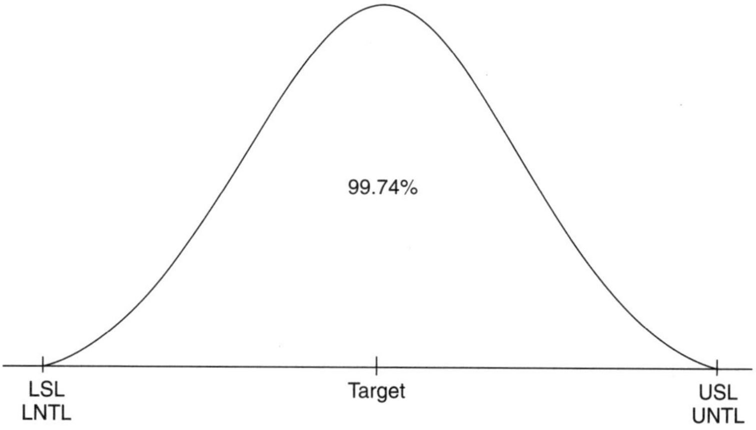

Figure 8.4 A process with process capability equal to one.

mined to be capable and operating in a state of statistical control. Additionally, PRE-control has its supporters and critics. Therefore, one must consider and balance these advantages and disadvantages prior to using PRE-control.

8.5.1 Advantages of PRE-control

Conditions may warrant the use of PRE-control, as has been discussed throughout this chapter. The following list provides the advantages of using this SQC tool:

- It is much easier for shop-floor operators to use than SPC
- There is a cost savings from reduced measurement, as compared with SPC
- The measurement devices needed to support PRE-control (go/no-go gages) are less expensive than measurement devices for continuous variables
- PRE-control does not require computation and charting, as does SPC
- PRE-control provides process performance data faster than SPC does (remember that SPC requires 25 subgroups/samples to be drawn, control limits to be calculated, and charting to be completed before any conclusions can be made about process performance)
- PRE-control is designed to ensure that defective products and services do not reach the customer (as compared with SPC, which is designed to detect assignable cause variation)

8.5.2 Disadvantages of PRE-control

PRE-control also presents certain disadvantages when compared with other SQC tools such as SPC. Montgomery (2005a, 475) summarizes these disadvantages:

- Because SPC is commonly discontinued when PRE-control begins, diagnostic information contained as patterns of assignable cause variation in control charts is lost
- Historical records of process performance (that is, records of why assignable cause variation occurred) over time are lost
- Small sample sizes with PRE-control reduce the ability to detect "even moderate-to-large shifts"
- PRE-control provides no information helpful in establishing statistical control or in reducing variability
- PRE-control is extremely sensitive to deviations from being in statistical control and being capable

- PRE-control "will likely lead to unnecessary tampering with the process"
- PRE-control will have "more false alarms or more missed signals than the control chart" (Wheeler and Chambers 1992, 82)

8.6 What Comes After PRE-control?

In Chapter 1 a point was made that the use of SQC tools should be tailored to the specific needs of a situation. This tailoring referred to how the various SQC tools are designed, implemented, and interpreted. This tailoring also referred to the use of the SQC tools relative to each other. Figure 1.1, and later Figure 8.1, was provided to help show the relationship among the SQC tools.

A quick review of Figure 8.1 reveals that use of acceptance sampling follows use of either (1) capability analysis and SPC, or (2) PRE-control. Acceptance sampling for variables and attributes is the subject of Chapter 9.

It should be noted that in order for acceptance sampling to be a valid SQC tool, there must be some objective evidence that a process is operating in a state of statistical control, is determined to be capable, and exhibits an acceptably low defect rate. It should also be noted that use of acceptance sampling may not be required to support production operations, because the consumer may elect not to use this SQC tool, perhaps in favor of mutually supportive, long-term supplier relationships based on the use of other tools, techniques, or methods.

9

Acceptance Sampling

9.1 The Intent of Acceptance Sampling

Acceptance sampling is a method for inspecting a product. Inspection can be done with screening (also called sorting, or 100 percent inspection), in which all units are inspected, or with sampling. *Acceptance sampling* is the process of inspecting a portion of the product in a lot for the purpose of making a decision regarding classification of the entire lot as either conforming or nonconforming to quality specifications.

Whether inspection is done with screening or with sampling, the results can be used for different purposes, as follows:

1. To distinguish between good lots and bad lots using acceptance sampling plans (as in incoming material inspection and final product inspection).
2. To distinguish between good products and bad products.
3. To determine the status of process control and whether the process is changing. This is usually done in conjunction with control charts.
4. To evaluate process capability. In this case, inspection is used to determine whether the process exhibits excessive variation and whether it is approaching or exceeding the specification limits.
5. To determine process adjustment. Based on inspection results of process output, as depicted by a histogram, for example, the process mean may require adjustment and/or process variation may need to be reduced. A process might require adjustment even though all the units produced to date conform to the quality standards agreed upon with the customer.

Originally published in a slightly different form in R. W. Berger, D. W. Benbow, A. K. Elshennawy, and H. F. Walker, eds., *The Certified Quality Engineer Handbook,* 2nd ed. (Milwaukee, WI: ASQ Quality Press, 2007), 190–242. Reprinted with permission.

6. To rate the accuracy of inspectors or inspection equipment by comparing the inspection results with the corresponding standards. An inspection operation can result in two types of error: classification of a conforming unit as nonconforming and classification of a nonconforming unit as conforming. The probabilities of both types of errors can be easily estimated using probability theory and other statistical methods.
7. To serve as a mechanism for evaluating vendors in terms of their products' quality. Vendors that consistently deliver high-quality products can receive preferred status involving reduced inspection and priority in bidding for new contracts, while vendors that do not stand up to quality requirements could be warned or discontinued altogether. This type of procedure is known as *vendor qualification* or *vendor certification.*

The last three uses of inspection might be seen as feedback about the production processes, the measurement processes, and the supplier.

9.2 Sampling Inspection versus 100 Percent Inspection

Sampling provides the economic advantage of lower inspection costs due to fewer units being inspected. In addition, the time required to inspect a sample is substantially less than that required for the entire lot, and there is less damage to the product due to reduced handling. Most inspectors find that selection and inspection of a random sample is less tedious and monotonous than inspection of the complete lot. Another advantage of sampling inspection is related to the supplier/customer relationship. By inspecting a small fraction of the lot and forcing the supplier to screen 100 percent in case of lot rejection (which is the case for rectifying inspection), the customer emphasizes that the supplier must be concerned with quality. On the other hand, the variability inherent in sampling results in sampling errors: rejection of lots of conforming quality and acceptance of lots of nonconforming quality.

Acceptance sampling is most appropriate when inspection costs are high and when 100 percent inspection is monotonous and can cause inspector fatigue and boredom, resulting in degraded performance and increased error rates. Obviously, sampling is the only choice available for destructive inspection. Rectifying sampling is a form of acceptance sampling. Sample units detected as nonconforming are discarded from the lot, replaced with conforming units, or repaired. Rejected lots are subject to 100 percent screening, which can involve discarding, replacing, or repairing units detected as nonconforming.

In certain situations, it is preferable to inspect 100 percent of the product. This would be the case for critical or complex products, where the cost of making the wrong decision would be too high. Screening is appropriate when the fraction nonconforming is extremely high. In this case, most of the lots would be rejected under acceptance sampling, and those accepted would be so as a result of statistical variations rather than better quality. Screening is also appropriate when the fraction nonconforming is not known and an estimate based on a large sample is needed.

9.3 Sampling Concepts

Sampling may be performed according to the type of quality characteristics to be inspected. There are three major categories of sampling plans: sampling plans for attributes, sampling plans for variables, and special sampling plans. It should be noted that acceptance sampling is not advised for processes in continuous production and in a state of statistical control. For these processes, Deming provides decision rules for selecting either 100 percent inspection or no inspection.[1]

9.3.1 Lot-by-Lot versus Average Quality Protection

For continuing processes, sampling plans based on average quality protection have characteristics calculated from the binomial and/or Poisson distributions. For processes not considered to be continuing, sampling plans based on lot-by-lot protection have characteristics calculated from the hypergeometric distribution, which takes the lot size into consideration.

Sampling plans based on the Poisson and binomial distributions are more common than those based on the hypergeometric distribution. This is due to the complexity of calculating plans based on the hypergeometric distribution. New software on personal computers, however, may eliminate this drawback.

9.3.2 The OC Curve

No matter which type of attribute sampling plan is considered, the most important evaluation tool is the OC curve.

The OC curve allows a sampling plan to be almost completely evaluated at a glance, giving a pictorial view of the probabilities of accepting lots submitted at varying levels of percent defective. The OC curve illustrates the risks involved in acceptance sampling. Figure 9.1 shows an OC curve for a sample size n of 50 drawn from an infinite lot size, with an acceptance number c of 3.

As can be seen by the OC curve, if the lot were 100 percent to specifications, the probability of acceptance P_a would also be 100 percent. But if the lot were 13.4 percent defective, there would be a 10 percent probability of acceptance. There are two types of OC curves to consider: (1) type A OC curves and (2) type B OC curves. Type A OC curves are used to calculate the probability of acceptance on a lot-by-lot basis when the lot is not a product of a continuous process. These OC curves are calculated using the hypergeometric distribution.

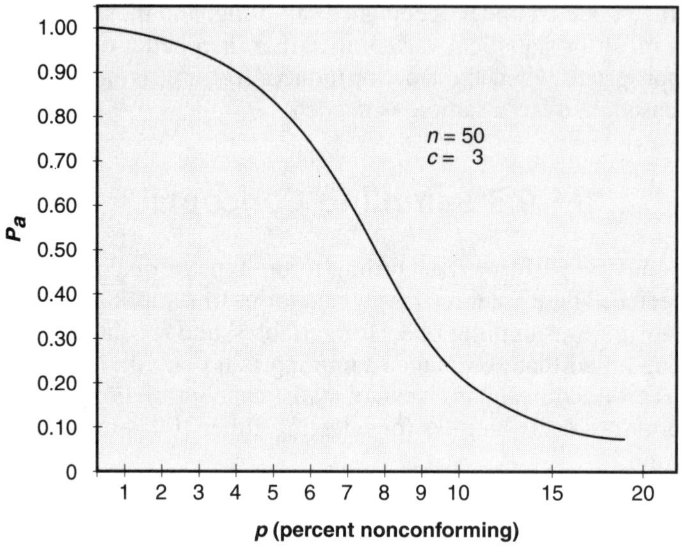

Figure 9.1 An OC curve.

Type B OC curves are used to evaluate sampling plans for a continuous process. These curves are based on the binomial and/or Poisson distributions when the requirements for usage are met. In general, the ANSI/ASQ Z1.4-2003 standard OC curves are based on the binomial distribution for sample sizes through 80 and the Poisson approximation to the binomial for sample sizes greater than 80.

9.3.3 Plotting the OC Curve

In the following examples, the points for the OC curve shown in Figure 9.1 will be calculated for products produced from a continuous process. The Poisson distribution will be used as an approximation to the binomial. The approximation is accurate if the sample size is at least 16, the population is at least 10 times the sample size, and the proportion defective is less than 0.1.[2] Because the process is continuous, the lot size is not considered during calculation. The sample size is 50, and the lot will be accepted if three or fewer nonconformances are found in the sample. To plot the OC curve, six to eight representative points for every fraction nonconforming should be used to draw the continuous curve through the points.

If the formula for the Poisson as an approximation to the binomial were used, one would be required to calculate

$$\sum_{x=0}^{r} \frac{(np)^x e^{-np}}{x!},$$

where x is the index of the summation, n is the sample size, p is the lot fraction nonconforming, and r is the number of nonconformances in the sample, for every fraction nonconforming for which a point is to be plotted. The letter c in Figure 9.1 is equivalent to r in the preceding equation.

Example 9.1 *For a sampling plan with* n = *50 and the acceptable number of nonconformances* c *is three or fewer, the following table may be constructed.*

p	np	P_a
0.01	0.50	0.998
0.02	1.00	0.981
0.03	1.50	0.934
0.05	2.50	0.758
0.07	3.50	0.537
0.08	4.00	0.433
0.09	4.50	0.342
0.10	5.00	0.265

For example, to calculate the first point, one should access Table A.6, "Poisson probabilities," in the appendix, for np = *(50) (0.01) = 0.50 and three or fewer nonconformances* c *and find a value of 0.99P* (P_a)*. Other points are calculated in the same way. These points can then be plotted, and a curve such as the one shown in Figure 9.1 can be drawn.*

Values for p (fraction defective) are chosen arbitrarily and are selected to result in a product of np that has a corresponding table value. Table A.6 lists values of 0, 1, 2, 3, . . . , n. These are the cumulative number of nonconformances. For example, the value under 0 for a given value of np is the probability of exactly zero nonconformances in the sample. This is P_a at $c = 0$ for a given value of np. The value listed under 1 is the probability of one or fewer nonconformances, the value under 2 is the probability of two or fewer nonconformances, and so on.

9.3.4 Acceptance Sampling by Attributes

Acceptance sampling by attributes is generally used for two purposes: (1) protection against accepting lots from a continuing process whose average quality deteriorates beyond an acceptable quality level, and (2) protection against isolated lots that may have levels of nonconformances greater than what can be considered acceptable. The most commonly used form of acceptance sampling plan is sampling by attributes. The most widely used standard of all attribute plans, although not necessarily the best, is ANSI/ASQ Z1.4-2003. The following sections provide more details on the characteristics of acceptance sampling and a discussion of military standards in acceptance sampling.

9.3.5 Acceptable Quality Limit

As part of the revision of ANSI/ASQC Z1.4-1993, *acceptable quality level* (AQL) has been changed to *acceptable quality limit* (AQL) in ANSI/ASQ Z1.4-2003 and is defined as the quality level that is the worst tolerable process average when a continuing series of lots is submitted for acceptance sampling. This means that a lot that has a fraction defective equal to the AQL has a high probability (generally in the area of 0.95, although it may vary) of being accepted. As a result, plans that are based on AQL, such as ANSI/ASQ Z1.4-2003, favor the producer in getting lots accepted that are in the general neighborhood of the AQL for fraction defective in a lot.

9.3.6 Lot Tolerance Percent Defective

The lot tolerance percent defective (LTPD), expressed in percent defective, is the poorest quality in an individual lot that should be accepted. The LTPD has a low probability of acceptance. In many sampling plans, the LTPD is the percent defective having a 10 percent probability of acceptance.

9.3.7 Producer's and Consumer's Risks

There are risks involved in using acceptance sampling plans. These risks are (1) producer's risk and (2) consumer's risk. These risks correspond with Type I and Type II errors in hypothesis testing. The definitions of producer's and consumer's risks are:

> *Producer's risk (α).* The producer's risk for any given sampling plan is the probability of rejecting a lot that is within the acceptable quality level.[3] This means that the producer faces the possibility (at level of significance α) of having a lot rejected even though the lot has met the requirements stipulated by the AQL level.
>
> *Consumer's risk (β).* The consumer's risk for any given sampling plan is the probability of acceptance (usually 10 percent) for a designated numerical value of relatively poor submitted quality.[4] The consumer's risk, therefore, is the probability of accepting a lot that has a quality level equal to the LTPD.

9.3.8 Average Outgoing Quality

The *average outgoing quality* (AOQ) is the expected average quality of outgoing products, including all accepted lots, plus all rejected lots that have been sorted 100 percent and have had all the nonconforming units replaced by conforming units.

There is a given AOQ for specific fractions nonconforming of submitted lots sampled under a given sampling plan. When the fraction nonconforming is very low, a large majority of the lots will be accepted as submitted. The few lots that are rejected will be sorted 100 percent and have all nonconforming units replaced with conforming units. Thus, the AOQ will always be less than the submitted quality. As the quality of submitted lots declines in relation to the AQL, the percentage of lots rejected increases in proportion to accepted lots. As these rejected lots are sorted and combined with accepted lots, an AOQ lower than the average fraction of nonconformances of submitted lots emerges. Therefore, when the level of quality of incoming lots is good, the AOQ is good; when the incoming quality is bad and most lots are rejected and sorted, the result is also good.

To calculate the AOQ for a specific fraction nonconforming and a sampling plan, the first step is to calculate the probability of accepting the lot at that level of fraction nonconforming. Then, multiply the probability of acceptance by the fraction nonconforming for the AOQ. Thus,

$$\text{AOQ} = P_a\, p[1 - (\text{sample size/lot size})].$$

If the desired result is a percentage, multiply by 100.

The average outgoing quality limit is the maximum AOQ for all possible levels of incoming quality.

9.3.9 Average Outgoing Quality Limit

The AOQ is a variable dependent on the quality level of incoming lots. When the AOQ is plotted for all possible levels of incoming quality, a curve as shown in Figure 9.2 results. The average outgoing quality limit (AOQL) is the highest value on the AOQ curve.

Assuming an infinite lot size, the AOQ may be calculated as AOQ = $P_a\, p$. Probability of acceptance (P_a) may be obtained from tables, as explained earlier, and then multiplied by p (associated value of fraction nonconforming) to produce a value for AOQ, as shown in Example 9.2, using the previous equation.

Example 9.2 *Given an OC curve points* (P_a *and* p) *as shown, construct the AOQ curve. Note that* P_a *and* p *are calculated as explained in the previous example.*

Probability of Acceptance (P_a)	Fraction Defective (p)	AOQ
0.998	0.01	0.00998
0.982	0.02	0.01964
0.937	0.03	0.02811
0.861	0.04	0.03444
0.760	0.05	0.03800
0.647	0.06	0.03882
0.533	0.07	0.03731
0.425	0.08	0.03400
0.330	0.09	0.02970
0.250	0.10	0.02500

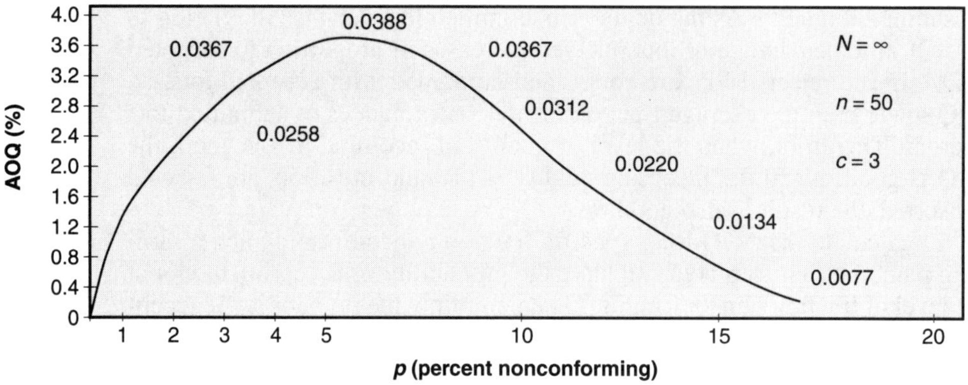

Figure 9.2 AOQ curve for $N = \infty$, $n = 50$, $c = 3$.

As can be seen, the AOQ rises until the incoming quality level of 0.06 nonconforming is reached. The maximum AOQ point is 0.03882, which is called the AOQL. This is the AOQL for an infinite lot size, sample size = 50, accept on three or fewer nonconformances.

9.3.10 Lot Size, Sample Size, and Acceptance Number

For any single sampling plan, the plan is completely described by the lot size, sample size, and acceptance number. In this section, the effect of changing the sample size, acceptance number, and lot size on the behavior of the sampling plan will be explored, along with the risks of constant percentage plans.

The effect on the OC curve caused by changing the sample size while holding all other parameters constant is shown in Figure 9.3. The probability of acceptance changes considerably as sample size changes. The P_a for the given sample sizes for a 10 percent nonconforming lot and an acceptance number of zero are shown in the following table.

Sample Size (n)	Probability of Acceptance (P_a%)
10	35
4	68
2	82
1	90

The effect of changing the acceptance number on a sampling plan while holding all other parameters constant is shown in Figure 9.4. Another point of interest is that for $c = 0$, the OC curve is concave in shape, while plans with larger acceptance numbers have a "reverse s" shape. Figure 9.4 and the following table show the effect of changing the acceptance number of a sampling plan on the indifference quality level (IQL: 50-50 chance of accepting a given percent defective).

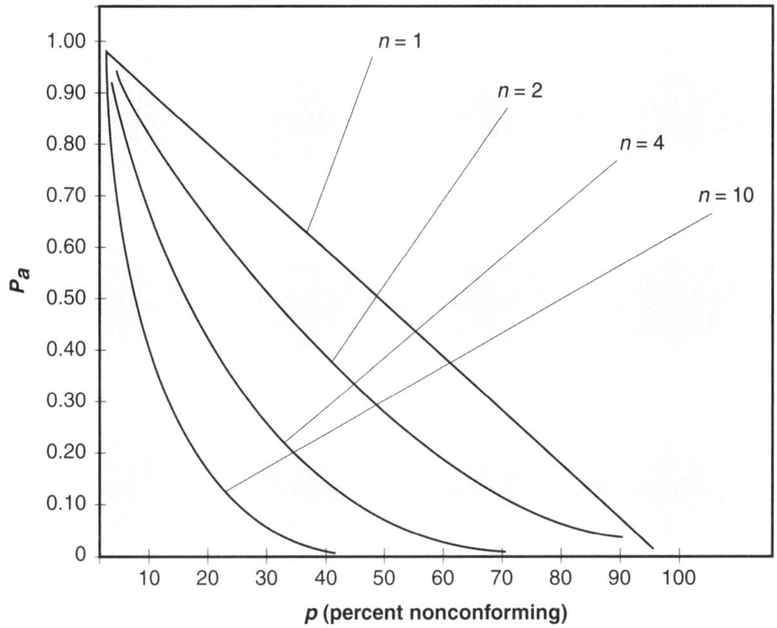

Figure 9.3 Effect on an OC curve of changing sample size (*n*) when acceptance number (*c*) is held constant.

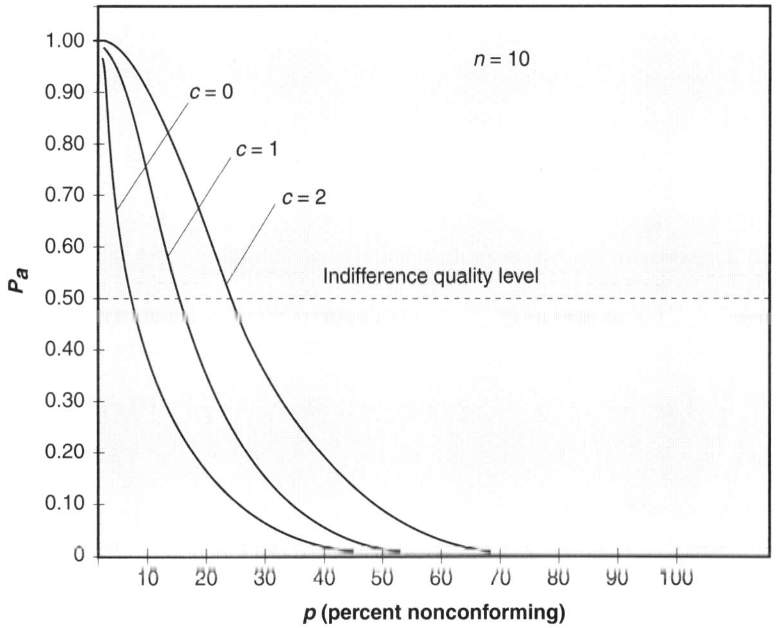

Figure 9.4 Effect of changing acceptance number (*c*) when sample size (*n*) is held constant.

Sample Size (n)	Acceptance Number (c)	Percent Defective at IQL
10	2	27
10	1	17
10	0	7

The parameter having the least effect on the OC curve is the lot size N. Figure 9.5 shows the changes in the OC curve for a sample size of 10, acceptance number of 0, and lot sizes of 100, 200, and 1000. For this reason, using the binomial and Poisson approximations, even when lot sizes are known (and are large compared with sample size), results in little error in accuracy. Some key probabilities of acceptance points for the three lot sizes follow. As can be seen, the differences due to lot size are minimal.

Fraction Defective (p)	Probability of Acceptance (P_a)	Lot Size (N)
0.10	0.330	100
0.30	0.023	100
0.50	0.001	100
0.10	0.340	200
0.30	0.026	200
0.50	0.001	200
0.10	0.347	1000
0.30	0.028	1000
0.50	0.001	1000

Computing the sample size as a percentage of the lot size has a large effect on risks and protection, as shown in Figure 9.6. In this case, plans having a sample size totaling 10 percent of the lot size are shown. As can be seen, the degree of protection changes dramatically with changes in lot size, which results in low protection for small lot sizes and gives excessively large sample requirements for large lot sizes.

9.4 Types of Attribute Sampling Plans

There are several types of attribute sampling plans in use, with the most common being single, double, multiple, and sequential sampling plans. The type of sampling plan used is determined by ease of use and administration, general quality level of incoming lots, average sample number, and so on.

9.4.1 Single Sampling Plans

When single sampling plans are used, the decision to either accept or reject the lot is based on the results of the inspection of a single sample of n items

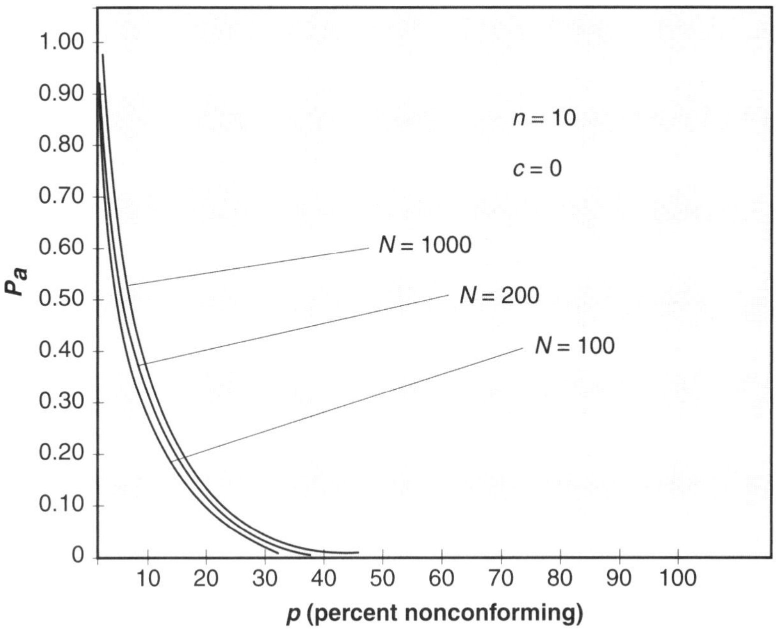

Figure 9.5 Effect of changing lot size (N) when acceptance number (c) and sample size (n) are held constant.

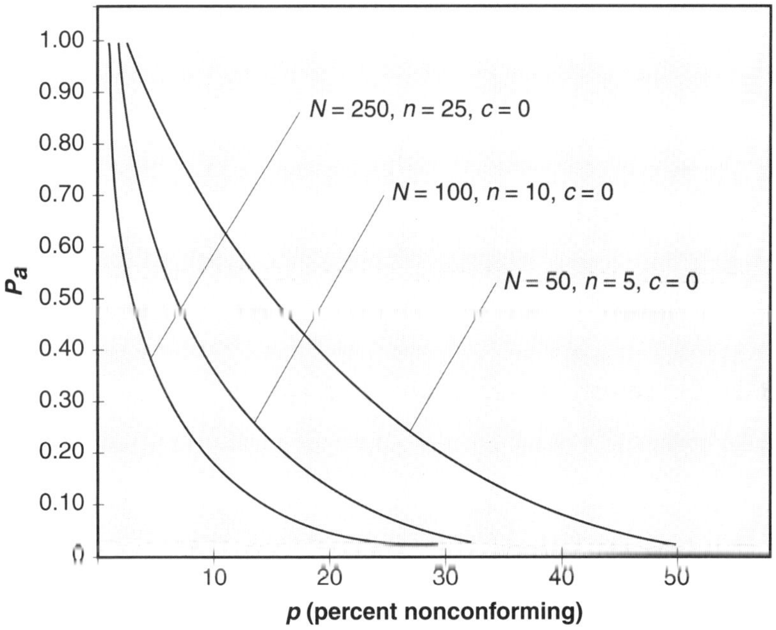

Figure 9.6 OC curves for sampling plans having the sample size equal to 10 percent of the lot size.

from a submitted lot. In the example shown earlier, the OC curve and the AOQ curve were calculated for a single sampling plan where $n = 50$ and $c = 3$. Single sampling plans have the advantage of ease of administration, but due to the unchanging sample size, they do not take advantage of the potential cost savings of reduced inspection when incoming quality is either excellent or poor.

9.4.2 Double Sampling Plans

When using double sampling plans, a smaller first sample is taken from the submitted lot, and one of three decisions is made: (1) accept the lot, (2) reject the lot, or (3) draw another sample. If a second sample is to be drawn, the lot will either be accepted or rejected after the second sample. Double sampling plans have the advantage of a lower total sample size when the incoming quality is either excellent or poor because the lot is either accepted or rejected on the first sample.

Example 9.3 *A double sampling plan is to be executed as follows: Take a first sample* (n_1) *of 75 units and set* c_1 *(the acceptance number for the first sample) = 0. The lot will be accepted based on the first sample results if no nonconformances are found in the first sample. If three nonconformances are found in the first sample, the lot will be rejected based on the first sample results. If, after analyzing the results of the first sample, one or two nonconformances are found, take a second sample* ($n_2 = 75$)*. The acceptance number for the second sample* (c_2) *is set to three. If the combined number of nonconformances in the first and second samples is three or fewer, the lot will be accepted; if the combined number of nonconformances is four or more, the lot will be rejected. The plan is represented in the following table.*

Sample Size	Acceptance Number (*c*)	Rejection Number (*r*)
$n_1 = 75$	$c_1 = 0$	$r_1 = 3$
$n_2 = 75$	$c_2 = 3$	$r_2 = 4$

9.4.3 OC Curve for a Double Sampling Plan

To calculate the OC curve for a double sampling plan, Table A.6 can again be utilized. To calculate probabilities of acceptance, some arbitrary points for p are chosen to cover the range of the OC curve. The fraction defective p is then multiplied by n_1 (the first sample) or n_2 (the second sample) to determine the expected value np.

The calculated value of np is then used with Table A.6 (as with the single sampling plan) to determine the necessary probabilities.

The generalized formula for calculating the probability of acceptance (P_a) is

$$P_a = p_0 + (p_1p_2 + p_1p_1 + p_1p_0) + (p_2p_1 + p_2p_0),$$

where

p_0 = probability of zero nonconformances in first sample

p_1p_2 = probability of one nonconformance in first sample times the probability of two nonconformances in the second sample, and so on.

Example 9.4 *For a double sampling plan where* $n_1 = 75$, $c_1 = 0$, $r_1 = 3$, $n_2 = 75$, $c_2 = 3$, *and* $r_2 = 4$, *show the computations for the OC curve.*

To determine the technique of plotting the OC curve, three points for p may be used (0.01, 0.04, and 0.08), although in practice, 6 to 10 should be used. The points for the OC curve are calculated using the generalized equation for each fraction nonconforming, selected as shown in the following table.

Generalized Equation Values	$p = 0.01$	$p = 0.04$	$p = 0.08$
p_0	0.4720	0.050	0.002
p_1p_0	0.1676	0.0075	0.00003
p_1p_1	0.1260	0.0222	0.000225
p_1p_2	0.0433	0.0334	0.000675
p_2p_0	0.0623	0.0112	0.00009
p_2p_1	0.0433	0.0334	0.000675
Totals for P_a	0.9145	0.1577	0.003695

These points are used to construct the OC curve for the double sampling plan, as shown in Figure 9.7.

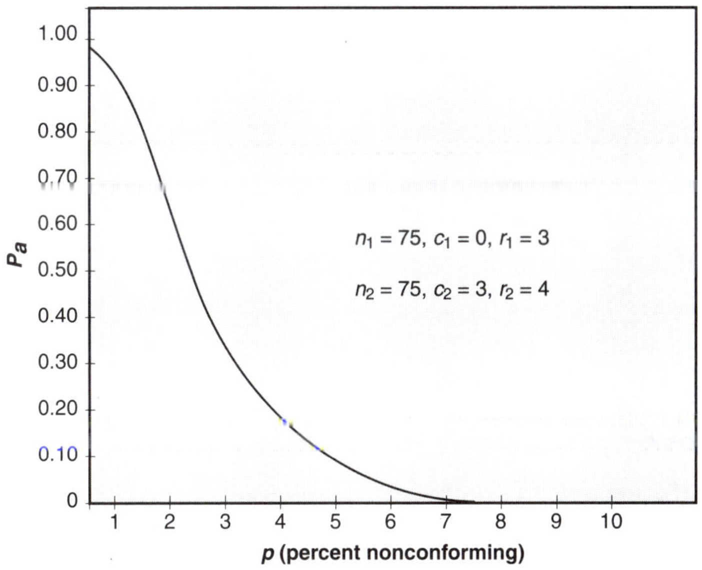

Figure 9.7 OC curve for double sampling plan where $n_1 = 75$, $c_1 = 0$, $r_1 = 3$, $n_2 = 75$, $c_2 = 3$, and $r_2 = 4$.

9.4.4 Multiple Sampling Plans

Multiple sampling plans work in the same way as double sampling plans but with an extension of the number of samples to be taken up to seven, according to ANSI/ASQ Z1.4-2003. In the same manner that double sampling is performed, acceptance or rejection of submitted lots may be reached before the seventh sample, depending on the acceptance/rejection criteria established for the plan.

9.4.5 AOQ and AOQL for Double and Multiple Plans

The AOQ curve and AOQL for double and multiple sampling plans are plotted and determined in the same manner as single sampling plans. An AOQ curve for a double sampling plan is shown in Figure 9.8, and the AOQL is approximately 1.3 percent.

9.4.6 Average Sample Number

The average sample number (ASN) is a determination of the expected average amount of inspection per lot for a given sampling plan. The ASN for single sampling plans is a constant value that is equal to the single sample size for the plan. The ASN for double sampling plans is the sum of the first sample size plus the second sample size times the probability that a second sample will be required. The ASN is also a function of fraction nonconforming when working with a double sampling plan. The double sampling plan ASN formula is

$$\text{ASN} = n_1 + n_2(P_2),$$

where

n_1 = size of first sample,

n_2 = size of second sample,

P_2 = probability of requiring a second sample.

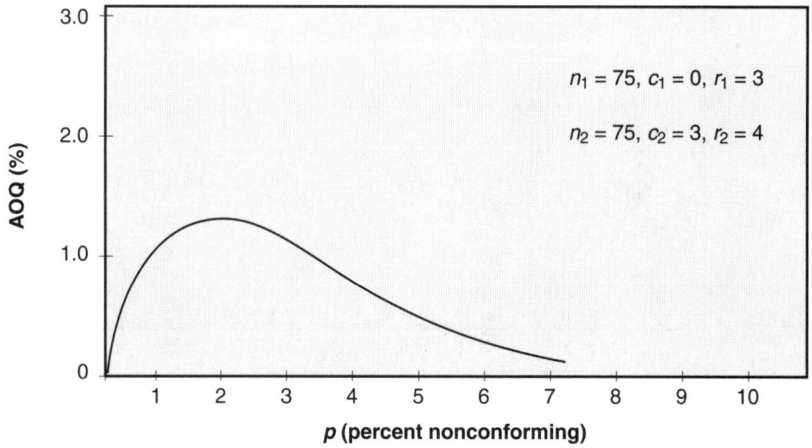

Figure 9.8 AOQ curve for double sampling plan.

Example 9.5 *The double sampling plan in the earlier section was*

$$n_1 = 75, \qquad c_1 = 0, \qquad r_1 = 3,$$

$$n_2 = 75, \qquad c_2 = 3, \qquad r_2 = 4.$$

- A second sample is required if, on the first sample, one or two nonconformances are noted
- If zero nonconformances are found in the first sample, the lot is accepted
- If three or more nonconformances are found in the first sample, the lot is rejected

Denote the probability of making a decision, accept or reject, on the first sample as $P(D_1)$*. Then,*

$$P(D_1) = P(0) + P\text{ (3 or more)},$$

$P(0)$ = The probability of 0 nonconformances on the first sample,

P (3 or more) = The probability of 3 or more nonconformances on the first sample,

$$P_2 = 1 - P(D_1), \text{ then ASN} = n_1 + n_2(P_2).$$

When using Table A.6 to calculate the probability of three or more nonconformances, remember that the probability is given by

(1 – probability of 2 or fewer nonconformances) in the sample.

The ASN will be plotted for several values of fraction nonconforming p*, and an ASN curve will be plotted. An example of the ASN calculation for the fraction nonconforming* p = *0.01 is shown in the following equation. Several other points need to be plotted for other values of* p*. Figure 9.9 shows an ASN curve for the example.*

When p = *0.01:*

$P(0)$ = Probability of 0 nonconformances in sample = 0.4724,

P (3 or more) = Probability of 3 or more nonconformances in sample = 0.0410,

$P(D_1)$ = Probability of a decision on the first sample (using the preceding equation) = 0.4724 + 0.0410 = 0.5134,

Then P_2 = Probability of requiring a second sample = 1 – 0.5134 = 0.4866.

Thus, the ASN is:

$$\text{ASN}(0.01) = \text{Average sample number for a lot quality } p = 0.01$$

$$= n_1 + n_2\,(P_2)$$

$$= 75 + 75\,(0.4866) = 111.50 \text{ or } 112.$$

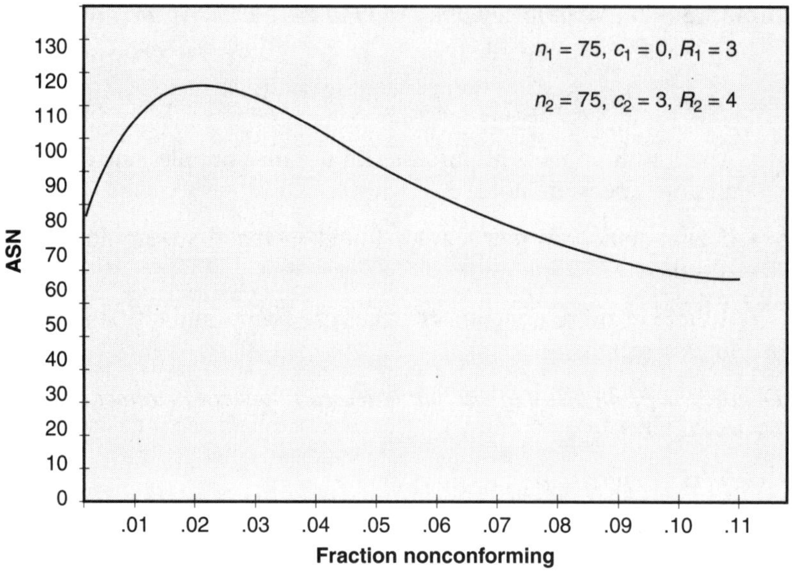

Figure 9.9 ASN curve for double sampling plan.

Values of ASN at different p *values (ASNp) may be calculated in a similar way, and the results are given in the following list. All values are rounded to the next highest integer.*

ASN(0.01) = 112	ASN(0.06) = 87
ASN(0.02) = 120	ASN(0.07) = 82
ASN(0.03) = 113	ASN(0.08) = 79
ASN(0.04) = 103	ASN(0.09) = 78
ASN(0.05) = 94	ASN(0.1) = 77

When comparing sampling plans with equal protection, double sampling plans will generally result in smaller average sample sizes when quality is excellent or poor. When quality is near the indifference level, double sampling plans could rarely result in greater ASN.

9.5 Sampling Standards and Plans

9.5.1 ANSI/ASQ Z1.4-2003

ANSI/ASQ Z1.4-2003 is a revision of ANSI/ASQC Z1.4-1993 that includes the following changes:[5]

1. Acceptable quality level (AQL) has been changed to acceptable quality limit (AQL).
2. The definition and explanation of AQL have been changed (see item 1 in this list).

3. The discontinuation of inspection rule has been changed. See later sections in this chapter.

4. ANSI/ASQC A2-1987 has been changed to ANSI/ASQ A3534-2-1993.

5. ANSI/ASQC Q3 has been changed to ASQC Q3-1988.

Other than these changes and changes to the footnotes of some tables, all tables, table numbers, and procedures used in MIL-STD-105E (which was canceled in 1995) and ANSI/ASQC Z1.4-1993 have been retained.

ANSI/ASQ Z1.4-2003 is probably the most commonly used standard for attribute sampling plans, but its wide recognition and acceptance could be due to government contracts stipulating the standard rather than its statistical importance. Producers submitting products at a nonconformance level within AQL have a high probability of having the lot accepted by the customer.

When using ANSI/ASQ Z1.4-2003, the characteristics under consideration should be classified. The general classifications are critical, major, and minor defects:

- A *critical defect* is a defect that judgment and experience indicate is likely to result in hazardous or unsafe conditions for the individuals using, maintaining, or depending on the product; or it is a defect that judgment and experience indicate is likely to prevent performance of the unit. In practice, critical characteristics are commonly inspected to an AQL level of 0.40 to 0.65 percent, if not 100 percent inspected. One hundred percent inspection is recommended for critical characteristics if possible. Acceptance numbers are always zero for critical defects.

- A *major defect* is a defect other than critical that is likely to result in failure or to reduce materially the usability of the unit of product for its intended purpose. In practice, AQL levels for major defects are generally about 1 percent.

- A *minor defect* is a defect that is not likely to reduce materially the usability of the unit of product for its intended purpose. In practice, AQL levels for minor defects generally range from 1.5 percent to 2.5 percent.

9.5.2 Levels of Inspection

There are seven levels of inspection used in ANSI/ASQ Z1.4-2003: reduced inspection, normal inspection, tightened inspection, and four levels of special inspection. The special inspection levels should be used only when small sample sizes are necessary and large risks can be tolerated. When using ANSI/ASQ Z1.4-2003, a set of switching rules must be followed as to the use of reduced, normal, and tightened inspection.

The following guidelines are taken from ANSI/ASQ Z1.4-2003:

Initiation of inspection. Normal inspection Level II will be used at the start of inspection unless otherwise directed by the responsible authority.

Continuation of inspection. Normal, tightened, or reduced inspection shall continue unchanged for each class of defect or defectives on successive lots or batches except where the following switching procedures require change. The switching procedures shall be applied to each class of defects or defectives independently.

Switching procedures. Switching rules are graphically shown in Figure 9.10.

Normal to tightened. When normal inspection is in effect, tightened inspection shall be instituted when two out of five consecutive lots or batches have been rejected on original inspection (that is, ignoring resubmitted lots or batches for this procedure).

Tightened to normal. When tightened inspection is in effect, normal inspection shall be instituted when five consecutive lots or batches have been considered acceptable on original inspection.

Normal to reduced. When normal inspection is in effect, reduced inspection shall be instituted providing that all of the following conditions are satisfied:

a. The preceding 10 lots or batches (or more), as indicated by the note on ANSI/ASQ Z1.4-2003 Table VIII, also shown as Figure 9.13 at the end of this chapter, have been on normal inspection and none have been rejected on original inspection.

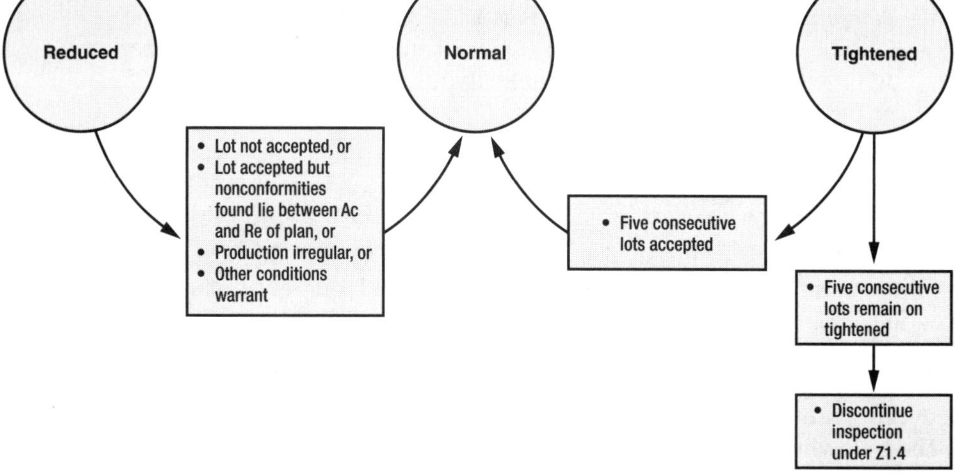

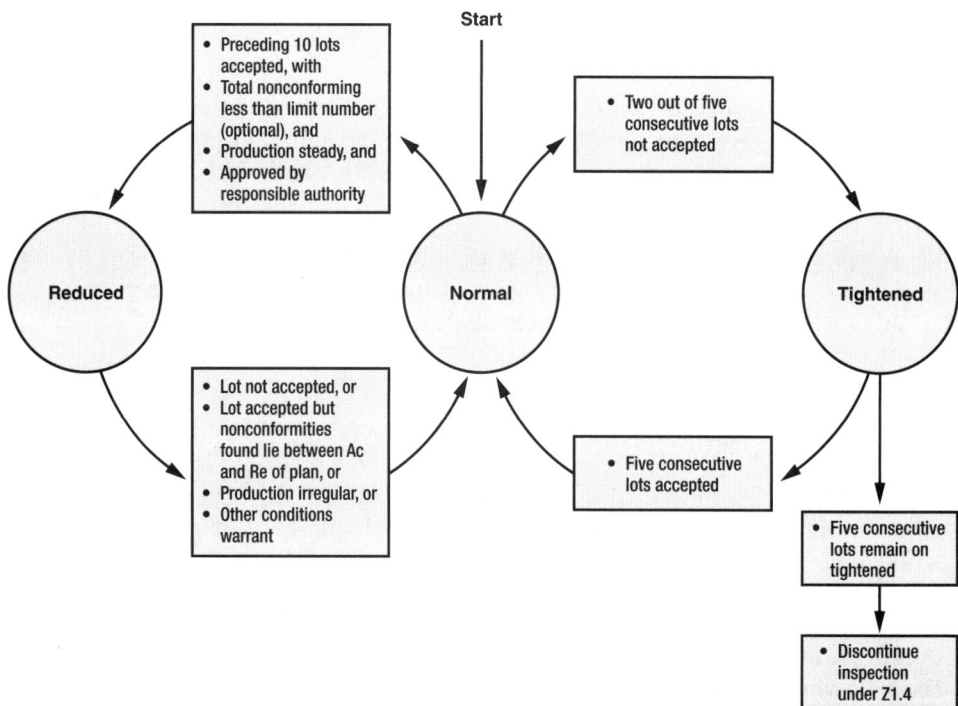

Figure 9.10 Switching rules for normal, tightened, and reduced inspection.

b. The total number of defectives (or defects) in the sample from the preceding 10 lots or batches (or such other number as was used for condition (a)) is equal to or less than the applicable number given in Table VIII of ANSI/ASQ Z1.4-2003 (shown as Figure 9.13 at the end of this chapter). If double or multiple sampling is in use, all samples inspected should be included, not first samples only.

c. Production is at a steady rate.

d. Reduced inspection is considered desirable by the responsible authority.

Reduced to normal. When reduced inspection is in effect, normal inspection shall be instituted if any of the following occur on original inspection:

a. A lot or batch is rejected.

b. A lot or batch is considered acceptable under reduced inspection but the sampling procedures terminated without either acceptance or rejection criteria having been met. In these circumstances, the lot or batch will be considered acceptable, but normal inspection will be reinstated starting with the new lot or batch.

c. Production becomes irregular or delayed.

d. Other conditions warrant that normal inspection shall be instituted.

Discontinuation of inspection. If the cumulative number of lots not accepted in a sequence of consecutive lots on tightened inspection reaches five, the acceptance procedures of this standard shall be discontinued. Inspection under the provisions of this standard shall not be resumed until corrective action has been taken. Tightened inspection shall then be used as "normal to tightened."

9.5.3 Types of Sampling

ANSI/ASQ Z1.4-2003 allows for three types of sampling:

1. Single sampling
2. Double sampling
3. Multiple sampling

The choice of the type of plan depends on many variables. Single sampling is the easiest to administer and perform, but it usually results in the largest average total inspection (ATI). Double sampling results in a lower ATI than single sampling, but it requires more decisions to be made, such as:

- Accept the lot after the first sample
- Reject the lot after the first sample
- Take a second sample

- Accept the lot after the second sample
- Reject the lot after the second sample

Multiple sampling plans further reduce the ATI, but they also increase the number of decisions to be made. As many as seven samples may be required before a decision to accept or reject the lot can be made. This type of plan requires the most administration.

A general procedure for selecting plans from ANSI/ASQ Z1.4-2003 is as follows:

1. Decide on an AQL.
2. Decide on the inspection level.
3. Determine the lot size.
4. Find the appropriate sample size code letter. See Table I from ANSI/ASQ Z1.4-2003, also shown as Figure 9.14 at the end of this chapter.
5. Determine the type of sampling plan to be used: single, double, or multiple.
6. Using the selected AQL and sample size code letter, enter the appropriate table to find the desired plan to be used.
7. Determine the normal, tightened, and reduced plans as required from the corresponding tables.

Example 9.6 *A lot of 1750 parts has been received and is to be checked to an AQL level of 1.5 percent. Determine the appropriate single, double, and multiple sampling plans for general inspection Level II.*

Steps to define the plans are as follows:

4.1 Using Table I on page 10 of ANSI/ASQ Z1.4-2003, also shown as Figure 9.14 at the end of this chapter, stipulates code letter K.

4.2 Normal inspection is applied. For code letter K, using Table II-A of ANSI/ASQ Z1.4-2003 on page 11 of the standard, also shown as Figure 9.15 at the end of this chapter, a sample of 125 is specified.

4.3 For double sampling, two samples of 80 may be required. Refer to Table III-A on page 14 of the standard, shown as Figure 9.16 at the end of this chapter.

4.4 For multiple sampling, at least two samples of 32 are required and it may take up to seven samples of 32 before an acceptance or rejection decision is made. Refer to Table IV-A on page 17 of the standard, shown as Figure 9.17 at the end of this chapter.

A breakdown of all three plans follows:

Sampling Plan		Sample(s) Size	Ac	Re
Single sampling		125	5	6
Double sampling	First	80	2	5
	Second	80	6	7
Multiple sampling	First	32	*	4
	Second	32	1	5
	Third	32	2	6
	Fourth	32	3	7
	Fifth	32	5	8
	Sixth	32	7	9
	Seventh	32	9	10

Ac = acceptance number (Ac)
Re = rejection number (Re)
* Acceptance not permitted at this sample size.

9.5.4 Dodge-Romig Tables

Dodge-Romig tables were designed as sampling plans to minimize ATI. These plans require an accurate estimate of the process average nonconforming in selection of the sampling plan to be used. The Dodge-Romig tables use the AOQL and LTPD values for plan selection rather than AQL as in ANSI/ASQ Z1.4-2003. When the process average nonconforming is controlled to requirements, Dodge-Romig tables result in lower ATI, but rejection of lots and sorting tend to minimize the gains if process quality deteriorates.

Note that if the process average nonconforming shows statistical control, acceptance sampling should not be used. The most economical course of action in this situation is either no inspection or 100 percent inspection.[6]

9.6 Variables Sampling Plans

Variables sampling plans use the actual measurements of sample products for decision making rather than classifying products as conforming or nonconforming, as in attribute sampling plans. Variables sampling plans are more complex in administration than attribute plans, thus they require more skill. They provide some benefits, however, over attribute plans:

1. Equal protection to an attribute sampling plan with a much smaller sample size. There are several types of variables sampling plans in use, three of these being the following: (1) σ known; (2) σ unknown but can be estimated using sample standard deviation s;

and (3) σ unknown and the range R is used as an estimator. If an attribute sampling plan sample size is determined, the variables plans previously listed can be compared as a percentage to the attribute plan.

Plan	Sample Size (percent)
Attribute	100
σ unknown, range method	60
σ unknown, s estimated from sample	40
σ known	15

2. Variables sampling plans allow the determination of how close to nominal or a specification limit the process is performing. Attribute plans either accept or reject a lot; variables plans give information on how well or poorly the process is performing.

Variables sampling plans, such as ANSI/ASQ Z1.9-2003, have some disadvantages and limitations:

1. The assumption of normality of the population from which the samples are being drawn
2. Unlike attribute sampling plans, separate characteristics on the same parts will have different averages and dispersions, resulting in a separate sampling plan for each characteristic
3. Variables plans are more complex in administration
4. Variables gauging is generally more expensive than attribute gauging

9.6.1 ANSI/ASQ Z1.9-2003

ANSI/ASQ Z1.9-2003 is a revision of ANSI/ASQC Z1.9-1993 that includes changing the term *acceptable quality level* (AQL) to *acceptable quality limit* (AQL), changing the definition and explanation of AQL, and changing the discontinuation of inspection rule, as explained previously in the ANSI/ASQ Z1.4-2003.

The most common standard for variables sampling plans is ANSI/ASQ Z1.9-2003, which has plans for (1) variability known, (2) variability unknown—standard deviation method, and (3) variability unknown—range method. Using the aforementioned methods, this sampling plan can be used to test for a single specification limit, a double (or bilateral) specification limit, estimation of the process average, and estimation of the dispersion of the parent population.

As in ANSI/ASQ Z1.4-2003, several AQL levels are used, and specific switching procedures for normal, reduced, or tightened inspection are followed. ANSI/ASQ Z1.9-2003 allows for the same AQL value for each specification limit of double specification limit plans or the use of different AQL values for each specification limit. The AQL values are designated ML for the LSL and MU for the USL.

There are two forms used for every specification limit ANSI/ASQ Z1.9-2003 plan: Form 1 and Form 2. Form 1 provides only acceptance or rejection criteria, whereas Form 2 estimates the percent below the LSL and the percent above the USL. These percentages are compared with the AQL for acceptance/rejection criteria. Figure 9.11 summarizes the structure and organization of ANSI/ASQ Z1.9-2003.

There are 14 AQL levels used in ANSI/ASQ Z1.9-2003 that are consistent with the AQL levels used in ANSI/ASQ Z1.4-2003. Section A of ANSI/ASQ Z1.9-2003 contains both an AQL conversion table and a table for selecting the desired inspection level. Inspection Level II should be used unless otherwise specified. See Section A7.1 of the standard for further information about levels.

Table A-3 on page 7 of ANSI/ASQ Z1.9-2003 contains the OC curves for the sampling plans in Sections B, C, and D.

Section B contains sampling plans used when the variability is unknown and the standard deviation method is used. Part I is used for a single specification limit, Part II is used for a double specification limit, and Part III is used for estimation of process average and criteria for reduced and tightened inspection.

Section C contains sampling plans used when the variability is unknown and the range method is used. Parts I, II, and III are the same as Parts I, II, and III in Section B.

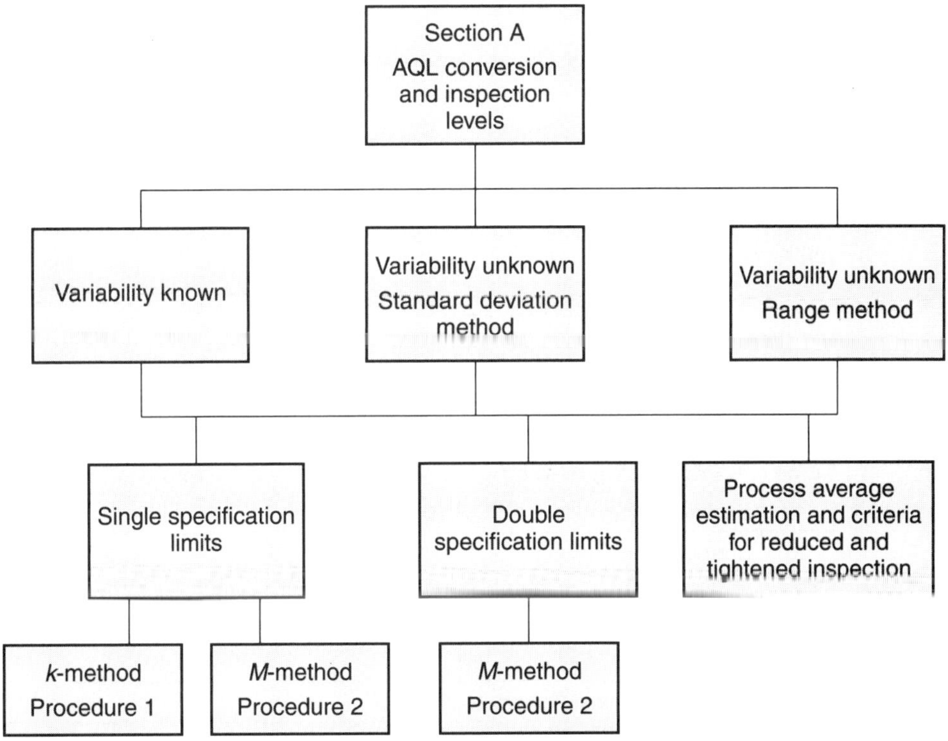

Figure 9.11 Structure and organization of ANSI/ASQ Z1.9-2003.

Section D contains sampling plans used when variability is known. Parts I, II, and III are the same as Parts I, II, and III in Section B.

9.6.1.1 Variability Unknown—Range Method

An example from Section C is used here to illustrate the use of the variability unknown—range method for a single specification limit. The quality indices for a single specification limit are

$$\frac{\left(U-\bar{X}\right)}{\bar{R}} \text{ or } \frac{\left(\bar{X}-L\right)}{\bar{R}},$$

where

U = upper specification limit
L = lower specification limit
$\bar{X}$ = sample average
$\bar{R}$ = average range of the sample

The acceptance criterion is a comparison of the quality $(U - \bar{X})/\bar{R}$ or $(\bar{X} - L)/\bar{R}$ to the acceptability constant k. If the calculated quantity is equal to or greater than k, the lot is accepted; if the calculated quantity is negative or less than k, the lot is rejected.

The following example illustrates the use of the variability unknown—range method, Form I variables sampling plan and is similar to examples from Section C of ANSI/ASQ Z1.9-2003.

Example 9.7 *The LSL for electrical resistance of a certain electrical component is 620 ohms. A lot of 100 items is submitted for inspection. Inspection Level IV, normal inspection, with AQL = 0.4 percent, is to be used. From ANSI/ASQ Z1.9-2003 Table A-2 and Table C-1, shown at the end of this chapter as Figure 9.18 and Figure 9.19, respectively, it is seen that a sample size of 10 is required. Suppose that values of the sample resistances (reading from left to right) are:*

$$645, 651, 621, 625, 658 \ (R = 658 - 621 = 37),$$

$$670, 673, 641, 638, 650 \ (R = 673 - 638 = 35).$$

Determine compliance with the acceptability criterion.

Line	Information Needed	Value	Explanation
1.	Sample size: n	10	
2.	Sum of measurement: ΣX	6472	
3.	Sample mean $\bar{X}$: $\Sigma X/n$	647.2	6472/10
4.	Average range $\bar{R}$: R/no. of subgroups	36	(37 + 35)/2
5.	Specification limit (lower): L	620	
6.	The quantity: $(\bar{X} - L)/\bar{R}$	.756	(647.2 – 620)/36

7.	Acceptability constant: *k*	.811	See Table C-1 (Figure 9.19 at the end of this chapter)
8.	Acceptability criterion: compare $(\bar{X} - L)/\bar{R}$ with *k*	.756 ≤ .811	

The lot does not meet the acceptability criterion, because $(\bar{X} - L)/\bar{R}$ *is less than* k.

Note: If a single USL U is given, then compute the quantity $(U - \bar{X})/\bar{R}$ *in line 6 and compare it with* k. *The lot meets the acceptability criterion if* $(U - \bar{X})/\bar{R}$ *is equal to or greater than* k.

9.6.1.2 Variability Unknown—Standard Deviation Method

In this section, a sampling plan is shown for the situation where the variability is not known and the standard deviation is estimated from the sample data. The sampling plan will be that for a double specification limit, and it is found in Section B of the standard with one AQL value for both upper and lower specification limits combined.

The acceptability criterion is based on comparing an estimated percent nonconforming with a maximum allowable percent nonconforming for the given AQL level. The estimated percent nonconforming is found in ANSI/ASQ Z1.9-2003 Table B-5, shown as Figure 9.20 at the end of this chapter.

The quality indices for this sampling plan are

$$Q_U = \frac{U - \bar{X}}{s} \text{ and } Q_L = \frac{\bar{X} - L}{s},$$

where

U = upper specification limit
L = lower specification limit
$\bar{X}$ = sample mean
s = estimate of lot standard deviation

The quality level of the lot is in terms of the lot percent defective. Three values are calculated: P_U, P_L, and p. P_U is an estimate of conformance with the USL; P_L is an estimate of conformance with the LSL; and p is the sum of P_U and P_L.

The value of p is then compared with the maximum allowable percent defective. If p is less than or equal to M (ANSI/ASQ Z1.9-2003 Table B-5, shown as Figure 9.20 at the end of this chapter), or if either Q_U or Q_L is negative, the lot is rejected. The following example illustrates the preceding procedure.

Example 9.8 *The minimum temperature of operation for a certain device is specified as 180°F. The maximum temperature is 209°F. A lot of 40 items is submitted for inspection. Inspection Level IV, normal inspection with*

AQL = 1 percent, is to be used. ANSI/ASQ Z1.9-2003 Table A-2, shown as Figure 9.18 at the end of this chapter, gives code letter D, which results in a sample size of five from ANSI/ASQC Z1.9-2003 Table B-3, shown as Figure 9.21 at the end of this chapter. The results of the five measurements in degrees Fahrenheit are as follows: 197, 188, 184, 205, and 201. Determine if the lot meets acceptance criteria.

	Information Needed	Value Obtained	Explanation
1.	Sample size: n	5	
2.	Sum of measurements: ΣX	975	
3.	Sum of squared measurements: ΣX^2	190,435	
4.	Correction factor: $(\Sigma X)^2/n$	190,125	9752/5
5.	Corrected sum of squares (SS): $\Sigma X^2 - CF$	310	190,435 – 190,125
6.	Variance (V): SS/(n – 1)	77.5	310/4
7.	Standard deviation s: $\sqrt{v}$	8.81	$\sqrt{77.5}$
8.	Sample mean $\bar{X}$: $\Sigma X/n$	195	975/5
9.	Upper specification limit: U	209	
10.	Lower specification limit: L	180	
11.	Quality index: $Q_U = (U - \bar{X})/s$	1.59	(209 – 195)/8.81
12.	Quality index: $Q_L = (\bar{X} - L)/s$	1.7	(195 – 180)/8.81
13.	Estimate of lot percent defective above U: P_U	2.19%	See Table B-5 (Figure 9.20 at the end of this chapter)
14.	Estimate of lot percent defective below L: P_L	0.66%	See Table B-5 (Figure 9.20 at the end of this chapter)
15.	Total estimate of percent defective in lot: $p = P_U + P_L$	2.85%	2.19 + 0.66
16.	Maximum allowable percent defective: M	3.32%	See Table B-3 (Figure 9.21 at the end of this chapter)
17.	Acceptability criterion: compare $p = P_U + P_L$ with M.	2.85% < 3.32%	

The lot meets the acceptability criterion because p = $P_U + P_L$ *is less than* M.

ANSI/ASQ Z1.9-2003 provides a variety of other examples for variables sampling plans.

9.7 Sequential Sampling Plans

When tests are either destructive in nature or costly, it may be advantageous to use sequential sampling plans popularized by Wald.[7] These plans have the advantage of greatly reduced sample sizes while giving good protection.

To determine a sequential sampling plan, the following parameters must be defined:

$$\alpha = \text{producer's risk}$$

$$\text{AQL} = \text{acceptable quality level} = p_1$$

$$\beta = \text{consumer's risk}$$

$$\text{RQL} = \text{rejectable (or unacceptable) quality level} = p_2$$

The following example uses $\alpha = 0.05$, AQL = 0.05, $\beta = 0.1$, and RQL = 0.2. This results in a plan that will have a 5 percent chance of rejecting a lot that is 5 percent nonconforming and a 10 percent chance of accepting a lot that is 20 percent nonconforming.

Figure 9.12 shows the accept, reject, and continue testing areas for a sequential sampling plan. The *y* axis represents the number of nonconforming units in the sample, and the *x* axis scales the number of units inspected.

The equations for the acceptance and rejection zone lines are

$$\text{Reject zone line} = sn + h_2,$$

$$\text{Accept zone line} = sn - h_1,$$

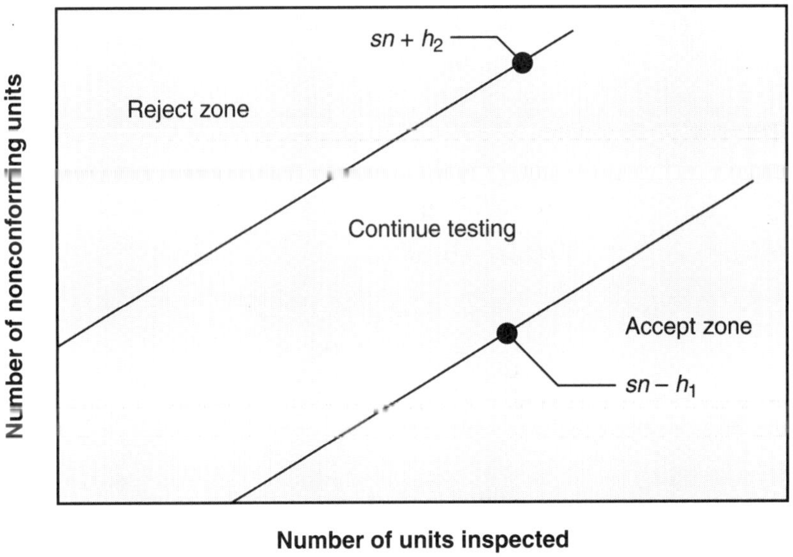

Figure 9.12 Decision areas for a sequential sampling plan.

where

n = sample size,

$$h_1 = \frac{b}{\log \frac{p_2(1-p_1)}{p_1(1-p_2)}},$$

$$h_2 = \frac{a}{\log \frac{p_2(1-p_1)}{p_1(1-p_2)}},$$

$$s = \frac{\log[(1-p_1)/(1-p_2)]}{\log \frac{p_2(1-p_1)}{p_1(1-p_2)}},$$

$$a = \log \frac{(1-\beta)}{\alpha},$$

$$b = \log \frac{(1-\alpha)}{\beta}.$$

Example 9.9 *Assume that the following values are desired for a sequential sampling plan:*

$$\alpha = 0.05,\ p_1\ (\text{AQL}) = 0.05,$$

$$\beta = 0.1,\ p_2\ (\text{RQL}) = 0.2.$$

Then:

$$a = \log \frac{1-0.10}{0.05} = 1.2553,$$

$$b = \log \frac{1-0.05}{0.10} = 0.9777,$$

$$s = \log \frac{\log[(1-0.05)/(1-0.20)]}{\log \frac{0.20(1-0.05)}{0.05(1-0.20)}} = 0.1103,$$

$$h_1 = \frac{0.9777}{\log \frac{0.20(1-0.05)}{0.05(1-0.20)}} = 1.4448,$$

$$h_2 = \frac{1.2553}{\log \frac{0.20(1-0.05)}{0.05(1-0.20)}} = 1.855.$$

$$\text{Reject line} = sn + h_2 = (0.1103)(n) + 1.855,$$

$$\text{Accept line} = sn - h_1 = (0.1103)(n) - 1.4448.$$

Points for Accept and Reject Lines*					
n	Acceptance Number	Rejection Number	*n*	Acceptance Number	Rejection Number
1	A	B	14	0	4
2	A	B	20	0	5
3	A	3	24	1	5
4	A	3	40	2	7
5	A	3	50	4	8
6	A	3			

* Accept values are rounded down to the nearest integer.
Note A: Acceptance not possible when acceptance number is negative.
Note B: Rejection not possible when rejection number is greater than sample number.

As can be seen by the preceding plan, rejecting the lot is not possible until the 3rd sample unit, and accepting the lot is withheld until the 14th sample unit.

9.8 Continuous Sampling Plans

Many production processes do not produce lots, and thus lot-by-lot acceptance sampling plans discussed earlier cannot be applied. In cases such as these, continuous sampling plans are developed. In continuous sampling plans, 100 percent inspection and sampling inspection are alternately applied. The most recent standard for developing continuous sampling plans is the MIL-STD-1235B.

Continuous sampling plans are characterized by two parameters: i is called the clearance number or the number of conforming units under 100 percent inspection, and f is the ratio of the units inspected to the total number of units produced or passing through the inspection station.

9.8.1 Types of Continuous Sampling Plans

There are two different standards for continuous sampling plans:

1. *Dodge's continuous sampling plans.* These include CSP-1 and CSP-2 sampling plans. These plans take AOQL as an index. That is, for every AOQL value, there are different combinations of i and f.

2. *MIL-STD-1235B.* These plans are selected using a sample size code letter and an AQL value. The standard includes CSP-1, CSP-2, CSP-F, CSP-T, and CSP-V plans.

9.8.1.1 Dodge's Continuous Sampling Plans

Dodge's CSP-1 continuous sampling plans operate as follows for a selected AOQL value:

1. Start with 100 percent inspection
2. When i (clearance number) consecutive number of units are found free from nonconformities, 100 percent inspection is then substituted with sampling inspection
   2.1. A fraction of f units is randomly selected and then inspected
      2.1.1. If one nonconformity is found, the 100 percent inspection procedure is to restart again and the cycle is repeated

Dodge's CSP-2 continuous sampling plans operate as follows for a selected value of AOQL:

1. Start with 100 percent inspection
2. When i (clearance number) consecutive number of units are found free from nonconformities, 100 percent inspection is then substituted with sampling inspection
   2.1. A fraction of f units is randomly selected and then inspected
      2.1.1. If one nonconformity is found, the sampling inspection continues and the following procedure (2.1.2) is initiated
      2.1.2. The number of conforming units (after finding the nonconformity) is counted
         2.1.2.1. If i consecutive number are found free of nonconformities, sampling inspection continues
         2.1.2.2. If one nonconformity is found, 100 percent inspection is reinstated

9.8.1.2 MIL-STD-1235B

The standard uses the same parameters, i and f, as previously defined. The standard includes CSP-1, CSP-2, CSP-F, CSP-T, and CSP-V plans.

CSP-1 and CSP-2 plans operate in the same way as Dodge's CSP-1 and CSP-2 plans, but they are selected based on a sample size code letter and an AQL value as a quality index. The sample size code letter is selected based on the number of units in the production interval.

CSP-F plans work the same way as CSP-1 plans, providing alternate sequences of 100 percent and sampling inspection procedures, but the difference is that AOQL and the number of units in the production interval are used in this case to characterize the plans. Once AOQL and f values are selected, go to the corresponding table to read i, the clearance number. CSP-F is a single-level continuous sampling scheme.

CSP-T plans provide reduced sampling frequency once the product shows superior quality. The CSP-T plan works as follows:

1. Start with 100 percent inspection
2. When i (clearance number) consecutive number of units are found free from nonconformities, 100 percent inspection is then substituted with sampling inspection
3. A fraction of f units is randomly selected and then inspected
   - 3.1. If one nonconformity is found, the inspector reinstates 100 percent inspection
   - 3.2. If the inspector finds i consecutive units free from nonconformities, the frequency f is reduced to $f/2$
     - 3.2.1. If one nonconformity is found, the inspector switches back to 100 percent inspection
     - 3.2.2. If the inspector finds i consecutive units free from nonconformities, the frequency f is reduced to $f/4$
       - 3.2.2.1. If one nonconformity is found, 100 percent inspection is reinstated

CSP-V plans work the same way as CSP-T plans but with reduced i instead of reduced f. The procedure is as follows:

1. Start with 100 percent inspection
2. When i (clearance number) consecutive number of units are found free from nonconformities, 100 percent inspection is then substituted with sampling inspection
3. A fraction of f units is randomly selected and then inspected
   - 3.1. If one nonconformity is found, the inspector reinstates 100 percent inspection
   - 3.2. If the inspector finds i consecutive units free from nonconformities, the inspection continues with inspecting the same fraction f
     - 3.2.1. If one nonconformity is found, the inspector switches back to 100 percent inspection
     - 3.2.2. If the inspector finds $i/3$, the sampling inspection continues with the same fraction f

9.9 Variables Plan When the Standard Deviation Is Known

There are applications for developing a variables plan when the standard deviation is known, as outlined in Burr.[8] These plans are based on the Z-test for testing for differences in means. The equation is

$$Z = \frac{\bar{X} - \mu}{\sigma / \sqrt{n}}.$$

The α and β risks and unacceptable process levels must be set prior to designing the test. The next example illustrates the procedure.

Example 9.10 *A pressure-sensing gage has a tensile strength requirement after staking of 30,000 pounds psi. The lot will be acceptable if no more than 2.5 percent of the units are below 29,000 pounds psi (β risk). The vendor also wants a high probability of acceptance of a lot that has a tensile strength of 31,000 pounds psi (α risk). The process standard deviation is known to be 4200 pounds psi. What sample size and sample mean are required to meet these given levels and risks?*

Utilizing the previous equation, then

$$\frac{\bar{X}-\mu}{\sigma/\sqrt{n}}=Z_\beta \text{ and } \frac{\bar{X}-\mu}{\sigma/\sqrt{n}}=-Z_\alpha.$$

The producer's risk (α) = 0.05 at 31,000 psi

The consumer's risk (β) = 0.10 at 29,000 psi

Substitute the given values into this equation:

$$\frac{\bar{X}-29{,}000}{4200/\sqrt{n}}=1.282 \text{ and } \frac{\bar{X}-31{,}000}{4200/\sqrt{n}}=-1.645$$

Subtracting the second equation from the first results in the following:

$$\frac{2000}{4200/\sqrt{n}}=2.927, \text{ which gives a value for } n=37.78 \text{ or } n=38$$

Substituting this value of n *into either equation will provide a solution for* $\bar{X}$*. If the known value for* n *is substituted into the first equation, the consumer's risk* (β) *will be maintained at the required level. If the known value for* n *is substituted into the second equation, the producer's risk* (α) *will be maintained at the required level. One or the other, but not both, will be at the average given level. To maintain the* α *risk:*

$$\bar{X}=31{,}000-1.645\left(4200/\sqrt{38}\right)$$

$$\bar{X}=29{,}879.21$$

Then $Z_\beta=\dfrac{29{,}879.21-29{,}000}{4200/\sqrt{38}}=1.2904$, which results in a β risk of 0.0985.

Therefore, the sampling plan as developed is:

Sample size $n = 38$
Accept the lot if $\bar{X} \geq 29{,}879.21$
Reject the lot if $\bar{X} < 29{,}879.21$

Number of Sample Units from Last 10 Lots or Batches	AQL																									
	0.010	0.015	0.025	0.040	0.065	0.10	0.15	0.25	0.40	0.65	1.0	1.5	2.5	4.0	6.5	10	15	25	40	65	100	150	250	400	650	1000
20–29	*	*	*	*	*	*	*	*	*	*	*	*	[illegible]	*	*	0	0	2	4	8	14	22	40	68	115	181
30–49	*	*	*	*	*	*	*	*	*	*	*	*	[illegible]	*	0	0	1	3	7	13	22	36	63	105	178	277
50–79	*	*	*	*	*	*	*	*	*	*	*	*	[illegible]	0	0	2	3	7	14	25	40	63	110	181	301	
80–129	*	*	*	*	*	*	*	*	*	*	*	*	[illegible]	0	2	4	7	14	24	42	68	105	181	297		
130–199	*	*	*	*	*	*	*	*	*	*	*	0	[illegible]	2	4	7	13	25	42	72	115	177	301	490		
200–319	*	*	*	*	*	*	*	*	*	*	0	0	[illegible]	4	8	14	22	40	68	115	181	277	471			
320–499	*	*	*	*	*	*	*	*	*	0	0	1	[illegible]	8	14	24	39	68	113	189						
500–799	*	*	*	*	*	*	*	*	0	0	2	3	[illegible]	14	25	40	63	110	181							
800–1249	*	*	*	*	*	*	*	0	0	2	4	7	14	24	42	68	105	181								
1250–1999	*	*	*	*	*	*	0	0	2	4	7	13	24	49	69	110	169									
2000–3149	*	*	*	*	*	0	0	2	4	8	14	22	40	68	115	181										
3150–4999	*	*	*	*	0	0	1	4	8	14	24	38	67	111	186											
5000–7999	*	*	*	0	0	2	3	7	14	25	40	63	110	181												
8000–12,499	*	*	0	0	2	4	7	14	24	42	68	105	181													
12,500–19,999	*	0	0	2	4	7	13	24	40	69	110	169														
20,000–31,499	0	0	2	4	8	14	22	40	68	115	181															
31,500 and over	0	1	4	8	14	24	38	67	111	186																

* = Denotes that the number of sample units from the last 10 lots or batches is not sufficient for reduced inspection for this AQL. In this instance, more than 10 lots or batches may be used for the calculation, provided that the lots or batches used are the most recent ones in sequence, that they have all been on normal inspection, and that none have been rejected while on original inspection.

Figure 9.13 ANSI/ASQ Z1.4-2003 Table VIII: Limit numbers for reduced inspection.

Lot or Batch Size	Special Inspection Levels				General Inspection Levels		
	S-1	S-2	S-3	S-4	I	II	III
2 to 8	A	A	A	A	A	A	B
9 to 15	A	A	A	A	A	B	C
16 to 25	A	A	B	B	B	C	D
26 to 50	A	B	B	C	C	D	E
51 to 90	B	B	C	C	C	E	F
91 to 150	B	B	C	D	D	F	G
151 to 280	B	C	D	E	E	G	H
281 to 500	B	C	D	E	F	H	J
501 to 1200	C	C	E	F	G	J	K
1201 to 3200	C	D	E	G	H	K	L
3201 to 10,000	C	D	F	G	J	L	M
10,001 to 35,000	C	D	F	H	K	M	N
35,001 to 150,000	D	E	G	J	L	N	P
150,001 to 500,000	D	E	G	J	M	P	Q
500,001 and over	D	E	H	K	N	Q	R

Figure 9.14 ANSI/ASQ Z1.4-2003 Table I: Sample size code letters.

Sample Size Code Letter	Sample Size	AQLs in Percent Nonconforming Items and Nonconformities per 100 Items (normal inspection)																									
		0.010	0.015	0.025	0.040	0.065	0.10	0.15	0.25	0.40	0.65	1.0	1.5	2.5	4.0	6.5	10	15	25	40	65	100	150	250	400	650	1000
		AcRe	AcRe	AcRe	AcRe	AcRe	AcRe	AcRe	AcRe	AcRe	AcRe	AcRe	AcRe	AcRe	AcRe	AcRe	AcRe	AcRe	AcRe	AcRe	AcRe	AcRe	AcRe	AcRe	AcRe	AcRe	AcRe
A	2	↓	↓	↓	↓	↓	↓	↓	↓	↓	↓	↓	↓	↓	↓	0 1	↓	↓	1 2	2 3	3 4	5 6	7 8	10 11	14 15	21 22	30 31
B	3	↓	↓	↓	↓	↓	↓	↓	↓	↓	↓	↓	↓	↓	0 1	↑	↓	1 2	2 3	3 4	5 6	7 8	10 11	14 15	21 22	30 31	44 45
C	5	↓	↓	↓	↓	↓	↓	↓	↓	↓	↓	↓	↓	0 1	↑	↓	1 2	2 3	3 4	5 6	7 8	10 11	14 15	21 22	30 31	44 45	↑
D	8	↓	↓	↓	↓	↓	↓	↓	↓	↓	↓	↓	0 1	↑	↓	1 2	2 3	3 4	5 6	7 8	10 11	14 15	21 22	30 31	44 45	↑	↑
E	13	↓	↓	↓	↓	↓	↓	↓	↓	↓	↓	0 1	↑	↓	1 2	2 3	3 4	5 6	7 8	10 11	14 15	21 22	30 31	44 45	↑	↑	↑
F	20	↓	↓	↓	↓	↓	↓	↓	↓	↓	0 1	↑	↓	1 2	2 3	3 4	5 6	7 8	10 11	14 15	21 22	↑	↑	↑	↑	↑	↑
G	32	↓	↓	↓	↓	↓	↓	↓	↓	0 1	↑	↓	1 2	2 3	3 4	5 6	7 8	10 11	14 15	21 22	↑	↑	↑	↑	↑	↑	↑
H	50	↓	↓	↓	↓	↓	↓	↓	0 1	↑	↓	1 2	2 3	3 4	5 6	7 8	10 11	14 15	21 22	↑	↑	↑	↑	↑	↑	↑	↑
J	80	↓	↓	↓	↓	↓	↓	0 1	↑	↓	1 2	2 3	3 4	5 6	7 8	10 11	14 15	21 22	↑	↑	↑	↑	↑	↑	↑	↑	↑
K	125	↓	↓	↓	↓	↓	0 1	↑	↓	1 2	2 3	3 4	5 6	7 8	10 11	14 15	21 22	↑	↑	↑	↑	↑	↑	↑	↑	↑	↑
L	200	↓	↓	↓	↓	0 1	↑	↓	1 2	2 3	3 4	5 6	7 8	10 11	14 15	21 22	↑	↑	↑	↑	↑	↑	↑	↑	↑	↑	↑
M	315	↓	↓	↓	0 1	↑	↓	1 2	2 3	3 4	5 6	7 8	10 11	14 15	21 22	↑	↑	↑	↑	↑	↑	↑	↑	↑	↑	↑	↑
N	500	↓	↓	0 1	↑	↓	1 2	2 3	3 4	5 6	7 8	10 11	14 15	21 22	↑	↑	↑	↑	↑	↑	↑	↑	↑	↑	↑	↑	↑
P	800	↓	0 1	↑	↓	1 2	2 3	3 4	5 6	7 8	10 11	14 15	21 22	↑	↑	↑	↑	↑	↑	↑	↑	↑	↑	↑	↑	↑	↑
Q	1250	0 1	↑	↓	1 2	2 3	3 4	5 6	7 8	10 11	14 15	21 22	↑	↑	↑	↑	↑	↑	↑	↑	↑	↑	↑	↑	↑	↑	↑
R	2000	↑	↑	1 2	2 3	3 4	5 6	7 8	10 11	14 15	21 22	↑	↑	↑	↑	↑	↑	↑	↑	↑	↑	↑	↑	↑	↑	↑	↑

↓ = Use first sampling plan below arrow. If sample size equals or exceeds lot size, carry out 100 percent inspection.

↑ = Use first sampling plan above arrow.

Ac = Acceptance number.

Re = Rejection number.

Figure 9.15 ANSI/ASQ Z1.4-2003 Table II-A: Single sampling plans for normal inspection.

Sample Size Code Letter	Sample	Sample Size	Cumulative Sample Size	AQLs (reduced inspection)																									
				0.010	0.015	0.025	0.040	0.065	0.10	0.15	0.25	0.40	0.65	1.0	1.5	2.5	4.0	6.5	10	15	25	40	65	100	150	250	400	650	1000
				AcRe	AcRe	AcRe	AcRe	AcRe	AcRe	AcRe	AcRe	AcRe	AcRe	AcRe	AcRe	AcRe	AcRe	AcRe	AcRe	AcRe	AcRe	AcRe	AcRe	AcRe	AcRe	AcRe	AcRe	AcRe	AcRe
A				↓	↓	↓	↓	↓	↓	↓	↓	↓	↓	↓	↓	↓	↓	*	↓	↓	+	+	+	+	+	+	+	+	+
B	First	2	2	↓	↓	↓	↓	↓	↓	↓	↓	↓	↓	↓	↓	↓	*	↑	↓	0 2	0 3	1 4	2 5	3 7	5 9	7 11	11 16	17 22	25 31
	Second	2	4																	1 2	3 4	4 5	6 7	8 9	12 13	18 19	26 27	37 38	56 57
C	First	3	3	↓	↓	↓	↓	↓	↓	↓	↓	↓	↓	↓	↓	*	↑	↓	0 2	0 3	1 4	2 5	3 7	5 9	7 11	11 16	17 22	25 31	↑
	Second	3	6																1 2	3 4	4 5	6 7	8 9	12 13	18 19	26 27	37 38	56 57	
D	First	5	5	↓	↓	↓	↓	↓	↓	↓	↓	↓	↓	↓	*	↑	↓	0 2	0 3	1 4	2 5	3 7	5 9	7 11	11 16	17 22	25 31	↑	↑
	Second	5	10															1 2	3 4	4 5	6 7	8 9	12 13	18 19	26 27	37 38	56 57		
E	First	8	8	↓	↓	↓	↓	↓	↓	↓	↓	↓	↓	*	↑	↓	0 2	0 3	1 4	2 5	3 7	5 9	7 11	11 16	17 22	25 31	↑	↑	↑
	Second	8	16														1 2	3 4	4 5	6 7	8 9	12 13	18 19	26 27	37 38	56 57			
F	First	13	13	↓	↓	↓	↓	↓	↓	↓	↓	↓	*	↑	↓	0 2	0 3	1 4	2 5	3 7	5 9	7 11	11 16	↑	↑	↑	↑	↑	↑
	Second	13	26													1 2	3 4	4 5	6 7	8 9	12 13	18 19	26 27						
G	First	20	20	↓	↓	↓	↓	↓	↓	↓	↓	*	↑	↓	0 2	0 3	1 4	2 5	3 7	5 9	7 11	11 16	↑	↑	↑	↑	↑	↑	↑
	Second	20	40												1 2	3 4	4 5	6 7	8 9	12 13	18 19	26 27							
H	First	32	32	↓	↓	↓	↓	↓	↓	↓	*	↑	↓	0 2	0 3	1 4	2 5	3 7	5 9	7 11	11 16	↑	↑	↑	↑	↑	↑	↑	↑
	Second	32	64											1 2	3 4	4 5	6 7	8 9	12 13	18 19	26 27								
J	First	50	50	↓	↓	↓	↓	↓	↓	*	↑	↓	0 2	0 3	1 4	2 5	3 7	5 9	7 11	11 16	↑	↑	↑	↑	↑	↑	↑	↑	↑
	Second	50	100										1 2	3 4	4 5	6 7	8 9	12 13	18 19	26 27									
K	First	80	80	↓	↓	↓	↓	↓	*	↑	↓	0 2	0 3	1 4	2 5	3 7	5 9	7 11	11 16	↑	↑	↑	↑	↑	↑	↑	↑	↑	↑
	Second	80	160									1 2	3 4	4 5	6 7	8 9	12 13	18 19	26 27										
L	First	125	125	↓	↓	↓	↓	*	↑	↓	0 2	0 3	1 4	2 5	3 7	5 9	7 11	11 16	↑	↑	↑	↑	↑	↑	↑	↑	↑	↑	↑
	Second	125	250								1 2	3 4	4 5	6 7	8 9	12 13	18 19	26 27											
M	First	200	200	↓	↓	↓	*	↑	↓	0 2	0 3	1 4	2 5	3 7	5 9	7 11	11 16	↑	↑	↑	↑	↑	↑	↑	↑	↑	↑	↑	↑
	Second	200	400							1 2	3 4	4 5	6 7	8 9	12 13	18 19	26 27												
N	First	315	315	↓	↓	*	↑	↓	0 2	0 3	1 4	2 5	3 7	5 9	7 11	11 16	↑	↑	↑	↑	↑	↑	↑	↑	↑	↑	↑	↑	↑
	Second	315	630						1 2	3 4	4 5	6 7	8 9	12 13	18 19	26 27													
P	First	500	500	↓	*	↑	↓	0 2	0 3	1 4	2 5	3 7	5 9	7 11	11 16	↑	↑	↑	↑	↑	↑	↑	↑	↑	↑	↑	↑	↑	↑
	Second	500	1000					1 2	3 4	4 5	6 7	8 9	12 13	18 19	26 27														
Q	First	800	800	*	↑	↓	0 2	0 3	1 4	2 5	3 7	5 9	7 11	11 16	↑	↑	↑	↑	↑	↑	↑	↑	↑	↑	↑	↑	↑	↑	↑
	Second	800	1600				1 2	3 4	4 5	6 7	8 9	12 13	18 19	26 27															
R	First	1250	1250	↑	↑	0 2	0 3	1 4	2 5	3 7	5 9	7 11	11 16	↑	↑	↑	↑	↑	↑	↑	↑	↑	↑	↑	↑	↑	↑	↑	↑
	Second	1250	2500			1 2	3 4	4 5	6 7	8 9	12 13	18 19	26 27																

↓ = Use first sampling plan below arrow. If sample size equals or exceeds lot or batch size, do 100 percent inspection.

↑ = Use first sampling plan above arrow.

Ac = Acceptance number.

Re = Rejection number.

* = Use corresponding single sampling plan.

\+ = Use corresponding single sampling plan or double sampling plan for code letter B.

Figure 9.16 ANSI/ASQ Z1.4-2003 Table III-A: Double sampling plans for normal inspection.

Sample Size Code Letter	Sample	Sample Size	Cumulative Sample Size	AQLs (normal inspection)																									
				0.010	0.015	0.025	0.040	0.065	0.10	0.15	0.25	0.40	0.65	1.0	1.5	2.5	4.0	6.5	10	15	25	40	65	100	150	250	400	650	1000
				AcRe	AcRe	AcRe	AcRe	AcRe	AcRe	AcRe	AcRe	AcRe	AcRe	AcRe	AcRe	AcRe	AcRe	AcRe	AcRe	AcRe	AcRe	AcRe	AcRe	AcRe	AcRe	AcRe	AcRe	AcRe	AcRe
A				↓	↓	↓	↓	↓	↓	↓	↓	↓	↓	↓	↓	↓	↓	*	↓	↓	*	*	*	*	*	*	*	*	*
B				↓	↓	↓	↓	↓	↓	↓	↓	↓	↓	↓	↓	↓	*	↑	↓	++	++	++	++	++	++	++	++	##	##
C				↓	↓	↓	↓	↓	↓	↓	↓	↓	↓	↓	↓	*	↑	↓	++	++	++	++	++	++	++	++	++	##	↑
D	First	2	2	↓	↓	↓	↓	↓	↓	↓	↓	↓	↓	↓	*	↑	↓	# 2	# 2	# 3	# 4	0 4	0 5	1 7	2 9	4 12	6 16	↑	↑
	Second	2	4															# 2	0 3	0 3	1 5	1 6	3 8	4 10	7 14	11 19	17 27		
	Third	2	6															0 2	0 3	1 4	2 6	3 8	6 10	8 13	13 19	19 27	29 39		
	Fourth	2	8															0 3	1 4	2 5	3 7	5 10	8 13	12 17	19 25	27 34	40 49		
	Fifth	2	10															1 3	2 4	3 6	5 8	7 11	11 15	17 20	25 29	36 40	53 58		
	Sixth	2	12															1 3	3 5	4 6	7 9	10 12	14 17	21 23	31 33	45 47	65 68		
	Seventh	2	14															2 3	4 5	6 7	9 10	13 14	18 19	25 26	37 38	53 54	77 78		
E	First	3	3	↓	↓	↓	↓	↓	↓	↓	↓	↓	↓	*	↑	↓	# 2	# 2	# 3	# 4	0 4	0 5	1 7	2 9	4 12	6 16	↑	↑	↑
	Second	3	6														# 2	0 3	0 3	1 5	1 6	3 8	4 10	7 14	11 19	17 27			
	Third	3	9														0 2	0 3	1 4	2 6	3 8	6 10	8 13	13 19	19 27	29 39			
	Fourth	3	12														0 3	1 4	2 5	3 7	5 10	8 13	12 17	19 25	27 34	40 49			
	Fifth	3	15														1 3	2 4	3 6	5 8	7 11	11 15	17 20	25 29	36 40	53 58			
	Sixth	3	18														1 3	3 5	4 6	7 9	10 12	14 17	21 23	31 33	45 47	65 68			
	Seventh	3	21														2 3	4 5	6 7	9 10	13 14	18 19	25 26	37 38	53 54	77 78			
F	First	5	5	↓	↓	↓	↓	↓	↓	↓	↓	↓	*	↑	↓	# 2	# 2	# 3	# 4	0 4	0 5	1 7	2 9	↑	↑	↑	↑	↑	↑
	Second	5	10													# 2	0 3	0 3	1 5	1 6	3 8	4 10	7 14						
	Third	5	15													0 2	0 3	1 4	2 6	3 8	6 10	8 13	13 19						
	Fourth	5	20													0 3	1 4	2 5	3 7	5 10	8 13	12 17	19 25						
	Fifth	5	25													1 3	2 4	3 6	5 8	7 11	11 15	17 20	25 29						
	Sixth	5	30													1 3	3 5	4 6	7 9	10 12	14 17	21 23	31 33						
	Seventh	5	35													2 3	4 5	6 7	9 10	13 14	18 19	25 26	37 38						
G	First	8	8	↓	↓	↓	↓	↓	↓	↓	↓	*	↑	↓	# 2	# 2	# 3	# 4	0 4	0 5	1 7	2 9	↑	↑	↑	↑	↑	↑	↑
	Second	8	16												# 2	0 3	0 3	1 5	1 6	3 8	4 10	7 14							
	Third	8	24												0 2	0 3	1 4	2 6	3 8	6 10	8 13	13 19							
	Fourth	8	32												0 3	1 4	2 5	3 7	5 10	8 13	12 17	19 25							
	Fifth	8	40												1 3	2 4	3 6	5 8	7 11	11 15	17 20	25 29							
	Sixth	8	48												1 3	3 5	4 6	7 9	10 12	14 17	21 23	31 33							
	Seventh	8	56												2 3	4 5	6 7	9 10	13 14	18 19	25 26	37 38							
H	First	13	13	↓	↓	↓	↓	↓	↓	↓	*	↑	↓	# 2	# 2	# 3	# 4	0 4	0 5	1 7	2 9	↑	↑	↑	↑	↑	↑	↑	↑
	Second	13	26											# 2	0 3	0 3	1 5	1 6	3 8	4 10	7 14								
	Third	13	39											0 2	0 3	1 4	2 6	3 8	6 10	8 13	13 19								
	Fourth	13	52											0 3	1 4	2 5	3 7	5 10	8 13	12 17	19 25								
	Fifth	13	65											1 3	2 4	3 6	5 8	7 11	11 15	17 20	25 29								
	Sixth	13	78											1 3	3 5	4 6	7 9	10 12	14 17	21 23	31 33								
	Seventh	13	91											2 3	4 5	6 7	9 10	13 14	18 19	25 26	37 38								
J	First	20	20	↓	↓	↓	↓	↓	↓	*	↑	↓	# 2	# 2	# 3	# 4	0 4	0 5	1 7	2 9	↑	↑	↑	↑	↑	↑	↑	↑	↑
	Second	20	40										# 2	0 3	0 3	1 5	1 6	3 8	4 10	7 14									
	Third	20	60										0 2	0 3	1 4	2 6	3 8	6 10	8 13	13 19									
	Fourth	20	80										0 3	1 4	2 5	3 7	5 10	8 13	12 17	19 25									
	Fifth	20	100										1 3	2 4	3 6	5 8	7 11	11 15	17 20	25 29									
	Sixth	20	120										1 3	3 5	4 6	7 9	10 12	14 17	21 23	31 33									
	Seventh	20	140										2 3	4 5	6 7	9 10	13 14	18 19	25 26	37 38									

↓ = Use first sampling plan below arrow. If sample size equals or exceeds lot or batch size, do 100 percent inspection.

↑ = Use first sampling plan above arrow.

* = Use corresponding single sampling plan.

++ = Use corresponding double sampling plan or multiple sampling plan for code letter D.

Ac = Acceptance number.

Re = Rejection number.

= Acceptance not permitted at this sample size.

= Use corresponding double sampling plan.

Figure 9.17 ANSI/ASQ Z1.4-2003 Table IV-A: Multiple sampling plans for normal inspection. *(continued)*

(continued)

Sample Size Code Letter	Sample	Sample Size	Cumulative Sample Size	AQLs (normal inspection)																									
				0.010	0.015	0.025	0.040	0.065	0.10	0.15	0.25	0.40	0.65	1.0	1.5	2.5	4.0	6.5	10	15	25	40	65	100	150	250	400	650	1000
				Ac Re	Ac Re	Ac Re	Ac Re	Ac Re	Ac Re	Ac Re	Ac Re	Ac Re	Ac Re	Ac Re	Ac Re	Ac Re	Ac Re	Ac Re	Ac Re	Ac Re	Ac Re	Ac Re	Ac Re	Ac Re	Ac Re	Ac Re	Ac Re	Ac Re	Ac Re
K	First	32	32	↓	↓	↓	↓	↓	*	↑	↓	# 2	# 2	# 3	# 4	0 4	0 5	1 7	2 9	↑	↑	↑	↑	↑	↑	↑	↑	↑	↑
	Second	32	64									# 2	0 3	0 3	1 5	1 6	3 8	4 10	7 14										
	Third	32	96									0 2	0 3	1 4	2 6	3 8	6 10	8 13	13 19										
	Fourth	32	128									0 3	1 4	2 5	3 7	5 10	8 13	12 17	19 25										
	Fifth	32	160									1 3	2 4	3 6	5 8	7 11	11 15	17 20	25 29										
	Sixth	32	192									1 3	3 5	4 6	7 9	10 12	14 17	21 23	31 33										
	Seventh	32	224									2 3	4 5	6 7	9 10	13 14	18 19	25 26	37 38										
L	First	50	50	↓	↓	↓	↓	*	↑	↓	# 2	# 2	# 3	# 4	0 4	0 5	1 7	2 9	↑	↑	↑	↑	↑	↑	↑	↑	↑	↑	↑
	Second	50	100								# 2	0 3	0 3	1 5	1 6	3 8	4 10	7 14											
	Third	50	150								0 2	0 3	1 4	2 6	3 8	6 10	8 13	13 19											
	Fourth	50	200								0 3	1 4	2 5	3 7	5 10	8 13	12 17	19 25											
	Fifth	50	250								1 3	2 4	3 6	5 8	7 11	11 15	17 20	25 29											
	Sixth	50	300								1 3	3 5	4 6	7 9	10 12	14 17	21 23	31 33											
	Seventh	50	350								2 3	4 5	6 7	9 10	13 14	18 19	25 26	37 38											
M	First	80	80	↓	↓	↓	*	↑	↓	# 2	# 2	# 3	# 4	0 4	0 5	1 7	2 9	↑	↑	↑	↑	↑	↑	↑	↑	↑	↑	↑	↑
	Second	80	160							# 2	0 3	0 3	1 5	1 6	3 8	4 10	7 14												
	Third	80	240							0 2	0 3	1 4	2 6	3 8	6 10	8 13	13 19												
	Fourth	80	320							0 3	1 4	2 5	3 7	5 10	8 13	12 17	19 25												
	Fifth	80	400							1 3	2 4	3 6	5 8	7 11	11 15	17 20	25 29												
	Sixth	80	480							1 3	3 5	4 6	7 9	10 12	14 17	21 23	31 33												
	Seventh	80	560							2 3	4 5	6 7	9 10	13 14	18 19	25 26	37 38												
N	First	125	125	↓	↓	*	↑	↓	# 2	# 2	# 3	# 4	0 4	0 5	1 7	2 9	↑	↑	↑	↑	↑	↑	↑	↑	↑	↑	↑	↑	↑
	Second	125	250						# 2	0 3	0 3	1 5	1 6	3 8	4 10	7 14													
	Third	125	375						0 2	0 3	1 4	2 6	3 8	6 10	8 13	13 19													
	Fourth	125	500						0 3	1 4	2 5	3 7	5 10	8 13	12 17	19 25													
	Fifth	125	625						1 3	2 4	3 6	5 8	7 11	11 15	17 20	25 29													
	Sixth	125	750						1 3	3 5	4 6	7 9	10 12	14 17	21 23	31 33													
	Seventh	125	875						2 3	4 5	6 7	9 10	13 14	18 19	25 26	37 38													
P	First	200	200	↓	*	↑	↓	# 2	# 2	# 3	# 4	0 4	0 5	1 7	2 9	↑	↑	↑	↑	↑	↑	↑	↑	↑	↑	↑	↑	↑	↑
	Second	200	400					# 2	0 3	0 3	1 5	1 6	3 8	4 10	7 14														
	Third	200	600					0 2	0 3	1 4	2 6	3 8	6 10	8 13	13 19														
	Fourth	200	800					0 3	1 4	2 5	3 7	5 10	8 13	12 17	19 25														
	Fifth	200	1000					1 3	2 4	3 6	5 8	7 11	11 15	17 20	25 29														
	Sixth	200	1200					1 3	3 5	4 6	7 9	10 12	14 17	21 23	31 33														
	Seventh	200	1400					2 3	4 5	6 7	9 10	13 14	18 19	25 26	37 38														
Q	First	315	315	*	↑	↓	# 2	# 2	# 3	# 4	0 4	0 5	1 7	2 9	↑	↑	↑	↑	↑	↑	↑	↑	↑	↑	↑	↑	↑	↑	↑
	Second	315	630				# 2	0 3	0 3	1 5	1 6	3 8	4 10	7 14															
	Third	315	945				0 2	0 3	1 4	2 6	3 8	6 10	8 13	13 19															
	Fourth	315	1260				0 3	1 4	2 5	3 7	5 10	8 13	12 17	19 25															
	Fifth	315	1575				1 3	2 4	3 6	5 8	7 11	11 15	17 20	25 29															
	Sixth	315	1890				1 3	3 5	4 6	7 9	10 12	14 17	21 23	31 33															
	Seventh	315	2205				2 3	4 5	6 7	9 10	13 14	18 19	25 26	37 38															
R	First	500	500	↑	↓	# 2	# 2	# 3	# 4	0 4	0 5	1 7	2 9	↑	↑	↑	↑	↑	↑	↑	↑	↑	↑	↑	↑	↑	↑	↑	↑
	Second	500	1000			# 2	0 3	0 3	1 5	1 6	3 8	4 10	7 14																
	Third	500	1500			0 2	0 3	1 4	2 6	3 8	6 10	8 13	13 19																
	Fourth	500	2000			0 3	1 4	2 5	3 7	5 10	8 13	12 17	19 25																
	Fifth	500	2500			1 3	2 4	3 6	5 8	7 11	11 15	17 20	25 29																
	Sixth	500	3000			1 3	3 5	4 6	7 9	10 12	14 17	21 23	31 33																
	Seventh	500	3500			2 3	4 5	6 7	9 10	13 14	18 19	25 26	37 38																

↓ = Use first sampling plan below arrow. If sample size equals or exceeds lot or batch size, do 100 percent inspection.

↑ = Use first sampling plan above arrow.

* = Use corresponding single sampling plan.

Ac = Acceptance number.

= Acceptance not permitted at this sample size.

Re = Rejection number.

Figure 9.17 ANSI/ASQ Z1.4-2003 Table IV-A: Multiple sampling plans for normal inspection.

(continued)

Lot Size			Inspection Levels				
			Special		General		
			S3	S4	I	II	III
2	to	8	B	B	B	B	C
9	to	15	B	B	B	B	D
16	to	25	B	B	B	C	E
26	to	50	B	B	C	D	F
51	to	90	B	B	D	E	G
91	to	150	B	C	E	F	H
151	to	280	B	D	F	G	I
281	to	400	C	E	G	H	J
401	to	500	C	E	G	I	J
501	to	1200	D	F	H	J	K
1201	to	3200	E	G	I	K	L
3201	to	10,000	F	H	J	L	M
10,001	to	35,000	G	I	K	M	N
35,001	to	150,000	H	J	L	N	P
150,001	to	500,000	H	K	M	P	P
500,001	and	over	H	K	N	P	P

Figure 9.18 4.20 ANSI/ASQ Z1.9-2003 Table A-2*: Sample size code letters.**

*The theory governing inspection by variables depends on the properties of the normal distribution; therefore, this method of inspection is applicable only when there is reason to believe that the frequency distribution is normal.

**Sample size code letters given in body of table are applicable when the indicated inspection levels are to be used.

Sample Size Code Letter	Sample Size	AQLs (normal inspection)											
		T	.10	.15	.25	.40	.65	1.00	1.50	2.50	4.00	6.50	10.00
		k	*k*	*k*	*k*	*k*	*k*	*k*	*k*	*k*	*k*	*k*	*k*
B	3	↓	↓	↓	↓	↓	↓	↓	↓	.587	.502	.401	.296
C	4	↓	↓	↓	↓	↓	↓	.651	.598	.525	.450	.364	.276
D	5	↓	↓	↓	↓	↓	.663	.614	.565	.498	.431	.352	.272
E	7	↓	↓	↓	.702	.659	.613	.569	.525	.465	.405	.336	.266
F	10	↓	↓	.916	.863	.811	.755	.703	.650	.579	.507	.424	.341
G	15	1.04	.999	.958	.903	.850	.792	.738	.684	.610	.536	.452	.368
H	25	1.10	1.05	1.01	.951	.896	.835	.779	.723	.647	.571	.484	.398
I	30	1.10	1.06	1.02	.959	.904	.843	.787	.730	.654	.577	.490	.403
J	40	1.13	1.08	1.04	.978	.921	.860	.803	.746	.668	.591	.503	.415
K	60	1.16	1.11	1.06	1.00	.948	.885	.826	.768	.689	.610	.521	.432
L	85	1.17	1.13	1.08	1.02	.962	.899	.839	.780	.701	.621	.530	.441
M	115	1.19	1.14	1.09	1.03	.975	.911	.851	.791	.711	.631	.539	.449
N	175	1.21	1.16	1.11	1.05	.994	.929	.868	.807	.726	.644	.552	.460
P	230	1.21	1.16	1.12	1.06	.996	.931	.870	.809	.728	.646	.553	.462
		.10	.15	.25	.40	.65	1.00	1.50	2.50	4.00	6.50	10.00	
		AQLs (tightened inspection)											

All AQL values are in percent nonconforming. *T* denotes plan used exclusively on tightened inspection and provides symbol for identification of appropriate OC curve.

↓ = Use first sampling plan below arrow, that is, both sample size and *k* value. When sample size equals or exceeds lot size, every item in the lot must be inspected.

Figure 9.19 ANSI/ASQ Z1.9-2003 Table C-1: Master table for normal and tightened inspection for plans based on variability unknown (single specification limit—Form 1).

Q_U or Q_L	Sample size														
	3	4	5	7	10	15	20	25	30	35	50	75	100	150	200
0	50.00	50.00	50.00	50.00	50.00	50.00	50.00	50.00	50.00	50.00	50.00	50.00	50.00	50.00	50.00
.1	47.24	46.67	46.44	46.26	46.16	46.10	46.08	46.06	46.05	46.05	46.04	46.03	46.03	46.02	46.02
.2	44.46	43.33	42.90	42.54	42.35	42.24	42.19	42.16	42.15	42.13	42.11	42.10	42.09	42.09	42.08
.3	41.63	40.00	39.37	38.87	38.60	38.44	38.37	38.33	38.31	38.29	38.27	38.25	38.24	38.23	38.22
.31	41.35	39.67	39.02	38.50	38.23	38.06	37.99	37.95	37.93	37.91	37.89	37.87	37.86	37.85	37.84
.32	41.06	39.33	38.67	38.14	37.86	37.69	37.62	37.58	37.55	37.54	37.51	37.49	37.48	37.47	37.46
.33	40.77	39.00	38.32	37.78	37.49	37.31	37.24	37.20	37.18	37.16	37.13	37.11	37.10	37.09	37.08
.34	40.49	38.67	37.97	37.42	37.12	36.94	36.87	36.83	36.80	36.78	36.75	36.73	36.72	36.71	36.71
.35	40.20	38.33	37.62	37.06	36.75	36.57	36.49	36.45	36.43	36.41	36.38	36.36	36.35	36.34	36.33
.36	39.91	38.00	37.28	36.69	36.38	36.20	36.12	36.08	36.05	36.04	36.01	35.98	35.97	35.96	35.96
.37	39.62	37.67	36.93	36.33	36.02	35.83	35.75	35.71	35.68	35.66	35.63	35.61	35.60	35.59	35.58
.38	39.33	37.33	36.58	35.98	35.65	35.46	35.38	35.34	35.31	35.29	35.26	35.24	35.23	35.22	35.21
.39	39.03	37.00	36.23	35.62	35.29	35.10	35.02	34.97	34.94	34.93	34.89	34.87	34.86	34.85	34.84
.40	38.74	36.67	35.88	35.26	34.93	34.73	34.65	34.60	34.58	34.56	34.53	34.50	34.49	34.48	34.47
.41	38.45	36.33	35.54	34.90	34.57	34.37	34.28	34.24	34.21	34.19	34.16	34.13	34.12	34.11	34.11
.42	38.15	36.00	35.19	34.55	34.21	34.00	33.92	33.87	33.85	33.83	33.79	33.77	33.76	33.75	33.74
.43	37.85	35.67	34.85	34.19	33.85	33.64	33.56	33.51	33.48	33.46	33.43	33.40	33.39	33.38	33.38
.44	37.56	35.33	34.50	33.84	33.49	33.28	33.20	33.15	33.12	33.10	33.07	33.04	33.03	33.02	33.01
.45	37.26	35.00	34.16	33.49	33.13	32.92	32.84	32.79	32.76	32.74	32.71	32.68	32.67	32.66	32.65
.46	36.96	34.67	33.81	33.13	32.78	32.57	32.48	32.43	32.40	32.38	32.35	32.32	32.31	32.30	32.29
.47	36.66	34.33	33.47	32.78	32.42	32.21	32.12	32.07	32.04	32.02	31.99	31.96	31.95	31.94	31.93
.48	36.35	34.00	33.12	32.43	32.07	31.85	31.77	31.72	31.69	31.67	31.63	31.61	31.60	31.58	31.58
.49	36.05	33.67	32.78	32.08	31.72	31.50	31.41	31.36	31.33	31.31	31.28	31.25	31.24	31.23	31.22
.50	35.75	33.33	32.44	31.74	31.37	31.15	31.06	31.01	30.98	30.96	30.93	30.90	30.89	30.88	30.87
.51	35.44	33.00	32.10	31.39	31.02	30.80	30.71	30.66	30.63	30.61	30.57	30.55	30.54	30.53	30.52
.52	35.13	32.67	31.76	31.04	30.67	30.45	30.36	30.31	30.28	30.26	30.23	30.20	30.19	30.18	30.17
.53	34.82	32.33	31.42	30.70	30.32	30.10	30.01	29.96	29.93	29.91	29.88	29.85	29.84	29.83	29.82
.54	34.51	32.00	31.08	30.36	29.98	29.76	29.67	29.62	29.59	29.57	29.53	29.51	29.49	29.48	29.48
.55	34.20	31.67	30.74	30.01	29.64	29.41	29.32	29.27	29.24	29.22	29.19	29.16	29.15	29.14	29.13
.56	33.88	31.33	30.40	29.67	29.29	29.07	28.98	28.93	28.90	28.88	28.85	28.82	28.81	28.80	28.79
.57	33.57	31.00	30.06	29.33	28.95	28.73	28.64	28.59	28.56	28.54	28.51	28.48	28.47	28.46	28.45
.58	33.25	30.67	29.73	28.99	28.61	28.39	28.30	28.25	28.22	28.20	28.17	28.14	28.13	28.12	28.11
.59	32.93	30.33	29.39	28.66	28.28	28.05	27.96	27.92	27.89	27.87	27.83	27.81	27.79	27.78	27.78
.60	32.61	30.00	29.05	28.32	27.94	27.72	27.63	27.58	27.55	27.53	27.50	27.47	27.46	27.45	27.44
.61	32.28	29.67	28.72	27.98	27.60	27.39	27.30	27.25	27.22	27.20	27.16	27.14	27.13	27.11	27.11
.62	31.96	29.33	28.39	27.65	27.27	27.05	26.96	26.92	26.89	26.87	26.83	26.81	26.80	26.78	26.78
.63	31.63	29.00	28.05	27.32	26.94	26.72	26.63	26.59	26.56	26.54	26.50	26.48	26.47	26.46	26.45
.64	31.30	28.67	27.72	26.99	26.61	26.39	26.31	26.26	26.23	26.21	26.18	26.15	26.14	26.13	26.12
.65	30.97	28.33	27.39	26.66	26.28	26.07	25.98	25.93	25.90	25.88	25.85	25.83	25.82	25.81	25.80
.66	30.63	28.00	27.06	26.33	25.96	25.74	25.66	25.61	25.58	25.56	25.53	25.51	25.49	25.48	25.48
.67	30.30	27.67	26.73	26.00	25.63	25.42	25.33	25.29	25.26	25.24	25.21	25.19	25.17	25.16	25.16
.68	29.96	27.33	26.40	25.68	25.31	25.10	25.01	24.97	24.94	24.92	24.89	24.87	24.86	24.85	24.84
.69	29.61	27.00	26.07	25.35	24.99	24.78	24.70	24.65	24.62	24.60	24.57	24.55	24.54	24.53	24.52

Figure 9.20 ANSI/ASQ Z1.9-2003 Table B-5: Table for estimating the lot percent nonconforming using standard deviation method. Values tabulated are read as percentages. *(continued)*

Q_U or Q_L	Sample size														
	3	4	5	7	10	15	20	25	30	35	50	75	100	150	200
.70	29.27	26.67	25.74	25.03	24.67	24.46	24.38	24.33	24.31	24.29	24.26	24.24	24.23	24.22	24.21
.71	28.92	26.33	25.41	24.71	24.35	24.15	24.06	24.02	23.99	23.98	23.95	23.92	23.91	23.90	23.90
.72	28.57	26.00	25.09	24.39	24.03	23.83	23.75	23.71	23.68	23.67	23.64	23.61	23.60	23.59	23.59
.73	28.22	25.67	24.76	24.07	23.72	23.52	23.44	23.40	23.37	23.36	23.33	23.31	23.30	23.29	23.28
.74	27.86	25.33	24.44	23.75	23.41	23.21	23.13	23.09	23.07	23.05	23.02	23.00	22.99	22.98	22.98
.75	27.50	25.00	24.11	23.44	23.10	22.90	22.83	22.79	22.76	22.75	22.72	22.70	22.69	22.68	22.68
.76	27.13	24.67	23.79	23.12	22.79	22.60	22.52	22.48	22.46	22.44	22.42	22.40	22.39	22.38	22.38
.77	26.76	24.33	23.47	22.81	22.48	22.30	22.22	22.18	22.16	22.14	22.12	22.10	22.09	22.08	22.08
.78	26.39	24.00	23.15	22.50	22.18	21.99	21.92	21.89	21.86	21.85	21.82	21.80	21.78	21.79	21.78
.79	26.02	23.67	22.83	22.19	21.87	21.70	21.63	21.59	21.57	21.55	21.53	21.51	21.50	21.49	21.49
.80	25.64	23.33	22.51	21.88	21.57	21.40	21.33	21.29	21.27	21.26	21.23	21.22	21.21	21.20	21.20
.81	25.25	23.00	22.19	21.58	21.27	21.10	21.04	21.00	20.98	20.97	20.94	20.93	20.92	20.91	20.91
.82	24.86	22.67	21.87	21.27	20.98	20.81	20.75	20.71	20.69	20.68	20.65	20.64	20.63	20.62	20.62
.83	24.47	22.33	21.56	29.97	29.68	20.52	20.46	20.42	20.40	20.39	20.37	20.35	20.35	20.34	20.34
.84	24.07	22.00	21.24	20.67	20.39	20.23	20.17	20.14	20.12	20.11	20.09	20.07	20.06	20.06	20.05
.85	23.67	21.67	20.93	20.37	20.10	19.94	19.89	19.86	19.84	19.82	19.80	19.79	19.78	19.78	19.77
.86	23.26	21.33	20.62	20.07	19.81	19.66	19.60	19.57	19.56	19.54	19.53	19.51	19.51	19.50	19.50
.87	22.84	21.00	20.31	19.78	19.52	19.38	19.32	19.30	19.28	19.27	19.25	19.24	19.23	19.23	19.22
.88	22.42	20.67	20.00	19.48	19.23	19.10	19.05	19.02	19.00	18.99	18.98	18.96	18.96	18.95	18.95
.89	21.99	20.33	19.69	19.19	18.95	18.82	18.77	18.74	18.73	18.72	18.70	18.69	18.69	18.68	18.68
.90	21.55	20.00	19.38	18.90	18.67	18.54	18.50	18.47	18.46	18.45	18.43	18.42	18.42	18.41	18.41
.91	21.11	19.67	19.07	18.61	18.39	18.27	18.23	18.20	18.19	18.18	18.17	18.16	18.15	18.15	18.15
.92	20.66	19.33	18.77	18.33	18.11	18.00	17.96	17.94	17.92	17.92	17.90	17.89	17.89	17.89	17.88
.93	20.19	19.00	18.46	18.04	17.84	17.73	17.69	17.67	17.66	17.65	17.64	17.63	17.63	17.62	17.62
.94	19.73	18.67	18.16	17.76	17.56	17.46	17.43	17.41	17.40	17.39	17.38	17.37	17.37	17.37	17.36
.95	19.25	18.33	17.86	17.48	17.29	17.20	17.17	17.16	17.14	17.13	17.12	17.12	17.11	17.11	17.11
.96	18.75	18.00	17.55	17.20	17.03	16.94	16.90	16.89	16.88	16.88	16.87	16.86	16.86	16.86	16.86
.97	18.25	17.67	17.25	16.92	16.76	16.68	16.65	16.63	16.62	16.62	16.61	16.61	16.61	16.61	16.60
.98	17.74	17.33	16.96	16.65	16.49	16.42	16.39	16.38	16.37	16.37	16.36	16.36	16.36	16.36	16.36
.99	17.21	17.00	16.66	16.37	16.23	16.16	16.14	16.13	16.12	16.12	16.12	16.11	16.11	16.11	16.11
1.00	16.67	16.67	16.36	16.10	15.97	15.91	15.89	15.88	15.88	15.87	15.87	15.87	15.87	15.87	15.87
1.01	16.11	16.33	16.07	15.83	15.72	15.66	15.64	15.63	15.63	15.63	15.63	15.62	15.62	15.62	15.62
1.02	15.53	16.00	15.78	15.56	15.46	15.41	15.40	15.39	15.39	15.38	15.38	15.38	15.38	15.39	15.39
1.03	14.93	15.67	15.48	15.30	15.21	15.17	15.15	15.15	15.15	15.15	15.15	15.15	15.15	15.15	15.15
1.04	14.31	15.33	15.19	15.03	14.96	14.92	14.91	14.91	14.91	14.91	14.91	14.91	14.91	14.91	14.91
1.05	13.66	15.00	14.91	14.77	14.71	14.68	14.67	14.67	14.67	14.67	14.68	14.68	14.68	14.68	14.68
1.06	12.98	14.67	14.62	14.51	14.46	14.44	14.44	14.44	14.44	14.44	14.45	14.45	14.45	14.45	14.45
1.07	12.27	14.33	14.33	14.26	14.22	14.20	14.20	14.21	14.21	14.21	14.22	14.22	14.22	14.23	14.22
1.08	11.51	14.00	14.05	14.00	13.97	13.97	13.97	13.98	13.98	13.98	13.99	13.99	14.00	14.00	14.00
1.09	10.71	13.67	13.76	13.75	13.73	13.74	13.74	13.75	13.75	13.76	13.77	13.77	13.77	13.78	13.78

Figure 9.20 ANSI/ASQ Z1.9-2003 Table B-5: Table for estimating the lot percent nonconforming using standard deviation method. Values tabulated are read as percentages. *(continued)*

Q_U or Q_L	Sample size														
	3	4	5	7	10	15	20	25	30	35	50	75	100	150	200
1.10	9.84	13.33	13.48	13.49	13.50	13.51	13.52	13.52	13.53	13.54	13.54	13.55	13.55	13.56	13.56
1.11	8.89	13.00	13.20	13.25	13.26	13.28	13.29	13.30	13.31	13.31	13.32	13.33	13.34	13.34	13.34
1.12	7.82	12.67	12.93	13.00	13.03	13.05	13.07	13.08	13.09	13.10	13.11	13.12	13.12	13.13	13.13
1.13	6.60	12.33	12.65	12.75	12.80	12.83	12.85	12.86	12.87	12.88	12.89	12.90	12.91	12.91	12.92
1.14	5.08	12.00	12.37	12.51	12.57	12.61	12.63	12.65	12.66	12.67	12.68	12.69	12.70	12.70	12.71
1.15	2.87	11.67	12.10	12.27	12.34	12.39	12.42	12.44	12.45	12.46	12.47	12.48	12.49	12.49	12.50
1.16	0.00	11.33	11.83	12.03	12.12	12.18	12.21	12.22	12.24	12.25	12.26	12.28	12.28	12.29	12.29
1.17	0.00	11.00	11.56	11.79	11.90	11.96	12.00	12.02	12.03	12.04	12.06	12.07	12.08	12.09	12.09
1.18	0.00	10.67	11.29	11.56	11.68	11.75	11.79	11.81	11.82	11.84	11.85	11.87	11.88	11.88	11.89
1.19	0.00	10.33	11.02	11.33	11.46	11.54	11.58	11.61	11.62	11.63	11.65	11.67	11.68	11.69	11.69
1.20	0.00	10.00	10.76	11.10	11.24	11.34	11.38	11.41	11.42	11.43	11.46	11.47	11.48	11.49	11.49
1.21	0.00	9.67	10.50	10.87	11.03	11.13	11.18	11.21	11.22	11.24	11.26	11.28	11.29	11.30	11.30
1.22	0.00	9.33	10.23	10.65	10.82	10.93	10.98	11.01	11.03	11.04	11.07	11.09	11.09	11.10	11.11
1.23	0.00	9.00	9.97	10.42	10.61	10.73	10.78	10.81	10.84	10.85	10.88	10.90	10.91	10.92	10.92
1.24	0.00	8.67	9.72	10.20	10.41	10.53	10.59	10.62	10.64	10.66	10.69	10.71	10.72	10.73	10.73
1.25	0.00	8.33	9.46	9.98	10.21	10.34	10.40	10.43	10.46	10.47	10.50	10.52	10.53	10.54	10.55
1.26	0.00	8.00	9.21	9.77	10.00	10.15	10.21	10.25	10.27	10.29	10.32	10.34	10.35	10.36	10.37
1.27	0.00	7.67	8.96	9.55	9.81	9.96	10.02	10.06	10.09	10.10	10.13	10.16	10.17	10.18	10.19
1.28	0.00	7.33	8.71	9.34	9.61	9.77	9.84	9.88	9.90	9.92	9.95	9.98	9.99	10.00	10.01
1.29	0.00	7.00	8.46	9.13	9.42	9.58	9.66	9.70	9.72	9.74	9.78	9.80	9.82	9.83	9.83
1.30	0.00	6.67	8.21	8.93	9.22	9.40	9.48	9.52	9.55	9.57	9.60	9.63	9.64	9.65	9.66
1.31	0.00	6.33	7.97	8.72	9.03	9.22	9.30	9.34	9.37	9.39	9.43	9.46	9.47	9.48	9.49
1.32	0.00	6.00	7.73	8.52	8.85	9.04	9.12	9.17	9.20	9.22	9.26	9.29	9.30	9.31	9.32
1.33	0.00	5.67	7.49	8.32	8.66	8.86	8.95	9.00	9.03	9.05	9.09	9.12	9.13	9.15	9.15
1.34	0.00	5.33	7.25	8.12	8.48	8.69	8.78	8.83	8.86	8.88	8.92	8.95	8.97	8.98	8.99
1.35	0.00	5.00	7.02	7.92	8.30	8.52	8.61	8.66	8.69	8.72	8.76	8.79	8.81	8.82	8.83
1.36	0.00	4.67	6.79	7.73	8.12	8.35	8.44	8.50	8.53	8.55	8.60	8.63	8.65	8.66	8.67
1.37	0.00	4.33	6.56	7.54	7.95	8.18	8.28	8.33	8.37	8.39	8.44	8.47	8.49	8.50	8.51
1.38	0.00	4.00	6.33	7.35	7.77	8.01	8.12	8.17	8.21	8.24	8.28	8.31	8.33	8.35	8.36
1.39	0.00	3.67	6.10	7.17	7.60	7.85	7.96	8.01	8.05	8.08	8.12	8.16	8.18	8.19	8.20
1.40	0.00	3.33	5.88	6.98	7.44	7.69	7.80	7.86	7.90	7.92	7.97	8.01	8.02	8.04	8.05
1.41	0.00	3.00	5.66	6.80	7.27	7.53	7.64	7.70	7.74	7.77	7.82	7.86	7.87	7.89	7.90
1.42	0.00	2.67	5.44	6.62	7.10	7.37	7.49	7.55	7.59	7.62	7.67	7.71	7.73	7.74	7.75
1.43	0.00	2.33	5.23	6.45	6.94	7.22	7.34	7.40	7.44	7.47	7.52	7.56	7.58	7.60	7.61
1.44	0.00	[illegible]	[illegible]	[illegible]	[illegible]	[illegible]	[illegible]	[illegible]	[illegible]	[illegible]	[illegible]	[illegible]	[illegible]	[illegible]	[illegible]
1.45	0.00	1.67	4.81	6.10	6.63	6.92	7.04	7.11	7.15	7.18	7.24	7.28	7.30	7.32	7.32
1.46	0.00	1.33	4.60	5.93	6.47	6.77	6.90	6.97	7.01	7.04	7.10	7.14	7.16	7.18	7.19
1.47	0.00	1.00	4,39	5.77	6.32	6.63	6.75	6.83	6.87	6.90	6.96	7.00	7.02	7.04	7.05
1.48	0.00	.67	4.19	5.60	6.17	6.48	6.61	6.69	6.73	6.77	6.82	6.86	6.88	6.90	6.91
1.49	0.00	.33	3.99	5.44	6.02	6.34	6.48	6.55	6.60	6.63	6.69	6.73	6.75	6.77	6.78

Figure 9.20 ANSI/ASQ Z1.9-2003 Table B-5: Table for estimating the lot percent nonconforming using standard deviation method. Values tabulated are read as percentages. *(continued)*

Q_U or Q_L	Sample size														
	3	4	5	7	10	15	20	25	30	35	50	75	100	150	200
1.50	0.00	0.00	3.80	5.28	5.87	6.20	6.34	6.41	6.46	6.50	6.55	6.60	6.62	6.64	6.65
1.51	0.00	0.00	3.61	5.13	5.73	6.06	6.20	6.28	6.33	6.36	6.42	6.47	6.49	6.51	6.52
1.52	0.00	0.00	3.42	4.97	5.59	5.93	6.07	6.15	6.20	6.23	6.29	6.34	6.36	6.38	6.39
1.53	0.00	0.00	3.23	4.82	5.45	5.80	5.94	6.02	6.07	6.11	6.17	6.21	6.24	6.26	6.27
1.54	0.00	0.00	3.05	4.67	5.31	5.67	5.81	5.89	5.95	5.98	6.04	6.09	6.11	6.13	6.15
1.55	0.00	0.00	2.87	4.52	5.18	5.54	5.69	5.77	5.82	5.86	5.92	5.97	5.99	6.01	6.02
1.56	0.00	0.00	2.69	4.38	5.05	5.41	5.56	5.65	5.70	5.74	5.80	5.85	5.87	5.89	5.90
1.57	0.00	0.00	2.52	4.24	4.92	5.29	5.44	5.53	5.58	5.62	5.68	5.73	5.75	5.78	5.79
1.58	0.00	0.00	2.35	4.10	4.79	5.16	5.32	5.41	5.46	5.50	5.56	5.61	5.64	5.66	5.67
1.59	0.00	0.00	2.19	3.96	4.66	5.04	5.20	5.29	5.34	5.38	5.45	5.50	5.52	5.55	5.56
1.60	0.00	0.00	2.03	3.83	4.54	4.92	5.08	5.17	5.23	5.27	5.33	5.38	5.41	5.43	5.44
1.61	0.00	0.00	1.87	3.69	4.41	4.81	4.97	5.06	5.12	5.16	5.22	5.27	5.30	5.32	5.33
1.62	0.00	0.00	1.72	3.57	4.30	4.69	4.86	4.95	5.01	5.04	5.11	5.16	5.19	5.21	5.23
1.63	0.00	0.00	1.57	3.44	4.18	4.58	4.75	4.84	4.90	4.94	5.01	5.06	5.08	5.11	5.12
1.64	0.00	0.00	1.42	3.31	4.06	4.47	4.64	4.73	4.79	4.83	4.90	4.95	4.98	5.00	5.01
1.65	0.00	0.00	1.28	3.19	3.95	4.36	4.53	4.62	4.68	4.72	4.79	4.85	4.87	4.90	4.91
1.66	0.00	0.00	1.15	3.07	3.84	4.25	4.43	4.52	4.58	4.62	4.69	4.74	4.77	4.80	4.81
1.67	0.00	0.00	1.02	2.95	3.73	4.15	4.32	4.42	4.48	4.52	4.59	4.64	4.67	4.70	4.71
1.68	0.00	0.00	0.89	2.84	3.62	4.05	4.22	4.32	4.38	4.42	4.49	4.55	4.57	4.60	4.61
1.69	0.00	0.00	0.77	2.73	3.52	3.94	4.12	4.22	4.28	4.32	4.39	4.45	4.47	4.50	4.51
1.70	0.00	0.00	0.66	2.62	3.41	3.84	4.02	4.12	4.18	4.22	4.30	4.35	4.38	4.41	4.42
1.71	0.00	0.00	0.55	2.51	3.31	3.75	3.93	4.02	4.09	4.13	4.20	4.26	4.29	4.31	4.32
1.72	0.00	0.00	0.45	2.41	3.21	3.65	3.83	3.93	3.99	4.04	4.11	4.17	4.19	4.22	4.23
1.73	0.00	0.00	0.36	2.30	3.11	3.56	3.74	3.84	3.90	3.94	4.02	4.08	4.10	4.13	4.14
1.74	0.00	0.00	0.27	2.20	3.02	3.46	3.65	3.75	3.81	3.85	3.93	3.99	4.01	4.04	4.05
1.75	0.00	0.00	0.19	2.11	2.93	3.37	3.56	3.66	3.72	3.77	3.84	3.90	3.93	3.95	3.97
1.76	0.00	0.00	0.12	2.01	2.83	3.28	3.47	3.57	3.63	3.68	3.76	3.81	3.84	3.87	3.88
1.77	0.00	0.00	0.06	1.92	2.74	3.20	3.38	3.48	3.55	3.59	3.67	3.73	3.76	3.78	3.80
1.78	0.00	0.00	0.02	1.83	2.66	3.11	3.30	3.40	3.47	3.51	3.59	3.64	3.67	3.70	3.71
1.79	0.00	0.00	0.00	1.74	2.57	3.03	3.21	3.32	3.38	3.43	3.51	3.56	3.59	3.62	3.63
1.80	0.00	0.00	0.00	1.65	2.49	2.94	3.13	3.24	3.30	3.35	3.43	3.48	3.51	3.54	3.55
1.81	0.00	0.00	0.00	1.57	2.40	2.86	3.05	31.6	3.22	3.27	3.35	3.40	3.43	3.46	3.47
1.82	0.00	0.00	0.00	1.49	2.32	2.79	2.98	3.08	3.15	3.19	3.27	3.33	3.36	3.38	3.40
1.83	0.00	0.00	0.00	1.41	2.25	2.71	2.90	3.00	3.07	3.11	3.19	3.25	3.28	3.31	3.32
1.84	0.00	0.00	0.00	1.34	2.17	2.63	2.82	2.93	2.99	3.04	3.12	3.18	3.21	3.23	3.25
1.85	0.00	0.00	0.00	1.26	2.09	2.56	2.75	2.85	2.92	2.97	3.05	3.10	3.13	3.16	3.17
1.86	0.00	0.00	0.00	1.19	2.02	2.48	2.68	2.78	2.85	2.89	2.97	3.03	3.06	3.09	3.10
1.87	0.00	0.00	0.00	1.12	1.95	2.41	2.61	2.71	2.78	2.82	2.90	2.96	2.99	3.02	3.03
1.88	0.00	0.00	0.00	1.06	1.88	2.34	2.54	2.64	2.71	2.75	2.83	2.89	2.92	2.95	2.96
1.89	0.00	0.00	0.00	0.99	1.81	2.28	2.47	2.57	2.64	2.69	2.77	2.83	2.85	2.88	2.90

Figure 9.20 ANSI/ASQ Z1.9-2003 Table B-5: Table for estimating the lot percent nonconforming using standard deviation method. Values tabulated are read as percentages.

(continued)

Q_U or Q_L	Sample size														
	3	4	5	7	10	15	20	25	30	35	50	75	100	150	200
1.90	0.00	0.00	0.00	0.93	1.75	2.21	2.40	2.51	2.57	2.62	2.70	2.76	2.79	2.82	2.83
1.91	0.00	0.00	0.00	0.87	1.68	2.14	2.34	2.44	2.51	2.56	2.63	2.69	2.72	2.75	2.77
1.92	0.00	0.00	0.00	0.81	1.62	2.08	2.27	2.38	2.45	2.49	2.57	2.63	2.66	2.69	2.70
1.93	0.00	0.00	0.00	0.76	1.56	2.02	2.21	2.32	2.38	2.43	2.51	2.57	2.60	2.63	2.64
1.94	0.00	0.00	0.00	0.70	1.50	1.96	2.15	2.25	2.32	2.37	2.45	2.51	2.54	2.56	2.58
1.95	0.00	0.00	0.00	0.65	1.44	1.90	2.09	2.19	2.26	2.31	2.39	2.45	2.48	2.50	2.52
1.96	0.00	0.00	0.00	0.60	1.38	1.84	2.03	2.14	2.20	2.25	2.33	2.39	2.42	2.44	2.46
1.97	0.00	0.00	0.00	0.56	1.33	1.78	1.97	2.08	2.14	2.19	2.27	2.33	2.36	2.39	2.40
1.98	0.00	0.00	0.00	0.51	1.27	1.73	1.92	2.02	2.09	2.13	2.21	2.27	2.30	2.33	2.34
1.99	0.00	0.00	0.00	0.47	1.22	1.67	1.86	1.97	2.03	2.08	2.16	2.22	2.25	2.27	2.29
2.00	0.00	0.00	0.00	0.43	1.17	1.62	1.81	1.91	1.98	2.03	2.10	2.16	2.19	2.22	2.23
2.01	0.00	0.00	0.00	0.39	1.12	1.57	1.76	1.86	1.93	1.97	2.05	2.11	2.14	2.17	2.18
2.02	0.00	0.00	0.00	0.36	1.07	1.52	1.71	1.81	1.87	1.92	2.00	2.06	2.09	2.11	2.13
2.03	0.00	0.00	0.00	0.32	1.03	1.47	1.66	1.76	1.82	1.87	1.95	2.01	2.04	2.06	2.08
2.04	0.00	0.00	0.00	0.29	0.98	1.42	1.61	1.71	1.77	1.82	1.90	1.96	1.99	2.01	2.03
2.05	0.00	0.00	0.00	0.26	0.94	1.37	1.56	1.66	1.73	1.77	1.85	1.91	1.94	1.96	1.98
2.06	0.00	0.00	0.00	0.23	0.90	1.33	1.51	1.61	1.68	1.72	1.80	1.86	1.89	1.92	1.93
2.07	0.00	0.00	0.00	0.21	0.86	1.28	1.47	1.57	1.63	1.68	1.76	1.81	1.84	1.87	1.88
2.08	0.00	0.00	0.00	0.18	0.82	1.24	1.42	1.52	1.59	1.63	1.71	1.77	1.79	1.82	1.84
2.09	0.00	0.00	0.00	0.16	0.78	1.20	1.38	1.48	1.54	1.59	1.66	1.72	1.75	1.78	1.79
2.10	0.00	0.00	0.00	0.14	0.74	1.16	1.34	1.44	1.50	1.54	1.62	1.68	1.71	1.73	1.75
2.11	0.00	0.00	0.00	0.12	0.71	1.12	1.30	1.39	1.46	1.50	1.58	1.63	1.66	1.69	1.70
2.12	0.00	0.00	0.00	0.10	0.67	1.08	1.26	1.35	1.42	1.46	1.54	1.59	1.62	1.65	1.66
2.13	0.00	0.00	0.00	0.08	0.64	1.04	1.22	1.31	1.38	1.42	1.50	1.55	1.58	1.61	1.62
2.14	0.00	0.00	0.00	0.07	0.61	1.00	1.18	1.28	1.34	1.38	1.46	1.51	1.54	1.57	1.58
2.15	0.00	0.00	0.00	0.06	0.58	0.97	1.14	1.24	1.30	1.34	1.42	1.47	1.50	1.53	1.54
2.16	0.00	0.00	0.00	0.05	0.55	0.93	1.10	1.20	1.26	1.30	1.38	1.43	1.46	1.49	1.50
2.17	0.00	0.00	0.00	0.04	0.52	0.90	1.07	1.16	1.22	1.27	1.34	1.40	1.42	1.45	1.46
2.18	0.00	0.00	0.00	0.03	0.49	0.87	1.03	1.13	1.19	1.23	1.30	1.36	1.39	1.41	1.42
2.19	0.00	0.00	0.00	0.02	0.46	0.83	1.00	1.09	1.15	1.20	1.27	1.32	1.35	1.38	1.39
2.20	0.000	0.000	0.000	0.015	0.437	0.803	0.968	1.160	1.120	1.160	1.233	1.287	1.314	1.340	1.352
2.21	0.000	0.000	0.000	0.010	0.413	0.772	0.936	1.028	1.087	1.128	1.199	1.253	1.279	1.305	1.318
2.22	0.000	0.000	0.000	0.006	0.389	0.734	0.905	0.996	1.054	1.095	1.166	1.219	1.245	1.271	1.284
2.23	0.000	0.000	0.000	0.003	0.366	0.715	0.874	0.965	1.023	1.063	1.134	1.186	1.212	1.238	1.250
2.24	0.000	0.000	0.000	0.002	0.345	0.687	0.845	0.935	0.992	1.032	1.102	1.154	1.180	1.205	1.218
2.25	0.000	0.000	0.000	0.001	0.324	0.660	0.816	0.905	0.962	1.002	1.071	1.123	1.148	1.173	1.186
2.26	0.000	0.000	0.000	0.000	0.304	0.634	0.789	0.876	0.933	0.972	1.041	1.092	1.117	1.142	1.155
2.27	0.000	0.000	0.000	0.000	0.285	0.609	0.762	0.848	0.904	0.943	1.011	1.062	1.087	1.112	1.124
2.28	0.000	0.000	0.000	0.000	0.267	0.585	0.735	0.821	0.876	0.915	0.982	1.033	1.058	1.082	1.095
2.29	0.000	0.000	0.000	0.000	0.250	0.561	0.710	0.794	0.849	0.887	0.954	1.004	1.029	1.053	1.065

Figure 9.20 ANSI/ASQ Z1.9-2003 Table B-5: Table for estimating the lot percent nonconforming using standard deviation method. Values tabulated are read as percentages.

(continued)

Q_U or Q_L	Sample size														
	3	4	5	7	10	15	20	25	30	35	50	75	100	150	200
2.30	0.000	0.000	0.000	0.000	0.233	0.538	0.685	0.769	0.823	0.861	0.927	0.977	1.001	1.025	1.037
2.31	0.000	0.000	0.000	0.000	0.218	0.516	0.661	0.743	0.797	0.834	0.900	0.949	0.974	0.998	1.009
2.32	0.000	0.000	0.000	0.000	0.203	0.495	0.637	0.719	0.772	0.809	0.874	0.923	0.947	0.971	0.982
2.33	0.000	0.000	0.000	0.000	0.189	0.474	0.614	0.695	0.748	0.784	0.848	0.897	0.921	0.944	0.956
2.34	0.000	0.000	0.000	0.000	0.175	0.454	0.592	0.672	0.724	0.760	0.824	0.872	0.895	0.919	0.930
2.35	0.000	0.000	0.000	0.000	0.163	0.435	0.571	0.650	0.701	0.736	0.799	0.847	0.870	0.893	0.905
2.36	0.000	0.000	0.000	0.000	0.151	0.416	0.550	0.628	0.678	0.714	0.776	0.823	0.846	0.869	0.880
2.37	0.000	0.000	0.000	0.000	0.139	0.398	0.530	0.606	0.656	0.691	0.753	0.799	0.822	0.845	0.856
2.38	0.000	0.000	0.000	0.000	0.128	0.381	0.510	0.586	0.635	0.670	0.730	0.777	0.799	0.822	0.833
2.39	0.000	0.000	0.000	0.000	0.118	0.364	0.491	0.566	0.614	0.648	0.709	0.754	0.777	0.799	0.810
2.40	0.000	0.000	0.000	0.000	0.109	0.348	0.473	0.546	0.594	0.628	0.687	0.732	0.755	0.777	0.787
2.41	0.000	0.000	0.000	0.000	0.100	0.332	0.455	0.527	0.575	0.608	0.667	0.711	0.733	0.755	0.766
2.42	0.000	0.000	0.000	0.000	0.091	0.317	0.437	0.509	0.555	0.588	0.646	0.691	0.712	0.734	0.744
2.43	0.000	0.000	0.000	0.000	0.083	0.302	0.421	0.491	0.537	0.569	0.627	0.670	0.692	0.713	0.724
2.44	0.000	0.000	0.000	0.000	0.076	0.288	0.404	0.474	0.519	0.551	0.608	0.651	0.672	0.693	0.703
2.45	0.000	0.000	0.000	0.000	0.069	0.275	0.389	0.457	0.501	0.533	0.589	0.632	0.653	0.673	0.684
2.46	0.000	0.000	0.000	0.000	0.063	0.262	0.373	0.440	0.484	0.516	0.571	0.613	0.634	0.654	0.664
2.47	0.000	0.000	0.000	0.000	0.057	0.249	0.359	0.425	0.468	0.499	0.553	0.595	0.615	0.636	0.646
2.48	0.000	0.000	0.000	0.000	0.051	0.237	0.345	0.409	0.452	0.482	0.536	0.577	0.597	0.617	0.627
2.49	0.000	0.000	0.000	0.000	0.046	0.226	0.331	0.394	0.436	0.466	0.519	0.560	0.580	0.600	0.609
2.50	0.000	0.000	0.000	0.000	0.041	0.214	0.317	0.380	0.421	0.451	0.503	0.543	0.563	0.582	0.592
2.51	0.000	0.000	0.000	0.000	0.037	0.204	0.305	0.366	0.407	0.436	0.487	0.527	0.546	0.565	0.575
2.52	0.000	0.000	0.000	0.000	0.033	0.193	0.292	0.352	0.392	0.421	0.472	0.511	0.530	0.549	0.559
2.53	0.000	0.000	0.000	0.000	0.029	0.184	0.280	0.339	0.379	0.407	0.457	0.495	0.514	0.533	0.542
2.54	0.000	0.000	0.000	0.000	0.026	0.174	0.268	0.326	0.365	0.393	0.442	0.480	0.499	0.517	0.527
2.55	0.000	0.000	0.000	0.000	0.023	0.165	0.257	0.314	0.352	0.379	0.428	0.465	0.484	0.502	0.511
2.56	0.000	0.000	0.000	0.000	0.020	0.156	0.246	0.302	0.340	0.366	0.414	0.451	0.469	0.487	0.496
2.57	0.000	0.000	0.000	0.000	0.017	0.148	0.236	0.291	0.327	0.354	0.401	0.437	0.455	0.473	0.482
2.58	0.000	0.000	0.000	0.000	0.015	0.140	0.226	0.279	0.316	0.341	0.388	0.424	0.441	0.459	0.468
2.59	0.000	0.000	0.000	0.000	0.013	0.133	0.216	0.269	0.304	0.330	0.375	0.410	0.428	0.445	0.454
2.60	0.000	0.000	0.000	0.000	0.011	0.125	0.207	0.258	0.293	0.318	0.363	0.398	0.415	0.432	0.441
2.61	0.000	0.000	0.000	0.000	0.009	0.118	0.198	0.248	0.282	0.307	0.351	0.385	0.402	0.419	0.428
2.62	0.000	0.000	0.000	0.000	0.008	0.112	0.189	0.238	0.272	0.296	0.339	0.373	0.390	0.406	0.415
2.63	0.000	0.000	0.000	0.000	0.007	0.105	0.181	0.229	0.262	0.285	0.328	0.361	0.378	0.394	0.402
2.64	0.000	0.000	0.000	0.000	0.006	0.099	0.172	0.220	0.252	0.275	0.317	0.350	0.366	0.382	0.390
2.65	0.000	0.000	0.000	0.000	0.005	0.094	0.165	0.211	0.242	0.265	0.307	0.339	0.355	0.371	0.379
2.66	0.000	0.000	0.000	0.000	0.004	0.088	0.157	0.202	0.233	0.256	0.296	0.328	0.344	0.359	0.367
2.67	0.000	0.000	0.000	0.000	0.003	0.083	0.150	0.194	0.224	0.246	0.286	0.317	0.333	0.348	0.356
2.68	0.000	0.000	0.000	0.000	0.002	0.078	0.143	0.186	0.216	0.237	0.277	0.307	0.322	0.338	0.345
2.69	0.000	0.000	0.000	0.000	0.002	0.073	0.136	0.179	0.208	0.229	0.267	0.297	0.312	0.327	0.335

Figure 9.20 ANSI/ASQ Z1.9-2003 Table B-5: Table for estimating the lot percent nonconforming using standard deviation method. Values tabulated are read as percentages. *(continued)*

Q_U or Q_L	Sample size													
	3	4	5	7	10	15	20	25	30	35	50	75	100	150	200
2.70	0.000	0.000	0.000	0.000	0.001	0.069	0.130	0.171	0.200	0.220	0.258	0.288	0.302	0.317	0.325
2.71	0.000	0.000	0.000	0.000	0.001	0.064	0.124	0.164	0.192	0.212	0.249	0.278	0.293	0.307	0.315
2.72	0.000	0.000	0.000	0.000	0.001	0.060	0.118	0.157	0.184	0.204	0.241	0.269	0.283	0.298	0.305
2.73	0.000	0.000	0.000	0.000	0.001	0.057	0.112	0.151	0.177	0.197	0.232	0.260	0.274	0.288	0.296
2.74	0.000	0.000	0.000	0.000	0.000	0.053	0.107	0.144	0.170	0.189	0.224	0.252	0.266	0.279	0.286
2.75	0.000	0.000	0.000	0.000	0.000	0.049	0.102	0.138	0.163	0.182	0.216	0.243	0.257	0.271	0.277
2.76	0.000	0.000	0.000	0.000	0.000	0.046	0.097	0.132	0.157	0.175	0.209	0.235	0.249	0.262	0.269
2.77	0.000	0.000	0.000	0.000	0.000	0.043	0.092	0.126	0.151	0.168	0.201	0.227	0.241	0.254	0.260
2.78	0.000	0.000	0.000	0.000	0.000	0.040	0.087	0.121	0.145	0.162	0.194	0.220	0.223	0.246	0.252
2.79	0.000	0.000	0.000	0.000	0.000	0.037	0.083	0.115	0.139	0.156	0.187	0.212	0.220	0.238	0.244
2.80	0.000	0.000	0.000	0.000	0.000	0.035	0.079	0.110	0.133	0.150	0.181	0.205	0.218	0.230	0.237
2.81	0.000	0.000	0.000	0.000	0.000	0.032	0.075	0.105	0.128	0.144	0.174	0.198	0.211	0.223	0.229
2.82	0.000	0.000	0.000	0.000	0.000	0.030	0.071	0.101	0.122	0.138	0.168	0.192	0.204	0.216	0.222
2.83	0.000	0.000	0.000	0.000	0.000	0.028	0.067	0.096	0.117	0.133	0.162	0.185	0.197	0.209	0.215
2.84	0.000	0.000	0.000	0.000	0.000	0.026	0.064	0.092	0.112	0.128	0.156	0.179	0.190	0.202	0.208
2.85	0.000	0.000	0.000	0.000	0.000	0.024	0.060	0.088	0.108	0.122	0.150	0.173	0.184	0.195	0.201
2.86	0.000	0.000	0.000	0.000	0.000	0.022	0.057	0.084	0.103	0.118	0.145	0.167	0.178	0.189	0.195
2.87	0.000	0.000	0.000	0.000	0.000	0.020	0.054	0.080	0.099	0.113	0.139	0.161	0.172	0.183	0.188
2.88	0.000	0.000	0.000	0.000	0.000	0.019	0.051	0.076	0.094	0.108	0.134	0.155	0.166	0.177	0.182
2.89	0.000	0.000	0.000	0.000	0.000	0.017	0.048	0.073	0.090	0.104	0.129	0.150	0.160	0.171	0.176
2.90	0.000	0.000	0.000	0.000	0.000	0.016	0.046	0.069	0.087	0.100	0.125	0.145	0.155	0.165	0.171
2.91	0.000	0.000	0.000	0.000	0.000	0.015	0.043	0.066	0.083	0.096	0.120	0.140	0.150	0.160	0.165
2.92	0.000	0.000	0.000	0.000	0.000	0.013	0.041	0.063	0.079	0.092	0.115	0.135	0.145	0.155	0.160
2.93	0.000	0.000	0.000	0.000	0.000	0.012	0.038	0.060	0.076	0.088	0.111	0.130	0.140	0.149	0.154
2.94	0.000	0.000	0.000	0.000	0.000	0.011	0.036	0.057	0.072	0.084	0.107	0.125	0.135	0.144	0.149
2.95	0.000	0.000	0.000	0.000	0.000	0.010	0.034	0.054	0.069	0.081	0.103	0.121	0.130	0.140	0.144
2.96	0.000	0.000	0.000	0.000	0.000	0.009	0.032	0.051	0.066	0.077	0.099	0.117	0.126	0.135	0.140
2.97	0.000	0.000	0.000	0.000	0.000	0.009	0.030	0.049	0.063	0.074	0.095	0.112	0.121	0.130	0.135
2.98	0.000	0.000	0.000	0.000	0.000	0.008	0.028	0.046	0.060	0.071	0.091	0.108	0.117	0.126	0.130
2.99	0.000	0.000	0.000	0.000	0.000	0.007	0.027	0.044	0.057	0.068	0.088	0.104	0.113	0.122	0.126
3.00	0.000	0.000	0.000	0.000	0.000	0.006	0.025	0.042	0.055	0.065	0.084	0.101	0.109	0.118	0.122
3.01	0.000	0.000	0.000	0.000	0.000	0.006	0.024	0.040	0.052	0.062	0.081	0.097	0.105	0.113	0.118
3.02	0.000	0.000	0.000	0.000	0.000	0.005	0.022	0.038	0.050	0.060	0.078	0.093	0.101	0.110	0.114
3.03	0.000	0.000	0.000	0.000	0.000	0.005	0.021	0.036	0.048	0.057	0.075	0.090	0.098	0.106	0.110
3.04	0.000	0.000	0.000	0.000	0.000	0.004	0.019	0.034	0.045	0.054	0.072	0.087	0.094	0.102	0.106
3.05	0.000	0.000	0.000	0.000	0.000	0.004	0.018	0.032	0.043	0.052	0.069	0.083	0.091	0.099	0.103
3.06	0.000	0.000	0.000	0.000	0.000	0.003	0.017	0.030	0.041	0.050	0.066	0.080	0.088	0.095	0.099
3.07	0.000	0.000	0.000	0.000	0.000	0.003	0.016	0.029	0.039	0.047	0.064	0.077	0.085	0.092	0.096
3.08	0.000	0.000	0.000	0.000	0.000	0.003	0.015	0.027	0.037	0.045	0.061	0.074	0.081	0.089	0.092
3.09	0.000	0.000	0.000	0.000	0.000	0.002	0.014	0.026	0.036	0.043	0.059	0.072	0.079	0.086	0.089

Figure 9.20 ANSI/ASQ Z1.9-2003 Table B-5: Table for estimating the lot percent nonconforming using standard deviation method. Values tabulated are read as percentages. *(continued)*

Q_U or Q_L	Sample size														
	3	4	5	7	10	15	20	25	30	35	50	75	100	150	200
3.10	0.000	0.000	0.000	0.000	0.000	0.002	0.013	0.024	0.034	0.041	0.056	0.069	0.076	0.083	0.086
3.11	0.000	0.000	0.000	0.000	0.000	0.002	0.012	0.023	0.032	0.039	0.054	0.066	0.073	0.080	0.083
3.12	0.000	0.000	0.000	0.000	0.000	0.002	0.011	0.022	0.031	0.038	0.052	0.064	0.070	0.077	0.080
3.13	0.000	0.000	0.000	0.000	0.000	0.002	0.011	0.021	0.029	0.036	0.050	0.061	0.068	0.074	0.077
3.14	0.000	0.000	0.000	0.000	0.000	0.001	0.010	0.019	0.028	0.034	0.048	0.059	0.065	0.071	0.075
3.15	0.000	0.000	0.000	0.000	0.000	0.001	0.009	0.018	0.026	0.033	0.046	0.057	0.063	0.069	0.072
3.16	0.000	0.000	0.000	0.000	0.000	0.001	0.009	0.017	0.025	0.031	0.044	0.055	0.060	0.066	0.069
3.17	0.000	0.000	0.000	0.000	0.000	0.001	0.008	0.016	0.024	0.030	0.042	0.053	0.058	0.064	0.067
3.18	0.000	0.000	0.000	0.000	0.000	0.001	0.007	0.015	0.022	0.028	0.040	0.050	0.056	0.062	0.065
3.19	0.000	0.000	0.000	0.000	0.000	0.001	0.007	0.015	0.021	0.027	0.038	0.049	0.054	0.059	0.062
3.20	0.000	0.000	0.000	0.000	0.000	0.001	0.006	0.014	0.020	0.026	0.037	0.047	0.052	0.057	0.060
3.21	0.000	0.000	0.000	0.000	0.000	0.000	0.006	0.013	0.019	0.024	0.035	0.045	0.050	0.055	0.058
3.22	0.000	0.000	0.000	0.000	0.000	0.000	0.005	0.012	0.018	0.023	0.034	0.043	0.048	0.053	0.056
3.23	0.000	0.000	0.000	0.000	0.000	0.000	0.005	0.011	0.017	0.022	0.032	0.041	0.046	0.051	0.054
3.24	0.000	0.000	0.000	0.000	0.000	0.000	0.005	0.011	0.016	0.021	0.031	0.040	0.044	0.049	0.052
3.25	0.000	0.000	0.000	0.000	0.000	0.000	0.004	0.010	0.015	0.020	0.030	0.038	0.043	0.048	0.050
3.26	0.000	0.000	0.000	0.000	0.000	0.000	0.004	0.009	0.015	0.019	0.028	0.037	0.042	0.046	0.048
3.27	0.000	0.000	0.000	0.000	0.000	0.000	0.004	0.009	0.014	0.018	0.027	0.035	0.040	0.044	0.046
3.28	0.000	0.000	0.000	0.000	0.000	0.000	0.003	0.008	0.013	0.017	0.026	0.034	0.038	0.042	0.045
3.29	0.000	0.000	0.000	0.000	0.000	0.000	0.003	0.008	0.012	0.016	0.025	0.032	0.037	0.041	0.043
3.30	0.000	0.000	0.000	0.000	0.000	0.000	0.003	0.007	0.012	0.015	0.024	0.031	0.035	0.039	0.042
3.31	0.000	0.000	0.000	0.000	0.000	0.000	0.003	0.007	0.011	0.015	0.023	0.030	0.034	0.038	0.040
3.32	0.000	0.000	0.000	0.000	0.000	0.000	0.002	0.006	0.010	0.014	0.022	0.029	0.032	0.036	0.038
3.33	0.000	0.000	0.000	0.000	0.000	0.000	0.002	0.006	0.010	0.013	0.021	0.027	0.031	0.035	0.037
3.34	0.000	0.000	0.000	0.000	0.000	0.000	0.002	0.006	0.009	0.013	0.020	0.026	0.030	0.034	0.036
3.35	0.000	0.000	0.000	0.000	0.000	0.000	0.002	0.005	0.009	0.012	0.019	0.025	0.029	0.032	0.034
3.36	0.000	0.000	0.000	0.000	0.000	0.000	0.002	0.005	0.008	0.011	0.018	0.024	0.028	0.031	0.033
3.37	0.000	0.000	0.000	0.000	0.000	0.000	0.002	0.005	0.008	0.011	0.017	0.023	0.026	0.030	0.032
3.38	0.000	0.000	0.000	0.000	0.000	0.000	0.001	0.004	0.007	0.010	0.016	0.022	0.025	0.029	0.031
3.39	0.000	0.000	0.000	0.000	0.000	0.000	0.001	0.004	0.007	0.010	0.016	0.021	0.024	0.028	0.029
3.40	0.000	0.000	0.000	0.000	0.000	0.000	0.001	0.004	0.007	0.009	0.015	0.020	0.023	0.027	0.028
3.41	0.000	0.000	0.000	0.000	0.000	0.000	0.001	0.003	0.006	0.009	0.014	0.020	0.022	0.026	0.027
3.42	0.000	0.000	0.000	0.000	0.000	0.000	0.001	0.003	0.006	0.008	0.014	0.019	0.022	0.025	0.026
3.43	0.000	0.000	0.000	0.000	0.000	0.000	0.001	0.003	0.005	0.008	0.013	0.018	0.021	0.024	0.025
3.44	0.000	0.000	0.000	0.000	0.000	0.000	0.001	0.003	0.005	0.007	0.012	0.017	0.020	0.023	0.024
3.45	0.000	0.000	0.000	0.000	0.000	0.000	0.001	0.003	0.005	0.007	0.012	0.016	0.019	0.022	0.023
3.46	0.000	0.000	0.000	0.000	0.000	0.000	0.001	0.002	0.005	0.007	0.011	0.016	0.018	0.021	0.022
3.47	0.000	0.000	0.000	0.000	0.000	0.000	0.001	0.002	0.004	0.006	0.011	0.015	0.018	0.020	0.022
3.48	0.000	0.000	0.000	0.000	0.000	0.000	0.001	0.002	0.004	0.006	0.010	0.014	0.017	0.019	0.021
3.49	0.000	0.000	0.000	0.000	0.000	0.000	0.000	0.002	0.004	0.005	0.010	0.014	0.016	0.019	0.020

Figure 9.20 ANSI/ASQ Z1.9-2003 Table B-5: Table for estimating the lot percent nonconforming using standard deviation method. Values tabulated are read as percentages. *(continued)*

Q_U or Q_L	Sample size														
	3	4	5	7	10	15	20	25	30	35	50	75	100	150	200
3.50	0.000	0.000	0.000	0.000	0.000	0.000	0.000	0.002	0.003	0.005	0.009	0.013	0.015	0.018	0.019
3.51	0.000	0.000	0.000	0.000	0.000	0.000	0.000	0.002	0.003	0.005	0.009	0.013	0.015	0.017	0.018
3.52	0.000	0.000	0.000	0.000	0.000	0.000	0.000	0.002	0.003	0.005	0.008	0.012	0.014	0.016	0.018
3.53	0.000	0.000	0.000	0.000	0.000	0.000	0.000	0.001	0.003	0.004	0.008	0.011	0.014	0.016	0.017
3.54	0.000	0.000	0.000	0.000	0.000	0.000	0.000	0.001	0.003	0.004	0.008	0.011	0.013	0.015	0.016
3.55	0.000	0.000	0.000	0.000	0.000	0.000	0.000	0.001	0.003	0.004	0.007	0.011	0.012	0.015	0.016
3.56	0.000	0.000	0.000	0.000	0.000	0.000	0.000	0.001	0.002	0.004	0.007	0.010	0.012	0.014	0.015
3.57	0.000	0.000	0.000	0.000	0.000	0.000	0.000	0.001	0.002	0.003	0.006	0.010	0.011	0.013	0.014
3.58	0.000	0.000	0.000	0.000	0.000	0.000	0.000	0.001	0.002	0.003	0.006	0.009	0.011	0.013	0.014
3.59	0.000	0.000	0.000	0.000	0.000	0.000	0.000	0.001	0.002	0.003	0.006	0.009	0.010	0.012	0.013
3.60	0.000	0.000	0.000	0.000	0.000	0.000	0.000	0.001	0.002	0.003	0.006	0.008	0.010	0.012	0.013
3.61	0.000	0.000	0.000	0.000	0.000	0.000	0.000	0.001	0.002	0.003	0.005	0.008	0.010	0.011	0.012
3.62	0.000	0.000	0.000	0.000	0.000	0.000	0.000	0.001	0.002	0.003	0.005	0.008	0.009	0.011	0.012
3.63	0.000	0.000	0.000	0.000	0.000	0.000	0.000	0.001	0.001	0.002	0.005	0.007	0.009	0.010	0.011
3.64	0.000	0.000	0.000	0.000	0.000	0.000	0.000	0.001	0.001	0.002	0.004	0.007	0.008	0.010	0.011
3.65	0.000	0.000	0.000	0.000	0.000	0.000	0.000	0.001	0.001	0.002	0.004	0.007	0.008	0.010	0.010
3.66	0.000	0.000	0.000	0.000	0.000	0.000	0.000	0.000	0.001	0.002	0.004	0.006	0.008	0.009	0.010
3.67	0.000	0.000	0.000	0.000	0.000	0.000	0.000	0.000	0.001	0.002	0.004	0.006	0.007	0.009	0.010
3.68	0.000	0.000	0.000	0.000	0.000	0.000	0.000	0.000	0.001	0.002	0.004	0.006	0.007	0.008	0.009
3.69	0.000	0.000	0.000	0.000	0.000	0.000	0.000	0.000	0.001	0.002	0.003	0.005	0.007	0.008	0.009
3.70	0.000	0.000	0.000	0.000	0.000	0.000	0.000	0.000	0.001	0.002	0.003	0.005	0.006	0.008	0.008
3.71	0.000	0.000	0.000	0.000	0.000	0.000	0.000	0.000	0.001	0.001	0.003	0.005	0.006	0.007	0.008
3.72	0.000	0.000	0.000	0.000	0.000	0.000	0.000	0.000	0.001	0.001	0.003	0.005	0.006	0.007	0.008
3.73	0.000	0.000	0.000	0.000	0.000	0.000	0.000	0.000	0.001	0.001	0.003	0.005	0.006	0.007	0.007
3.74	0.000	0.000	0.000	0.000	0.000	0.000	0.000	0.000	0.001	0.001	0.003	0.004	0.005	0.006	0.007
3.75	0.000	0.000	0.000	0.000	0.000	0.000	0.000	0.000	0.001	0.001	0.002	0.004	0.005	0.006	0.007
3.76	0.000	0.000	0.000	0.000	0.000	0.000	0.000	0.000	0.001	0.001	0.002	0.004	0.005	0.006	0.007
3.77	0.000	0.000	0.000	0.000	0.000	0.000	0.000	0.000	0.001	0.001	0.002	0.004	0.005	0.006	0.006
3.78	0.000	0.000	0.000	0.000	0.000	0.000	0.000	0.000	0.000	0.001	0.002	0.004	0.004	0.005	0.006
3.79	0.000	0.000	0.000	0.000	0.000	0.000	0.000	0.000	0.000	0.001	0.002	0.003	0.004	0.005	0.006
3.80	0.000	0.000	0.000	0.000	0.000	0.000	0.000	0.000	0.000	0.001	0.002	0.003	0.004	0.005	0.006
3.81	0.000	0.000	0.000	0.000	0.000	0.000	0.000	0.000	0.000	0.001	0.002	0.003	0.004	0.005	0.005
3.82	0.000	0.000	0.000	0.000	0.000	0.000	0.000	0.000	0.000	0.001	0.002	0.003	0.004	0.005	0.005
3.83	0.000	0.000	0.000	0.000	0.000	0.000	0.000	0.000	0.000	0.001	0.002	0.003	0.004	0.004	0.005
3.84	0.000	0.000	0.000	0.000	0.000	0.000	0.000	0.000	0.000	0.001	0.001	[illegible]	[illegible]	[illegible]	[illegible]
3.85	0.000	0.000	0.000	0.000	0.000	0.000	0.000	0.000	0.000	0.001	0.001	0.002	0.003	0.004	0.004
3.86	0.000	0.000	0.000	0.000	0.000	0.000	0.000	0.000	0.000	0.000	0.001	0.002	0.003	0.004	0.004
3.87	0.000	0.000	0.000	0.000	0.000	0.000	0.000	0.000	0.000	0.000	0.001	0.002	0.003	0.004	0.004
3.88	0.000	0.000	0.000	0.000	0.000	0.000	0.000	0.000	0.000	0.000	0.001	0.002	0.003	0.003	0.004
3.89	0.000	0.000	0.000	0.000	0.000	0.000	0.000	0.000	0.000	0.000	0.001	0.002	0.003	0.003	0.004
3.90	0.000	0.000	0.000	0.000	0.000	0.000	0.000	0.000	0.000	0.000	0.001	0.002	0.003	0.003	0.004

Figure 9.20 ANSI/ASQ Z1.9-2003 Table B-5: Table for estimating the lot percent nonconforming using standard deviation method. Values tabulated are read as percentages. *(continued)*

Sample Size Code Letter	Sample Size	AQLs (normal inspection)											
		T	.10	.15	.25	.40	.65	1.00	1.50	2.50	4.00	6.50	10.00
		M	*M*	*M*	*M*	*M*	*M*	*M*	*M*	*M*	*M*	*M*	*M*
B	3	↓	↓	↓	↓	↓	↓	↓	↓	7.59	18.86	26.94	33.69
C	4	↓	↓	↓	↓	↓	↓	1.49	5.46	10.88	16.41	22.84	29.43
D	5	↓	↓	↓	↓	0.041	1.34	3.33	5.82	9.80	14.37	20.19	26.55
E	7	↓	0.005	0.087	0.421	1.05	2.13	3.54	5.34	8.40	12.19	17.34	23.30
F	10	0.077	0.179	0.349	0.714	1.27	2.14	3.27	4.72	7.26	10.53	15.17	20.73
G	15	0.186	0.311	0.491	0.839	1.33	2.09	3.06	4.32	6.55	9.48	13.74	18.97
H	20	0.228	0.356	0.531	0.864	1.33	2.03	2.93	4.10	6.18	8.95	13.01	18.07
I	25	0.250	0.378	0.551	0.874	1.32	2.00	2.86	3.97	5.98	8.65	12.60	17.55
J	35	0.253	0.373	0.534	0.833	1.24	1.87	2.66	3.70	5.58	8.11	11.89	16.67
K	50	0.243	0.355	0.503	0.778	1.16	1.73	2.47	3.44	5.21	7.61	11.23	15.87
L	75	0.225	0.326	0.461	0.711	1.06	1.59	2.27	3.17	4.83	7.10	10.58	15.07
M	100	0.218	0.315	0.444	0.684	1.02	1.52	2.18	3.06	4.67	6.88	10.29	14.71
N	150	0.202	0.292	0.412	0.636	0.946	1.42	2.05	2.88	4.42	6.56	9.86	14.18
P	200	0.204	0.294	0.414	0.637	0.945	1.42	2.04	2.86	4.39	6.52	9.80	14.11
		.10	.15	.25	.40	.65	1.00	1.50	2.50	4.00	6.50	10.00	
		AQLs (tightened inspection)											

All AQL values are in percent nonconforming. *T* denotes plan used exclusively on tightened inspection and provides symbol for identification of appropriate OC curve.

↓ = Use first sampling plan below arrow; that is, both sample size and *M* value. When sample size equals or exceeds lot size, every item in the lot must be inspected.

Figure 9.21 ANSI/ASQ Z1.9-2003 Table B-3: Master table for normal and tightened inspection for plans based on variability unknown (double specification limit and Form 2—single specification limit).

Notes

1. W. E. Deming, *Out of the Crisis* (Cambridge, MA: MIT Center for Advanced Engineering, 1986).
2. J. M. Juran and F. N. Gryna Jr., *Quality Planning and Analysis* (New York: McGraw-Hill, 1980).
3. ASQ Statistics Division, *Glossary and Tables for Statistical Quality Control,* 4th ed. (Milwaukee, WI: ASQ Quality Press, 2004).
4. Ibid.
5. *ANSI/ASQ Z1.4-2003, Sampling Procedures and Tables for Inspection by Attributes* (Milwaukee, WI: ASQ Quality Press, 2003).
6. Deming, *Crisis.*
7. A. Wald, *Sequential Analysis* (New York: Dover, 1973).
8. W. Burr, *Statistical Quality Control Methods* (New York: Marcel Dekker, 1976).

10

Computer Resources to Support SQC: MINITAB

In the past two decades, the use of technology to analyze complicated data has increased substantially, which not only has made the analysis much easier, but also has reduced the time required to complete the analysis. To facilitate statistical analysis, many companies use personal computer (PC)–based statistical application software. Several software packages are available, including BMDP, JMP, MINITAB, SAS, SPSS, and SYSTAT, to name a few. A great deal of effort has been expended in the development of these software packages to create graphical user interfaces that allow software users to complete statistical analysis activities without having to know a computer programming or scripting language. We believe that publishing a book about applied statistics without acknowledging and addressing the importance and usefulness of statistical software is not in the best interests of the reader. Accordingly, in this and the next chapter, we will briefly discuss two very popular statistical packages: MINITAB and JMP. It is our explicit intent not to endorse either software package, as each has different strengths and features/capabilities.

10.1 Using MINITAB—Version 14

MINITAB has the option of using commands from the menu bar, typing in Session commands, or using both. As shown in Figure 10.1 in the Windows environment, it has the look and feel of most other Windows applications, where the menu options help you to easily navigate through the software.

Once you are in MINITAB, you will see the heading MINITAB - Untitled and three windows:

1. The **Data window** (Worksheet) is used to enter data in columns labeled C1, C2, C3, . . . , C4000.
2. The **Session window** displays the output and also allows you to enter commands when using the command language.

3. The **Project Manager window** (minimized at start-up) displays project folders, which enables you to navigate through them and manipulate as necessary.

Getting Started with MINITAB

In this section we will briefly discuss how to use the MINITAB pull-down menus to analyze statistical data. Once you log on to your PC and open up MINITAB, you will see the screen shown in Figure 10.1. The pull-down menus appear at the top of the screen. Menu commands include:

File Edit Data Calc Stat Graph Editor Tools Window Help

By clicking any of these menu commands, you arrive at options included in that command. For example, if you click on **File**, you get the drop-down menu shown in Figure 10.2. The first option, **New**, allows you to create a new worksheet.

Creating a New Worksheet

Creating a new worksheet means to enter new data in the data window. The data window consists of four thousand columns, which are labeled C1, C2, . . . , C4000. The data can be entered in one or more columns, depending on the setup of the problem. In each column immediately below the labels, there

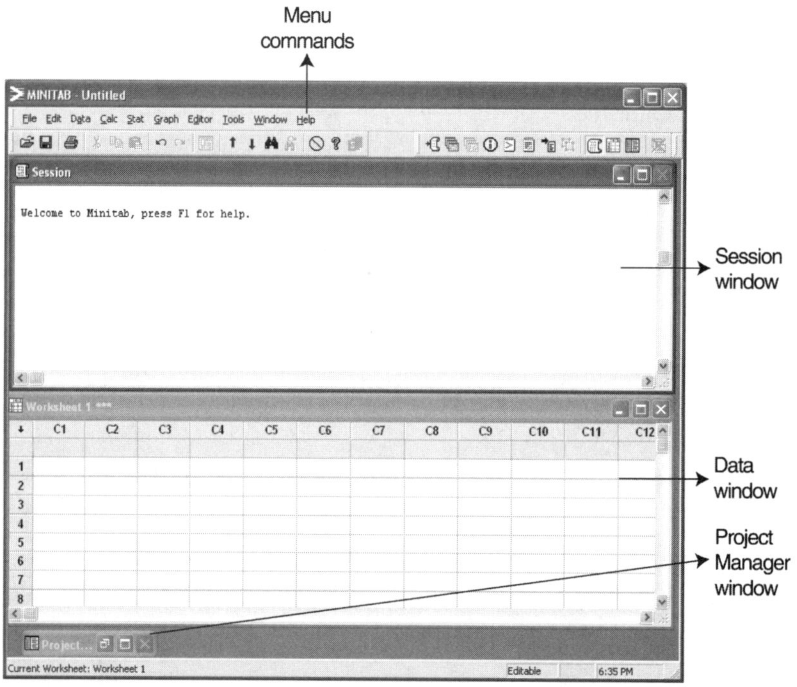

Figure 10.1 The welcome screen in MINITAB.

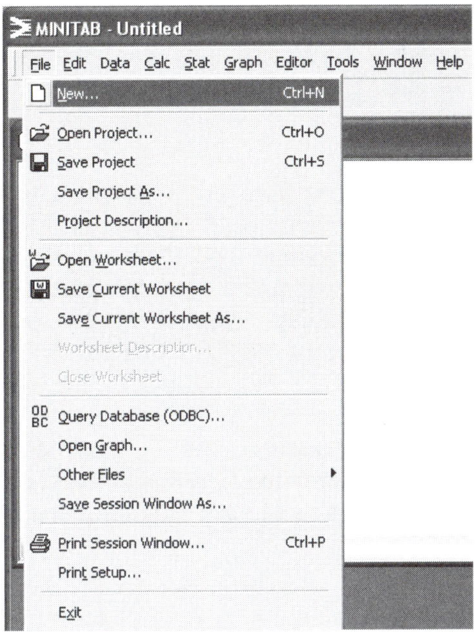

Figure 10.2 Showing the menu command options.

is one cell that is not labeled, whereas the rest of the cells are labeled 1, 2, 3, and so on. In the unlabeled cell, you can enter the variable name, such as part name, shift, lot number, and so on. Data are then entered in the labeled cells, using one cell for each data point. If a numerical observation is missing, MINITAB will automatically replace the missing value with a star (*).

Saving a Data File

Using the command **File > Save Current Worksheet As** allows saving the current data file. When you enter this command, a dialog box titled **Save Worksheet As** appears. Type the file name in the box next to **File Name**, select the drive location for the file, and then click **Save**.

Retrieving a Saved MINITAB Data File

Using the command **File > Open Worksheet** prompts the dialog box **Open Worksheet** to appear. Select the drive and directory where the file was saved by clicking the down arrow next to the **Look in** box, enter the file name in the box next to **FILE NAME**, and then click **Open**. The data will appear in the same format you had entered earlier.

Saving a MINITAB Project

Using the command **File > Save Project** saves the ongoing project in a MINITAB Project (MPJ) file to the designated directory with the name you choose. Saving the project saves *all* windows opened in the project, along with the contents of each window.

Print Options

To print the contents in any specific window, you need to make the window active by clicking on it, and then use the command **File > Print Session Window. . .(Graph. . ., Worksheet. . .)**.

If you want to print multiple graphs on a single page, highlight the graphs in the **Graph** folder in the Project Manager window by right-clicking on each and choose **Print**. The **Print Multiple Graphs** dialog box appears. To change the page orientation of the multiple graphs, use **File > Page Setup** to adjust the printing options.

The construction of several main tools of SPC using MINITAB is discussed in *Applied Statistics for the Six Sigma Green Belt*. In this book, however, we will discuss only the construction of various control charts using MINITAB and JMP.

10.2 The Shewhart Xbar-R Control Chart

To construct a Shewhart Xbar-R chart, first enter the data in one column of the Worksheet window. Then from the Menu Command, select **Stat > Control Charts > Variable Charts for Subgroups > Xbar-R**. The dialog box **Xbar-R Chart** shown in Figure 10.3 immediately appears. We illustrate construction of the Xbar-R chart with the following example.

Example 10.1 *Consider the data on the diameter measurements of ball bearings used in the wheels of heavy construction equipment shown in Table 3.4 of Example 3.4 in Chapter 3. Then use the following steps to construct the Xbar-R control chart.*

Solution:

1. Enter all the data in column C1 of the Worksheet window. Note that you have the option to enter the data in rows of columns such that each row contains data from one subgroup. This option is usually preferred when the sample size is variable. We shall consider this option for constructing an Xbar-R control chart with unequal sample sizes.
2. Click **Stat** from the Menu Command.
3. Select **Control Charts** from the pull-down menu in the **Stat** command menu.
4. Select **Variable Charts for Subgroups** from the **Control Charts** command menu.

5. Click **Xbar-R** from the **Variable Charts for Subgroups** command menu. The dialog box **Xbar-R Chart** shown in Figure 10.3 immediately appears.

6. From the dialog box **Xbar-R Chart**, choose the option "All observations for a chart are in one column."

7. Enter C1 in the next box.

8. Enter the sample size in the box next to the Subgroup sizes.

9. In the dialog box **Xbar-R Chart**, options such as Scale and Labels are available. If you select Labels, a new dialog box will appear and you can enter the title of an Xbar-R chart and any footnotes you would like to see on the output of the Xbar-R chart. Then click **OK**. By default, the title will be *Xbar-R Chart for C1* or *Xbar-R Chart for "name of the variable"* if you have given such a name in column C1 of the data window. Use Xbar-R Options. . . if you want to specify the values of the population mean and population standard deviation instead of estimating them by using the given data. Then click **OK** in the Xbar-R Chart dialog box. The desired Xbar-R control chart will appear in the Session window. In our example, the Xbar-R Chart dialog box will look as shown in Figure 10.3, and the output of the Xbar-R chart is as shown in Figure 3.10 in Chapter 3.

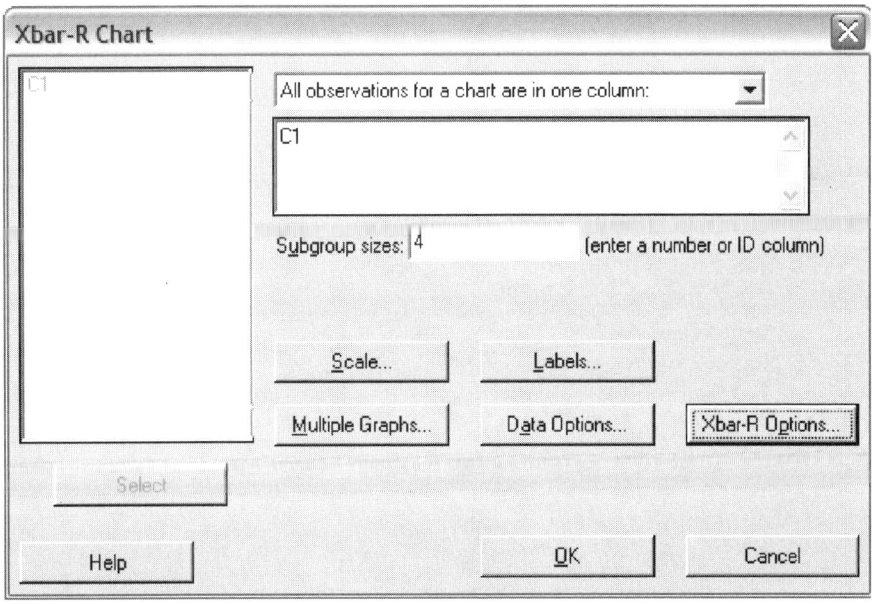

Figure 10.3 MINITAB window showing the Xbar-R Chart dialog box.

10.3 The Shewhart Xbar-R Control Chart When Process Mean μ and Process Standard Deviation σ Are Known

To construct a Shewhart Xbar-R control chart when process mean μ and process standard deviation σ are known, follow steps 1 through 8 of the solution shown in Example 10.1. Then click Xbar-R Options. . . . A new dialog box, shown in Figure 10.4, will appear. In the boxes next to Mean and Standard deviation, enter the specified values and then click **OK**. Then click **OK** again in the Xbar-R Chart dialog box. The desired Xbar-R control chart will appear in the Session window.

10.4 The Shewhart Control Chart for Individual Observations

To construct a Shewhart control chart for individual observations, first enter the data in one column, say C1, of the Worksheet window. Then from the Menu Command, select **Stat > Control Charts > Variable Charts for Individuals > I-MR**. The dialog box **Individuals-Moving Range Chart**, shown in Figure 10.5, appears. We illustrate the construction of a Shewhart control chart for individual observations with the following example.

Example 10.2 *Consider the data on the diameter measurements of ball bearings used in the wheels of heavy construction equipment shown in Table 3.5 of Example 3.6 in Chapter 3. Then use the following steps to construct the Shewhart control chart for individual observations.*

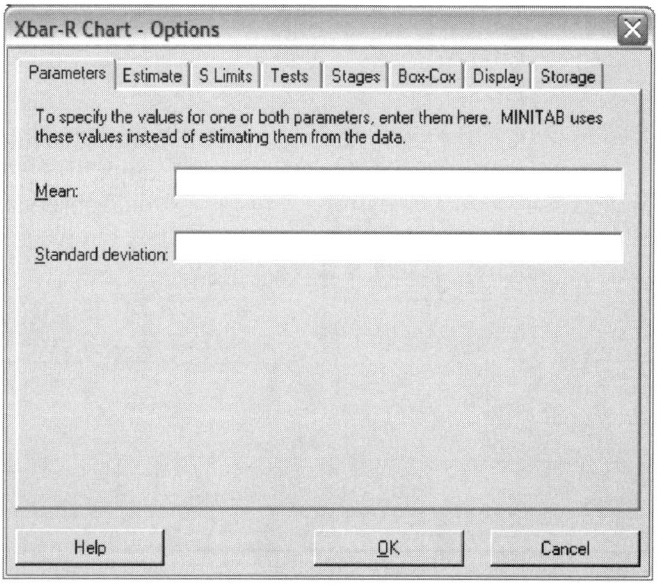

Figure 10.4 MINITAB window showing the Xbar-R Chart - Options dialog box.

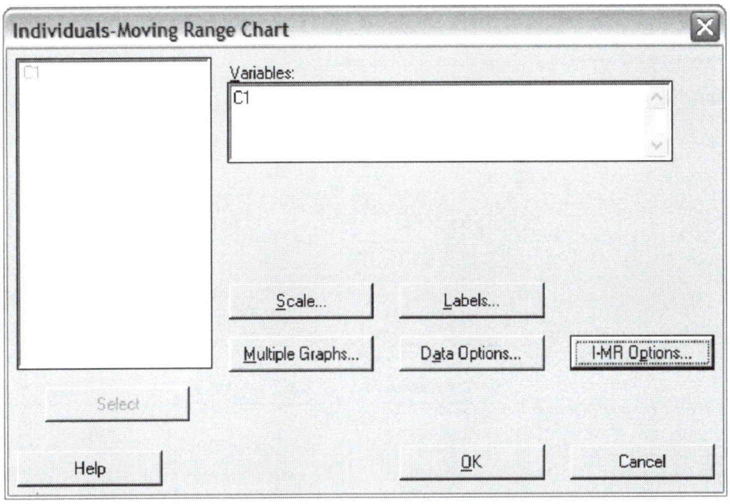

Figure 10.5 MINITAB window showing the Individuals-Moving Range Chart dialog box.

Solution:

1. Enter all the data in column C1 of the data (Worksheet) window. Click **Stat** from the Menu Command.
2. Select **Control Charts** from the pull-down menu in the **Stat** command menu.
3. Select **Variable Charts for Individuals** from the **Control Charts** command menu.
4. Click **I-MR** from the **Variable Charts for Individuals** command menu. The dialog box **Individuals-Moving Range Chart**, shown in Figure 10.5, immediately appears.
5. Enter C1 in the box next to Variables.

Select the other options from the dialog box **Individuals Moving Range Chart** in the same manner as discussed in step 9 of Example 10.1. Then click **OK**. The output of the Shewhart control chart for individual observations will appear in the Session window. The control chart for our example is shown in Figure 3.11 of Chapter 3.

10.5 The Shewhart Xbar-S Control Chart—Equal Sample Size

To construct a Shewhart Xbar-S control chart for equal sample size, first enter the data in one column, say C1, of the Worksheet window. Then from the Menu Command, select **Stat > Control Charts > Variable Charts for Subgroups > Xbar-S**. The dialog box **Xbar-S Chart** shown in Figure 10.6 appears. We illustrate the construction of the Shewhart Xbar-S control chart with the following example.

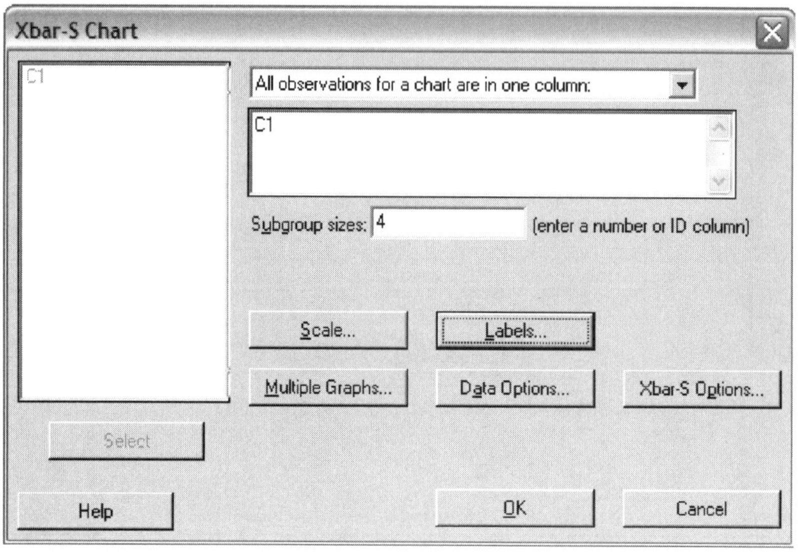

Figure 10.6 MINITAB window showing the Xbar-S Chart dialog box.

Example 10.3 *Consider the data on the diameter measurements of ball bearings used in the wheels of heavy construction equipment shown in Table 3.4 of Example 3.4 in Chapter 3. Then use the following steps to construct the Xbar-S control chart.*

Solution:

1. Enter all the data in column C1 of the Worksheet window. Note that as in the case of the Xbar-R chart, you have the option to enter the data in rows of columns such that each row contains data from one subgroup. This option is usually preferred when the sample size is variable. We will consider this option for constructing the Xbar-S control chart with unequal sample sizes.

2. Click **Stat** from the Menu Command.

3. Select **Control Charts** from the pull-down menu in the **Stat** command menu.

4. Select **Variable Charts for Subgroups** from the **Control Charts** command menu.

5. Click **Xbar-S** from the **Variable Charts for Subgroups** command menu. The dialog box **Xbar-S Chart** shown in Figure 10.6 appears.

6. From the dialog box **Xbar-S Chart**, choose the option "All observations for a chart are in one column."

7. Enter C1 in the next box.

8. Enter the sample size in the box next to the Subgroup sizes.

9. In the dialog box **Xbar-S Chart**, options such as Scale and Labels are available. If you select Labels, a new dialog box will appear and you can enter the title of an Xbar-S chart and any footnotes you would like to see on the output of the Xbar-S chart. Then click **OK**. By default, the title will be *Xbar-S Chart for C1* or *Xbar-S Chart for "name of the variable"* if you have given such a name in column C1 of the data window. Use Xbar-S Options. . . if you want to specify the values of the population mean and population standard deviation instead of estimating them by using the given data. Then click **OK** in the Xbar-S Chart dialog box. The desired Xbar-S control chart will appear in the Session window. In our example, the Xbar-S Chart dialog box will look as shown in Figure 10.6, and the output of the Xbar-S chart is as shown in Figure 3.12 in Chapter 3.

10.6 The Shewhart Xbar-S Control Chart—Sample Size Variable

To construct a Shewhart Xbar-S control chart for variable sample size, first enter the data in rows of the Worksheet window, using a separate row for each subgroup. Then from the Menu Command, select **Stat > Control Charts > Variable Charts for Subgroups > Xbar-S**. The dialog box **Xbar-S Chart** shown in Figure 10.7 appears. We illustrate the construction of a Shewhart Xbar-S control chart with variable sample size with the following example.

Example 10.4 *Consider the data on finished inside diameter measurements of piston rings shown in Table 3.6 of Example 3.8 in Chapter 3. Then use the following steps to construct the Xbar-S control chart.*

Solution:

1. Enter all the data in columns C1 through C10 of the Worksheet window. Note that as in the case of the Xbar-S chart with equal sample size, you have the option to enter the data in one column, say C1, and then in column C2 identify each observation by entering the corresponding sample numbers. For example, the first 10 observations in column C1 come from sample one; therefore, the first 10 entries in column C2 should be 1.

2. Click **Stat** from the Menu Command.

3. Select **Control Charts** from the pull-down menu in the **Stat** command menu.

4. Select **Variable Charts for Subgroups** from the **Control Charts** command menu.

5. Click **Xbar-S** from the **Variable Charts for Subgroups** command menu. The dialog box **Xbar-S Chart** shown in Figure 10.7 appears.
6. From the dialog box **Xbar-S Chart**, choose the option "Observations for a subgroup are in one row of columns."

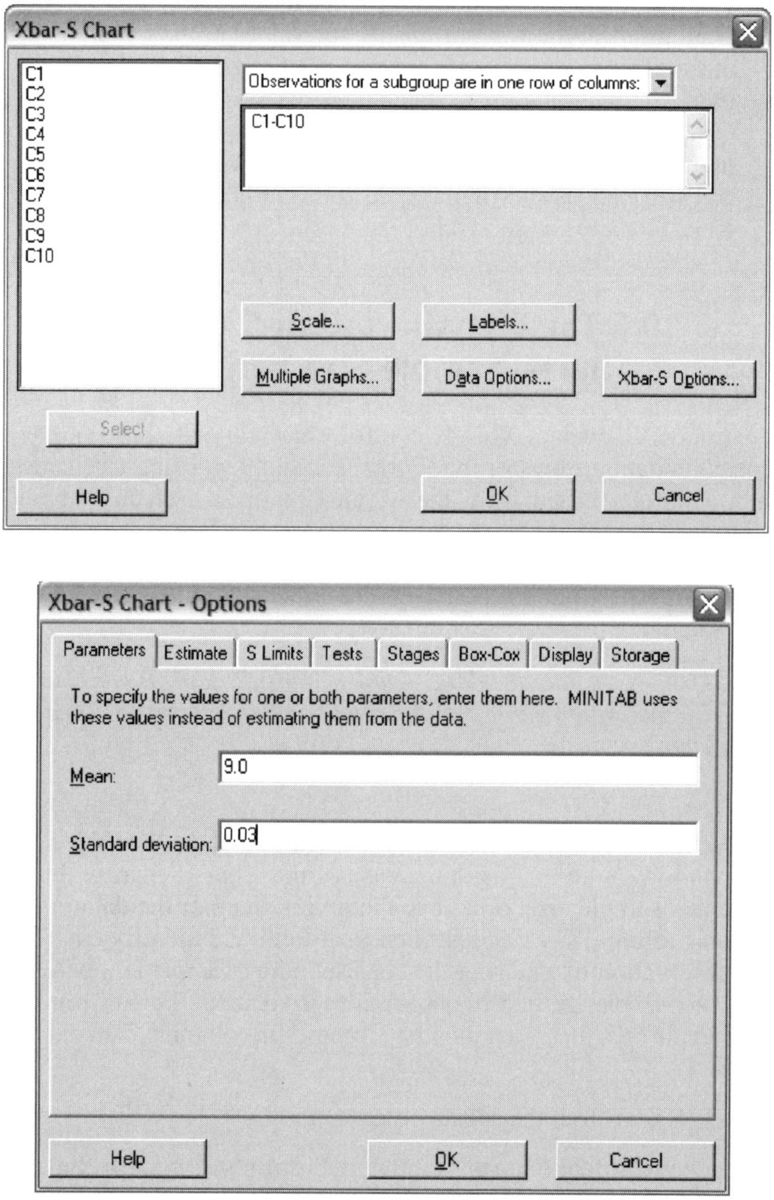

Figure 10.7 MINITAB windows showing the Xbar-S Chart and Xbar-S Chart – Options dialog boxes.

7. Enter C1-C10 in the next box, because the largest sample size is 10.

8. In the dialog box **Xbar-S Chart**, options such as Scale and Labels are available. If you select Labels, a new dialog box will appear and you can enter the title of an Xbar-S chart and any footnotes you would like to see on the output of the Xbar-S chart. Then click **OK**. By default, the title will be *Xbar-S Chart for C1-C10* or *Xbar-S Chart for "name of the variable"* if you have entered the data in one column, say C1, and have given such a name in column C1 of the data window. Use Xbar-S Options. . . if you want to specify the values of the population mean and population standard deviation instead of estimating them by using the given data as, for example, in the present example. Then click **OK** in the Xbar-S chart dialog box. The desired Xbar-S control chart will appear in the Session window. In our example, the Xbar-S chart and Xbar-S Options dialog boxes will look as shown in Figure 10.7, and the output of the Xbar-S chart is as shown in Figure 3.13 in Chapter 3.

10.7 Process Capability Analysis

To construct a process capability analysis chart, first enter the data in one column, say C1, of the Worksheet window. Then from the Menu Command, select **Stat > Quality Tools > Capability Analysis > Normal**. Then the dialog box **Capability Analysis (Normal Distribution)**, shown in Figure 10.8, appears. We illustrate the capability analysis of a process with the following example.

Example 10.5 *Consider a quality characteristic of a process that is normally distributed. Suppose that the process is stable with respect to the 3σ control limits. Furthermore, suppose that the data of 25 samples, each of size five, from this process are as shown in Table 10.1. Also, we are given that the LSL = 0.95 and the USL = 1.05. Perform the capability analysis of the process.*

Solution:

1. Enter all the data in columns C1 through C5 of the Worksheet window. Note that in this case you have the option to enter the data in one column, say, C1.

2. Click **Stat** from the Menu Command.

3. Select **Quality Tools > Normal** from the pull-down menu in the **Stat** command menu.

4. Select **Capability Analysis** from the **Control Charts** command menu.

5. Click **Normal** (or the distribution of the process characteristic) from the **Capability Analysis** command menu. The dialog box **Capability Analysis (Normal Distribution)**, shown in Figure 10.8, immediately appears.

6. From the **Capability Analysis (Normal Distribution)** dialog box, next to **Data are arranged as**, select either **Single column** or **Subgroups across rows of**, depending on how you entered the data in step 1, and then enter the column number or column numbers in which you have entered the data.

7. Click **OK**. The capability analysis output will appear as shown in Figure 10.9.

Table 10.1 Data of 25 samples, each of size five, from a given process.

Sample Number	Observations				
1	0.97076	0.98518	1.01204	0.97892	0.99094
2	0.99455	0.96904	0.99770	0.97502	0.98483
3	0.99538	0.99765	0.96011	1.03059	0.98048
4	1.00332	0.98891	0.98018	1.01699	1.00391
5	1.03023	0.98663	1.01498	0.97483	0.99836
6	0.98491	1.00487	0.96951	0.99613	1.03365
7	0.98894	1.00631	0.98630	0.98115	0.96755
8	0.93771	0.99017	1.03221	1.01045	1.01297
9	1.00103	1.01641	0.97683	1.00149	1.03012
10	1.01493	1.02220	1.00179	1.01556	1.01080
11	1.01606	0.96502	1.00546	0.99259	0.96857
12	0.98266	0.99031	0.99349	1.00499	1.03806
13	0.95560	1.00033	1.01098	0.99380	1.04496
14	0.97406	1.01305	0.97556	0.98493	1.00347
15	1.03027	0.97009	1.00151	0.99929	0.98366
16	1.02527	1.01652	1.02743	0.99951	0.99565
17	1.02837	1.01676	0.97056	0.95207	1.03254
18	0.98646	0.99434	1.00163	0.98811	1.01234
19	0.96072	1.02716	1.01030	1.04141	0.96355
20	1.03511	0.94637	1.00852	0.99454	1.00620
21	0.99550	0.98307	1.00948	1.00793	1.04035
22	0.98397	1.03082	0.98643	1.00540	0.97880
23	0.99934	0.99544	1.00959	1.00664	1.02905
24	1.00286	1.00777	1.01661	0.99793	1.03805
25	0.96557	0.98535	0.99911	1.03566	1.00453

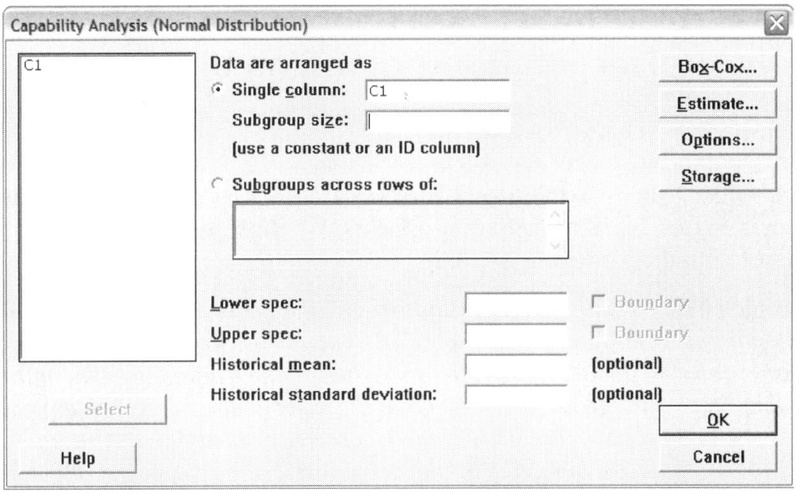

Figure 10.8 MINITAB window showing the Capability Analysis (Normal Distribution) dialog box.

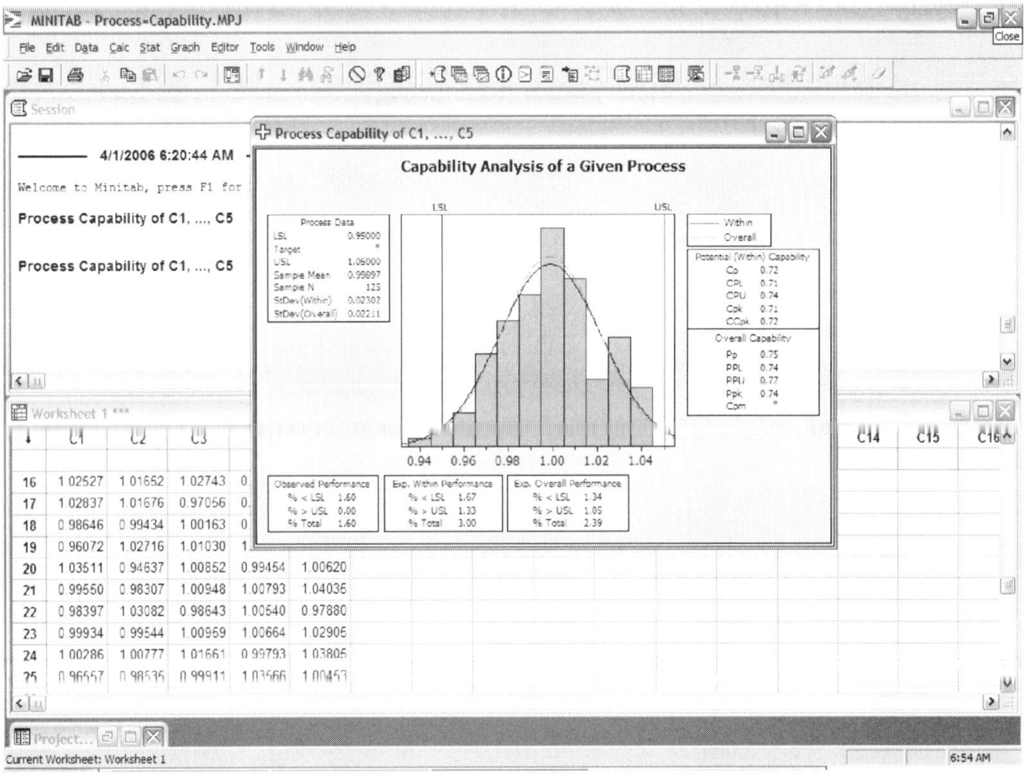

Figure 10.9 MINITAB windows showing the process capability analysis.

10.8 The *p* Chart: Control Chart for Fraction Nonconforming Units

To construct a *p* chart, first enter the data (number of nonconforming units) in one column, say C1, of the Worksheet window. Then from the Menu Command, select **Stat > Attributes Charts > P. . . .** The dialog box **P Chart** shown in Figure 10.10 immediately appears. We illustrate the construction of a *p* chart with the following example.

Example 10.6 *A semiconductor industry tracks the number of nonconforming computer chips produced each day. A team of Six Sigma Green Belts wants to improve the overall quality by reducing the fraction of nonconforming computer chips. To achieve this goal, the team decides to set up a* p *chart, and in order to do so, the Six Sigma Green Belts inspect a sample of 1000 chips each day over a period of 30 days. Table 4.2 of Example 4.1 in Chapter 4 gives the number of nonconforming chips out of 1000 inspected chips each day during the study period.*

Solution:

1. Enter all the data (number of nonconforming chips given in Table 4.2 in Chapter 4) in column C1 of the Worksheet window. Click **Stat** from the Menu Command.
2. Select **Control Charts** from the pull-down menu in the **Stat** command menu.
3. Select **Attributes Charts** from the **Control Charts** command menu.

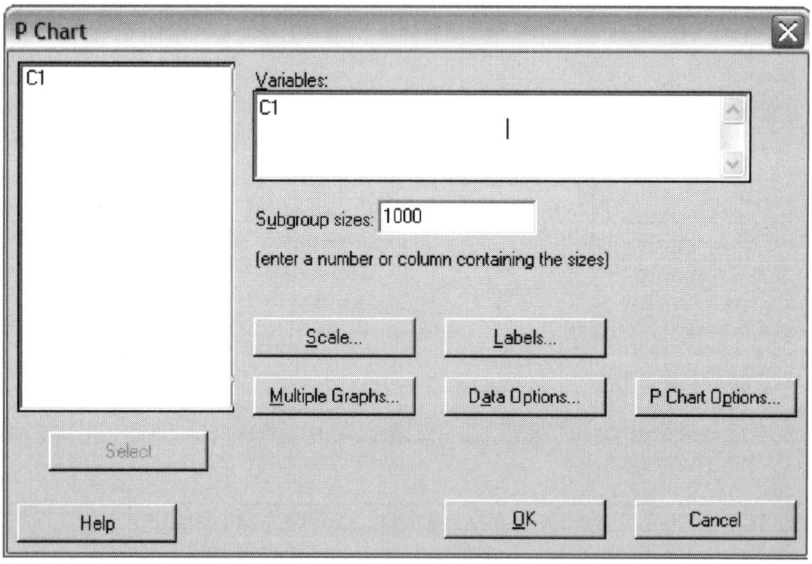

Figure 10.10 MINITAB window showing the P Chart dialog box.

4. Click **P**. . . from the **Attributes Charts** command menu. The dialog box **P Chart** shown in Figure 10.10 appears.
5. Enter C1 in the box next to Variables.
6. Enter the sample size in the box next to the Subgroup sizes.
7. In the dialog box **P Chart**, options such as Scale and Labels are available. If you select Labels, a new dialog box will appear and you can enter the title of a *p* chart and any footnotes you would like to see on the output of the *p* chart. Then click **OK**. By default, the title will be *P Chart for C1* or *P Chart for "name of the variable"* if you have given such a name in column C1 of the data window. Use P Chart Options. . . if you want to specify the values of fraction of nonconforming in the population instead of estimating them using the given data. Then click **OK** in the **P Chart** dialog box. The desired *p* control chart will appear in the Session window. Thus, in our example, the output of the *p* chart is shown in Figure 4.1 in Chapter 4.

10.9 The *p* Chart: Control Chart for Fraction Nonconforming Units with Variable Sample Size

Constructing a *p* chart with variable sample size is the same as constructing a *p* chart with fixed sample size, except in this case we enter the data on number of nonconforming units in column C1 and the corresponding sample sizes in column C2; and in step 6, instead of entering the sample size in the box next to the Subgroup sizes, we enter C2.

10.10 The *np* Chart: Control Chart for Nonconforming Units

In an *np* chart we plot the number of nonconforming units in an inspected sample. The *np* chart is very similar to the *p* chart, except that in the *p* chart we plot the fraction nonconforming units in each inspected sample. Moreover, in a *p* chart the sample sizes could be equal or unequal, whereas in an *np* chart, the sample sizes are equal. Otherwise, a *p* chart and an *np* chart can be implemented under the same circumstances. We summarize here some specific points that are important for an *np* chart:

- The inspection sample sizes should be equal
- The sample size should be large enough to include some nonconforming units

Record the sample size and number of nonconforming units (*np*) in each sample and plot the number of nonconforming units on the control chart.

To construct an *np* control chart, follow all the steps for a *p* control chart in section 10.8.

10.11 The c Chart

In many situations, we are interested in studying the number of nonconformities in a sample, which is also called the inspection unit, rather than studying the fraction nonconforming or total number of nonconforming in the sample. To construct the *c* chart, first enter the data (number of nonconformities) in one column, say C1, of the Worksheet window. Then from the Menu Command, select **Stat > Attributes Charts > C. . .** The dialog box **C Chart**, shown in Figure 10.11, immediately appears. We illustrate the construction of a *c* chart with the following example.

Example 10.7 *A paper mill has detected that almost 90 percent of rejected paper rolls are due to nonconformities of two types: holes and wrinkles in the paper. The Six Sigma Green Belt team in the mill decides to set up control charts to reduce or eliminate the number of these nonconformities. To set up the control charts, the team collects data by taking random samples of five rolls each day for 30 days and counting the number of nonconformities (holes and wrinkles) in each sample. The data are shown in Table 4.4 of Example 4.4 in Chapter 4. Set up a* c *control chart using these data.*

Solution:

1. Enter all the data (number of nonconformities given in Table 4.4 in Chapter 4) in column C1 of the Worksheet window. Click **Stat** from the Menu Command.
2. Select **Control Charts** from the pull-down menu in the **Stat** command menu.
3. Select **Attributes Charts** from the **Control Charts** command menu.
4. Click **C**. . . from the **Attributes Charts** command menu. The dialog box **C Chart**, shown in Figure 10.11, appears.
5. Enter C1 in the box next to Variables.
6. In the dialog box **C Chart**, options such as Scale and Labels are available. If you select Labels, a new dialog box will appear and you can enter the title of a *c* chart and any footnotes you would like to see on the output of the *c* chart. Then click **OK**. By default, the title will be *C Chart for C1* or *C Chart for "name of the variable"* if you have given such a name, say "nonconformities," in column C1 of the data window. Use C Chart Options. . . if you want to specify the mean value of nonconformities in the population instead of estimating it using the given data. Then click **OK** in the **C chart** dialog box. The desired *c* control chart will appear in the Session window. Thus, in our example, the output of the *c* chart is shown in Figure 4.4 in Chapter 4.

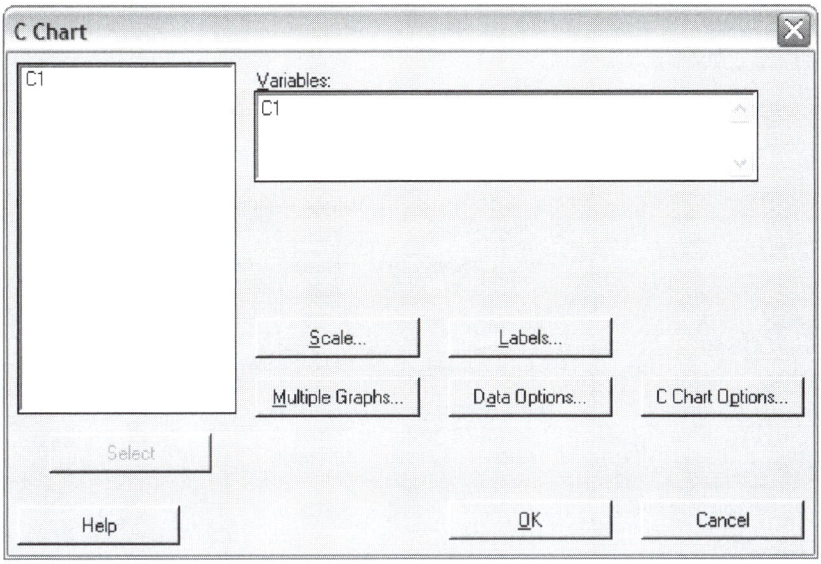

Figure 10.11 MINITAB window showing the C Chart dialog box.

10.12 The *u* Chart

The *u* chart is essentially the *c* chart, except that the *u* chart is always based on the number of nonconformities per inspection unit. In other words, the actual sample size may be different from one or may vary, but the control limits of the *u* chart are always determined based on one inspection unit. For example, if *n* is constant, one can use either a *c* chart or a *u* chart. We illustrate the construction of a *u* chart with the following example.

Example 10.8 *A Six Sigma Green Belt team in a semiconductor industry found that the printed boards for laptops have nonconformities of several types, such as shorted trace, open trace, cold solder joint, and solder short. In order to monitor nonconformities in the printed boards for laptops, the team members want to set up a u chart; therefore, they collect data by selecting samples of five inspection units, each inspection unit consisting of 30 boards. The data, which are shown in Table 4.5 of Example 4.5 in Chapter 4, are collected over a period of 30 days.*

Solution:

1. Enter all the data (number of nonconformities given in Table 4.5 in Chapter 4) in column C1 of the Worksheet window. Click **Stat** from the Menu Command.
2. Select **Control Charts** from the pull-down menu in the **Stat** command menu.
3. Select **Attributes Charts** from the **Control Charts** command menu.

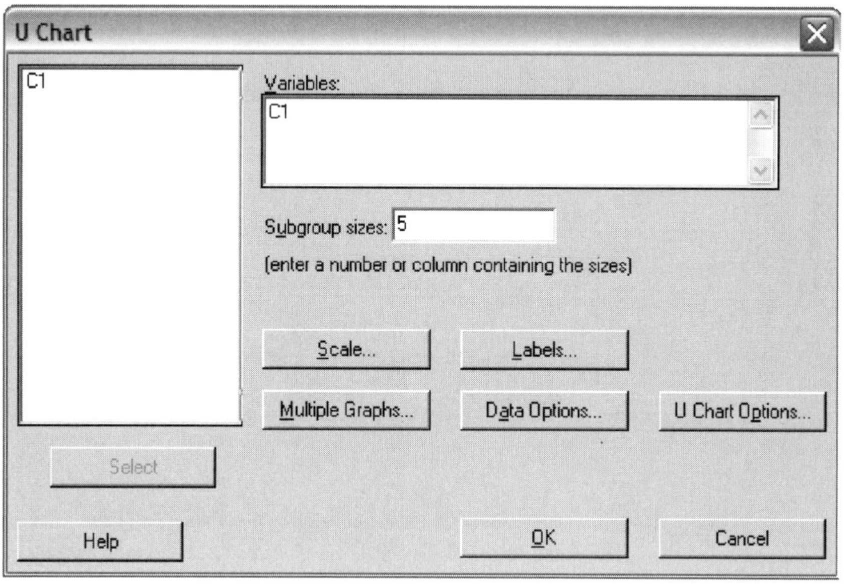

Figure 10.12 MINITAB window showing the U Chart dialog box.

4. Click U. . . from the **Attributes Charts** command menu. The dialog box **U Chart**, shown in Figure 10.12, appears.
5. Enter C1 in the box next to Variables.
6. Enter the sample size in the box next to Subgroup sizes.
7. In the dialog box **U Chart**, options such as Scale and Labels are available. If you select Labels, a new dialog box will appear and you can enter the title of a *u* chart and any footnotes you would like to see on the output of the *u* chart. Then click **OK**. By default, the title will be *U Chart for C1* or *U Chart for "name of the variable"* if you have given such a name, say "nonconformities," in column C1 of the data window. Use U Chart Options. . . if you want to specify the mean value of nonconformities per unit in the population instead of estimating it using the given data. Then click **OK** in the **U chart** dialog box. The desired *u* control chart will appear in the Session window. Thus, in our example, the output of the *u* chart is shown in Figure 4.5 in Chapter 4.

10.13 The *u* Chart: Variable Sample Size

Constructing a *u* chart with variable sample size is the same as constructing a *u* chart with fixed sample size, except in this case we enter the data on number of nonconforming in column C1 and the corresponding sample sizes in column C2; and in step 6, instead of entering the sample size in the box next to the Subgroup sizes, we enter C2. For an example of a *u* chart, see Figure 4.6 in Chapter 4.

10.14 Designing a CUSUM Control Chart

CUSUM charts are very effective in detecting small shifts. Unlike the $\bar{X}$ Shewhart control charts, CUSUM control charts can be designed to detect one-sided or two-sided shifts. These charts are defined by two parameters, *k* and *h*, which are called the *reference value* and the *decision interval*, respectively, and are defined in section 5.2.1. The two-sided process control by using a CUSUM control chart is achieved by concurrently using two one-sided CUSUM control charts. In both one-sided CUSUM charts one can use the same or different reference values depending on whether the upward and downward shifts are equally important. We discuss the construction of CUSUM control charts with the following example.

Example 10.9 *Consider a manufacturing process of auto parts. We are interested in studying a quality characteristic of the parts manufactured by the process. Let the quality characteristic when the process is under control be normally distributed with mean 20 and standard deviation 2. The data shown in Table 5.1 of Example 5.1 in Chapter 5 give the first 10 random samples of size four, which are taken when the process is stable and producing the parts with mean value 20 and standard deviation 2. The last 10 random samples, again of size four, were taken from that process after its mean experienced an upward shift of one standard deviation, resulting in a new process with mean 22. Construct a Shewhart CUSUM control chart for the data in Table 5.1.*

Solution:

1. Enter all the data in Table 5.1 of Chapter 5 in columns C1 through C4 (observations for each subgroup are entered in one row of columns) of the Worksheet window. Click **Stat** from the Menu Command.
2. Select **Control Charts** from the pull-down menu in the **Stat** command menu.
3. Select **Time Weighted Charts** from the **Control Charts** command menu.
4. Click **CUSUM** from the **Control Charts** command menu. The dialog box **CUSUM Chart**, shown in Figure 10.13, appears.
5. From the dialog box **CUSUM Chart**, choose the option "Observations for a subgroup are in one row of columns."
6. Enter C1-C4 in the next box, because the sample size is four.
7. Enter the target value in the box next to Target, which in our example is 20.

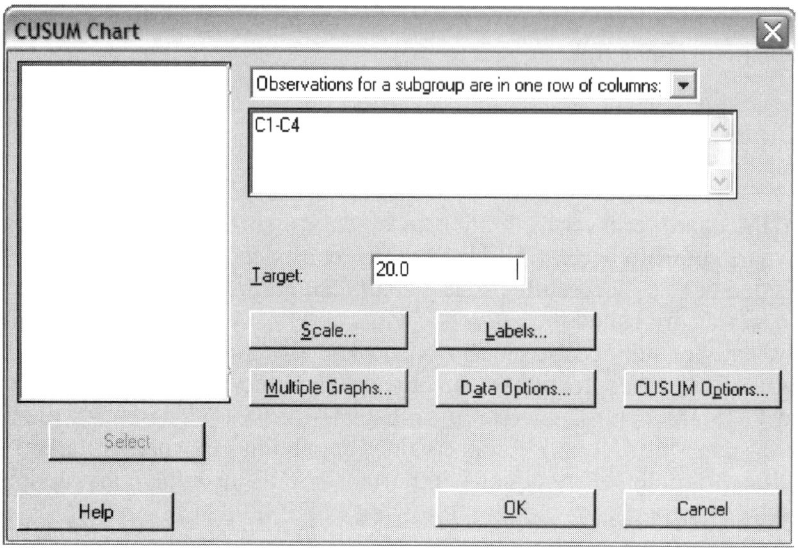

Figure 10.13 MINITAB window showing the CUSUM Chart dialog box.

8. In the dialog box **CUSUM Chart**, options such as Scale and Labels are available. If you select Labels, a new dialog box will appear and you can enter the title of a CUSUM chart and any footnotes you would like to see on the output of the CUSUM chart. Then click **OK**. By default, the title will be *CUSUM Chart for C1-C4.*

9. Select CUSUM Options . . . and the dialog box **CUSUM Chart – Options**, shown in Figure 10.14, will appear. In this dialog box are various options, but we will be using only a few of them, namely, **Parameters**, **Estimate**, **Plan/Type**, and **Storage**.

   a. **Parameters:** This option is used to specify a value for the standard deviation. Enter the specified value in the box next to "Standard deviation." MINITAB will use this value instead of estimating it from the data.

   b. **Estimate:** This option presents various methods for estimating the standard deviation. For example, you may choose moving range, Rbar, Sbar, pooled standard deviation, or others.

   c. **Plan/Type:** Under this option you choose the type of CUSUM chart you would like to prepare, that is, tabular CUSUM, V-mask CUSUM, and the suboption of FIR CUSUM, and reset after each signal. You also choose the appropriate values of the parameters *h* and *k*. For a tabular CUSUM chart, check the circles next to "one sided (LCL, UCL)."

   d. **Storage:** Under this option, many of the choices are used when you want to prepare a V-mask CUSUM chart. For a tabular

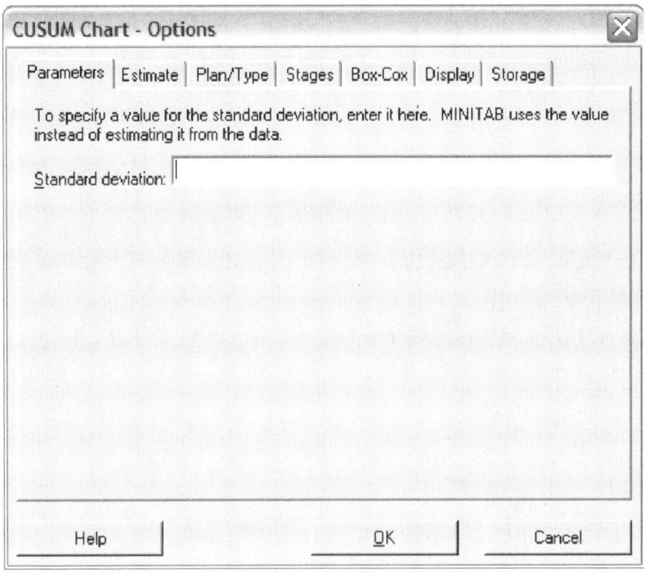

Figure 10.14 MINITAB window showing the CUSUM Chart - Options dialog box.

CUSUM, you need to check the boxes next to "point plotted," "center line value," and "control limit."

Using these steps, a tabular CUSUM control chart for the data in Table 5.1 is constructed, which is presented in Table 5.3, and its graph is shown in Figure 5.3. The center line value and control limits are shown in Figure 5.3.

10.15 The FIR Feature for a CUSUM Control Chart

Lucas and Crosier (1982) introduced the FIR feature, which improves the sensitivity at process start-up or immediately after any control action has been taken. In standard CUSUM control charts, we use the initial value $S_0 = 0$, but in a CUSUM control chart with the FIR feature, the starting value of S_0 is set up at some value greater than zero. Lucas and Crosier recommend setting up the starting value of S_0 at $h/2$. The procedure to construct a CUSUM control chart with FIR using MINITAB is exactly the same as discussed in Example 10.9, except in step 9(c) we must check the box next to "use FIR" and enter the value of S_0 in the box next to "Standard deviation." For an example of a CUSUM control chart using the FIR feature, see Example 5.4 in Chapter 5.

10.16 The MA Control Chart

The MA control chart is usually more effective in detecting small shifts in process mean than the Shewhart chart. However, it is usually not as effective as the CUSUM and EWMA charts. We illustrate the construction of an MA control chart with the following example.

Example 10.10 *Consider the data in Table 5.4 of Example 5.3 in Chapter 5 on the manufacturing process of auto parts. Design an MA control chart for these data with span* m = *4 and interpret the results.*

Solution:

1. Enter all the data in Table 5.4 in column C1 of the Worksheet window. Click **Stat** from the Menu Command.
2. Select **Control Charts** from the pull-down menu in the **Stat** command menu.
3. Select **Time Weighted Charts** from the **Control Charts** command menu.
4. Click **Moving Average. . .** from the **Control Charts** command menu. The dialog box **Moving Average Chart**, shown in Figure 10.15, appears.
5. From the dialog box **Moving Average Chart**, choose the option "All observations for a chart are in one column."
6. Enter C1 in the next box. (If the sample size is $n > 1$, then enter the data in columns C1 through Cn and in step 5 choose the option "Observations for a subgroup are in one row of columns.")
7. In the box next to Subgroup sizes, enter 1, or the appropriate value of n if the sample size is greater than 1.
8. In the box next to Length of MA, enter 4, or any other specified value of span.
9. In the dialog box **Moving Average Chart**, options such as Scale and Labels are available. If you select Labels, a new

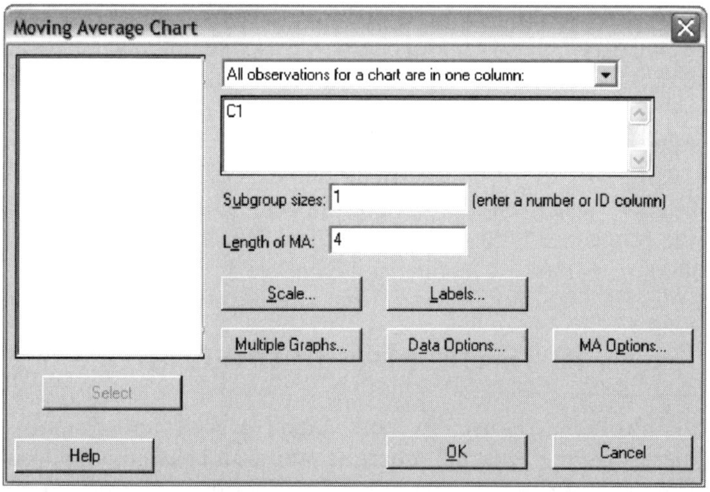

Figure 10.15 MINITAB window showing the Moving Average Chart dialog box.

dialog box will appear and you can enter the title of a Moving Average chart and any footnotes that you would like to see on the output of the Moving Average chart. Then click **OK**. By default, the title will be *Moving Average Chart for C1.*

10. Select MA Options . . . and the dialog box **Moving Average Chart – Options** will appear. In this dialog box are various options, but we will be using only a few of them, namely, **Parameters**, **Estimate**, **S Limits**, and **Storage**.
    a. **Parameters:** This option is used to specify a value of the mean and a value of the standard deviation. Enter the specified values in the boxes next to "Mean" and "Standard deviation." MINITAB will use this value instead of estimating it from the data.
    b. **Estimate:** This option presents various methods for estimating the mean and the standard deviation. For example, you may choose moving range, Rbar, Sbar, and others.
    c. **S Limits:** Under this option you choose, for example, control limits, bounds on control limits, and sample size.
    d. **Storage:** Under this option, check the boxes next to "point plotted," "center line value," and "control limit" and then click **OK**. Finally, click **OK** in the **Moving Average Chart** dialog box.

Using these steps, the MA control chart for the data in Table 5.4 is constructed. It is presented in Table 5.7, and its graph is shown in Figure 5.7. The center line value and control limits are shown in Figure 5.7.

10.17 The EWMA Control Chart

The EWMA control chart is very useful for processes in which only one observation per period may be available. We discuss the construction of an EWMA control chart using MINITAB with the following example.

Example 10.11 *Consider the data in Table 5.4 of Example 5.3 in Chapter 5 on the manufacturing process of auto parts. Design an EWMA control chart for these data with* $\lambda = 0.20$, $L = 2.962$, $\mu_0 = 20$, *and* $\sigma = 2$ *and interpret the results.*

Solution:

1. Enter all the data in Table 5.4 in column C1 of the Worksheet window. Click **Stat** from the Menu Command.
2. Select **Control Charts** from the pull-down menu in the **Stat** command menu.
3. Select **Time Weighted Charts** from the **Control Charts** command menu.

4. Click **EWMA. . .** from the **EWMA Chart** command menu. The dialog box **EWMA Chart**, shown in Figure 10.16, immediately appears.

5. From the dialog box **EWMA Chart**, choose the option "All observations for a chart are in one column."

6. Enter C1 in the next box. (If the sample size is $n > 1$, then enter the data in columns C1 through Cn and in step 5 choose the option "Observations for a subgroup are in one row of columns.")

7. In the box next to Subgroup sizes, enter 1, or the appropriate value of n if sample size is greater than 1.

8. Enter the specified value of λ (weight of EWMA) in the box next to **Weight of EWMA**.

9. In the dialog box **EWMA Chart**, options such as Scale and Labels are available. If you select Labels, a new dialog box will appear and you can enter the title of an EWMA chart and any footnotes you would like to see on the output of the EWMA chart. Then click **OK**. By default, the title will be *EWMA Chart for C1*.

10. Select EWMA Options. . . . The dialog box **EWMA Chart – Options** will appear. In this dialog box are various options, but we will be using only a few of them, namely, **Parameters**, **Estimate**, **S Limits**, and **Storage**.

    a. **Parameters:** This option is used to specify a value of the mean and a value of the standard deviation. Enter the specified values in the boxes next to "Mean" and "Standard

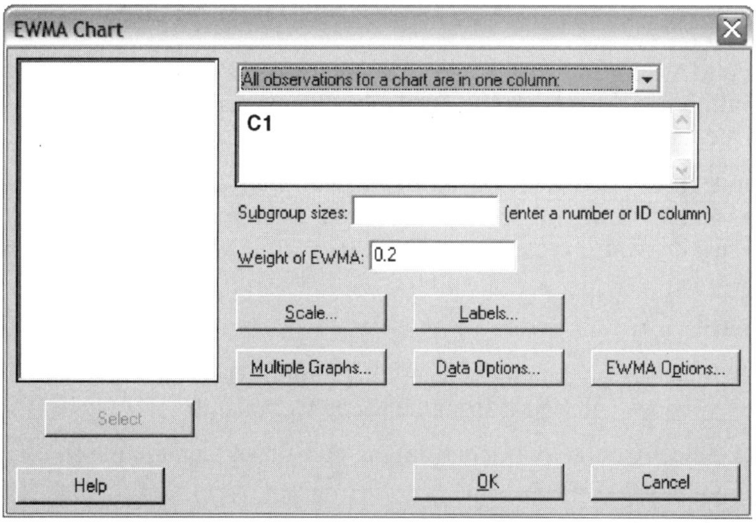

Figure 10.16 MINITAB window showing the EWMA Chart dialog box.

deviation." MINITAB will use this value instead of estimating it from the data.

b. **Estimate:** This option presents various methods for estimating the standard deviation. For example, you may choose Average moving range, Rbar, Sbar, Pooled standard deviation, or others.

c. **S Limits:** Under this option you choose, for example, Display control limits, bounds on control limits, and sample size. In this example, under the option Display control limits, enter the value of $L = 2.962$ in the box next to "These multiples of the standard deviation."

d. **Storage:** Under this option, check the boxes next to "point plotted," "center line value," and "control limit" and then click **OK**. Finally, click **OK** in the **EWMA Chart** dialog box.

Using these steps, the EWMA control chart for the data in Table 5.4 is constructed. It is presented in Table 5.9, and its graph is shown in Figure 5.8. The center line value and control limits are shown in Figure 5.8.

10.18 Measurement System Capability Analysis

The measurement system plays an important role in any effort to improve a process. In any process, the total process variation consists of two sources:

- Part-to-part variation
- Measurement system variation

If the measurement system variation is large compared with part-to-part variation, the measurement system cannot adequately discriminate between parts for complete process evaluation. In other words, the measurement system is not capable. It becomes very important to perform measurement system capability analysis.

Suppose we measure a quality characteristic of a part and let t be the total observed value of the quality characteristic, p be its true value, and e be the measurement error. Then, we have

$$t = p + e. \tag{10.1}$$

Assume now that the true value of the quality characteristic and the measurement error are normally distributed with mean μ and 0 and variances σ_p^2 and σ_m^2, respectively. Then it can be shown that

$$\sigma_t^2 = \sigma_p^2 + \sigma_m^2, \tag{10.2}$$

where σ_t^2 is the variance of the total observed values. Furthermore, the error variance σ_m^2 usually consists of two components: one due to gage variation (repeatability) and the other due to operator variation (reproducibility). The purpose of measurement system capability analysis is to separate these components and analyze them. In other words, we have

$$\sigma^2_{\text{measurement error}} = \sigma^2_{\text{reproducibilty}} + \sigma^2_{\text{repeatability}}.$$

To study these components, we usually use the ANOVA technique, which is also known as Gage R&R study. When using the ANOVA technique, we commonly deal with two types of situations: (1) when each operator measures the same specimens of a part, and (2) when each operator measures different specimens of a part. The designs used under these situations are known as *crossed* and *nested* designs, respectively. The following section discusses the Gage R&R study using MINITAB and crossed designs. We do not discuss nested designs here, as they are beyond the scope of this book.

10.18.1 Measurement System Capability Analysis (Using Crossed Designs)

A manufacturer of tubes used in automotive applications has installed a new measuring gage. The Six Sigma Green Belt team is interested in determining how well the new gage measures the inside diameter of the tube. In other words, the team is interested in performing the measurement system capability analysis. We discuss the measurement system capability analysis with the following example.

Example 10.12 *A manufacturer of bolts (parts) used in automotive applications has installed a new measuring gage. In order to perform the MSA on the new gage, the quality manager randomly selects three Six Sigma Green Belts from the quality control department, who decide to take a random sample of 10 bolts. Each Six Sigma Green Belt takes three measurements on each bolt, which is selected randomly. The data obtained are shown in Table 10.2.*

- *Estimate the repeatability and reproducibility of the measurement system.*
- *Estimate how much of the total process variation is due to the measurement system.*
- *If the tube diameter specifications are 70 ± 10, what can we say about the discrimination power of the measurement system? In other words, is the measurement system capable of discriminating between different parts?*

Solution: We have already discussed this example earlier, in Chapter 7. Here we discuss step by step how to set up MINITAB to find the solution to this or any other similar problem.

1. Following the steps discussed in section 10.1, start up MINITAB. The screen titled MINITAB – UNTITLED will appear first.

Table 10.2 Data on an experiment involving three operators, 10 bolts, and three measurements (in mm) on each bolt by each operator.

Bolt (Parts) Number	Operator 1			Operator 2			Operator 3		
	Trial 1	Trial 2	Trial 3	Trial 1	Trial 2	Trial 3	Trial 1	Trial 2	Trial 3
1	26	22	26	21	23	21	24	22	26
2	28	26	28	24	29	26	24	25	24
3	28	31	28	28	27	28	32	30	27
4	35	33	31	35	31	30	34	35	31
5	37	35	38	36	38	35	35	34	35
6	40	38	40	40	38	40	36	37	38
7	39	42	41	40	39	43	43	41	43
8	42	43	46	42	46	42	43	44	45
9	50	52	50	53	52	53	49	53	49
10	28	31	28	28	27	28	32	30	27
	$\bar{R}_1 = 3.0$ $\bar{x}_1 = 35.33$			$\bar{R}_2 = 2.5$ $\bar{x}_2 = 34.67$			$\bar{R}_3 = 3.0$ $\bar{x}_3 = 34.93$		

2. Enter the data using column C1 for the part numbers, column C2 for the operators, and column C3 for the observed values of the parts.
3. Select from the bar menu of the screen MINITAB – UNTITLED, **Stat > Quality Tools > Gage Study > Gage R&R Study (Crossed) . . .** and the screen MINITAB – UNTITLED with these selections is shown in Figure 10.17.
4. Click once on **Gage R&R Study (Crossed). . . .** The dialog box **Gage R&R Study (Crossed)**, shown in Figure 10.18, appears.

Double-click on C1, C2, and C3 in the square box within the dialog box **Gage R&R Study (Crossed)**, and the entries from the square box will move to the boxes next to Part numbers, Operators, and Measurement data, respectively. Check the circle next to **ANOVA**. Then click on **Options. . ..** The dialog box **Gage R&R Study (Crossed) – Options**, shown in Figure 10.19, appears. Enter 6 in the box next to **Study variation** (some authors use 5.15, for instance, Barrentine [2003]) .

Check the circle next to **Upper spec – Lower spec**, and in the box next to it enter the value of the specification band. Enter the value of alpha of your choice next to **Alpha to remove interaction term** (for example, we entered 0.25). Note that the interaction term (part*operator) will appear in

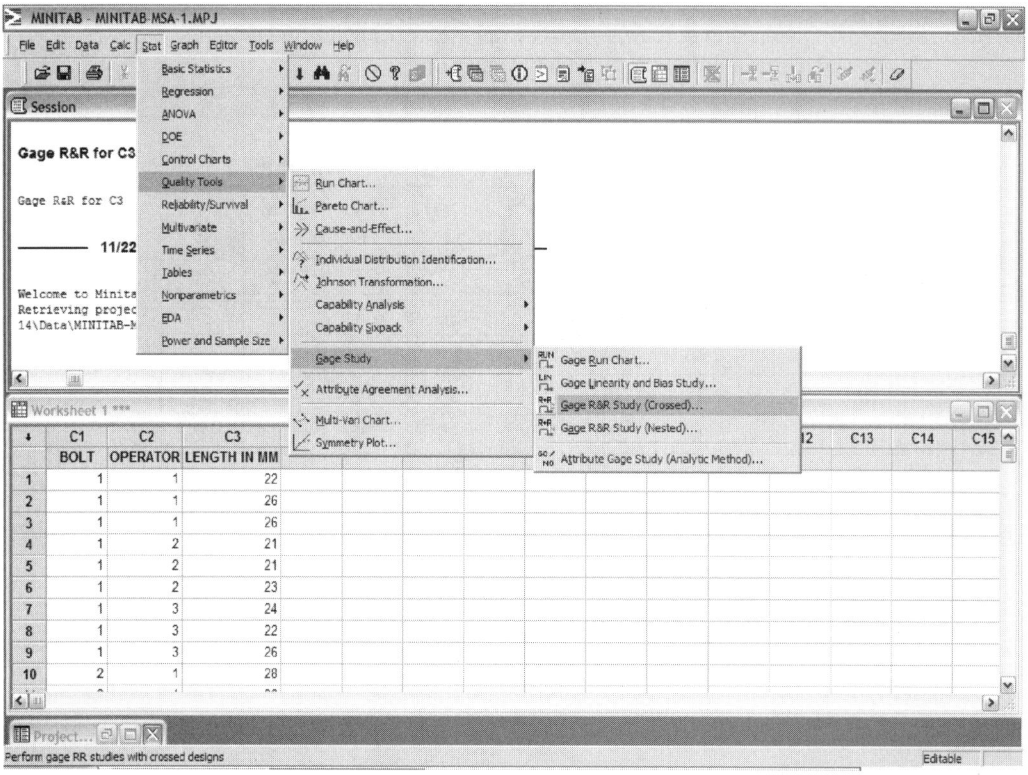

Figure 10.17 Screen showing the selections Stat > Quality Tools > Gage Study > Gage R&R Study (Crossed). . .

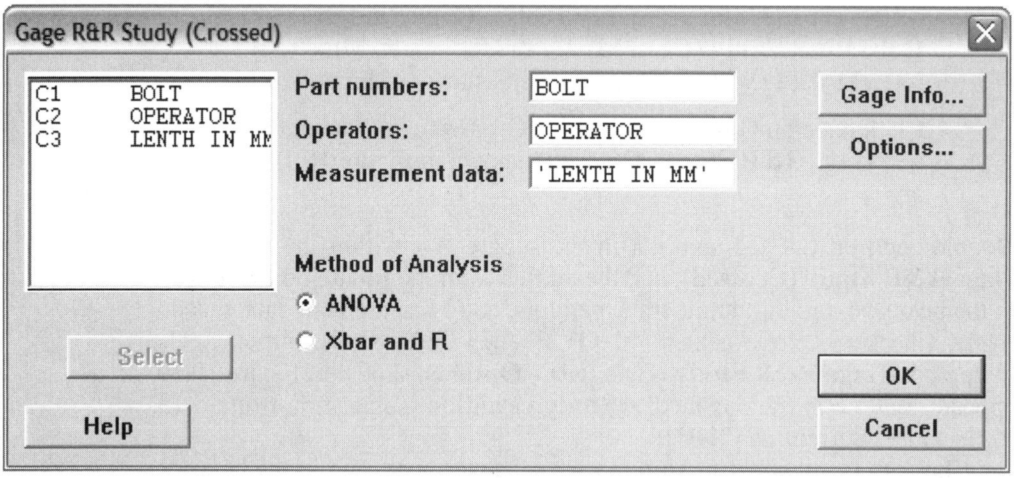

Figure 10.18 Gage R&R Study (Crossed) dialog box.

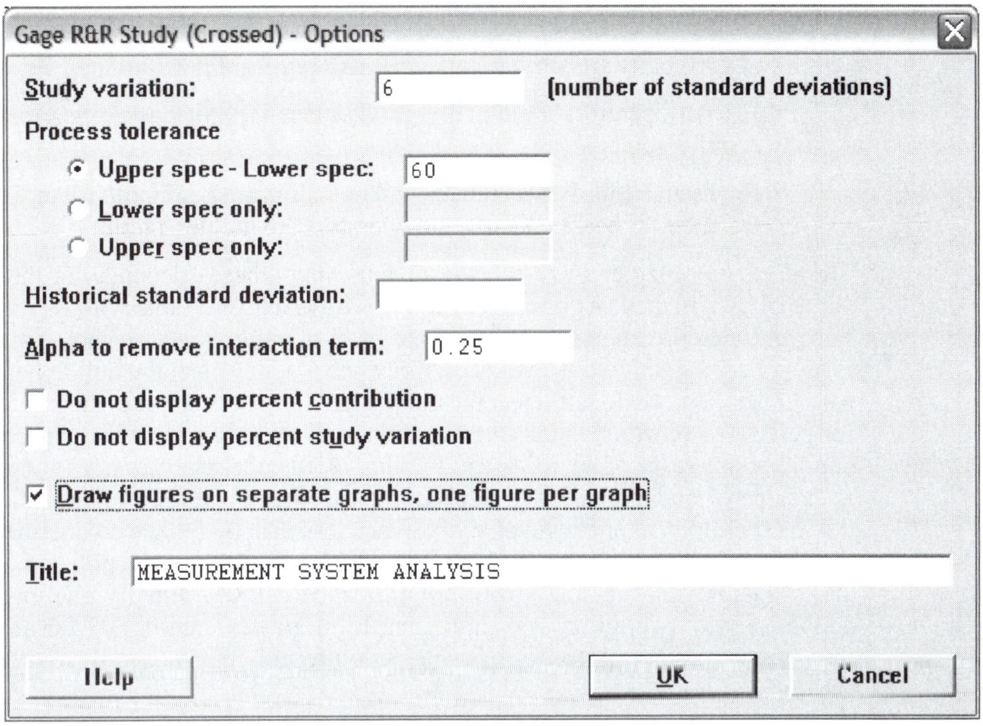

Figure 10.19 Gage R&R Study (Crossed) - Options dialog box.

the analysis only if the *p* value is less than or equal to the value you enter in the box next to **Alpha to remove interaction term**. If you wish, check the box next to **Draw figures on separate graphs, one figure per graph**. Otherwise, all the figures will appear on one graph. Finally, if you wish, you can enter the title of your project next to **Title**, and click **OK**. Then click **OK** in the dialog box **Gage R&R Study (Crossed)**. The output, including ANOVA tables and all the following graphs, will appear in the Session Window. We discussed this example earlier, in Chapter 7. However, for the sake of continuation of our discussion, we represent it here.

Gage R&R Study—ANOVA Method

Two-Way ANOVA Table with Interaction

Source	DF	SS	MS	F	P
Part Numbers	9	6135.73	681.748	165.532	0.000
Operators	2	6.76	3.378	0.820	0.456
Part Numbers*Operators	18	74.13	4.119	1.477	0.131
Repeatability	60	167.33	2.789		
Total	89	6383.95			

Alpha to remove interaction term = 0.25

In the Two-Way ANOVA Table with Interaction, we test three hypotheses:

- H_0: All parts are similar versus H_1: All parts are not similar
- H_0: All operators are equally good versus H_1: All operators are not equally good
- H_0: Interactions between parts and operators are negligible versus H_1: Interactions between parts and operators are not negligible

The decision whether to reject any of these hypotheses depends on the *p* value (shown in the last column of the Two-Way ANOVA Table with Interaction) and the corresponding value of the level of significance. If the *p* value is less than or equal to the level of significance (σ), we reject the null hypothesis. Otherwise, we do not reject the null hypothesis. For example, the *p* value for parts is zero, which means we reject the null hypothesis that the parts are similar at any level of significance. In other words, the measurement system is capable of distinguishing the different parts. The *p* value for operators is 0.456. Therefore, at any level of significance less than 0.456, we do not reject the null hypothesis that the operators are equally good (in most applications, an acceptable value of the level of significance is 0.05). Finally, the interactions are not negligible at a significant level greater than 0.131. Because the chosen value of alpha is 0.25, interaction term is not removed from the ANOVA.

Two-Way ANOVA Table without Interaction

Source	DF	SS	MS	F	P
Part Numbers	9	6135.73	681.748	220.222	0.000
Operators	2	6.76	3.378	1.091	0.341
Repeatability	78	241.47	3.096		
Total	89	6383.96			

```
Alpha to remove interaction term = 0.1
```

Because in this case the value of α is less than 0.131, the interaction term is removed from the Two-Way ANOVA Table without Interaction. In this case, the SS (sum of squares) and DF (degrees of freedom) are merged with corresponding terms of repeatability, which act as an error due to uncontrollable factors. The interpretation for parts and operators is the same as in the Two-Way ANOVA Table with Interaction. However, it is important to note that the *p* values can change from one ANOVA table to another. For example, the *p* values for operators are different in the two tables. We will not discuss here the reason for these changes in the *p* values, as it is beyond the scope of this book.

Gage R&R

%Contribution		
Source	VarComp	(of VarComp)
Total Gage R&R	3.2321	4.12
Repeatability	2.7889	3.55
Reproducibility	0.4432	0.56
Operators	0.0000	0.00
Operators*Part Numbers	0.4432	0.56
Part-to-Part	75.2922	95.88
Total Variation	78.5243	100.00

Process tolerance = 60

The first column in the Gage R&R MINITAB printout provides the breakdown of the variance components (estimates of variances). The second column provides percent contribution of the variance components, which becomes the basis of a Gage R&R study using the ANOVA method. For example, the total variation due to gage is 4.12 percent, of which 3.55 percent variation is contributed by the repeatability and the remaining 0.56 percent is contributed by the reproducibility. The variation due to parts is 95.88 percent of the total variation. This implies that the measurement system is very capable.

Note that the percent contributions are calculated simply by dividing the variance components by the total variation and then multiplying by 100. Thus, the percent contribution due to repeatability, for example, is given by

$$\frac{2.7889}{78.5243} \times 100 = 3.55\%.$$

Source	StdDev (SD)	Study Var (6 * SD)	%Study Var (%SV)	%Tolerance (SV/Toler)
Total Gage R&R	1.79780	10.7868	20.29	17.98
Repeatability	1.67000	10.0200	18.85	16.70
Reproducibility	0.66574	3.9944	7.51	6.66
Operators	0.00000	0.0000	0.00	0.00
Operators*Part Numbers	0.66574	3.9944	7.51	6.66
Part-to-Part	8.67711	52.0626	97.92	86.77
Total Variation	8.86139	53.1684	100.00	88.61

Number of distinct categories = 6

The preceding MINITAB printout provides various percent contributions using estimates of standard deviations, which are obtained by taking the square root of the variance components. The comparison with standard deviation does make more sense because the standard deviation uses the same units as those of the measurements. The study variation (that is, measurement system variation, which is equivalent to the process variation in the study of process control) is obtained by multiplying the standard deviation by 6. The percent study variations are calculated by dividing the standard deviation by the total variation and then multiplying by 100. The percent contribution due to part-to-part, for example, is given by

$$\frac{8.67711}{8.86139}\times 100 = 97.92\%.$$

The percent tolerance is obtained by dividing the (6*SD) by the process tolerance and the multiplying by 100. Thus, the process tolerance of total Gage R&R, for example, is given by

$$\frac{10.7868}{60}\times 100 = 17.98\%.$$

Note that the total percent tolerances in this example do not add up to 100. Rather, the total sum is 88.61, which means the total variation is using 88.61 percent of the specification band.

The last entry in the MINITAB printout is the number of distinct categories, which in this case is 6. The number of distinct categories can be determined as follows:

$$\begin{aligned}\text{Number of distinct categories} &= \text{Integral part of}\left(\frac{\text{part-to-part SD}}{\text{total Gage R\&R SD}}\times 1.4142\right)\\ &= \text{Integral part of}\left(\frac{8.67711}{1.79780}\times 1.4142\right)\\ &= 6.\end{aligned}$$

Under AIAG's recommendations, a measurement system is capable if the number of categories is greater than or equal to five. In this example, the measurement system is capable of separating the parts into the different categories in which they belong. This quantity is equivalent to the one defined in Montgomery (2005b) and is referred to as signal-to-noise ratio (SNR), that is,

$$\text{SNR} = \sqrt{\frac{2\rho_p}{1-\rho_p}}, \qquad \text{where } \rho_p = \frac{\sigma_p^2}{1-\rho_p^2}.$$

Graphical Representation of Gage R&R Study

Figure 10.20 shows the various percent contributions of Gage R&R, repeatability, reproducibility, and part-to-part variations, which we discussed in the previous section.

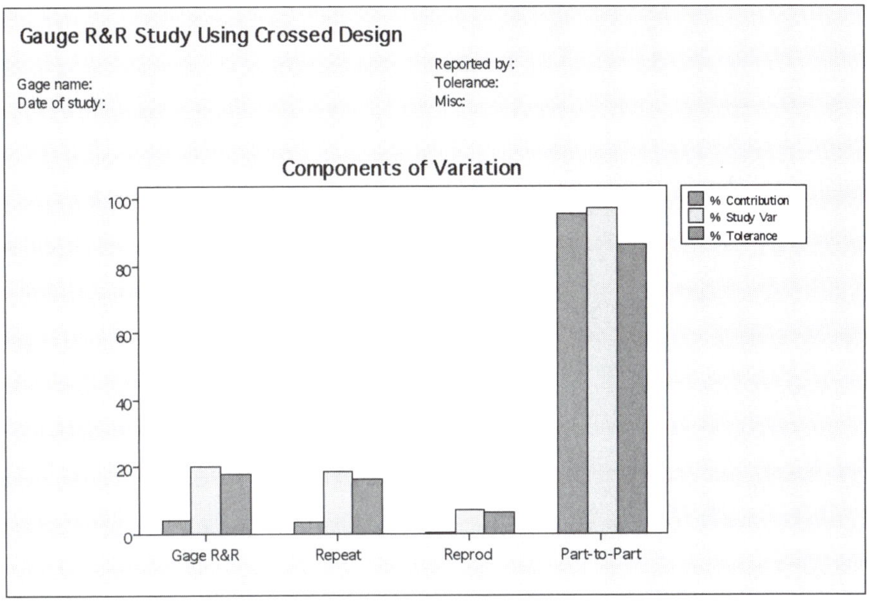

Figure 10.20 Percent contribution of variance components for the data in Example 10.12.

As usual, in Figure 10.21 we first interpret the R chart. All the data points are within the control limits, which indicates that the operators are measuring consistently. The $\bar{X}$ chart shows many points beyond the control limits, but this does not mean the measurement system is out of control. Rather, this indicates the narrower control limits because the variation due to repeatability is small and the measurement system is capable distinguishing the different parts.

Figure 10.22 plots the average of each part by any single operator. In this graph we have three lines because we have three operators. These lines intersect one another, but they are also very close to one another. This implies that there is some interaction between the operators and the parts, which is significant only at 0.131 or greater.

In Figure 10.23 the clear circles represent the measurements by each operator, and the dark circles represent the means. The spread of measurements for each operator is almost the same. The means fall on a horizontal line, which indicates that the average measurement for each operator is also the same. Thus, in this example, the operators are measuring the parts consistently. In other words, the variation due to reproducibility is low.

In Figure 10.23, the clear circles represent the measurements on each part, and the dark circles represent the mean for each part. In this case, the spread of measurements for each part is not exactly the same but is nonetheless very small. This means that each part is measured with the same precision and accuracy. Greater variability among the means indicates that the measurement system is quite capable of distinguishing the parts belonging to different categories. Combining the outcomes of Figures 10.23 and 10.24, we can say that, overall, the Gage R&R variability is not very significant.

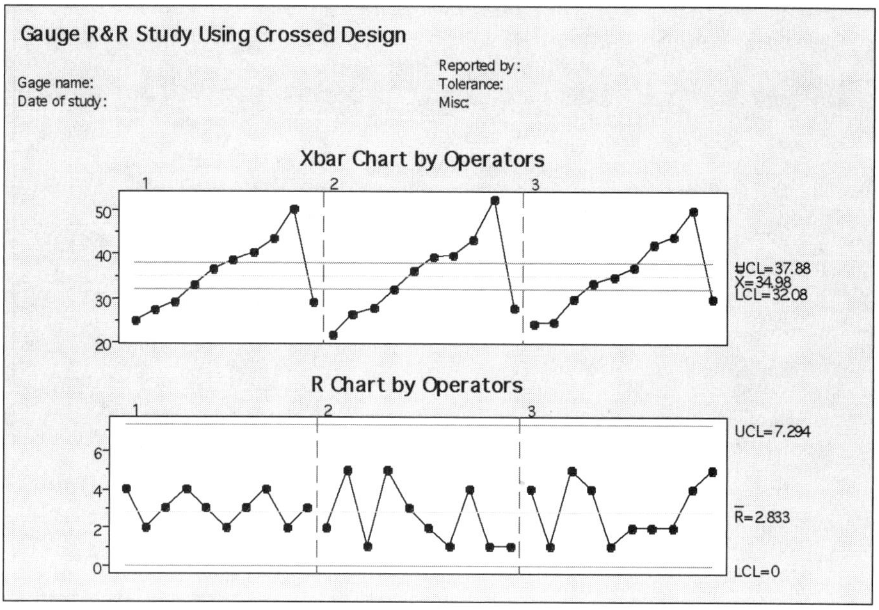

Figure 10.21 $\bar{X}$ and *R* charts for the data in Example 10.12.

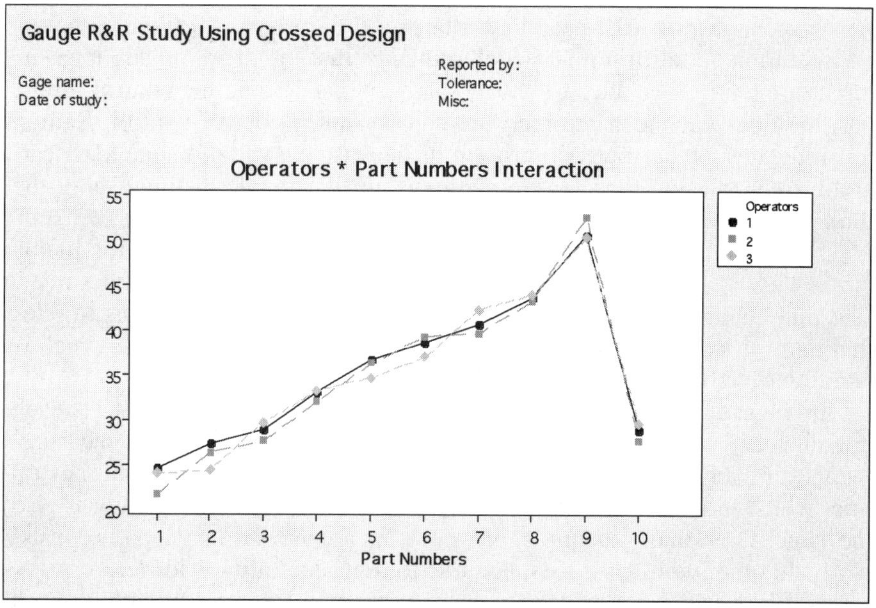

Figure 10.22 Interaction between operators and parts for the data in Example 10.12.

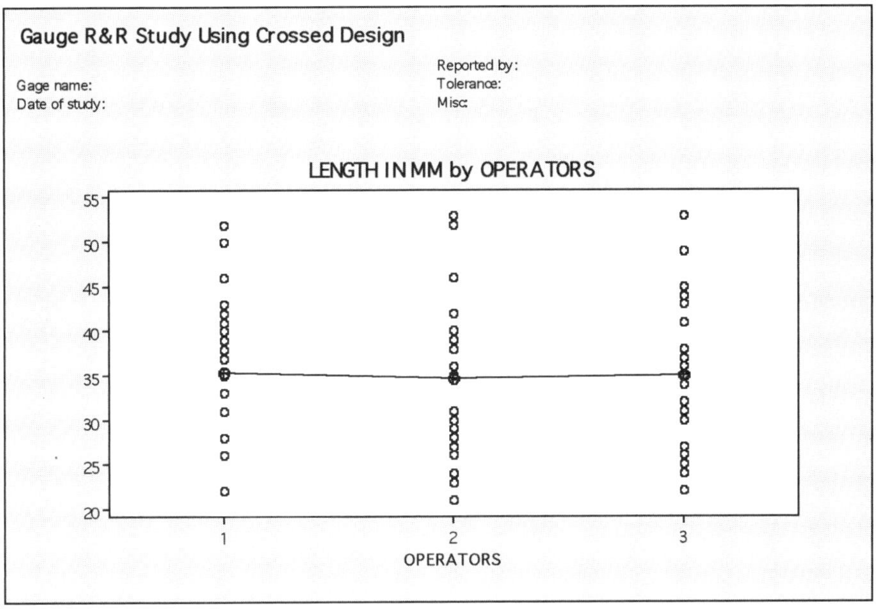

Figure 10.23 Scatter plot for measurements versus operators.

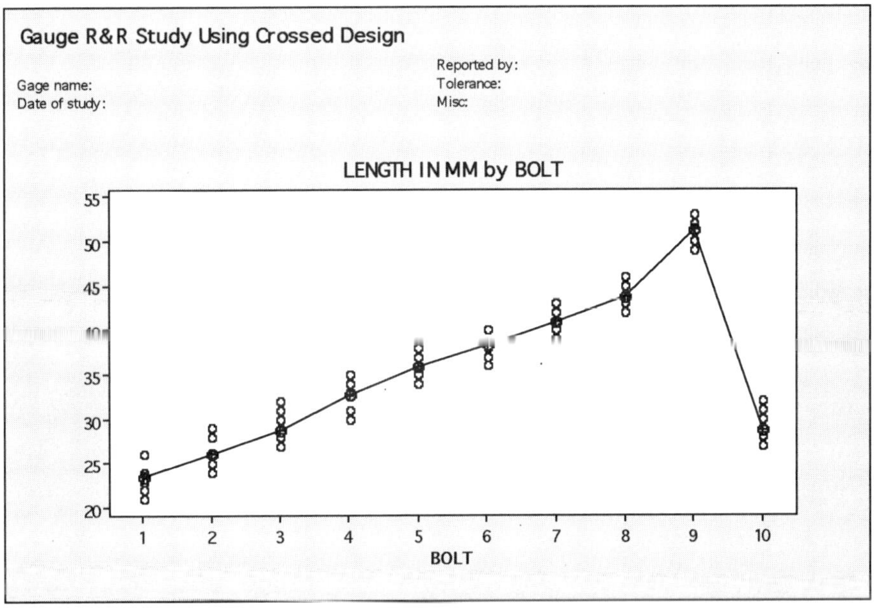

Figure 10.24 Scatter plot for measurements versus parts (bolts).

11

Computer Resources to Support SQC: JMP

Use of all the SQC tools discussed in this book began with hand calculation. Aside from the tediousness of the calculations, data transcription, and calculation errors, the amount of time required to complete the calculations and related graphing drove the need for computer support of SQC applications. Now there are many desktop statistical application software packages available to support SQC, and the focus of this chapter is on one of those software packages: JMP. In this chapter we will limit our discussion of topics to demonstrating the use of JMP for the tools and techniques discussed throughout this book, and we will emphasize the use of JMP for phase I and II SPC charts, process capability, and MSA. We will not discuss the use of JMP for acceptance sampling or PRE-control, as JMP is not specifically designed in Version 6.0 to support these SQC tools and techniques.

It is not our intent as authors to endorse any one software package, as each package has particular strengths and areas for improvement. We do, however, feel the need to introduce JMP as a software package that is very popular, that is statistically very powerful, and that supports the statistical content discussed in each of the four books in the Six Sigma Green Belt series. In order to gain the most benefit from the material in this chapter, readers should have basic computing literacy.

11.1 Using JMP—Version 6.0

When launching JMP, you will see the screen shown in Figure 11.1, which identifies JMP Starter as the topmost heading, indicating that there are no open files. Immediately below the drop-down menu is a dialog box, also with the heading of JMP Starter.

The JMP Starter is designed to assist new(er) JMP users by providing easily accessible prompts for and brief descriptions of the most common functions needed to start a JMP session. The JMP Starter is organized around categories of functions whereby you can select any of the categories of functions listed on the left side of Figure 11.1. The current category displayed is **File**, and the functions corresponding to the File category are shown in

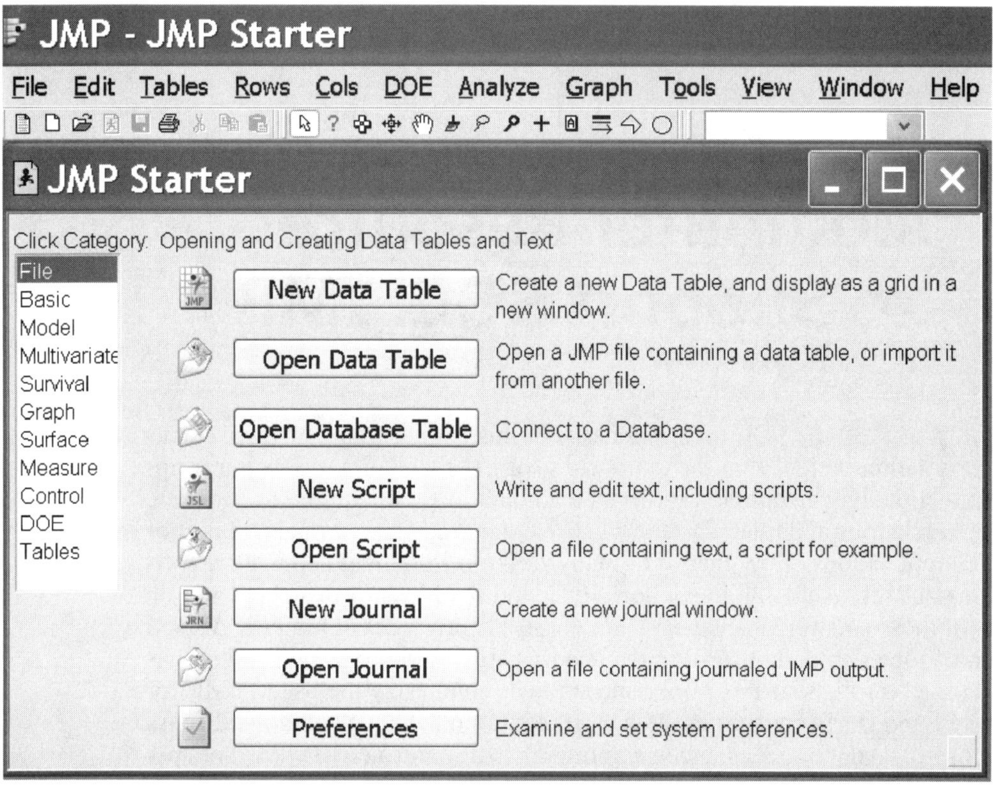

Figure 11.1 JMP Starter display.

the remainder of the dialog box. Each category displays a different set of functions.

In addition to the JMP Starter, JMP functions can be used by accessing the drop-down menus located at the top of the initial display, as can be seen in Figure 11.1 and Figure 11.2.

Clicking on any of the drop-down menu commands reveals a set of functions associated with that command. Examples of drop-down menu commands and associated functions are shown in Figures 11.3 and 11.4.

As can be seen in Figure 11.3, the **File, Edit,** and **Tables** commands have many functions that, for purposes of this chapter, are focused on file processing.

If you are familiar with Microsoft Windows products, the drop-down menus will appear quite familiar. As you gain familiarity with JMP, you may wish to disable the JMP Starter, which you can do by accessing **File > Preferences** and then deselecting the JMP Starter box.

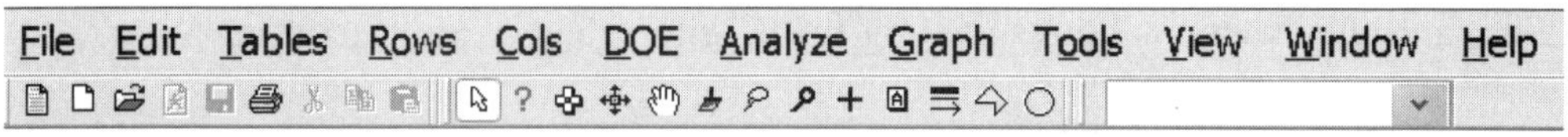

Figure 11.2 JMP drop-down menus.

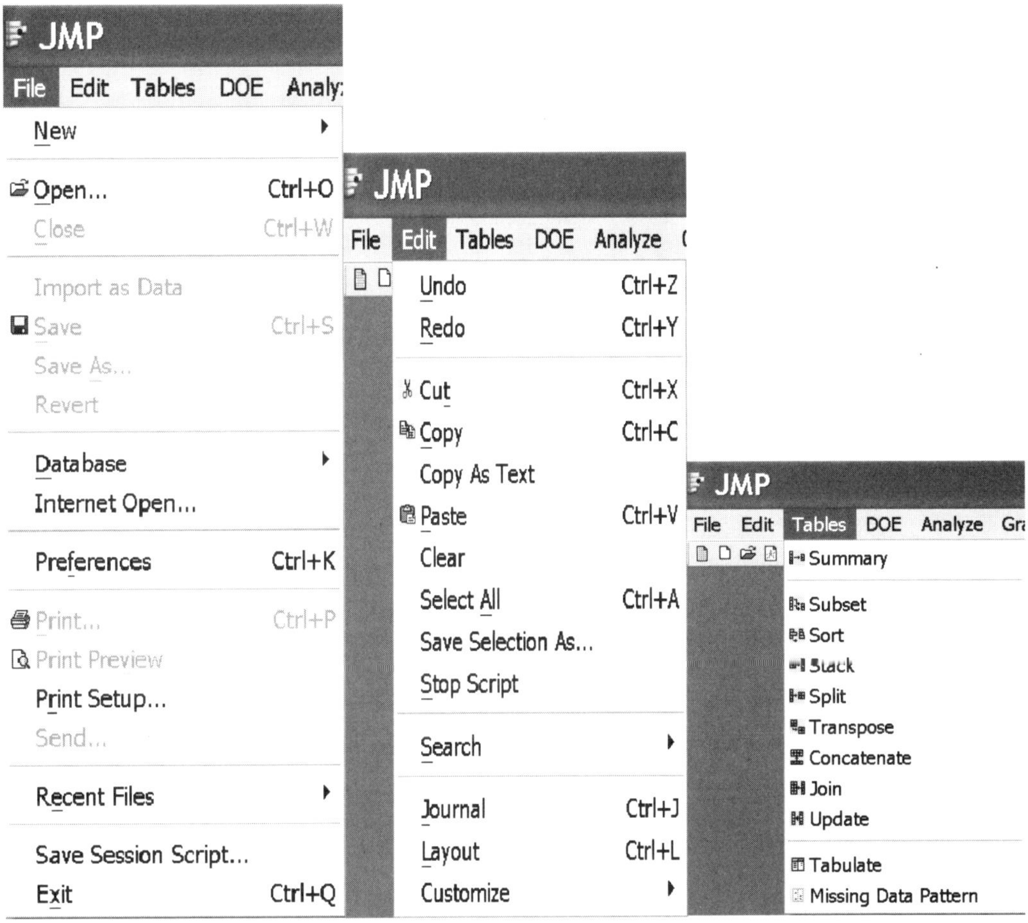

Figure 11.3 JMP file processing commands.

As can be seen in Figure 11.4, the **DOE**, **Analyze**, and **Graph** commands have many functions that, for the purposes of this chapter, are focused on statistical analysis.

Getting Started with JMP

To begin a JMP session, you will need to complete one of the following three steps:

1. Create a new data table
2. Open an existing JMP file
3. Create a new journal

As the intent of this chapter is to introduce readers to the use of JMP for SQC applications, creating new data tables and opening existing JMP files will be discussed. Creating journals is considered to be an advanced feature beyond the scope of this chapter. For more information on the many

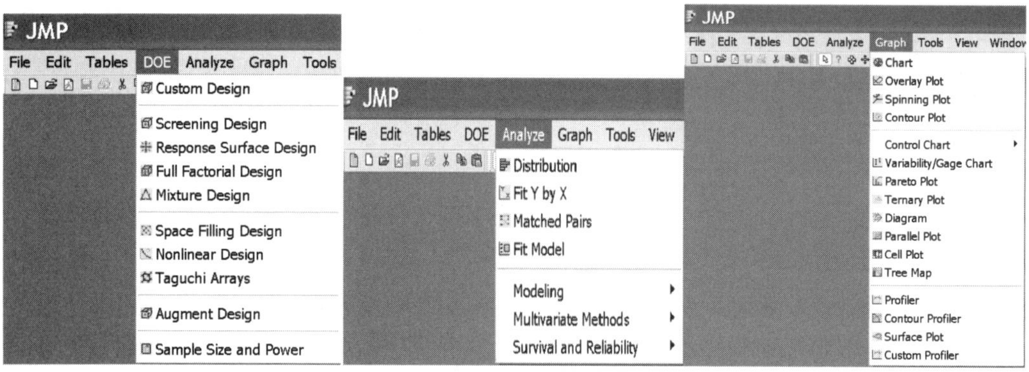

Figure 11.4 JMP statistical analysis commands.

advanced features of JMP, refer to the online help options within JMP, the JMP system documentation, or the book *JMP Start Statistics* (3rd edition; Thompson-Brooks/Cole Publishers).

Creating a New Data Table

Creating a new data table establishes a workspace empty of data, formatting, or labels. The steps required to create a new data table are identified in Figure 11.5.

As can be seen in Figure 11.5, to create a new data table, select the **File** drop-down menu, select the **New** command, and select **Data Table**. A new data table, which looks much like a Microsoft Excel worksheet, appears, as is shown in Figure 11.6.

Within the data table, column headings may be changed by double-clicking the heading and retyping the desired heading. New columns may be added by right-clicking in the workspace and selecting the option "New column." Descriptive statistics about the rows and columns defined are presented on the left of the display.

Lastly, it should be noted that blue arrows on any JMP display indicate the presence of a toggle switch, whereby clicking on the switch turns the display on or off. Red arrows on any JMP display indicate the presence of additional features or functions that may be selected. Selecting a red arrow reveals a drop-down menu of additional features or functions.

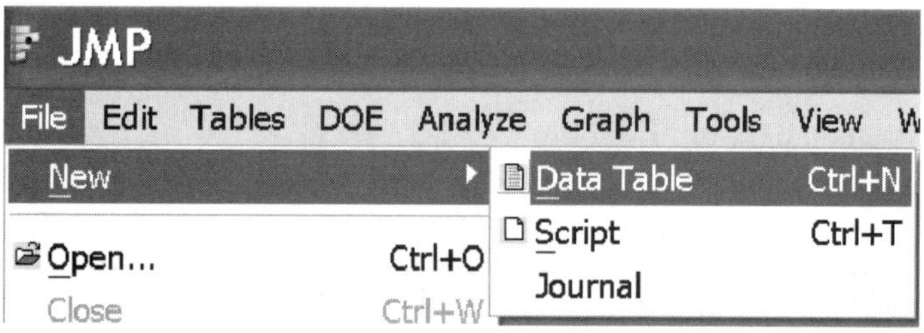

Figure 11.5 Creating a new data table.

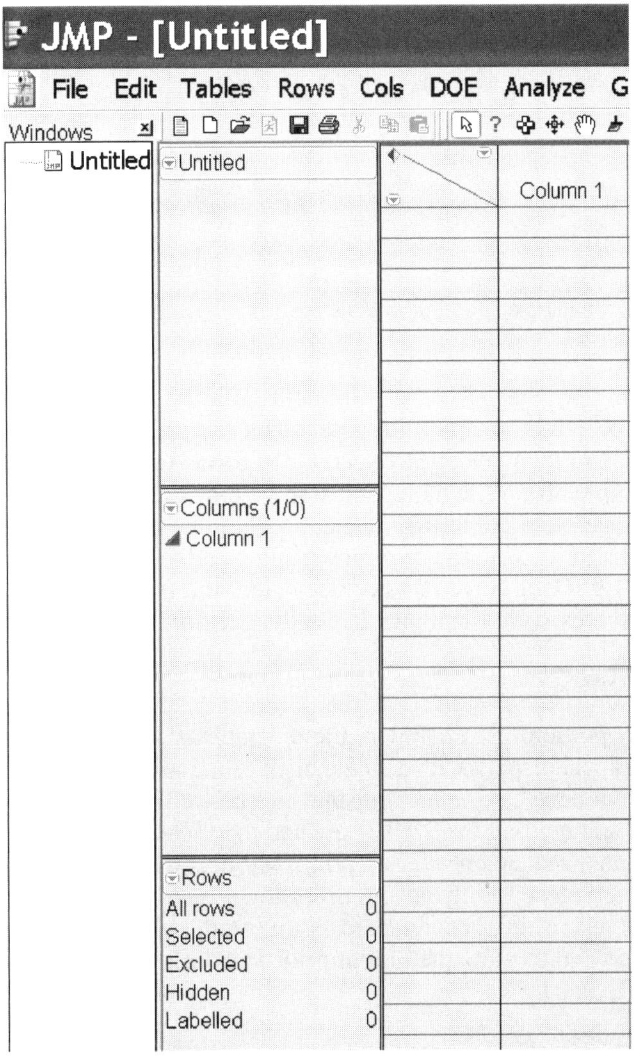

Figure 11.6 A new data table.

Opening an Existing JMP File

To open an existing JMP file, follow the steps in Figure 11.7. Select **File** from the drop-down menu and then select **Open**. Once the Open command has been selected, you can browse files in locations established in the system configuration.

Saving JMP Files

To save JMP files, use either the JMP Starter or the drop-down menu commands. The steps required to save a newly created JMP file are identified in Figure 11.8.

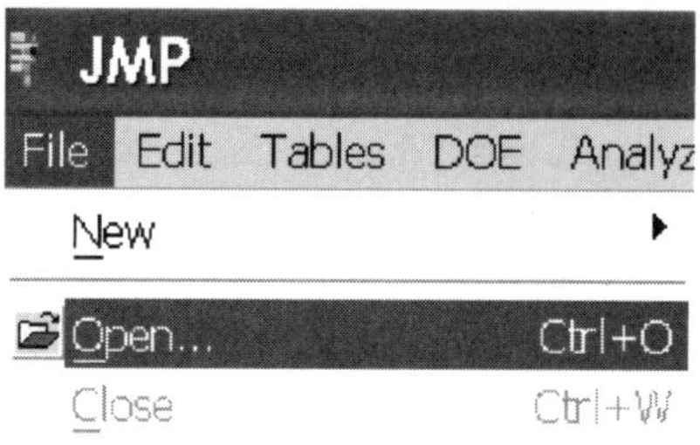

Figure 11.7 Opening an existing JMP file.

There are two ways to save a JMP file. If a file has not been previously saved, as would be the case with a new data file, select **File** from the drop-down menu and then select **Save As**. Once **Save As** has been selected, you will be prompted for a file name and storage location.

If a file has been previously saved, as would be the case with an existing data file, select **File** from the drop-down menu and then select **Save**, as shown in Figure 11.9. Once **Save** has been selected, the file will automatically be saved with the existing file name and in the existing storage location.

Print Options

To print any portion of a JMP data file or graphical display, select the entire table or graphical display with a single click of the mouse. If only certain portions of a data table or graphical display are desired, select the desired items by pressing and holding the SHIFT key and then selecting each of the desired items to print. The steps needed to print JMP data or graphs are identified in Figure 11.10. Select **File** from the drop-down menu and then select **Print**. Assuming that a printer is connected, configured, and on line, the output will print. If you want to view the output prior to printing, select **Print Preview** from the **File** menu.

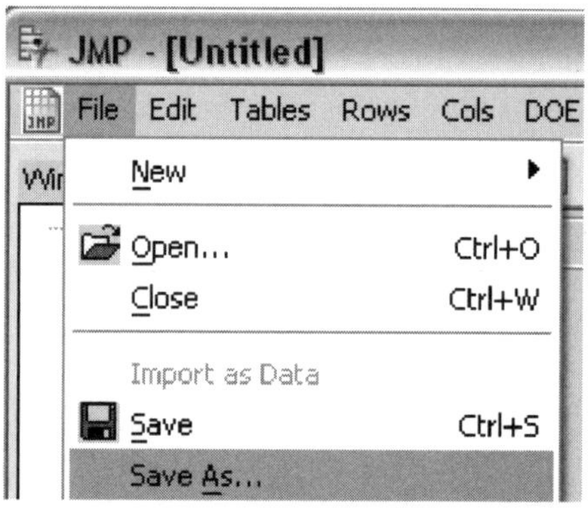

Figure 11.8 Saving a newly created JMP file.

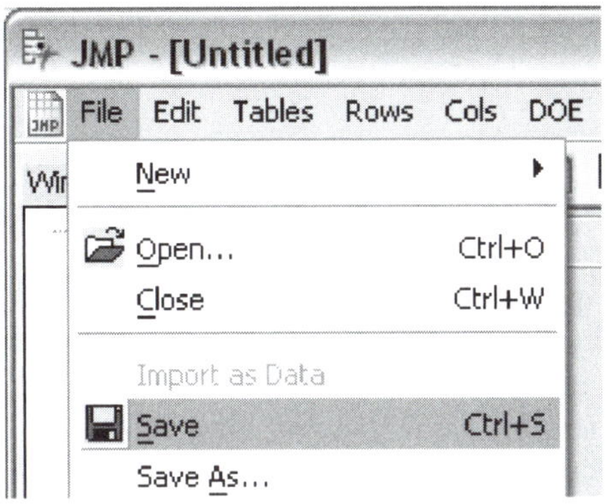

Figure 11.9 Saving an existing JMP file.

Using JMP Images for Reporting

One particularly useful feature of JMP is that images of data or graphics may be readily used in documents generated for reporting purposes. To use JMP images, simply select the desired images, as was described in the subsection "Print Options," right-click on them, and select Copy. Once the images are copied, launch your word processing software, such as Microsoft Word, and

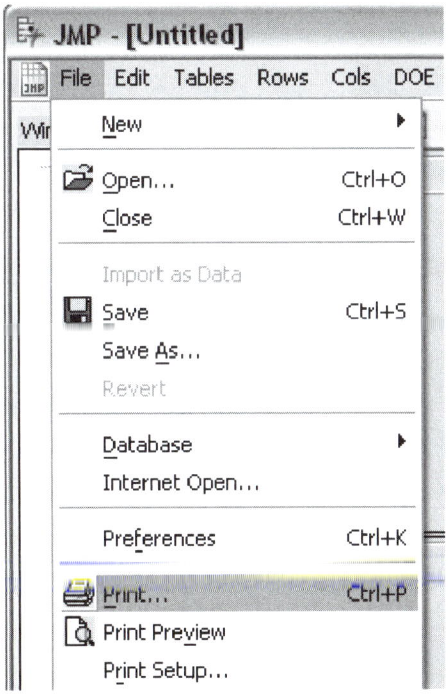

Figure 11.10 Printing JMP output.

then open your document and paste the images. This powerful feature eliminates the need for import/export functions.

11.2 The Shewhart XBar and R Control Chart

To create an XBar and R chart we begin by entering data into column 1 of a new data table. Once the data have been entered, we generate the chart by following the steps identified in Figure 11.11.

As can be seen in Figure 11.11, we first select **Graph** from the drop-down menu, then select **Control Chart**, and then **XBar**. A dialog box will be presented, as shown in Figure 11.12.

The dialog box in Figure 11.12 requires us to select a variable. The data table in this case contains only one variable, which is identified as "Column 1" in the Select Columns box, located in the upper left section of the dialog box. At this point, we would select the variable (click with the mouse) and assign it to the Process block, located in the upper center section of the dialog box, which indicates that a numeric variable is required.

Three additional points about the dialog box should be noted at this time. First, in an effort to anticipate the most frequently requested control chart, JMP automatically assumes we want to create an XBar and R chart. If any other type of variables control chart is desired, we must select the new

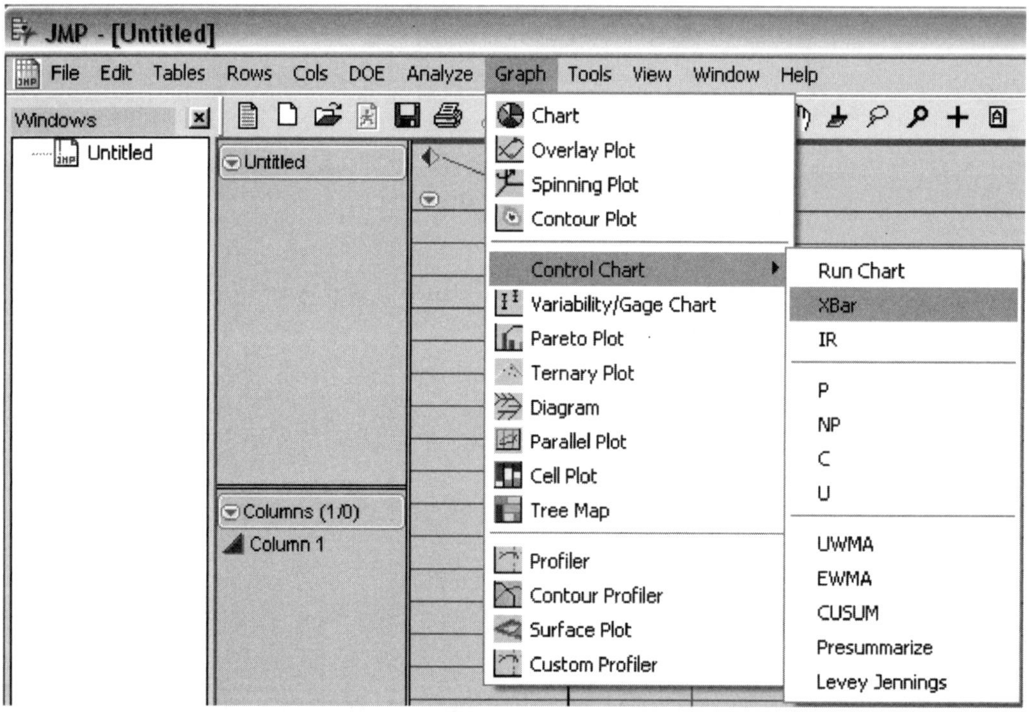

Figure 11.11 Generating an XBar and R chart.

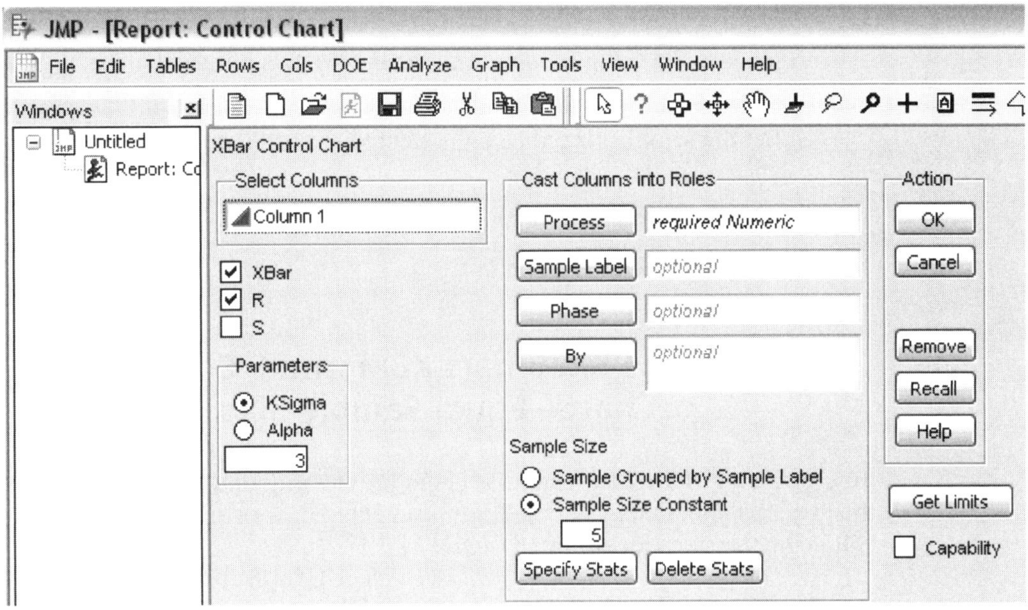

Figure 11.12 XBar chart dialog box.

chart type here. Second, the KSigma parameter is automatically set to three. KSigma refers to the selection of scaling factors based on +/– three standard deviations—which is the most common scaling factor used. Third, the sample size is automatically set to five. It is critically important that we ensure that the sample size defined in this block matches the sample size defined in the data table. It is common to collect sample sizes other than five, which are then recorded in the data table. If the actual sample size recorded in the data table does not match the sample size selected in the dialog box, JMP will calculate a control chart based on the sample sizes defined in the dialog box.

Once we complete our interaction with the dialog box, we select the **OK** function in the Action block, located in the upper right corner of the dialog box, and the control chart is generated and displayed.

Example 11.1 *Consider the data on the diameter measurements of ball bearings used in the wheels of heavy construction equipment shown in Table 3.4 of Example 3.4 in Chapter 3. Use the following steps to construct the XBar and R control chart.*

Solution:

1. Enter the data in column 1 of the data table.
2. Select **Graph** from the drop-down menu.
3. Select the **Control Chart** function.
4. Select the **XBar** chart option. The dialog box **XBar Control Chart** shown in Figure 11.12 appears.

5. Check the **R** option.
6. Choose the **KSigma** option in the Parameters box, and make sure "3" is entered as the parameter.
7. Set the sample size to be consistent with the sample size entered in the data table.
8. Assign a variable to be modeled in the Process field.
9. Select **OK** in the Action box.

11.3 The Shewhart XBar and S Control Chart—Equal Sample Size

To create an XBar and S chart we begin by entering data into column 1 of a new data table. Once the data have been entered, we generate the chart by following the steps identified in Figure 11.13.

As can be seen in Figure 11.13, we select **Graph** from the drop-down menu, then select **Control Chart**, and then **XBar**. Once the XBar chart has been selected, a dialog box will be presented, as shown in Figure 11.14.

The dialog box shown in Figure 11.14 requires us to select a chart type. An **R** chart is the default setting, and to generate an **S** chart, we must select the appropriate box, as is seen in the left section of the dialog box. Next, we must select a variable. The data table in this case contains only one variable, which is identified as "Column 1" in the Select Columns box, located in the upper left section of the dialog box. At this point, we would select the variable (click with the mouse) and assign it to the Process field, located in the upper center section of the dialog box, which indicates that a numeric variable is required.

Two additional points about the dialog box should be noted at this time. First, the KSigma parameter is automatically set to three. KSigma refers to the selection of scaling factors based on +/– three standard deviations—which is the most common scaling factor used. Second, the sample size is automatically set to five. It is critically important that we ensure that the sample size defined in this block matches the sample size defined in the data table. It is common to collect sample sizes other than five, which are then recorded in the data table. If the actual sample size recorded in the data table does not match the sample size selected in the dialog box, JMP will calculate a control chart based on the sample sizes defined in the dialog box.

Once we complete our interaction with the dialog box, we click **OK** in the Action block, located in the upper right corner of the dialog box, and the control chart is generated and displayed.

Example 11.2 *Consider the data on the diameter measurements of ball bearings used in the wheels of heavy construction equipment shown in Table 3.4 of Example 3.4 in Chapter 3. Then use the following steps to construct the XBar and S control chart.*

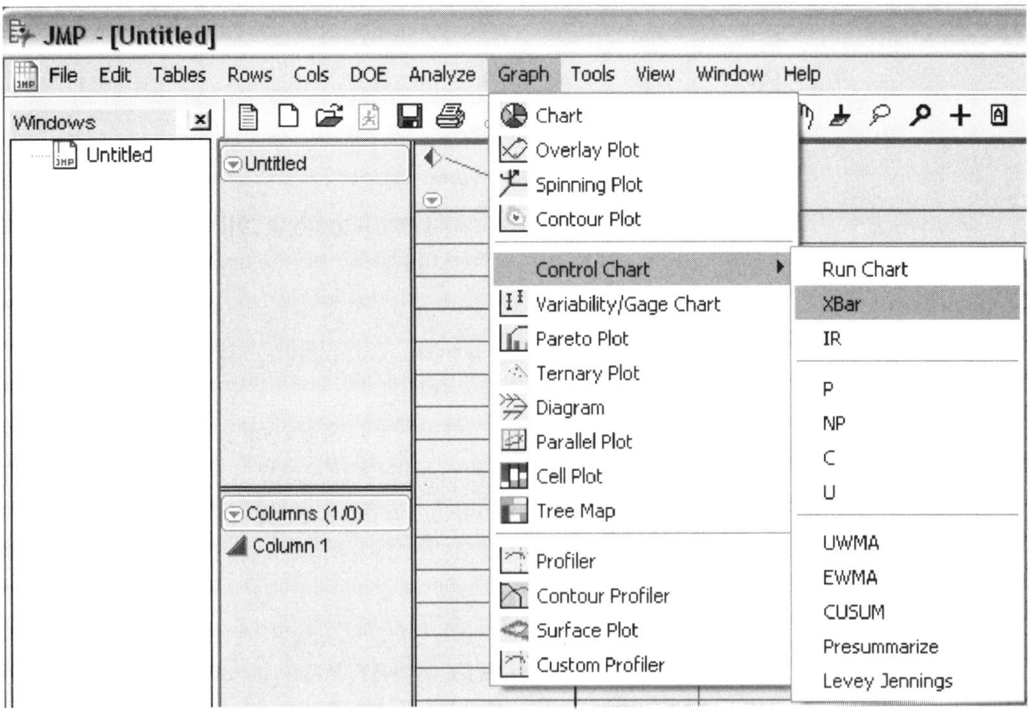

Figure 11.13 Generating an XBar and S chart.

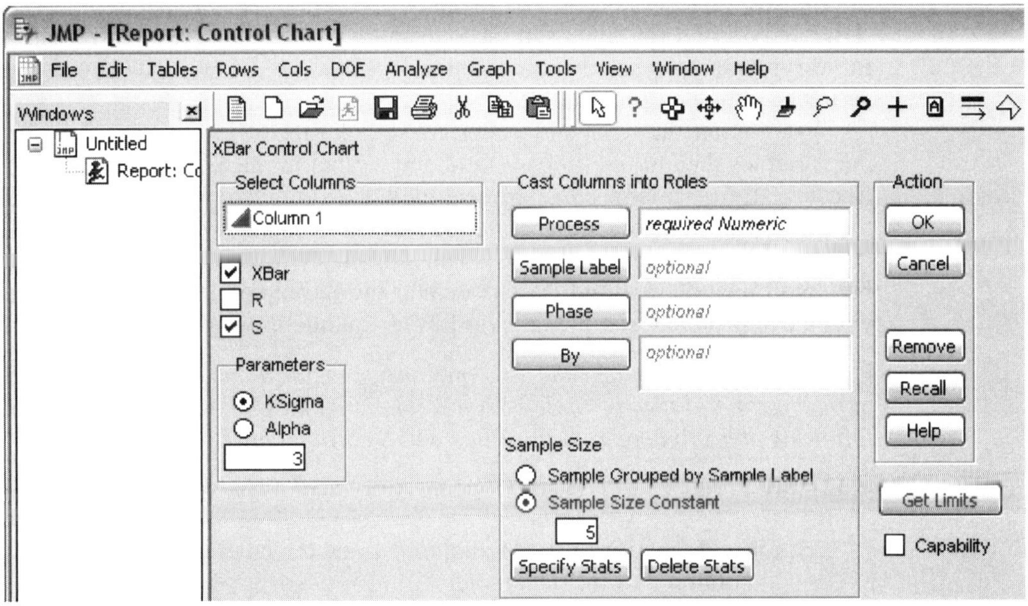

Figure 11.14 XBar chart dialog box.

Solution:

1. Enter the data in column 1 of the data table.
2. Select **Graph** from the drop-down menu.
3. Select the **Control Chart** function.
4. Select the **XBar** chart option. The dialog box **XBar Control Chart** shown in Figure 11.14 appears.
5. Check the **S** option.
6. Choose the **KSigma** option in the Parameters box, and make sure "3" is entered as the parameter.
7. Set the sample size to be consistent with the sample size entered in the data table.
8. Assign a variable to be modeled in the Process field.
9. Select **OK** in the Action box.

11.4 The Shewhart XBar and S Control Chart—Sample Size Variable

To generate an XBar and S chart with sample size variable, we follow the same procedural steps that were described for the XBar and S chart for equal sample size in section 11.3. The primary differences between generating an XBar and S chart for equal sample size and generating an XBar and S chart for varying sample size become apparent when we are presented with the dialog box shown in Figure 11.15.

To complete the XBar and S chart for sample size varying, we must assign the variables data in the Process field and a label in the Sample Label field. Because all the variables data are recorded in a single column, JMP requires the use of a second column labeling the data as belonging to a specific sample (for example, sample 1, sample 2). The **Sample Grouped by Sample Label** button is then selected, and JMP associates the amount of data in each sample with the appropriate sample label in further calculations.

Example 11.3 *Consider the data on finished inside diameter measurements of piston rings shown in Table 3.6 of Example 3.8 in Chapter 3. Then use the following steps to construct the XBar and S control chart.*

Solution:

1. Enter the variables data in column 1 and the label (sample) data in column 2 of the data table.
2. Select **Graph** from the drop-down menu.
3. Select the **Control Chart** function.

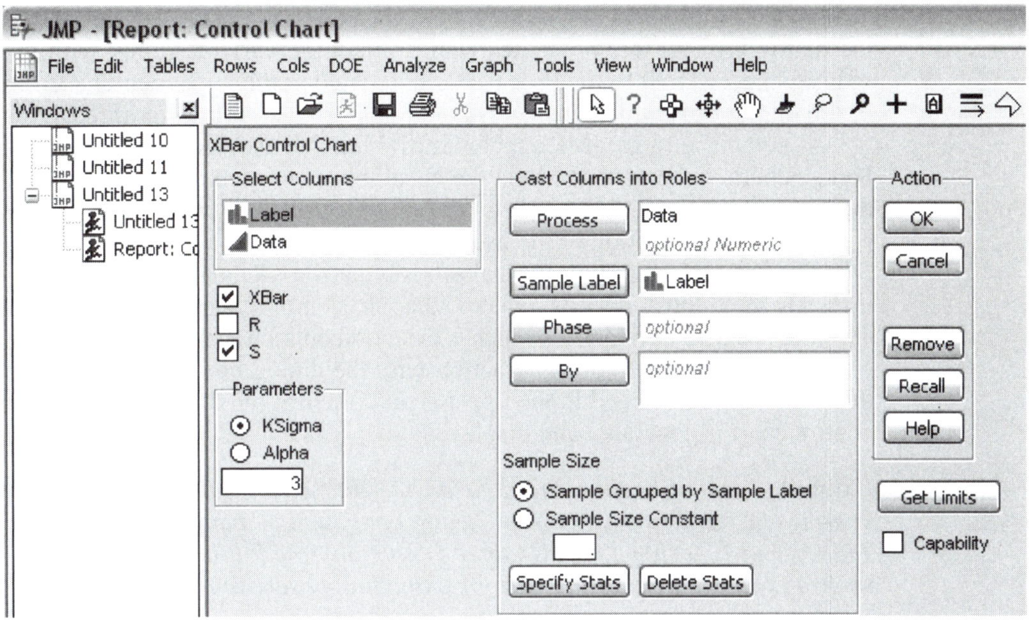

Figure 11.15 XBar and S chart dialog box.

4. Select the **XBar** chart option. The dialog box **XBar Control Chart** shown in Figure 11.15 appears.
5. Check the **S** option.
6. Choose the **KSigma** option in the Parameters box, and make sure "3" is entered as the parameter.
7. Assign the variable to be modeled in the Process box.
8. Assign the label in the Sample Label field (the **Sample Grouped by Sample Label** button will automatically be enabled).
9. Select **OK** in the Action box.

11.5 The Shewhart Control Chart for Individual Observations

To create a control chart for individual observations, we begin by entering data into column 1 of a new data table. Once the data have been entered, we generate the chart by following the steps identified in Figure 11.16.

As can be seen in Figure 11.16, we select **Graph** from the drop-down menu, then select the **Control Chart** function, and then select **IR**. Once the **IR** chart has been selected, a dialog box will be presented, as shown in Figure 11.17.

The dialog box shown in Figure 11.17 requires us to select a variable. The data table in this case contains only one variable, which is identified as

"Column 1" in the Select Columns box, located in the upper left section of the dialog box. At this point, we would select the variable (click with the mouse) and assign it to the Process field, located in the upper center section of the dialog box, which indicates that a numeric variable is required.

As default settings, JMP enables **Individual Measurement** and **Moving Range** charts to be generated via the check boxes located on the left side of the dialog box. JMP also defaults to a moving range of two, which can be changed at the discretion of the user.

An additional point about the dialog box is that the KSigma parameter is automatically set to three. KSigma refers to the selection of scaling factors based on +/– three standard deviations—which is the most common scaling factor used.

Once we complete our interaction with the dialog box, we click **OK** in the Action block, located in the upper right corner of the dialog box, and the control chart is generated and displayed.

Example 11.4 *Consider the data on the diameter measurements of ball bearings used in the wheels of heavy construction equipment shown in Table 3.5 of Example 3.6 in Chapter 3. Then use the following steps to construct the Shewhart control chart for individual observations.*

Solution:

1. Enter the data in column 1 of the data table.
2. Select **Graph** from the drop-down menu.

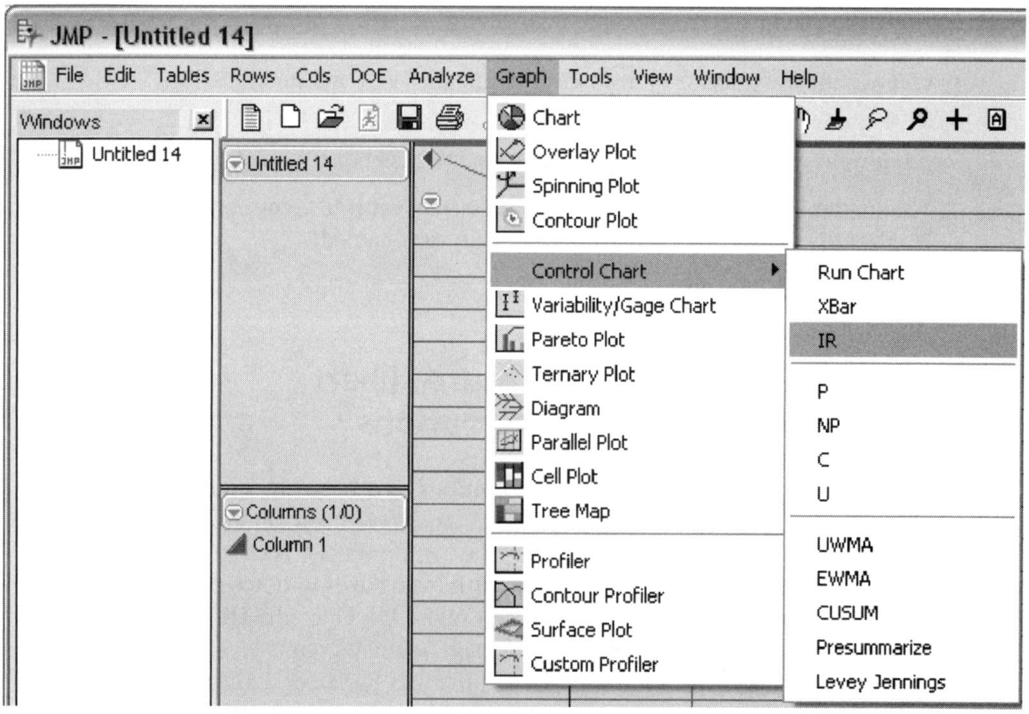

Figure 11.16 Generating a control chart for individual observations.

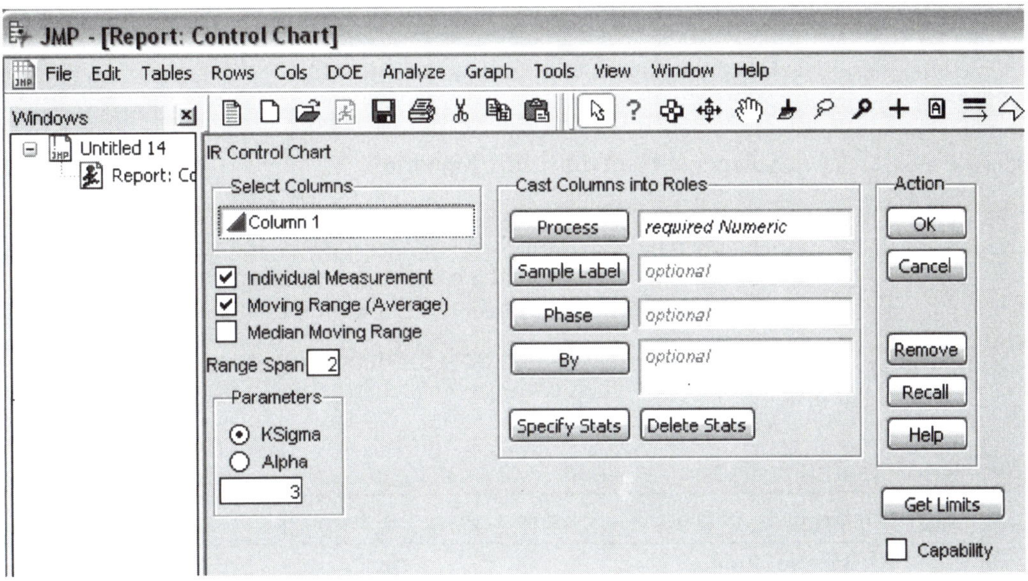

Figure 11.17 IR chart dialog box.

3. Select the **Control Chart** function.
4. Select the **IR** chart option. The dialog box **IR Control Chart**, shown in Figure 11.17, appears.
5. Check the **Individual Measurement** and **Moving Range** options.
6. Define the range in the Range Span field.
7. Choose the **KSigma** option in the Parameters box, and make sure "3" is entered as the parameter.
8. Assign the variable to be modeled in the **Process** field.
9. Select **OK** in the Action box.

11.6 Process Capability Analysis

A process capability analysis in JMP is conducted in the context of a data set that is being evaluated for process control. This means that in the dialog box presented for any of the control charts, a check box for a process capability analysis is presented, enabling the analysis. We illustrate the capability analysis of a process with the following example.

Example 11.5 *Consider a quality characteristic of a process that is normally distributed. Suppose that the process is stable with respect to the 3σ control limits. Furthermore, suppose that the data of 25 samples, each of size five, from this process are as shown in Table 11.1. Also, we are given that the LSL = 0.95 and the USL = 1.05. Perform the capability analysis of the process.*

Solution:

1. Enter the data in column 1 of the data table.
2. Select **Graph** from the drop-down menu.
3. Select the **Control Chart** function.
4. Select any of the control chart options. A dialog box associated with the type of control chart selected appears. For the data in this example, an XBar and S chart was selected and the process capability analysis was enabled, as is seen in Figure 11.18.
5. Complete the interaction with the dialog box as has been explained for each of the control chart types.

Table 11.1 Data of 25 samples, each of size five, from a given process.

Sample Number	Observations				
1	0.97076	0.98518	1.01104	0.97892	0.99094
2	0.99455	0.96904	0.99770	0.97502	0.98483
3	0.99538	0.99765	0.96011	1.03059	0.98048
4	1.00332	0.98891	0.98018	1.01699	1.00391
5	1.03023	0.98663	1.01498	0.97483	0.99836
6	0.98491	1.00487	0.96951	0.99613	1.03365
7	0.98894	1.00631	0.98630	0.98115	0.96755
8	0.93771	0.99017	1.03221	1.01045	1.01197
9	1.00103	1.01641	0.97683	1.00149	1.03011
10	1.01493	1.02220	1.00179	1.01556	1.01080
11	1.01606	0.96502	1.00546	0.99259	0.96857
12	0.98266	0.99031	0.99349	1.00499	1.03806
13	0.95560	1.00033	1.01098	0.99380	1.04496
14	0.97406	1.01305	0.97556	0.98493	1.00347
15	1.03027	0.97009	1.00151	0.99929	0.98366
16	1.02527	1.01652	1.02743	0.99951	0.99565
17	1.02837	1.01676	0.97056	0.95207	1.03254
18	0.98646	0.99434	1.00163	0.98811	1.01134
19	0.96072	1.02716	1.01030	1.04141	0.96355
20	1.03511	0.94637	1.00852	0.99454	1.00620
21	0.99550	0.98307	1.00948	1.00793	1.04035
22	0.98397	1.03082	0.98643	1.00540	0.97880
23	0.99934	0.99544	1.00959	1.00664	1.02905
24	1.00286	1.00777	1.01661	0.99793	1.03805
25	0.96557	0.98535	0.99911	1.03566	1.00453

6. Check the Capability option on the right side of the dialog box.
7. Select **OK** in the Action box. A process capability analysis dialog box appears, as is presented in Figure 11.19.
8. Define the specification limits and target value in accordance with the example instructions.
9. Check the **Long Term Sigma** box for C_p and C_{pk}.
10. Select **OK**, and the analysis output appears, as shown in Figure 11.20.

11.7 The *p* Chart: Control Chart for Fraction Nonconforming Units with Constant Sample Size

To create a *p* chart we begin by entering data (the number of nonconforming units) into column 1 of a new data table. Once the data have been entered, we generate the chart by following the steps identified in Figure 11.21.

As can be seen in Figure 11.21, we select **Graph** from the drop-down menu, then select the **Control Chart** function, and then select **P**. Once the ***p*** chart has been selected, a dialog box is presented, as shown in Figure 11.22.

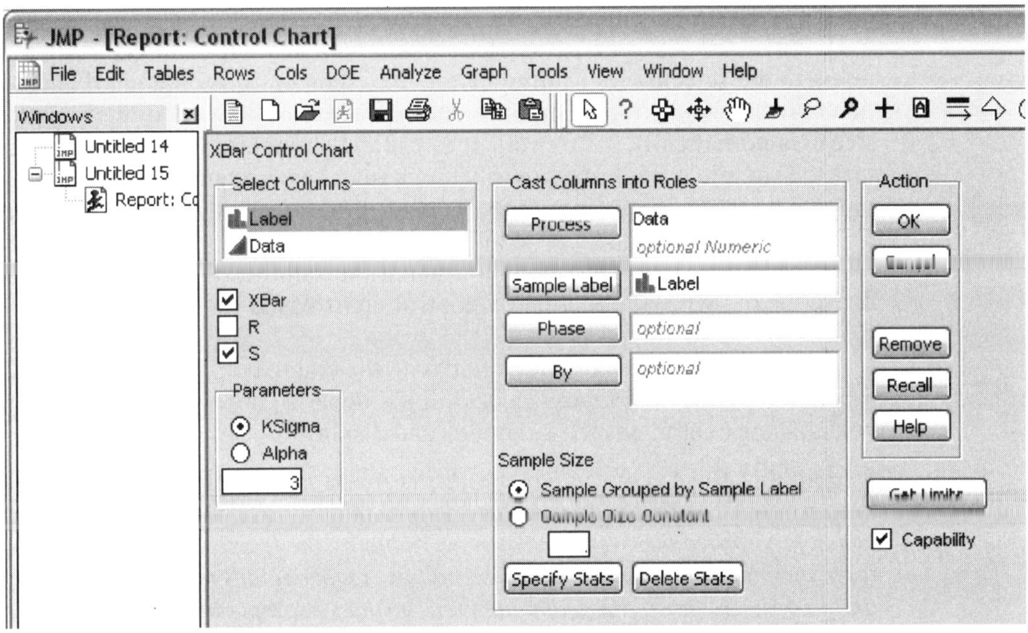

Figure 11.18 Capability analysis based on an XBar and S chart for Example 11.5.

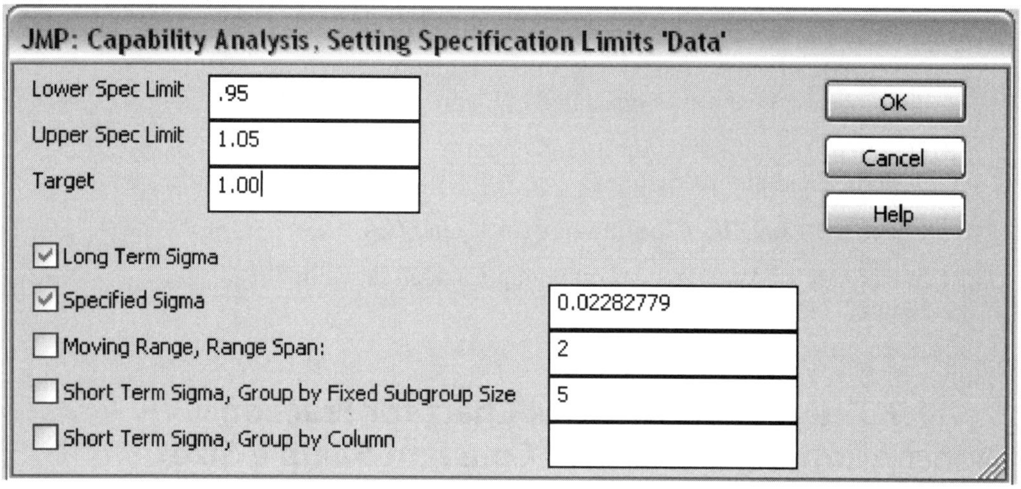

Figure 11.19 Process capability analysis dialog box.

The dialog box in Figure 11.22 requires us to select a variable. The data table in this case contains three variables, which are identified as "Lot," "Lot Size," and "# defects" in the Select Columns box, located in the upper left section of the dialog box. At this point, we would select the variable "# defects" (click with the mouse) and assign it to the Process field, located in the upper center section of the dialog box, which indicates that a numeric variable is required.

Two additional points about the dialog box should be noted at this time. First, the KSigma parameter is automatically set to three. KSigma refers to the selection of scaling factors based on +/– three standard deviations—which is the most common scaling factor used. Second, the sample size is automatically set to 100. It is critically important that we ensure that the sample size defined in this block matches the sample size defined in the data table. It is common to collect sample sizes other than 100 for a *p* chart, which are then recorded in the data table. If the actual sample size recorded in the data table does not match the sample size selected in the dialog box, JMP will calculate a control chart based on the sample sizes defined in the dialog box.

Once we complete our interaction with the dialog box, we select the **OK** function in the Action block, located in the upper right corner of the dialog box, and the control chart is generated and displayed.

Example 11.6 *A semiconductor industry tracks the number of nonconforming computer chips produced each day. A team of Six Sigma Green Belts wants to improve the overall quality by reducing the fraction of nonconforming computer chips. To achieve this goal, the team decides to set up a* p *chart, and in order to do so, the team members inspect a sample of 1000 chips each day over a period of 30 days. Table 4.2 of Example 4.1 in Chapter 4 gives the number of nonconforming chips out of 1000 inspected chips each day during the study period.*

Distributions

Data

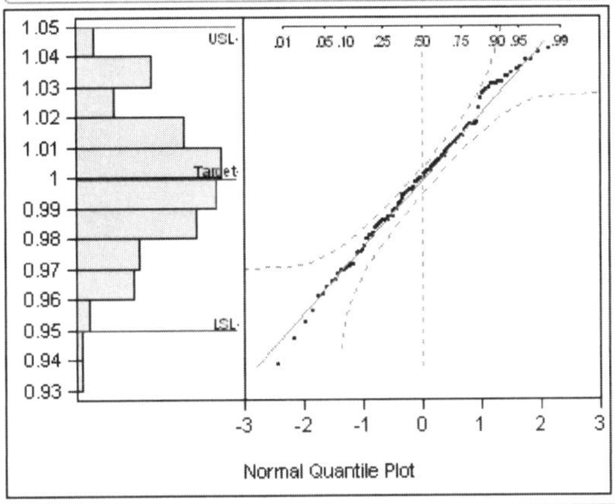

Capability Analysis

Specification	Value	Portion	% Actual
Lower Spec Limit	0.95	Below LSL	1.6000
Upper Spec Limit	1.05	Above USL	0.0000
Spec Target	1	Total Outside	1.6000

Overall, Sigma = 0.02206

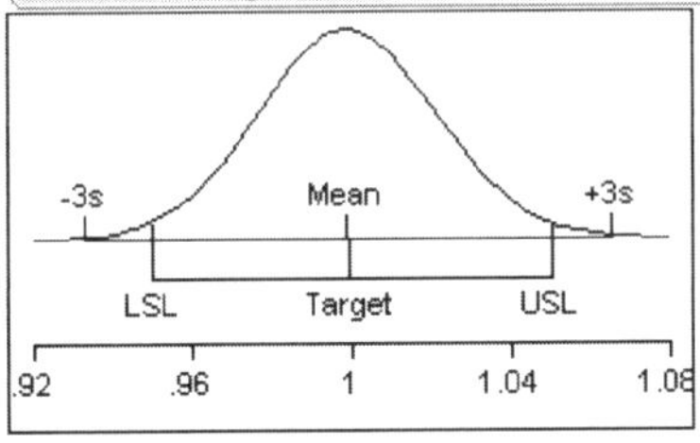

Capability	Index	Lower CI	Upper CI
CP	0.755	0.661	0.849
CPK	0.740	0.631	0.849
CPM	0.755	0.661	0.848
CPL	0.740	0.630	0.848
CPU	0.771	0.658	0.883

Portion	Percent	PPM	Sigma Quality
Below LSL	1.3228	13227.536	3.719
Above USL	1.0360	10360.475	3.813
Total Outside	2.3588	23588.011	3.485

Benchmark Z	Index
Z Bench	1.985
Z LSL	2.219
Z USL	2.313

Control Chart, Sigma = 0.02283

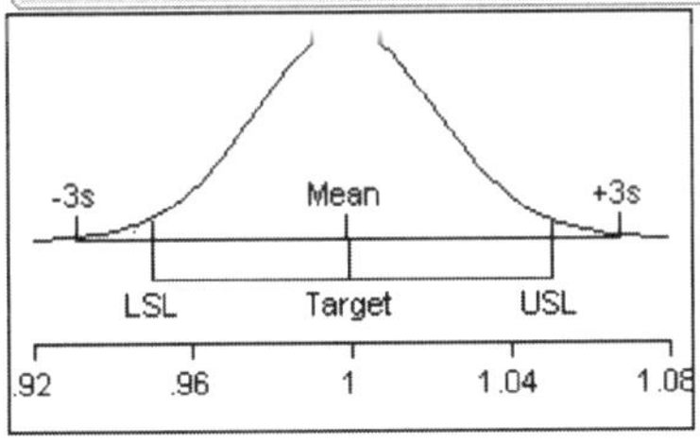

Capability	Index	Lower CI	Upper CI
CP	0.730	0.639	0.821
CPK	0.715	0.609	0.821
CPM	0.729	0.639	0.819
CPL	0.715	0.608	0.821
CPU	0.745	0.635	0.854

Portion	Percent	PPM	Sigma Quality
Below LSL	1.5973	15972.518	3.645
Above USL	1.2691	12691.358	3.736
Total Outside	2.8664	28663.876	3.401

Benchmark Z	Index
Z Bench	1.901
Z LSL	2.145
Z USL	2.236

Figure 11.20 Process capability analysis output.

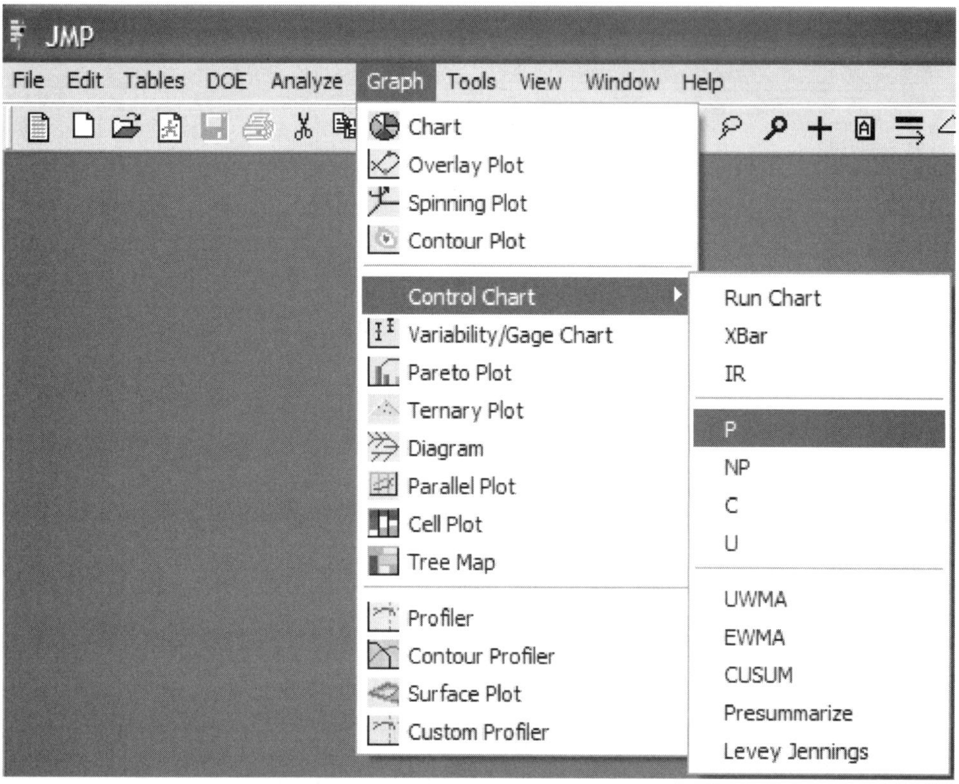

Figure 11.21 Generating a *p* chart.

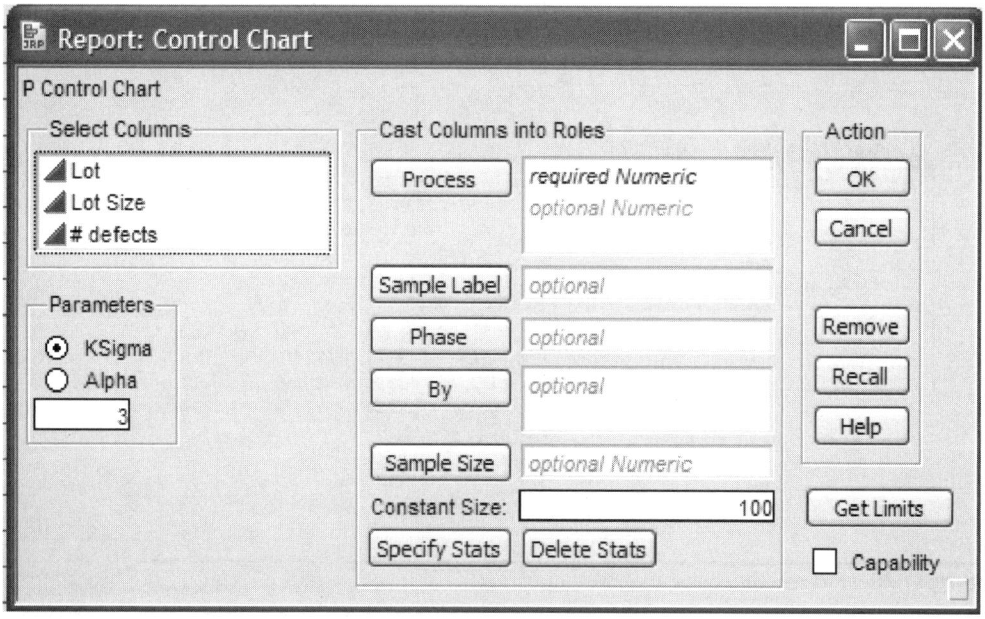

Figure 11.22 *p* chart dialog box.

Solution:

1. Enter the data (number of nonconforming units given in Table 4.2 in Chapter 4) in column 1 of the data table.
2. Select **Graph** from the drop-down menu.
3. Select the **Control Chart** function.
4. Select the **P** chart option. The dialog box titled **P Control Chart**, shown in Figure 11.22, appears.
5. Choose the **KSigma** option in the Parameters box, and make sure "3" is entered as the parameter.
6. Set the sample size to be consistent with the sample size entered in the data table.
7. Assign a variable to be modeled in the Process field.
8. Select **OK** in the Action field.

11.8 The *p* Chart: Control Chart for Fraction Nonconforming Units with Sample Size Varying

To generate a *p* chart with sample size varying, we use the same procedure as for a *p* chart with constant sample size. In the case of a sample size varying, we enter the sample numbers in column 1 and the corresponding nonconforming data in column 2, and in step 7 we assign the sample numbers entered in column 1 to the Sample Label field and the nonconforming data entered in column 2 to the Process Field.

11.9 The *np* Chart: Control Chart for Nonconforming Units

To create an *np* chart we plot the number of nonconforming units in an inspected sample. The *np* chart is very similar to the *p* chart except that in the *p* chart we plot the fraction nonconforming units in each inspected sample. Sample sizes in an *np* chart must be equal. We summarize here some specific points that are important for *np* charts:

- The inspection sample sizes should be equal
- The sample size should be large enough to include some nonconforming units

Record the sample size and number of nonconforming units (*np*) in each sample and plot the number of nonconforming units on the control chart.

To generate an *np* control chart, follow all the steps for creating a *p* control chart outlined in section 11.7.

11.10 The *c* Chart

The *c* chart is used for studying the number of nonconformities in a sample. In this case, we are studying the number of nonconformities in a unit of production, also referred to as an inspection unit, rather than studying the fraction nonconforming or total number of nonconforming units in the sample.

To create a *c* chart we begin by entering data (the number of nonconformities) into column 1 of a new data table. Once the data have been entered, we generate the chart by following the steps identified in Figure 11.23.

As can be seen in Figure 11.23, we select **Graph** from the drop-down menu, then select the **Control Chart** function, and then select **C**. Once the ***c*** chart has been selected, a dialog box will be presented, as shown in Figure 11.24.

The dialog box in Figure 11.24 requires us to select a variable. The data table in this case contains three variables, which are identified as "Lot," "Lot Size," and "# nonconformities" in the Select Columns box, located in the upper left section of the dialog box. At this point, we would select the variable "# nonconformities" (click with the mouse) and assign it to the Process field, located in the upper center section of the dialog box, which indicates a numeric variable is required. We then select **OK** to generate the chart. We illustrate how to create a *c* chart with the following example.

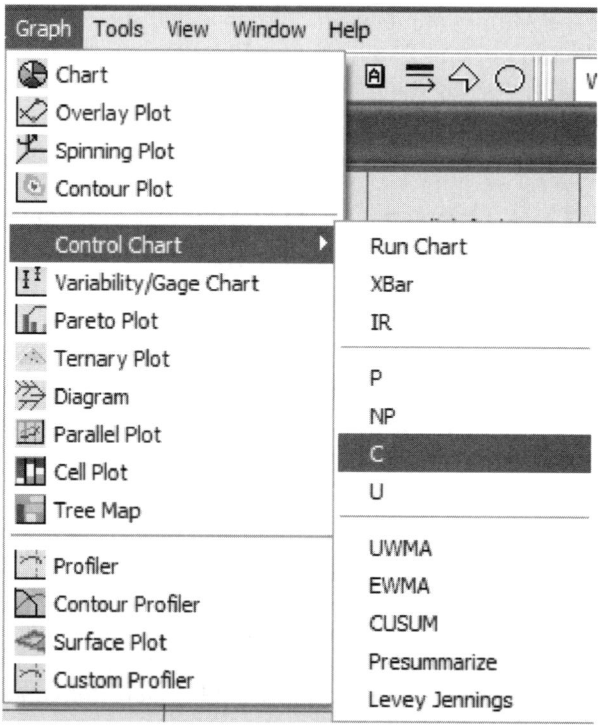

Figure 11.23 Generating a c chart.

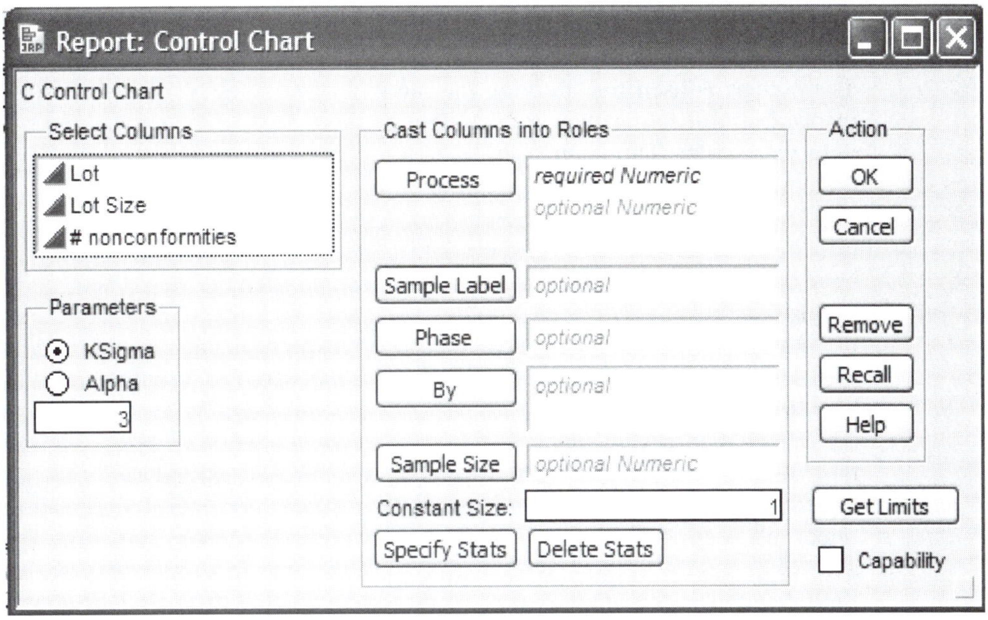

Figure 11.24 c chart dialog box.

Example 11.7 *A paper mill has detected that almost 90 percent of rejected paper rolls are due to nonconformities of two types: holes and wrinkles in the paper. The Six Sigma Green Belt team in the mill decides to set up control charts to reduce or eliminate the number of these nonconformities. To set up the control charts the team collects data by taking random sample of five rolls each day for 30 days and counting the number of nonconformities (holes and wrinkles) in each sample. The data are shown in Table 4.4 of Example 4.4 in Chapter 4. Set up a* c *control chart using these data.*

Solution:

1. Enter the data (number of nonconformities given in Table 4.4 in Chapter 4) in column 1 of the data table.
2. Select **Graph** from the drop-down menu.
3. Select the **Control Chart** function.
4. Select the **C** chart option. The dialog box **C Control Chart**, shown in Figure 11.24, appears.
5. Choose the **KSigma** option in the Parameters box, and make sure "3" is entered as the parameter.
6. Set the sample size to be consistent with the sample size entered in the data table.
7. Assign a variable to be modeled in the Process field.
8. Select **OK** in the Action box.

11.11 The *u* Chart with Constant Sample Size

The *u* chart is used for studying the number of nonconformities in a single inspection unit rather than in a sample of inspection units, as was the case with the *c* chart. The control limits in a *u* chart are based on the number of nonconformities in a single inspection unit.

To create a *u* chart we begin by entering data (the number of nonconformities per inspection unit) into column 1 of a new data table. Once the data have been entered, we generate the chart by following the steps identified in Figure 11.25.

As can be seen in Figure 11.25, we select **Graph** from the drop-down menu, then select the **Control Chart** function, and then select **U**. Once the *u* chart has been selected, a dialog box will be presented, as shown in Figure 11.26.

The dialog box in Figure 11.26 requires us to select a variable. The data table in this case contains three variables, which are identified as "Lot," "Lot Size," and "# nonconformities" in the Select Columns box, located in the upper left section of the dialog box. At this point, we would select the variable "# nonconformities" (click with the mouse) and assign it to the Process field, located in the upper center section of the dialog box, which indicates a numeric variable is required. We then select **OK** to generate the chart. We illustrate how to create a *u* chart with the following example.

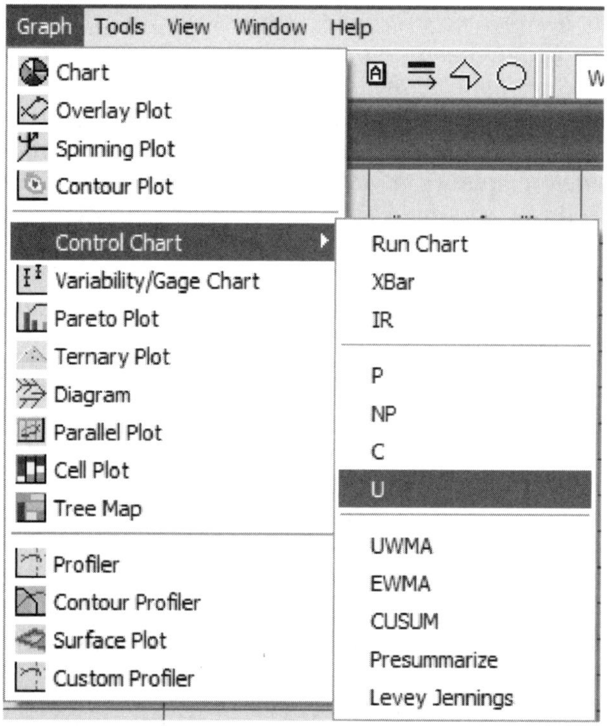

Figure 11.25 Generating a *u* chart.

Example 11.8 *A Six Sigma Green Belt team in a semiconductor industry found that the printed boards for laptops have nonconformities of several types, such as shorted trace, open trace, cold solder joint, and solder short. In order to monitor nonconformities in the printed boards for laptops, the Six Sigma Green Belt team wants to set up a* u *chart. Therefore, they collect data by selecting samples of five inspection units, where each inspection unit consists of 30 boards. The data, which are shown in Table 4.5 of Example 4.5 in Chapter 4, are collected over a period of 30 days.*

Solution:

1. Enter the data (number of nonconformities given in Table 4.5 in Chapter 4) in column 1 of the data table.
2. Select **Graph** from the drop-down menu.
3. Select the **Control Chart** function.
4. Select the **U** chart option. The dialog box **U Control Chart**, shown in Figure 11.26, appears.
5. Choose the **KSigma** option in the Parameters box, and make sure "3" is entered as the parameter.
6. Set the sample size to be consistent with the sample size entered in the data table.
7. Assign a variable to be modeled in the Process field.
8. Select **OK** in the Action box.

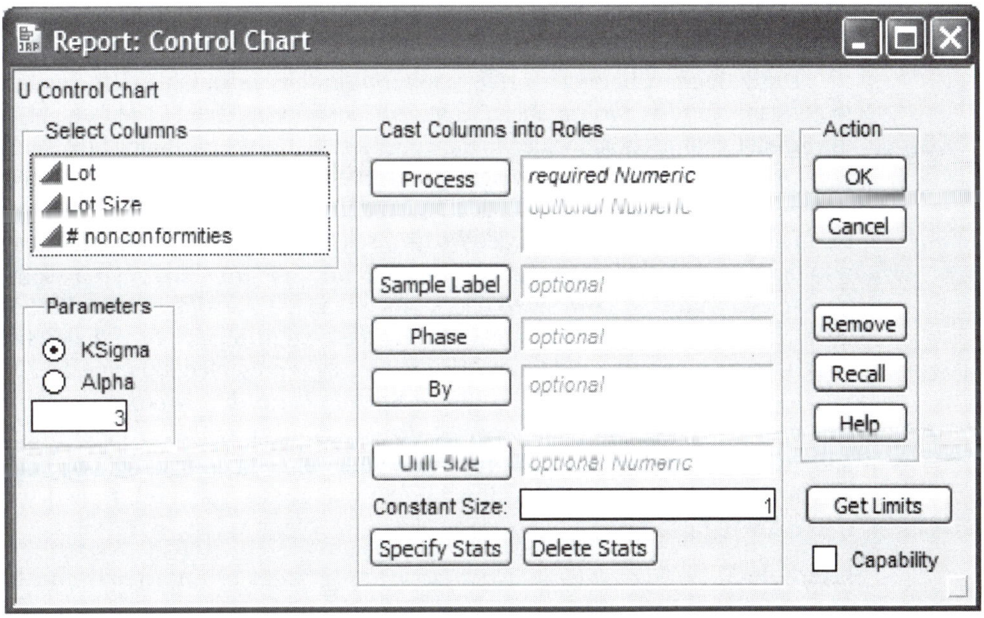

Figure 11.26 *u* chart dialog box.

11.12 The *u* Chart: Control Chart for Fraction Nonconforming Units with Sample Size Varying

To generate a *u* chart with sample size varying, we use the same procedure as for the *u* chart with constant sample size. In the case of a sample size varying, we enter the sample numbers in column 1 and the corresponding nonconformities data in column 2, and in step 7 we assign the sample numbers entered in column 1 to the sample lable field and the nonconforming data entered in column 2 to the Process field.

11.13 The CUSUM Chart

CUSUM charts are very effective in detecting small shifts. Unlike the $\bar{X}$ Shewhart control charts, CUSUM control charts can be designed to detect one-sided or two-sided shifts. These charts are defined by two parameters, k and h, which are called the *reference value* and the *decision interval*, respectively, and are defined in section 5.2.1. The two-sided process control by using a CUSUM control chart is achieved by concurrently using two one-sided CUSUM control charts. In both one-sided CUSUM charts we can use the same or different reference values depending on whether the upward and downward shifts are equally important.

To create a CUSUM chart we begin by entering sample numbers in column 1 and process data in column 2 of a new data table. Once the data have been entered, we generate the chart by following the steps identified in Figure 11.27.

As can be seen in Figure 11.27, we select **Graph** from the drop-down menu, then select the **Control Chart** function, and then select **CUSUM**. Once the CUSUM chart has been selected, a dialog box will be presented, as shown in Figure 11.28.

The dialog box in Figure 11.28 requires us to select a variable. The data table in this case contains two variables, which are identified as "hour" and "weight," in the Select Columns box, located in the upper left section of the dialog box. At this point, we select the variable "weight" (click with the mouse) and assign it to the Process field, located in the upper center section of the dialog box, which indicates that a numeric variable is required. We then select the variable "hour" and assign it to the Sample Label field. We specify a one-sided or two-sided chart by selecting or deselecting the **Two-Sided** check box on the left side of the dialog box. We could then click the **Specify Stats** button at the bottom center of the dialog box, which would generate an additional dialog box, as is presented in Figure 11.29.

As can be seen in Figure 11.29, the **Specify Stats** dialog box allows us to specify a Target, Delta (difference to detect), Shift, process variable Sigma, and a Head Start. Once the desired parameters have been inserted, we select **OK** to generate the chart. We illustrate how to create a CUSUM chart with the following example.

Example 11.9 *Consider a manufacturing process of auto parts. We are interested in studying a quality characteristic of the parts manufactured by the process. Let the quality characteristic when the process is under control be*

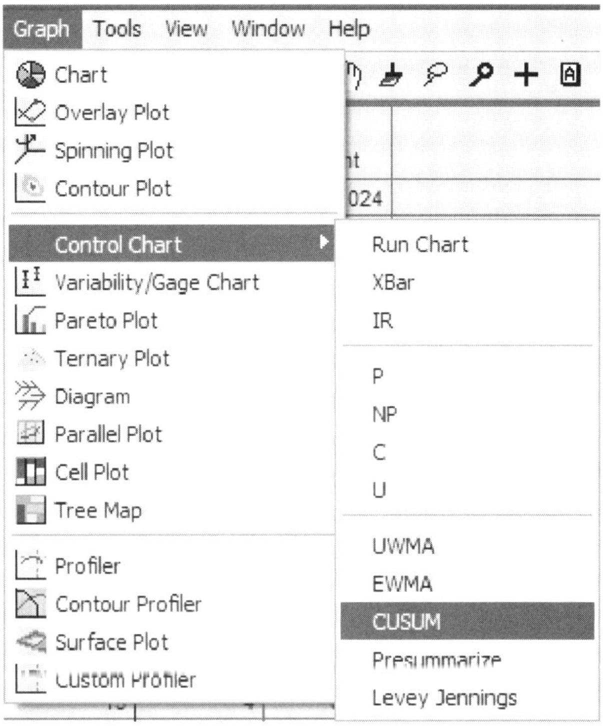

Figure 11.27 Generating a CUSUM chart.

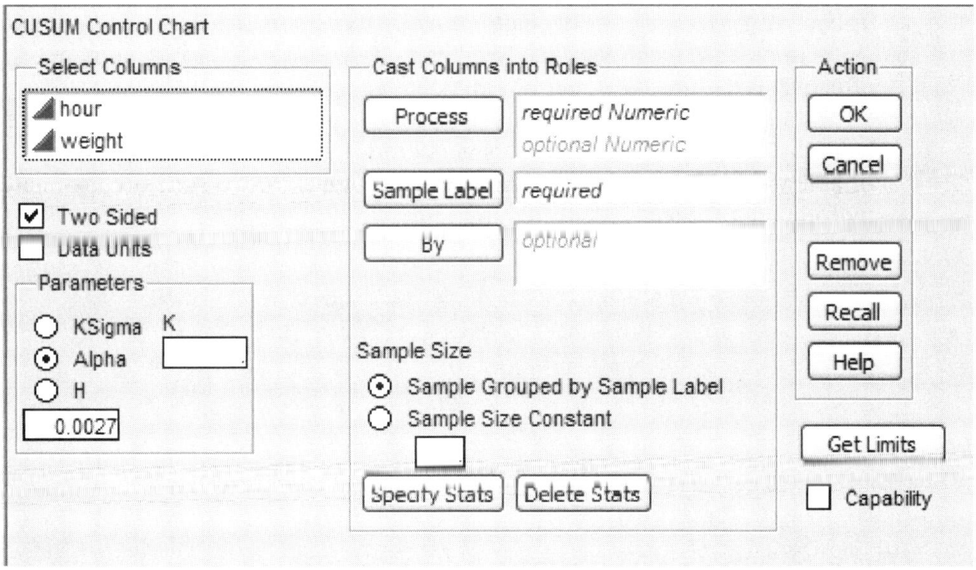

Figure 11.28 CUSUM chart dialog box.

normally distributed with mean 20 and standard deviation 2. The data shown in Table 5.1 of Example 5.1 in Chapter 5 give the first 10 random samples of size four, which are taken when the process is stable and producing the parts with mean value 20 and standard deviation 2. The last 10 random samples, again of size four, were taken from that process after its mean experienced an upward shift of one standard deviation, resulting in a new process with mean 22. Construct a Shewhart CUSUM control chart for the data in Table 5.1.

Solution:

1. Enter the sample number and data in Table 5.1 in columns 1 and 2, respectively, of the data table.
2. Select **Control Chart** from the **Graph** drop-down menu.
3. Select the **CUSUM** option. The dialog box **CUSUM Control Chart**, shown in Figure 11.28, immediately appears.
4. Select the **Two Sided** check box.
5. Click the **Specify Stats** button.
6. Enter the target value = 20, standard deviation $\sigma = 2$, and Delta = 1.
7. Select **OK** and the CUSUM control chart consistent with the data from Table 5.1 will be generated.

11.14 The Uniformly Weighted Moving Average Chart

The moving average control chart is usually more effective in detecting small shifts in process mean than the Shewhart chart. However, it is usually not as effective as the CUSUM and EWMA charts.

To create a uniformly weighted moving average (UWMA) chart, we begin by entering sample numbers in column 1 and process data in column 2 of a new data table. Once the data have been entered, we generate the chart by following the steps identified in Figure 11.30.

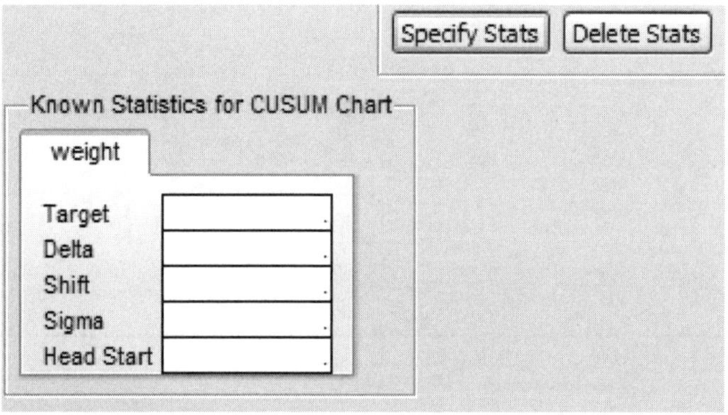

Figure 11.29 Specify Stats dialog box.

As can be seen in Figure 11.30, we select **Graph** from the drop-down menu, then select the **Control Chart** function, and then select **UWMA**. Once the UWMA chart has been selected, a dialog box will be presented, as shown in Figure 11.31.

The dialog box in Figure 11.31 requires us to select a variable. The data table in this case contains three variables, which are identified as "Sample," "Gap," and "Status" in the Select Columns box, located in the upper left section of the dialog box. At this point, we select the variable "Gap" (click with the mouse) and assign it to the Process field, located in the upper center section of the dialog box, which indicates that a numeric variable is required. We then select the variable "Sample" and assign it to the Sample Label field. Finally, we select a span for the moving average (3 in this case) and establish a constant sample size (5 in this case). We then select **OK** to generate the chart. We illustrate how to create a UWMA chart with the following example.

Example 11.10 *Consider the data in Table 5.4 of Example 5.3 in Chapter 5 on the manufacturing process of auto parts. Design a UWMA control chart for these data with span m = 4 and interpret the results.*

Solution:

1. Enter the sample number and data in Table 5.4 in columns 1 and 2, respectively, of the data table.
2. Select **Control Chart** from the **Graph** drop-down menu.
3. Select the **UWMA** option. The dialog box **UWMA Control Chart**, shown in Figure 11.31, appears.

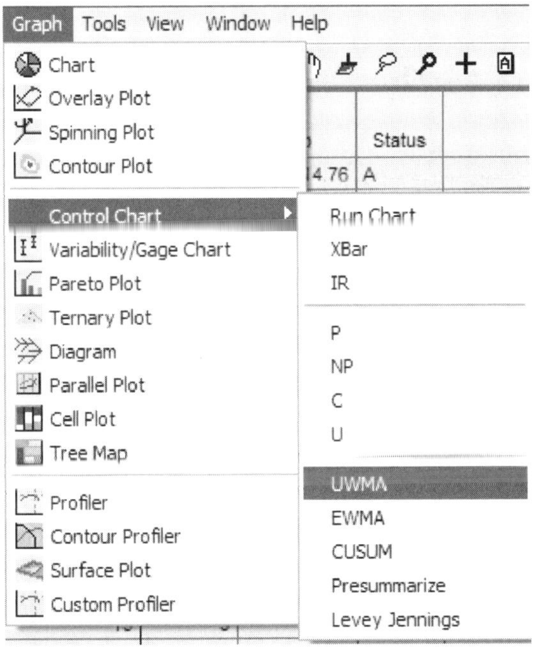

Figure 11.30 Generating a UWMA chart.

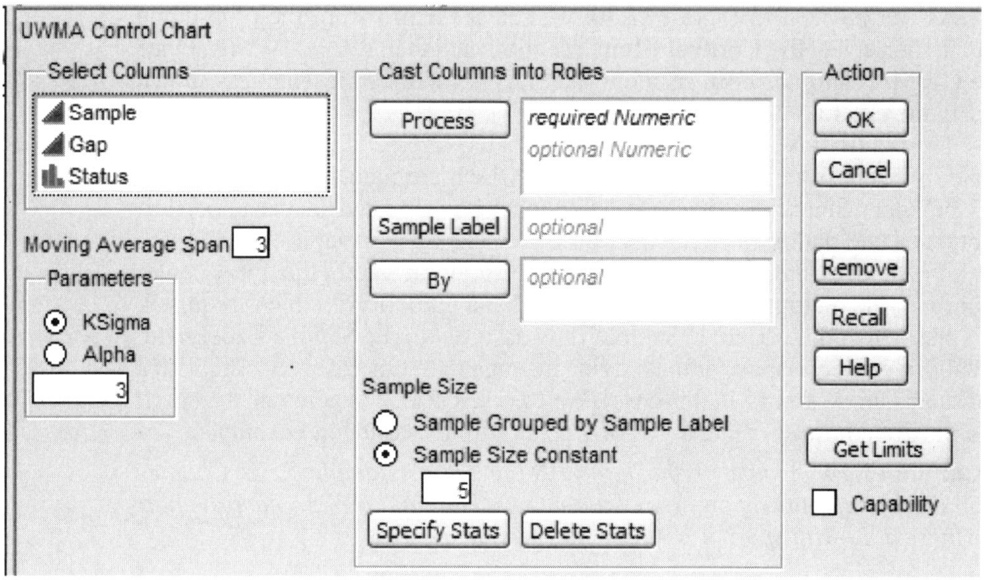

Figure 11.31 UWMA chart dialog box.

4. Enter 4, or any other specified value, in the Moving Average Span field.
5. Enter the sample size in the box below Sample Size Constant.
6. Select **OK** and the UWMA control chart consistent with the data from Table 5.4 will be generated.

11.15 The EWMA Control Chart

The EWMA control chart is very useful for processes in which only one observation per period may be available. To create an EWMA chart we begin by entering sample numbers in column 1 and process data in column 2 of a new data table. Once the data have been entered, we generate the chart by following the steps identified in Figure 11.32.

As can be seen in Figure 11.32, we select **Graph** from the drop-down menu, then select the **Control Chart** function, and then select **EWMA**. Once the EWMA chart has been selected, a dialog box will be presented, as shown in Figure 11.33.

The dialog box in Figure 11.33 requires us to select a variable. The data table in this case contains three variables, which are identified as "Sample," "Gap," and "Status" in the Select Columns box, located in the upper left section of the dialog box. At this point, we select the variable "Gap" (click with the mouse) and assign it to the Process field, located in the upper center section of the dialog box, which indicates that a numeric variable is required. We then select the variable "Sample" and assign it to the Sample Label field. Once the variables have been assigned, we specify the weighting factor in the Weight field, located on the left of the dialog box (0.2 is the default). Finally,

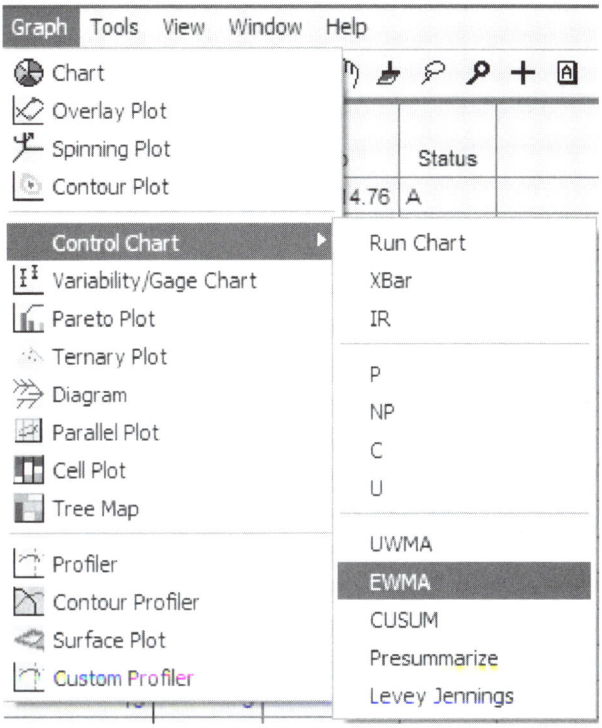

Figure 11.32 Generating an EWMA chart.

we can click **Specify Stats** if we want to specify a mean and standard deviation for the process variable. We then select **OK** to generate the chart. We illustrate how to create an EWMA chart with the following example.

Example 11.11 *Consider the data in Table 5.4 of Example 5.3 in Chapter 5 on the manufacturing process of auto parts. Design an EWMA control chart for these data with* $\lambda = 0.20$, $L = 2.962$, $\mu_0 = 20$, *and* $\sigma = 2$ *and interpret the results.*

Solution:

1. Enter the sample number and data in Table 5.4 in columns 1 and 2, respectively, of the data table.
2. Select **Control Chart** from the **Graph** drop-down menu.
3. Select the **EWMA** option. The dialog box **EWMA Control Chart**, shown in Figure 11.33, immediately appears.
4. Assign the process and sample variables.
5. Enter the desired weighting factor (0.2 in this case).
6. Click the **Specify Stats** button.
7. Assign the process mean and standard deviation.
8. Select **OK** and the EWMA control chart consistent with the data from Table 5.4 will be generated.

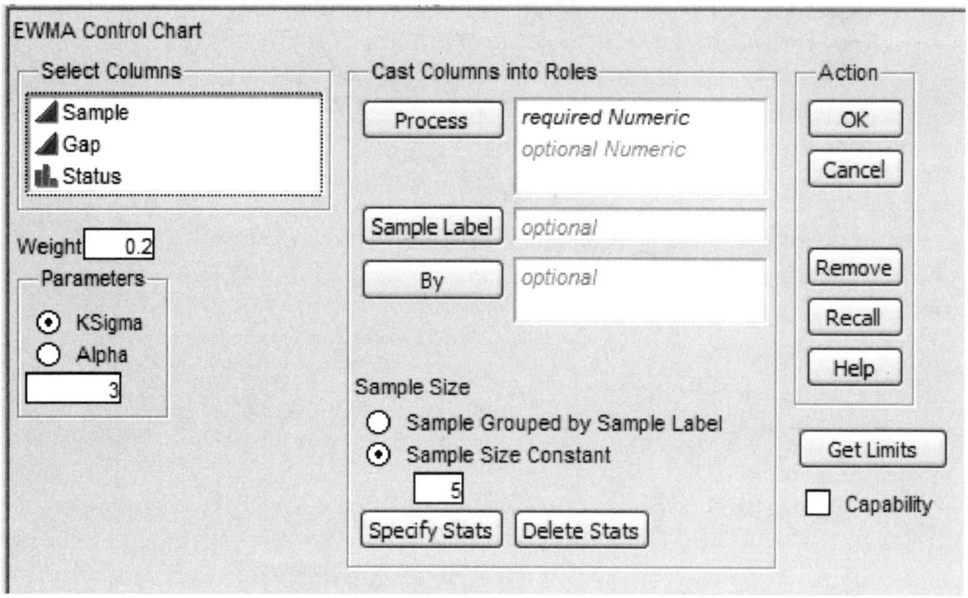

Figure 11.33 EWMA chart dialog box.

11.16 Measurement System Capability Analysis

The measurement system plays an important role in any efforts to improve a process. In any process, the total process variation consists of two sources:

- Part-to-part variation
- Measurement system variation

If the measurement system variation is large compared with part-to-part variation, the measurement system cannot adequately discriminate between parts for complete process evaluation. In other words, the measurement system is not capable. Thus, it becomes very important to perform measurement systems capability analysis.

Suppose we measure a quality characteristic of a part and let t be the total observed value of the quality characteristic, p be its true value, and e be the measurement error. Then, we have

$$t = p + e. \tag{11.1}$$

Assume now that the true value of the quality characteristic and the measurement error are normally distributed with mean μ and 0 and variances σ_p^2 and σ_m^2, respectively. Then it can easily be shown that

$$\sigma_t^2 = \sigma_p^2 + \sigma_m^2, \tag{11.2}$$

where σ_t^2 is the variance of the total observed values. Furthermore, the error variance σ_m^2 usually consists of two components: one due to gage variation (repeatability) and the other due to operator variation (reproducibility). The purpose of measurement system capability analysis is to separate these components and analyze them. In other words, we have

$$\sigma^2_{\text{measurement error}} = \sigma^2_{\text{reproducibilty}} + \sigma^2_{\text{repeatability}}.$$

To study these components, we usually use the ANOVA technique, which is also known as Gage R&R study. When using the ANOVA technique, we commonly deal with two types of situations: (1) when each operator measures the same specimens of a part, and (2) when each operator measures different specimens of a part. The designs used in these situations are known as *crossed* and *nested* designs, respectively. The following section discusses the Gage R&R study using JMP and crossed designs. We do not discuss nested designs here, as they are beyond the scope of this book.

11.16.1 Measurement System Capability Analysis (Using Crossed Designs)

A manufacturer of tubes used in automotive applications has installed a new measuring gage. The Six Sigma Green Belt team is interested in determining how well the new gage measures the inside diameter of the tube. In other words, the team is interested in performing the measurement system capability analysis. We discuss the measurement system capability analysis with the following example.

Example 11.12 *A manufacturer of bolts (parts) used in automotive applications has installed a new measuring gage. In order to perform the MSA on the new gage, the quality manager randomly selects three Six Sigma Green Belt operators from the department of quality control, who decide to take a random sample of 10 bolts. Each operator takes three measurements on each bolt, which is selected randomly. The data obtained are shown in Table 11.2.*

- *Estimate the repeatability and reproducibility of the measurement system.*
- *Estimate how much of the total process variation is due to the measurement system.*
- *If the tube diameter specifications are 70 ± 10, what can we say about the discrimination power of the measurement system? In other words, is the measurement system capable of discriminating between different parts?*

Solution: We have already discussed this example earlier, in Chapter 7. Here we discuss step by step how to set up JMP to find the solution to this or any other similar problem.

1. Following the steps discussed in section 11.1, start up JMP. The JMP Starter or the initial JMP start-up platform will appear first.

2. Enter the data in a new data table, using column 1 for the part numbers, column 2 for the operators, and column 3 for the observed values of the parts.

3. Select **Graph** from the drop-down menu, and then select the **Variability/Gage Chart** option, as shown in Figure a11.34. A Gage R&R dialog box is presented, as shown in Figure 11.35.

4. Complete the dialog box by assigning the variable "Length in MM" as the Y, Response, and assign the variables "Bolt" and "Operator" as the X, Grouping. Next, in the Model Type box located in the lower left corner of the dialog box, set the model type to "Crossed." Once complete, the dialog box should appear as shown in Figure 11.36.

5. Choose **OK** to proceed with the analysis. Variability charts for the Y, Response variable "Length in MM" are generated, as shown in Figure 11.37.

6. Having generated the variability charts, as shown in Figure 11.37, select the red drop-down arrow located in the upper left corner of the variability charts window. Select both **Variance Components** and **Gage Studies** from the drop-

Table 11.2 Data on an experiment involving three operators, 10 bolts, and three measurements (in mm) on each bolt by each operator.

Bolt (Parts) Number	Operator 1			Operator 2			Operator 3		
	Trial 1	Trial 2	Trial 3	Trial 1	Trial 2	Trial 3	Trial 1	Trial 2	Trial 3
1	26	22	26	21	23	21	24	22	26
2	28	26	28	24	29	26	24	25	24
3	28	31	28	28	27	28	32	30	27
4	35	33	31	35	31	30	34	35	31
5	37	35	38	36	38	35	35	34	35
6	40	38	40	40	38	40	36	37	38
7	39	42	41	40	39	43	43	41	43
8	42	43	46	42	46	42	43	44	45
9	50	52	50	53	52	53	49	53	49
10	28	31	28	28	27	28	32	30	27
	$\bar{R}_1 = 3.0$ $\bar{x}_1 = 35.33$			$\bar{R}_2 = 2.5$ $\bar{x}_2 = 34.67$			$\bar{R}_3 = 3.0$ $\bar{x}_3 = 34.93$		

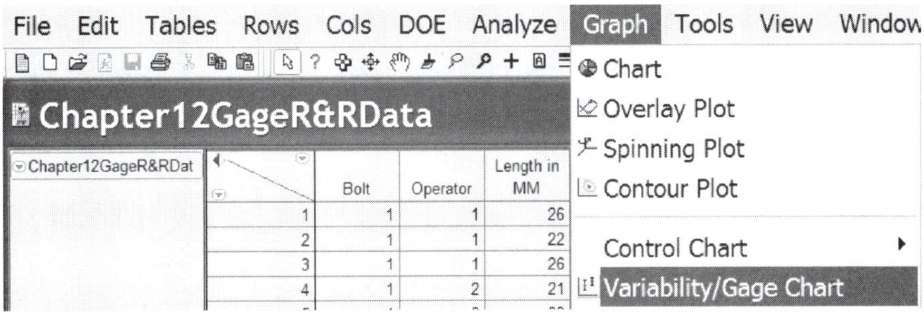

Figure 11.34 Initiating a Gage R&R.

down menu, which is shown in Figure 11.38. The variance components, shown in Figure 11.39, are generated as output. To generate the Gage R&R, a dialog box is presented, as shown in Figure 11.40.

7. Enter "6" in the K, Sigma Multiplier field (some authors use 5.15, Barrentine [2003]).

8. Enter "70 +/– 10" in the Tolerance Interval field. Then select **OK**. The output shown in Figure 11.41 will appear.

We discussed this example in Chapter 7 and again in Chapter 10. It should be noted that the treatment of Gage R&R as presented in this chapter is an introduction to the use of JMP. There are many additional features and capabilities of JMP as it pertains to MSA and Gage R&R. To learn more about the capabilities of JMP, see the online help within JMP, which provides instruction on use of the software as well as instruction on applicable statistical theory and interpretation.

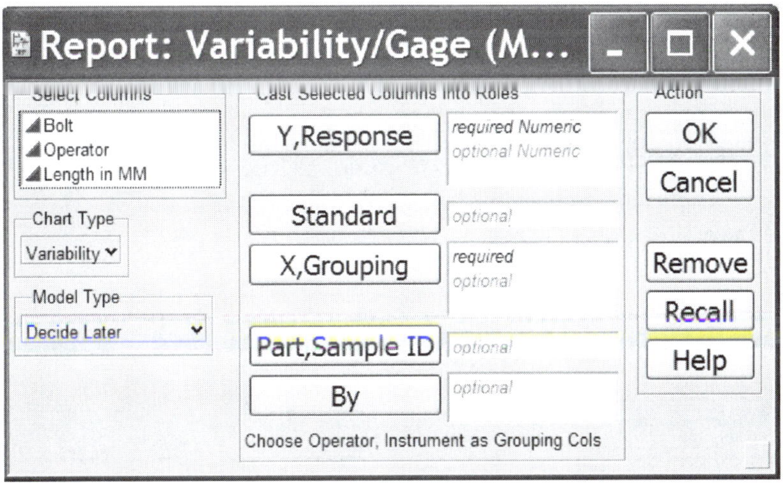

Figure 11.35 Gage R&R dialog box.

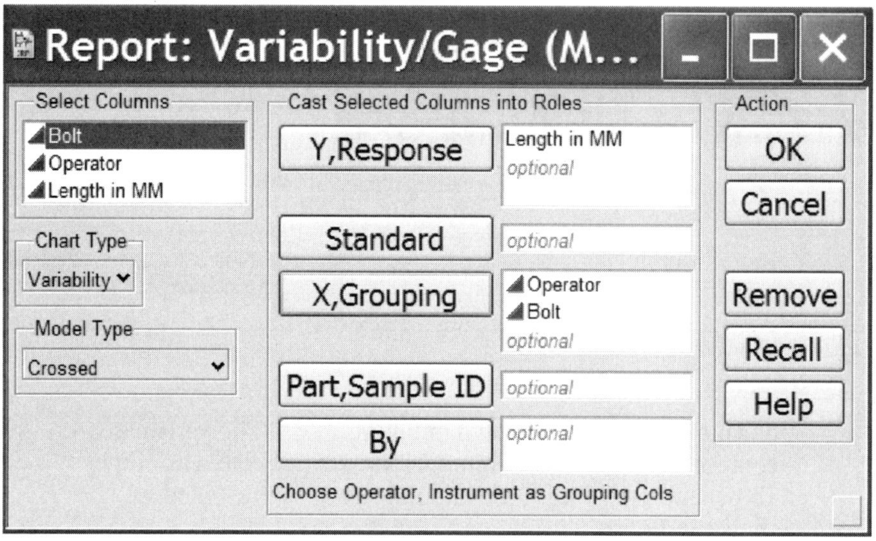

Figure 11.36 Completed Gage R&R dialog box.

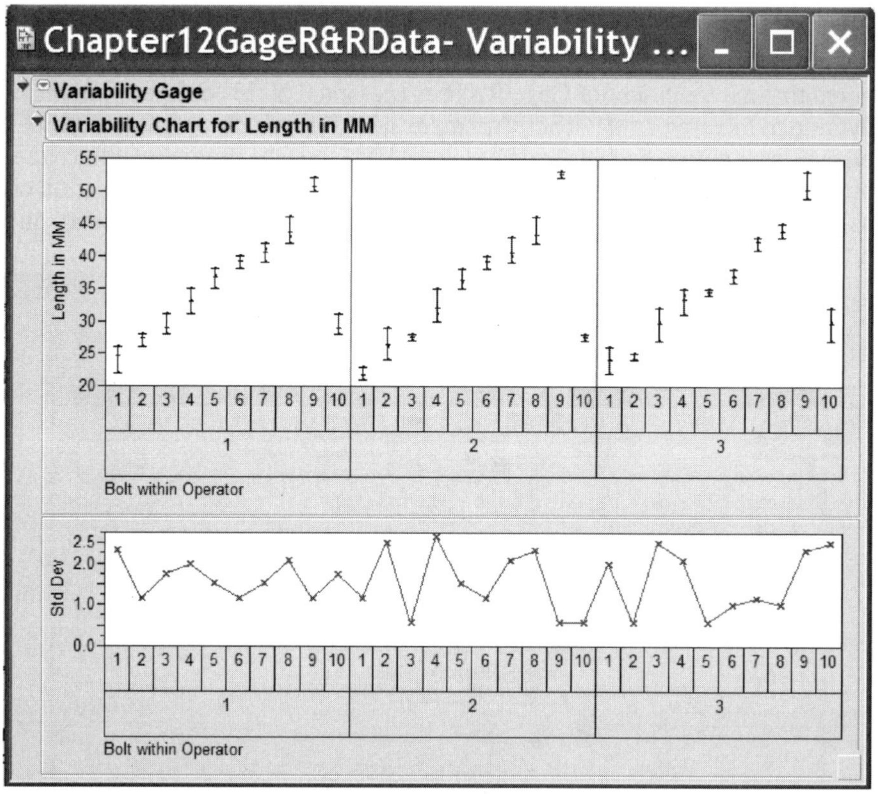

Figure 11.37 Y, Response variability charts.

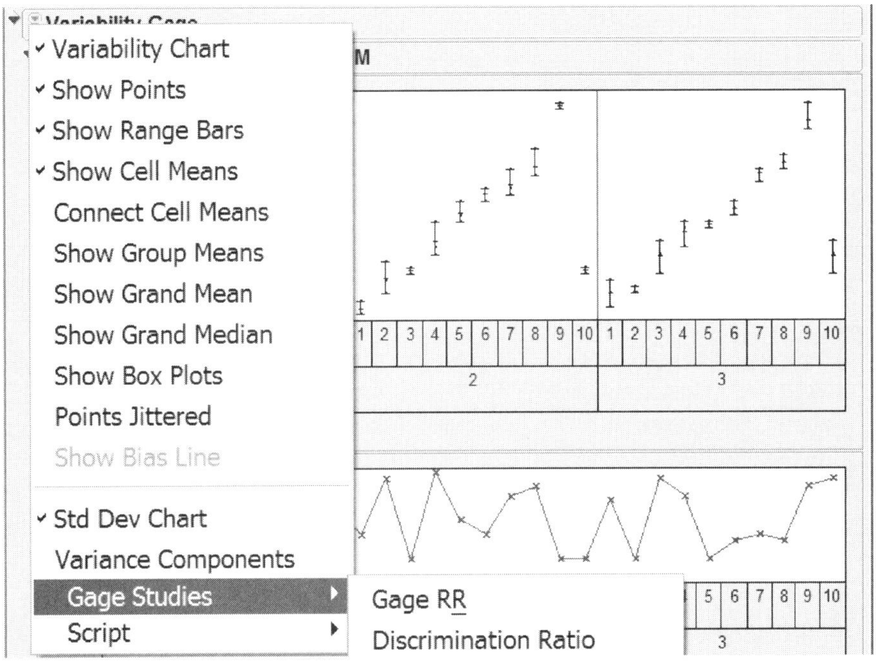

Figure 11.38 Continuing the Gage R&R.

Variance Components

Component	Var Component	% of Total Plot%	Sqrt(Var Comp)
Operator	0.000000	0.0	0.0000
Bolt	75.935665	95.9	8.7141
Operator*Bolt	0.322222	0.4069	0.5676
Within	2.922222	3.7	1.7095
Total	79.180110	100.0	8.8983

Figure 11.39 Variance components.

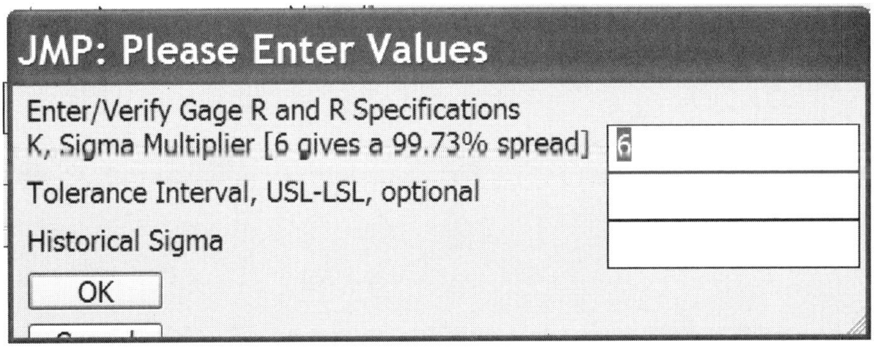

Figure 11.40 Gage R&R dialog box.

Gage R&R

Measurement		Variation		which is k*sqrt of
Repeatability	(EV)	10.256705	Equipment variation	V(Within)
Operator*Bolt	(IV)	3.405877	Interaction variation	V(Operator*Bolt)
Reproducibility	(AV)	3.405877	Appraiser variation	V(Operator) + V(Operator*Bolt)
Gage R&R	(RR)	10.807405	Measurement variation	V(Within) + V(Operator) + V(Operator*Bolt)
Part Variation	(PV)	52.284644	Part variation	V(Bolt)
Total Variation	(TV)	53.389924	Total variation	V(Within) + V(Operator) + V(Operator*Bolt) + V(Bolt)

6	K
20.2424	% Gage R&R = 100*(RR/TV)
0.2067	Precision to Part Variation = RR/PV
6	Number of Distinct Categories = 1.41(PV/RR)

Using column 'Operator' for Operator, and column 'Bolt' for Part.

Variance Components for Gage R&R

Component	Var Component	% of Total Plot%
Gage R&R	3.244444	4.10
Repeatability	2.922222	3.69
Reproducibility	0.322222	0.41
Part-to-Part	75.935665	95.90

Figure 11.41 Gage R&R output.

Appendix

Statistical Factors and Tables

Table A.1 Random numbers.

051407	989018	492019	104768	575186	245627	286990	734378	453966	057822
269053	276922	626639	672429	195157	261315	654257	422375	431234	118589
367431	749277	842766	168999	210133	816278	847625	664969	065701	024018
124630	013237	179229	435437	550763	752891	089084	292255	199266	557418
235703	291002	385271	207907	360800	276579	676139	769805	783328	436849
690077	456559	436334	395621	700837	781531	186054	821361	983046	055051
064522	297716	600883	381178	169364	100801	596694	928310	703015	277547
764938	805569	604184	977595	363240	078850	996467	690208	334904	842078
875941	644067	510442	811601	829395	040948	746376	609475	676581	258998
758163	303864	360595	406956	613170	659663	165049	285017	508337	823585
805127	590014	144389	672585	094987	111625	331838	818612	481421	401552
525959	799809	141968	625825	297508	334761	860898	960450	785312	746866
351524	456015	143766	420487	368857	730553	815900	317512	047606	283084
940666	599608	558502	853032	057656	056246	479494	975590	713502	116101
557125	106544	069601	752609	897074	240681	209045	145960	683943	437854
190980	359006	623535	763922	122217	220988	416186	312541	738818	490698
992339	518042	207523	781965	792693	594357	758633	193427	143471	502953
915848	881688	291695	447687	462282	802405	706686	055756	580658	814693
197116	180139	716829	291097	056602	424613	236547	415732	423617	644397
118122	936037	305685	509440	108748	215414	684961	684762	362416	133571
283321	359369	900968	211269	865878	952056	233151	978019	775520	968944
474018	149319	582300	362831	346320	692174	547654	948322	384851	801187
809947	466717	020564	975865	223465	112251	403475	222629	379671	270475
224102	479858	549809	622585	751051	468493	018852	493268	146506	178368

(continued)

Table A.1 Random numbers. *(continued)*

366694	104709	967459	251556	079166	652152	505645	639175	028598	404765
734814	311724	026072	962867	814804	190999	740559	023023	327014	811488
319937	808873	539157	307523	098627	909137	770359	114529	881772	145209
036430	039847	167620	072545	428240	600695	003392	565195	332140	503965
894345	168655	706409	748967	876037	365212	660673	571480	558421	426590
227929	567801	552407	365578	580152	897712	858336	400702	406915	830437
720918	315830	269847	043686	006433	277134	378624	907969	762816	959970
291797	701820	728789	699785	715058	750720	536696	611293	544362	402326
564482	758563	645279	943094	588786	125794	749337	615120	568039	899783
236422	473016	993530	507143	335475	436568	798873	027549	940155	530141
689701	926465	003731	242454	058491	385395	519231	042314	955428	238312
857239	581295	661440	496859	529204	410573	528164	003660	587030	270332
209684	798568	429214	353484	193667	287780	342053	706113	193544	818766
780527	198360	307604	179501	891015	513358	300694	204837	681840	231955
753734	619631	790026	637123	101453	454308	147441	686401	027541	945805
823316	720549	567136	213060	266102	621525	708377	251598	278505	802855
967448	479578	890643	687587	046236	580267	798545	062865	752600	335860
582204	247423	235450	566691	086168	455891	197764	140909	747406	253775
801682	781300	754834	224141	068082	893656	002893	039025	414661	882745
386489	999069	053767	557623	688263	306146	836909	609168	823938	499821
242456	974476	979505	641408	240580	428127	532147	666926	018437	291907
935535	398184	874762	563669	548471	998446	436267	489528	430501	311211
838423	749391	911628	800272	143947	918833	130208	783122	827365	308491
821829	694139	038590	889019	212883	739878	121333	242205	312241	777086
589642	722828	677276	169636	465933	525376	836387	969518	231291	330460
634530	779956	167305	517950	851658	764485	341043	689067	402153	061227

Table A.2 Factors helpful in constructing control charts for variables.

n	A	A_2	A_3	C_4	$1/C_4$	B_3	B_4	B_5	B_6	d_2	$1/d_2$	d_3	D_1	D_2	D_3	D_4
2	2.12130	1.88060	2.65870	0.79788	1.25332	0.00000	3.26657	0.00000	2.60633	1.128	0.88652	0.853	0.000	3.687	0.0000	3.26862
3	1.73205	1.02307	1.95440	0.88623	1.12838	0.00000	2.56814	0.00000	2.27597	1.693	0.59067	0.888	0.000	4.357	0.0000	2.57354
4	1.50000	0.72851	1.62810	0.92132	1.08540	0.00000	2.26603	0.00000	2.08774	2.059	0.48567	0.880	0.000	4.699	0.0000	2.28218
5	1.34164	0.57680	1.42729	0.93999	1.06384	0.00000	2.08895	0.00000	1.96360	2.326	0.42992	0.864	0.000	4.918	0.0000	2.11436
6	1.22474	0.48332	1.28713	0.95153	1.05094	0.03033	1.96967	0.02886	1.87420	2.534	0.39463	0.848	0.000	5.078	0.0000	2.00395
7	1.13389	0.41934	1.18191	0.95937	1.04235	0.11770	1.88230	0.11292	1.80582	2.704	0.36982	0.833	0.205	5.203	0.0758	1.92419
8	1.06066	0.37255	1.09910	0.96503	1.03624	0.18508	1.81492	0.17861	1.75145	2.847	0.35125	0.820	0.387	5.307	0.1359	1.86407
9	1.00000	0.33670	1.03166	0.96931	1.03166	0.23912	1.76088	0.23179	1.70683	2.970	0.33670	0.808	0.546	5.394	0.1838	1.81616
10	0.94868	0.30821	0.97535	0.97266	1.02811	0.28372	1.71628	0.27596	1.66936	3.078	0.32489	0.797	0.687	5.469	0.2232	1.77680
11	0.90453	0.28507	0.92739	0.97535	1.02527	0.32128	1.67872	0.31336	1.63734	3.173	0.31516	0.787	0.812	5.534	0.2559	1.74409
12	0.86603	0.26582	0.88591	0.97756	1.02296	0.35352	1.64648	0.34559	1.60953	3.258	0.30694	0.778	0.924	5.592	0.2836	1.71639
13	0.83205	0.24942	0.84954	0.97941	1.02102	0.38162	1.61838	0.37377	1.58505	3.336	0.29976	0.770	1.026	5.646	0.3076	1.69245
14	0.80178	0.23533	0.81734	0.98097	1.01940	0.40622	1.59378	0.39849	1.56345	3.407	0.29351	0.763	1.118	5.696	0.3282	1.67185
15	0.77460	0.22310	0.78854	0.98232	1.01800	0.42826	1.57174	0.42069	1.54395	3.472	0.28802	0.756	1.204	5.740	0.3468	1.65323
16	0.75000	0.21234	0.76260	0.98348	1.01680	0.44783	1.55217	0.44043	1.52653	3.532	0.28313	0.750	1.282	5.782	0.3630	1.63703
17	0.72761	0.20279	0.73905	0.98451	1.01573	0.46574	1.53426	0.45852	1.51050	3.588	0.27871	0.744	1.356	5.820	0.3779	1.62207
18	0.70711	0.19426	0.71758	0.98541	1.01481	0.48185	1.51815	0.47482	1.49600	3.640	0.27473	0.739	1.423	5.857	0.3909	1.60907
19	0.68825	0.18657	0.69787	0.98621	1.01398	0.49656	1.50344	0.48971	1.48271	3.689	0.27108	0.734	1.487	5.891	0.4031	1.59691
20	0.67082	0.17960	0.67970	0.98693	1.01324	0.51015	1.48985	0.50348	1.47038	3.735	0.26774	0.729	1.548	5.922	0.4145	1.58554
21	0.65465	0.17328	0.66289	0.98758	1.01258	0.52272	1.47728	0.51623	1.45893	3.778	0.26469	0.724	1.606	5.950	0.4251	1.57491
22	0.63960	0.16748	0.64726	0.98817	1.01197	0.53440	1.46560	0.52808	1.44826	3.819	0.26185	0.720	1.659	5.979	0.4344	1.56559
23	0.62554	0.16214	0.63269	0.98870	1.01143	0.54514	1.45486	0.53898	1.43842	3.858	0.25920	0.716	1.710	6.006	0.4432	1.55677
24	0.61237	0.15869	0.61906	0.98919	1.01093	0.55527	1.44473	0.54927	1.42911	3.859	0.25913	0.712	1.723	5.995	0.4465	1.55351
25	0.60000	0.15263	0.60628	0.98964	1.01047	0.56478	1.43522	0.55893	1.42035	3.931	0.25439	0.708	1.807	6.055	0.4597	1.54032

Table A.3 Values of K_1 for computing repeatability using the range method.

	Number of Trials													
n	**2**	**3**	**4**	**5**	**6**	**7**	**8**	**9**	**10**	**11**	**12**	**13**	**14**	**15**
1	3.65	2.70	2.30	2.08	1.93	1.82	1.74	1.67	1.62	1.57	1.54	1.51	1.48	1.47
2	4.02	2.85	2.40	2.15	1.98	1.86	1.77	1.71	1.65	1.60	1.56	1.52	1.49	1.47
3	4.19	2.91	2.43	2.16	2.00	1.87	1.78	1.71	1.66	1.60	1.57	1.53	1.50	1.47
4	4.26	2.94	2.44	2.17	2.00	1.88	1.79	1.72	1.66	1.61	1.57	1.53	1.50	1.48
5	4.33	2.96	2.45	2.18	2.01	1.89	1.79	1.72	1.66	1.61	1.57	1.54	1.51	1.48
6	4.36	2.98	2.46	2.19	2.01	1.89	1.79	1.72	1.66	1.61	1.57	1.54	1.51	1.48
7	4.40	2.98	2.46	2.19	2.02	1.89	1.79	1.72	1.66	1.61	1.57	1.54	1.51	1.48
8	4.44	2.99	2.48	2.19	2.02	1.89	1.79	1.73	1.67	1.61	1.57	1.54	1.51	1.48
9	4.44	2.99	2.48	2.20	2.02	1.89	1.80	1.73	1.67	1.62	1.57	1.54	1.51	1.48
10	4.44	2.99	2.48	2.20	2.02	1.89	1.80	1.73	1.67	1.62	1.57	1.54	1.51	1.48
11	4.44	3.01	2.48	2.20	2.02	1.89	1.80	1.73	1.67	1.62	1.57	1.54	1.51	1.48
12	4.48	3.01	2.49	2.20	2.02	1.89	1.81	1.73	1.67	1.62	1.57	1.54	1.51	1.48
13	4.48	3.01	2.49	2.20	2.02	1.90	1.81	1.73	1.67	1.62	1.57	1.54	1.51	1.48
14	4.48	3.01	2.49	2.20	2.03	1.90	1.81	1.73	1.67	1.62	1.57	1.54	1.51	1.48
15	4.48	3.01	2.49	2.20	2.03	1.90	1.81	1.73	1.67	1.62	1.58	1.54	1.51	1.48
$n \geq 16$	4.56	3.05	2.50	2.21	2.04	1.91	1.81	1.73	1.67	1.62	1.58	1.54	1.51	1.48

n = (# of parts (samples)) × (# of operators)

Table A.4 Values of K_2 for computing reproducibility using the range method.

Number of Operators												
3	4	5	6	7	8	9	10	11	12	13	14	15
2.70	2.30	2.08	1.93	1.82	1.74	1.67	1.62	1.57	1.54	1.51	1.48	1.47

Table A.5 Binomial probabilities.

Tabulated values are $P(X=x)=\binom{n}{x}p^x(1-p)^{n-x}$.

		p										
n	*x*	.05	.10	.20	.30	.40	.50	.60	.70	.80	.90	.95
1	0	.950	.900	.800	.700	.600	.500	.400	.300	.200	.100	.050
	1	.050	.100	.200	.300	.400	.500	.600	.700	.800	.900	.950
2	0	.902	.810	.640	.490	.360	.250	.160	.090	.040	.010	.003
	1	.095	.180	.320	.420	.480	.500	.480	.420	.320	.180	.095
	2	.003	.010	.040	.090	.160	.250	.360	.490	.640	.810	.902
3	0	.857	.729	.512	.343	.216	.125	.064	.027	.008	.001	.000
	1	.136	.243	.384	.441	.432	.375	.288	.189	.096	.027	.007
	2	.007	.027	.096	.189	.288	.375	.432	.441	.384	.243	.135
	3	.000	.001	.008	.027	.064	.125	.216	.343	.512	.729	.857
4	0	.815	.656	.410	.240	.130	.062	.025	.008	.002	.000	.000
	1	.171	.292	.410	.412	.346	.250	.154	.076	.026	.004	.001
	2	.014	.048	.154	.265	.345	.375	.346	.264	.154	.048	.014
	3	.000	.004	.025	.075	.154	.250	.346	.412	.409	.292	.171
	4	.000	.000	.001	.008	.025	.063	.129	.240	.409	.656	.815
5	0	.774	.591	.328	.168	.078	.031	.010	.002	.000	.000	.000
	1	.204	.328	.410	.360	.259	.156	.077	.028	.006	.001	.000
	2	.021	.073	.205	.309	.346	.312	.230	.132	.051	.008	.001
	3	.001	.008	.051	.132	.230	.312	.346	.308	.205	.073	.021
	4	.000	.000	.006	.028	.077	.156	.259	.360	.410	.328	.204
	5	.000	.000	.000	.003	.010	.031	.078	.168	.328	.590	.774
6	0	.735	.531	.262	.118	.047	.016	.004	.001	.000	.000	.000
	1	.232	.354	.393	.302	.187	.094	.037	.010	.002	.000	.000
	2	.031	.098	.246	.324	.311	.234	.138	.059	.015	.001	.000
	3	.002	.015	.082	.185	.276	.313	.277	.185	.082	.015	.002
	4	.000	.001	.015	.059	.138	.234	.311	.324	.246	.098	.031
	5	.000	.000	.002	.010	.037	.094	.186	.302	.393	.354	.232
	6	.000	.000	.000	.001	.004	.015	.047	.118	.262	.531	.735

(continued)

Table A.5 Binomial probabilities. *(continued)*

Tabulated values are $P(X = x) = \binom{n}{x} p^x (1-p)^{n-x}$.

		p										
n	*x*	.05	.10	.20	.30	.40	.50	.60	.70	.80	.90	.95
7	0	.698	.478	.210	.082	.028	.008	.002	.000	.000	.000	.000
	1	.257	.372	.367	.247	.131	.055	.017	.004	.000	.000	.000
	2	.041	.124	.275	.318	.261	.164	.077	.025	.004	.000	.000
	3	.004	.023	.115	.227	.290	.273	.194	.097	.029	.003	.000
	4	.000	.003	.029	.097	.194	.273	.290	.227	.115	.023	.004
	5	.000	.000	.004	.025	.077	.164	.261	.318	.275	.124	.041
	6	.000	.000	.000	.004	.017	.055	.131	.247	.367	.372	.257
	7	.000	.000	.000	.000	.002	.008	.028	.082	.210	.478	.698
8	0	.663	.430	.168	.058	.017	.004	.001	.000	.000	.000	.000
	1	.279	.383	.335	.198	.089	.031	.008	.001	.000	.000	.000
	2	.052	.149	.294	.296	.209	.109	.041	.010	.001	.000	.000
	3	.005	.033	.147	.254	.279	.219	.124	.048	.009	.000	.000
	4	.000	.005	.046	.136	.232	.273	.232	.136	.046	.005	.000
	5	.000	.000	.009	.047	.124	.219	.279	.254	.147	.033	.005
	6	.000	.000	.001	.010	.041	.110	.209	.296	.294	.149	.052
	7	.000	.000	.000	.001	.008	.031	.089	.198	.335	.383	.279
	8	.000	.000	.000	.000	.001	.004	.017	.057	.168	.430	.664
9	0	.630	.387	.134	.040	.010	.002	.000	.000	.000	.000	.000
	1	.298	.387	.302	.156	.061	.018	.004	.000	.000	.000	.000
	2	.063	.172	.302	.267	.161	.070	.021	.004	.000	.000	.000
	3	.008	.045	.176	.267	.251	.164	.074	.021	.003	.000	.000
	4	.001	.007	.066	.172	.251	.246	.167	.073	.017	.001	.000
	5	.000	.001	.017	.073	.167	.246	.251	.172	.066	.007	.001
	6	.000	.000	.003	.021	.074	.164	.251	.267	.176	.045	.008
	7	.000	.000	.000	.004	.021	.070	.161	.267	.302	.172	.063
	8	.000	.000	.000	.000	.004	.018	.060	.156	.302	.387	.298
	9	.000	.000	.000	.000	.000	.002	.010	.040	.134	.387	.630
10	0	.599	.349	.107	.028	.006	.001	.000	.000	.000	.000	.000
	1	.315	.387	.268	.121	.040	.010	.002	.000	.000	.000	.000
	2	.075	.194	.302	.234	.121	.044	.011	.001	.000	.000	.000
	3	.010	.057	.201	.267	.215	.117	.042	.009	.001	.000	.000
	4	.001	.011	.088	.200	.251	.205	.111	.037	.006	.000	.000

(continued)

Table A.5 Binomial probabilities. *(continued)*

Tabulated values are $P(X=x)=\binom{n}{x}p^x(1-p)^{n-x}$.

		p										
n	*x*	.05	.10	.20	.30	.40	.50	.60	.70	.80	.90	.95
	5	.000	.002	.026	.103	.201	.246	.201	.103	.026	.002	.000
	6	.000	.000	.006	.037	.111	.205	.251	.200	.088	.011	.001
	7	.000	.000	.001	.009	.042	.117	.215	.267	.201	.057	.011
	8	.000	.000	.000	.001	.011	.044	.121	.234	.302	.194	.075
	9	.000	.000	.000	.000	.002	.010	.040	.121	.268	.387	.315
	10	.000	.000	.000	.000	.000	.001	.006	.028	.107	.349	.599
11	0	.569	.314	.086	.020	.004	.001	.000	.000	.000	.000	.000
	1	.329	.384	.236	.093	.027	.005	.001	.000	.000	.000	.000
	2	.087	.213	.295	.200	.089	.027	.005	.001	.000	.000	.000
	3	.014	.071	.222	.257	.177	.081	.023	.004	.000	.000	.000
	4	.001	.016	.111	.220	.237	.161	.070	.017	.002	.000	.000
	5	.000	.003	.039	.132	.221	.226	.147	.057	.010	.000	.000
	6	.000	.000	.010	.057	.147	.226	.221	.132	.039	.003	.000
	7	.000	.000	.002	.017	.070	.161	.237	.220	.111	.016	.001
	8	.000	.000	.000	.004	.023	.081	.177	.257	.222	.071	.014
	9	.000	.000	.000	.001	.005	.027	.089	.200	.295	.213	.087
	10	.000	.000	.000	.000	.001	.005	.027	.093	.236	.384	.329
	11	.000	.000	.000	.000	.000	.001	.004	.020	.086	.314	.569
12	0	.540	.282	.069	.014	.002	.000	.000	.000	.000	.000	.000
	1	.341	.377	.206	.071	.017	.003	.000	.000	.000	.000	.000
	2	.099	.230	.283	.168	.064	.016	.003	.000	.000	.000	.000
	3	:017	.085	.236	.240	.142	.054	.012	.002	.000	.000	.000
	4	.002	.021	.133	.231	.213	.121	.042	.008	.001	.000	.000
	5	.000	.004	.053	.159	.227	.193	.101	.030	.003	.000	.000
	6	.000	.001	.016	.079	.177	.226	.177	.079	.016	.001	.000
	7	.000	.000	.003	.029	.101	.193	.227	.159	.053	.004	.000
	8	.000	.000	.001	.008	.042	.121	.213	.231	.133	.021	.002
	9	.000	.000	.000	.001	.013	.054	.142	.240	.236	.085	.017
	10	.000	.000	.000	.000	.003	.016	.064	.168	.283	.230	.099
	11	.000	.000	.000	.000	.000	.003	.017	.071	.206	.377	.341
	12	.000	.000	.000	.000	.000	.000	.002	.014	.069	.282	.540

(continued)

Table A.5 Binomial probabilities. *(continued)*

Tabulated values are $P(X = x) = \binom{n}{x} p^x (1-p)^{n-x}$.

		p										
n	***x***	**.05**	**.10**	**.20**	**.30**	**.40**	**.50**	**.60**	**.70**	**.80**	**.90**	**.95**
13	0	.513	.254	.055	.010	.001	.000	.000	.000	.000	.000	.000
	1	.351	.367	.179	.054	.011	.002	.000	.000	.000	.000	.000
	2	.111	.245	.268	.139	.045	.010	.001	.000	.000	.000	.000
	3	.021	.010	.246	.218	.111	.035	.007	.001	.000	.000	.000
	4	.003	.028	.154	.234	.185	.087	.024	.003	.000	.000	.000
	5	.000	.006	.069	.180	.221	.157	.066	.014	.001	.000	.000
	6	.000	.001	.023	.103	.197	.210	.131	.044	.006	.000	.000
	7	.000	.000	.006	.044	.131	.210	.197	.103	.023	.001	.000
	8	.000	.000	.001	.014	.066	.157	.221	.180	.069	.006	.000
	9	.000	.000	.000	.003	.024	.087	.184	.234	.154	.028	.003
	10	.000	.000	.000	.001	.007	.035	.111	.218	.246	.100	.021
	11	.000	.000	.000	.000	.001	.010	.045	.139	.268	.245	.111
	12	.000	.000	.000	.000	.000	.000	.011	.054	.179	.367	.351
	13	.000	.000	.000	.000	.000	.000	.001	.0100	.055	.254	.513
14	0	.488	.229	.044	.007	.001	.000	.000	.000	.000	.000	.000
	1	.359	.356	.154	.041	.007	.001	.000	.000	.000	.000	.000
	2	.123	.257	.250	.113	.032	.006	.001	.000	.000	.000	.000
	3	.026	.114	.250	.194	.085	.022	.003	.000	.000	.000	.000
	4	.004	.035	.172	.229	.155	.061	.014	.001	.000	.000	.000
	5	.000	.008	.086	.196	.207	.122	.041	.007	.000	.000	.000
	6	.000	.001	.032	.126	.207	.183	.092	.023	.002	.000	.000
	7	.000	.000	.009	.062	.157	.210	.157	.062	.010	.000	.000
	8	.000	.000	.002	.023	.092	.183	.207	.126	.032	.001	.000
	9	.000	.000	.0003	.0066	.0408	.1222	.2066	.1963	.0860	.0078	.000
	10	.000	.000	.000	.001	.014	.061	.155	.229	.172	.035	.004
	11	.000	.000	.000	.000	.003	.022	.085	.194	.250	.114	.026
	12	.000	.000	.000	.000	.001	.006	.032	.113	.250	.257	.123
	13	.000	.000	.000	.000	.000	.001	.007	.041	.154	.356	.359
	14	.000	.000	.000	.000	.000	.000	.001	.007	.044	.229	.488

(continued)

Table A.5 Binomial probabilities. *(continued)*

Tabulated values are $P(X = x) = \binom{n}{x} p^x (1-p)^{n-x}$.

		p										
n	**x**	**.05**	**.10**	**.20**	**.30**	**.40**	**.50**	**.60**	**.70**	**.80**	**.90**	**.95**
15	0	.463	.206	.035	.005	.001	.000	.000	.000	.000	.000	.000
	1	.366	.343	.132	.031	.005	.001	.000	.000	.000	.000	.000
	2	.135	.267	.231	.092	.022	.003	.000	.000	.000	.000	.000
	3	.031	.129	.250	.170	.063	.014	.002	.000	.000	.000	.000
	4	.005	.043	.188	.219	.127	.042	.007	.001	.000	.000	.000
	5	.001	.011	.103	.206	.186	.092	.025	.003	.000	.000	.000
	6	.000	.002	.043	.147	.207	.153	.061	.012	.001	.000	.000
	7	.000	.000	.014	.081	.177	.196	.118	.035	.004	.000	.000
	8	.000	.000	.004	.035	.118	.196	.177	.081	.014	.000	.000
	9	.000	.000	.001	.012	.061	.153	.207	.147	.043	.002	.000
	10	.000	.000	.000	.003	.025	.092	.186	.206	.103	.011	.001
	11	.000	.000	.000	.001	.007	.042	.127	.219	.188	.043	.005
	12	.000	.000	.000	.000	.002	.014	.063	.170	.250	.129	.031
	13	.000	.000	.000	.000	.000	.003	.022	.092	.231	.267	.135
	14	.000	.000	.000	.000	.000	.001	.005	.031	.132	.343	.366
	15	.000	.000	.000	.000	.000	.000	.001	.005	.035	.206	.463

Table A.6 Poisson probabilities.

Tabulated values are $P(X = x) = \frac{e^{-\lambda}\lambda^{x}}{x!}$.

	λ									
x	**0.1**	**0.2**	**0.3**	**0.4**	**0.5**	**0.6**	**0.7**	**0.8**	**0.9**	**1.0**
0	.905	.819	.741	.670	.607	.549	.497	.449	.407	.368
1	.091	.164	.222	.268	.303	.329	.348	.360	.366	.368
2	.005	.016	.033	.054	.076	.099	.122	.144	.165	.184
3	.000	.001	.003	.007	.013	.020	.028	.038	.049	.061
4	.000	.000	.000	.000	.002	.003	.005	.008	.011	.015
5	.000	.000	.000	.000	.000	.000	.001	.001	.002	.003
6	.000	.000	.000	.000	.000	.000	.000	.000	.000	.001
7	.000	.000	.000	.000	.000	.000	.000	.000	.000	.000

	λ									
x	**1.1**	**1.2**	**1.3**	**1.4**	**1.5**	**1.6**	**1.7**	**1.8**	**1.9**	**2.0**
0	.333	.301	.273	.247	.223	.202	.183	.165	.150	.135
1	.366	.361	.354	.345	.335	.323	.311	.298	.284	.271
2	.201	.217	.230	.242	.251	.258	.264	.268	.270	.271
3	.074	.087	.100	.113	.126	.138	.150	.161	.171	.180
4	.020	.026	.032	.040	.047	.055	.064	.072	.081	.090
5	.005	.006	.008	.011	.014	.018	.022	.026	.031	.036
6	.001	.001	.002	.003	.004	.005	.006	.008	.010	.012
7	.000	.000	.000	.001	.001	.001	.002	.002	.003	.003
8	.000	.000	.000	.000	.000	.000	.000	.001	.001	.001
9	.000	.000	.000	.000	.000	.000	.000	.000	.000	.000

	λ									
x	**2.1**	**2.2**	**2.3**	**2.4**	**2.5**	**2.6**	**2.7**	**2.8**	**2.9**	**3.0**
0	.123	.111	.100	.091	.082	.074	.067	.061	.055	.050
1	.257	.244	.231	.218	.205	.193	.182	.170	.160	.149
2	.270	.268	.265	.261	.257	.251	.245	.238	.231	.224
3	.189	.197	.203	.209	.214	.218	.221	.223	.224	.224
4	.099	.108	.117	.125	.134	.141	.149	.156	.162	.168
5	.042	.048	.054	.060	.067	.074	.080	.087	.094	.101
6	.015	.017	.021	.024	.028	.032	.036	.041	.046	.050
7	.004	.006	.007	.008	.010	.012	.014	.016	.019	.022
8	.001	.002	.002	.003	.003	.004	.005	.006	.007	.008

(continued)

Table A.6 Poisson probabilities. *(continued)*

Tabulated values are $P(X = x) = \frac{e^{-\lambda}\lambda^x}{x!}$.

	λ									
x	**2.1**	**2.2**	**2.3**	**2.4**	**2.5**	**2.6**	**2.7**	**2.8**	**2.9**	**3.0**
9	.000	.000	.001	.001	.001	.001	.001	.002	.002	.003
10	.000	.000	.000	.000	.000	.000	.000	.001	.001	.001
11	.000	.000	.000	.000	.000	.000	.000	.000	.000	.000
12	.000	.000	.000	.000	.000	.000	.000	.000	.000	.000

	λ									
x	**3.1**	**3.2**	**3.3**	**3.4**	**3.5**	**3.6**	**3.7**	**3.8**	**3.9**	**4.0**
0	.045	.041	.037	.033	.030	.027	.025	.022	.020	.018
1	.140	.130	.122	.114	.106	.098	.092	.085	.079	.073
2	.217	.209	.201	.193	.185	.177	.169	.162	.154	.147
3	.224	.223	.221	.219	.213	.209	.205	.200	.195	.195
4	.173	.178	.182	.186	.191	.193	.194	.195	.195	.195
5	.107	.114	.120	.132	.138	.143	.148	.152	.156	.156
6	.056	.061	.066	.077	.083	.088	.094	.099	.104	.104
7	.025	.028	.031	.039	.043	.047	.051	.055	.060	.060
8	.010	.011	.013	.017	.019	.022	.024	.027	.030	.030
9	.003	.004	.005	.007	.008	.009	.010	.012	.013	.013
10	.001	.001	.002	.002	.002	.003	.003	.004	.005	.005
11	.000	.000	.001	.001	.001	.001	.001	.001	.002	.002
12	.000	.000	.000	.000	.000	.000	.000	.000	.001	.001
13	.000	.000	.0000	.000	.000	.000	.000	.000	.000	.000
14	.000	.000	.000	.000	.000	.000	.000	.000	.000	.000

	λ									
x	**4.1**	**4.2**	**4.3**	**4.4**	**4.5**	**4.6**	**4.7**	**4.8**	**4.9**	**5.0**
0	.017	.015	.014	.012	.011	.010	.009	.008	.007	.007
1	.068	.063	.058	.054	.050	.046	.043	.040	.037	.034
2	.139	.132	.125	.119	.113	.106	.101	.095	.089	.084
3	.190	.185	.180	.174	.169	.163	.157	.152	.146	.140
4	.195	.194	.193	.192	.190	.188	.185	.182	.179	.176
5	.160	.163	.166	.169	.171	.173	.174	.175	.175	.176
6	.109	.114	.119	.124	.128	.132	.136	.140	.143	.146
7	.064	.069	.073	.078	.082	.087	.091	.096	.100	.104

(continued)

Table A.6 Poisson probabilities. *(continued)*

Tabulated values are $P(X = x) = \frac{e^{-\lambda}\lambda^{x}}{x!}$.

	λ									
x	**4.1**	**4.2**	**4.3**	**4.4**	**4.5**	**4.6**	**4.7**	**4.8**	**4.9**	**5.0**
8	.033	.036	.039	.043	.046	.050	.054	.058	.061	.065
9	.015	.017	.019	.021	.023	.026	.028	.031	.033	.036
10	.006	.007	.008	.009	.010	.012	.013	.015	.016	.018
11	.002	.003	.003	.004	.004	.005	.006	.006	.007	.008
12	.009	.001	.001	.001	.002	.002	.002	.003	.003	.003
13	.000	.000	.000	.001	.001	.001	.001	.001	.001	.001
14	.000	.000	.000	.000	.000	.000	.000	.000	.000	.000
15	.000	.000	.000	.000	.000	.000	.000	.000	.000	.000

	λ									
x	**5.1**	**5.2**	**5.3**	**5.4**	**5.5**	**5.6**	**5.7**	**5.8**	**5.9**	**6.0**
0	.006	.006	.005	.005	.004	.004	.003	.003	.003	.002
1	.031	.029	.027	.024	.022	.021	.019	.018	.016	.015
2	.079	.075	.070	.066	.062	.058	.054	.051	.048	.045
3	.135	.129	.124	.119	.113	.108	.103	.099	.094	.089
4	.172	.168	.164	.160	.156	.152	.147	.143	.138	.134
5	.175	.175	.174	.173	.171	.170	.168	.166	.163	.161
6	.149	.151	.154	.156	.157	.158	.159	.160	.161	.161
7	.109	.113	.116	.120	.123	.127	.130	.133	.135	.138
8	.069	.073	.077	.081	.085	.089	.093	.096	.100	.103
9	.039	.042	.045	.049	.052	.055	.059	.062	.065	.069
10	.020	.022	.024	.026	.029	.031	[illegible]	[illegible]	[illegible]	.041
11	.009	.010	.012	.013	.014	.016	.017	.019	.021	.023
12	.004	.005	.005	.006	.007	.007	.008	.009	.010	.011
13	.002	.002	.002	.002	.003	.003	.004	.004	.005	.005
14	.001	.001	.001	.001	.001	.001	.002	.002	.002	.002
15	.000	.000	.000	.000	.000	.000	.001	.001	.001	.001
16	.000	.000	.000	.000	.000	.000	.000	.000	.000	.000
17	.000	.000	.000	.000	.000	.000	.000	.000	.000	.000

(continued)

Table A.6 Poisson probabilities. *(continued)*

Tabulated values are $P(X = x) = \frac{e^{-\lambda}\lambda^x}{x!}$.

	λ									
x	**6.1**	**6.2**	**6.3**	**6.4**	**6.5**	**6.6**	**6.7**	**6.8**	**6.9**	**7.0**
0	.002	.002	.002	.002	.002	.001	.001	.001	.001	.001
1	.014	.013	.012	.011	.010	.010	.008	.008	.007	.007
2	.042	.040	.036	.034	.032	.029	.028	.026	.024	.022
3	.085	.081	.077	.073	.069	.065	.062	.058	.055	.052
4	.129	.125	.121	.116	.112	.108	.103	.099	.095	.091
5	.158	.155	.152	.149	.145	.142	.139	.135	.131	.128
6	.160	.160	.159	.159	.158	.156	.155	.153	.151	.149
7	.140	.142	.144	.145	.146	.147	.148	.149	.149	.149
8	.107	.110	.113	.116	.119	.122	.124	.126	.128	.130
9	.072	.076	.079	.083	.086	.089	.092	.095	.098	.101
10	.044	.047	.050	.053	.056	.059	.062	.065	.068	.071
11	.024	.026	.029	.031	.033	.035	.038	.040	.043	.045
12	.012	.014	.015	.016	.018	.019	.021	.023	.025	.026
13	.006	.007	.007	.008	.009	.010	.011	.012	.013	.014
14	.003	.003	.003	.004	.004	.005	.005	.006	.006	.007
15	.001	.001	.001	.002	.002	.002	.002	.003	.003	.003
16	.000	.001	.001	.001	.001	.001	.001	.001	.001	.001
17	.000	.000	.000	.000	.000	.000	.000	.000	.001	.001
18	.000	.000	.000	.000	.000	.000	.000	.000	.000	.000
19	.000	.000	.000	.000	.000	.000	.000	.000	.000	.000

Table A.7 Standard normal distribution.

Tabulated values are $P(0 \leq Z \leq z)$ = shaded area under the standard normal curve.

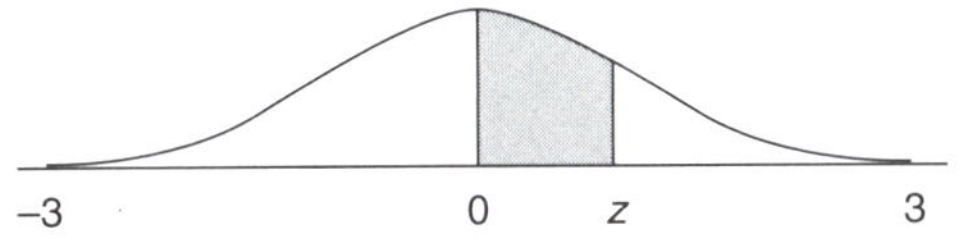

z	.00	.01	.02	.03	.04	.05	.06	.07	.08	.09
0.0	.0000	.0040	.0080	.0120	.0160	.0199	.0239	.0279	.0319	.0359
0.1	.0398	.0438	.0478	.0517	.0557	.0596	.0636	.0675	.0714	.0753
0.2	.0793	.0832	.0871	.0910	.0948	.0987	.1026	.1064	.1103	.1141
0.3	.1179	.1217	.1255	.1293	.1331	.1368	.1406	.1443	.1480	.1517
0.4	.1554	.1591	.1628	.1664	.1700	.1736	.1772	.1808	.1844	.1879
0.5	.1915	.1950	.1985	.2019	.2054	.2088	.2123	.2157	.2190	.2224
0.6	.2257	.2291	.2324	.2357	.2389	.2422	.2454	.2486	.2517	.2549
0.7	.2580	.2611	.2642	.2673	.2704	.2734	.2764	.2794	.2823	.2852
0.8	.2881	.2910	.2939	.2967	.2995	.3023	.3051	.3078	.3106	.3133
0.9	.3159	.3186	.3212	.3238	.3264	.3289	.3315	.3340	.3365	.3389
1.0	.3413	.3438	.3461	.3485	.3508	.3531	.3554	.3577	.3599	.3621
1.1	.3643	.3665	.3686	.3708	.3729	.3749	.3770	.3790	.3810	.3830
1.2	.3849	.3869	.3888	.3907	.3925	.3944	.3962	.3980	.3997	.4015
1.3	.4032	.4049	.4066	.4082	.4099	.4115	.4131	.4147	.4162	.4177
1.4	.4192	.4207	.4222	.4236	.4251	.4265	.4279	.4292	.4306	.4319
1.5	.4332	.4345	.4357	.4370	.4382	.4394	.4406	.4418	.4429	.4441
1.6	.4452	.4463	.4474	.4484	.4495	.4505	.4515	.4525	.4535	.4545
1.7	.4554	.4564	.4573	.4582	.4591	.4599	.4608	.4616	.4625	.4633
1.8	.4641	.4649	.4656	.4664	.4671	.4678	.4686	.4693	.4699	.4706
1.9	.4713	.4719	.4726	.4732	.4738	.4744	.4750	.4756	.4761	.4767
2.0	.4772	.4778	.4783	.4788	.4793	.4798	.4803	.4808	.4812	.4817
2.1	.4821	.4826	.4830	.4834	.4838	.4842	.4846	.4850	.4854	.4857
2.2	.4861	.4864	.4868	.4871	.4875	.4878	.4881	.4884	.4887	.4890
2.3	.4893	.4896	.4898	.4901	.4904	.4906	.4909	.4911	.4913	.4916
2.4	.4918	.4920	.4922	.4925	.4927	.4929	.4931	.4932	.4934	.4936
2.5	.4938	.4940	.4941	.4943	.4945	.4946	.4948	.4949	.4951	.4952
2.6	.4953	.4955	.4956	.4957	.4959	.4960	.4961	.4962	.4963	.4964
2.7	.4965	.4966	.4967	.4968	.4969	.4970	.4971	.4972	.4973	.4974
2.8	.4974	.4975	.4976	.4977	.4977	.4978	.4979	.4979	.4980	.4981
2.9	.4981	.4982	.4982	.4983	.4984	.4984	.4985	.4985	.4986	.4986
3.0	.4987	.4987	.4987	.4988	.4988	.4989	.4989	.4989	.4990	.4990

For negative values of *z*, the probabilities are found by using the symmetric property.

Table A.8 Critical values of χ^2 with ν degrees of freedom.

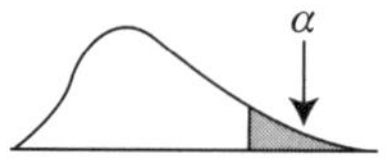

χ^2_{α}

ν	$\chi^2_{0.995}$	$\chi^2_{0.990}$	$\chi^2_{0.975}$	$\chi^2_{0.950}$	$\chi^2_{0.900}$
1	0.00004	0.00016	0.00098	0.00393	0.01589
2	0.0100	0.0201	0.0506	0.1026	0.2107
3	0.0717	0.1148	0.2158	0.3518	0.5844
4	0.2070	0.2971	0.4844	0.7107	1.0636
5	0.4117	0.5543	0.8312	1.1455	1.6103
6	0.6757	0.8720	1.2373	1.6354	2.2041
7	0.9893	1.2390	1.6899	2.1674	2.8331
8	1.3444	1.6465	2.1797	2.7326	3.4895
9	1.7349	2.0879	2.7004	3.3251	4.1682
10	2.1559	2.5582	3.2470	3.9403	4.8652
11	2.6032	3.0535	3.8158	4.5748	5.5778
12	3.0738	3.5706	4.4038	5.2260	6.3038
13	3.5650	4.1069	5.0087	5.8919	7.0415
14	4.0747	4.6604	5.6287	6.5706	7.7895
15	4.6009	5.2294	6.2621	7.2609	8.5468
16	5.1422	5.8122	6.9077	7.9616	9.3122
17	5.6972	6.4078	7.5642	8.6718	10.085
18	6.2648	7.0149	8.2308	9.3905	10.865
19	6.8440	7.6327	8.9066	10.1170	11.6509
20	7.4339	8.2604	9.5908	10.8508	12.4426
21	8.0337	8.8972	10.2829	11.5913	13.2396
22	8.6427	9.5425	10.9823	12.3380	14.0415
23	9.2604	10.1957	11.6885	13.0905	14.8479
24	9.8862	10.8564	12.4011	13.8484	15.6587
25	10.5197	11.5240	13.1197	14.6114	16.4734
26	11.1603	12.1981	13.8439	15.3791	17.2919
27	11.8076	12.8786	14.5733	16.1513	18.1138
28	12.4613	13.5648	15.3079	16.9279	18.9392
29	13.1211	14.2565	16.0471	17.7083	19.7677
30	13.7867	14.9535	16.7908	18.4926	20.5992
40	20.7065	22.1643	24.4331	26.5093	29.0505
50	27.9907	29.7067	32.3574	34.7642	37.6886
60	35.5346	37.4848	40.4817	43.1879	46.4589
70	43.2752	45.4418	48.7576	51.7393	55.3290
80	51.1720	53.5400	57.1532	60.3915	64.2778
90	59.1963	61.7541	65.6466	69.1260	73.2912
100	67.3276	70.0648	74.2219	77.9295	82.3581

(continued)

Table A.8 Critical values of χ^2 with ν degrees of freedom. *(continued)*

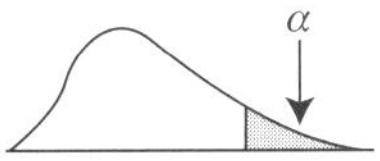

χ^2_α

ν	$\chi^2_{0.100}$	$\chi^2_{0.050}$	$\chi^2_{0.025}$	$\chi^2_{0.010}$	$\chi^2_{0.005}$
1	2.7055	3.8415	5.0239	6.6349	7.8794
2	4.6052	5.9915	7.3778	9.2103	10.5966
3	6.2514	7.8147	9.3484	11.3449	12.8381
4	7.7794	9.4877	11.1433	13.2767	14.8602
5	9.2364	11.0705	12.8325	15.0863	16.7496
6	10.6446	12.5916	14.4494	16.8119	18.5476
7	12.0170	14.0671	16.0128	18.4753	20.2777
8	13.3616	15.5073	17.5346	20.0902	21.9550
9	14.6837	16.9190	19.0228	21.6660	23.5893
10	15.9871	18.3070	20.4831	23.2093	25.1882
11	17.2750	19.6751	21.9200	24.7250	26.7569
12	18.5494	21.0261	23.3367	26.2170	28.2995
13	19.8119	22.3621	24.7356	27.6883	29.8194
14	21.0642	23.6848	26.1190	29.1413	31.3193
15	22.3072	24.9958	27.4884	30.5779	32.8013
16	23.5418	26.2962	28.8454	31.9999	34.2672
17	24.7690	27.5871	30.1910	33.4087	35.7185
18	25.9894	28.8693	31.5264	34.8053	37.1564
19	27.2036	30.1435	32.8523	36.1908	38.5822
20	28.4120	31.4104	34.1696	37.5662	39.9968
21	29.6151	32.6705	35.4789	38.9321	41.4010
22	30.8133	33.9244	36.7807	40.2894	42.7956
23	32.0069	35.1725	38.0757	41.6384	44.1813
24	[illegible]	[illegible]	[illegible]	[illegible]	[illegible]
25	34.3816	37.6525	40.6465	44.3141	46.9278
26	35.5631	38.8852	41.9232	45.6417	48.2899
27	36.7412	40.1133	43.1944	46.9630	49.6449
28	37.9159	41.3372	44.4607	48.2782	50.9933
29	39.0875	42.5569	45.7222	49.5879	52.3356
30	40.2560	43.7729	46.9792	50.8922	53.6720
40	51.8050	55.7585	59.3417	63.6907	66.7659
50	63.1671	67.5048	71.4202	76.1539	79.4900
60	74.3970	79.0819	83.2976	88.3794	91.9517
70	85.5271	90.5312	95.0231	100.4251	104.2148
80	96.5782	101.8795	106.6285	112.3288	116.3210
90	107.5650	113.1452	118.1360	124.1162	128.2290
100	118.4980	124.3421	129.5613	135.8070	140.1697

Table A.9 Critical values of t with ν degrees of freedom.

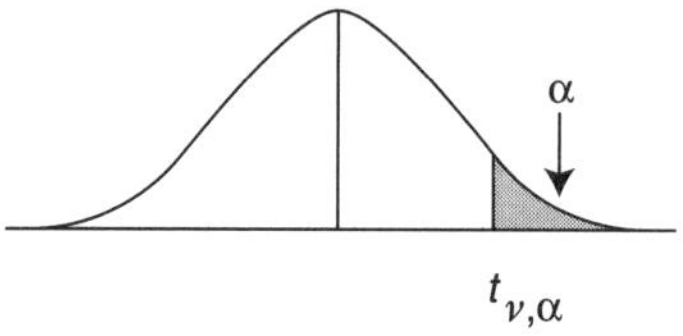

ν	$t_{.100}$	$t_{.050}$	$t_{.025}$	$t_{.010}$	$t_{.005}$	$t_{.0005}$
1	3.078	6.314	12.706	31.821	63.657	636.619
2	1.886	2.920	4.303	6.965	9.925	31.599
3	1.638	2.353	3.182	4.541	5.841	12.924
4	1.533	2.132	2.776	3.747	4.604	8.610
5	1.476	2.015	2.571	3.365	4.032	6.869
6	1.440	1.943	2.447	3.143	3.707	5.959
7	1.415	1.895	2.365	2.998	3.499	5.408
8	1.397	1.860	2.306	2.896	3.355	5.041
9	1.383	1.833	2.262	2.821	3.250	4.781
10	1.372	1.812	2.228	2.764	3.169	4.587
11	1.363	1.796	2.201	2.718	3.106	4.437
12	1.356	1.782	2.179	2.681	3.055	4.318
13	1.350	1.771	2.160	2.650	3.012	4.221
14	1.345	1.761	2.145	2.624	2.977	4.140
15	1.341	1.753	2.131	2.602	2.947	4.073
16	1.337	1.746	2.120	2.583	2.921	4.015
17	1.333	1.740	2.110	2.567	2.898	3.965
18	1.330	1.734	2.101	2.552	2.878	3.922
19	1.328	1.729	2.093	2.539	2.861	3.883
20	1.325	1.725	2.086	2.528	2.845	3.850
21	1.323	1.721	2.080	2.518	2.831	3.819
22	1.321	1.717	2.074	2.508	2.819	3.792
23	1.319	1.714	2.069	2.500	2.807	3.768
24	1.318	1.711	2.064	2.492	2.797	3.745
25	1.316	1.708	2.060	2.485	2.787	3.725
26	1.315	1.706	2.056	2.479	2.779	3.707
27	1.314	1.703	2.052	2.473	2.771	3.690
28	1.313	1.701	2.048	2.467	2.763	3.674
29	1.311	1.699	2.045	2.462	2.756	3.659
30	1.310	1.697	2.042	2.457	2.750	3.646
40	1.303	1.684	2.021	2.423	2.704	3.551

(continued)

Table A.9 Critical values of t with ν degrees of freedom. *(continued)*

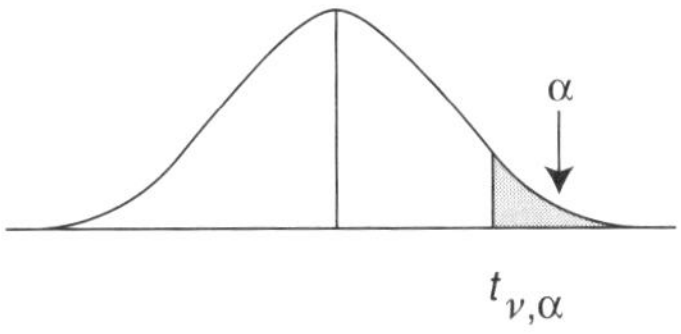

ν	$t_{.100}$	$t_{.050}$	$t_{.025}$	$t_{.010}$	$t_{.005}$	$t_{.0005}$
60	1.296	1.671	2.000	2.390	2.660	3.460
80	1.292	1.664	1.990	2.374	2.639	3.416
100	1.290	1.660	1.984	2.364	2.626	3.390
120	1.289	1.658	1.980	2.358	2.617	3.373
∞	1.282	1.645	1.960	2.326	2.576	3.291

Critical points of t for lower tail areas are found by using the symmetric property.

Table A.10 Critical values of F with numerator and denominator degrees of freedom ν_1,ν_2, respectively ($\alpha = 0.10$).

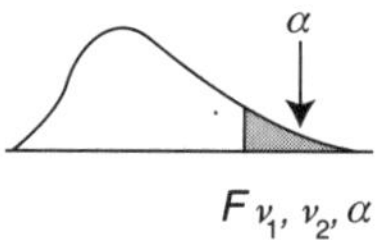

ν_2 \ ν_1	1	2	3	4	5	6	7	8	9	10
1	39.86	49.50	53.59	55.83	57.24	58.20	58.91	59.44	59.86	60.19
2	8.53	9.00	9.16	9.24	9.29	9.33	9.35	9.37	9.38	9.39
3	5.54	5.46	5.39	5.34	5.31	5.28	5.27	5.25	5.24	5.23
4	4.54	4.32	4.19	4.11	4.05	4.01	3.98	3.95	3.94	3.92
5	4.06	3.78	3.62	3.52	3.45	3.40	3.37	3.34	3.32	3.30
6	3.78	3.46	3.29	3.18	3.11	3.05	3.01	2.98	2.96	2.94
7	3.59	3.26	3.07	2.96	2.88	2.83	2.78	2.75	2.72	2.70
8	3.46	3.11	2.92	2.81	2.73	2.67	2.62	2.59	2.56	2.54
9	3.36	3.01	2.81	2.69	2.61	2.55	2.51	2.47	2.44	2.42
10	3.29	2.92	2.73	2.61	2.52	2.46	2.41	2.38	2.35	2.32
11	3.23	2.86	2.66	2.54	2.45	2.39	2.34	2.30	2.27	2.25
12	3.18	2.81	2.61	2.48	2.39	2.33	2.28	2.24	2.21	2.19
13	3.14	2.76	2.56	2.43	2.35	2.28	2.23	2.20	2.16	2.14
14	3.10	2.73	2.52	2.39	2.31	2.24	2.19	2.15	2.12	2.10
15	3.07	2.70	2.49	2.36	2.27	2.21	2.16	2.12	2.09	2.06
16	3.05	2.67	2.46	2.33	2.24	2.18	2.13	2.09	2.06	2.03
17	3.03	2.64	2.44	2.31	2.22	2.15	2.10	2.06	2.03	2.00
18	3.01	2.62	2.42	2.29	2.20	2.13	2.08	2.04	2.00	1.98
19	2.99	2.61	2.40	2.27	2.18	2.11	2.06	2.02	1.98	1.96
20	2.97	2.59	2.38	2.25	2.16	2.09	2.04	2.00	1.96	1.94
25	2.92	2.53	2.32	2.18	2.09	2.02	1.97	1.93	1.89	1.87
30	2.88	2.49	2.28	2.14	2.05	1.98	1.93	1.88	1.85	1.82
35	2.85	2.46	2.25	2.11	2.02	1.95	1.90	1.85	1.82	1.79
40	2.84	2.44	2.23	2.09	2.00	1.93	1.87	1.83	1.79	1.76
45	2.82	2.42	2.21	2.07	1.98	1.91	1.85	1.81	1.77	1.74
50	2.81	2.41	2.20	2.06	1.97	1.90	1.84	1.80	1.76	1.73
60	2.79	2.39	2.18	2.04	1.95	1.87	1.82	1.77	1.74	1.71
70	2.78	2.38	2.16	2.03	1.93	1.86	1.80	1.76	1.72	1.69
80	2.77	2.37	2.15	2.02	1.92	1.85	1.79	1.75	1.71	1.68
90	2.76	2.36	2.15	2.01	1.91	1.84	1.78	1.74	1.70	1.67
100	2.76	2.36	2.14	2.00	1.91	1.83	1.78	1.73	1.69	1.66
∞	2.71	2.30	2.08	1.94	1.85	1.77	1.72	1.67	1.63	1.60

To find the critical value of F when α is under the lower tail denoted by $F_{\nu_1,\nu_2,1-\alpha}$, we use the following formula:

$F_{\nu_1,\nu_2,1-\alpha} = 1/F_{\nu_2,\nu_1,\alpha}$. Example: $F_{\nu_1,\nu_2,1-.10} = 1/F_{\nu_2,\nu_1,.10}$.

(continued)

Table A.10 Critical values of *F* with numerator and denominator degrees of freedom ν_1, ν_2, respectively ($\alpha = 0.10$). *(continued)*

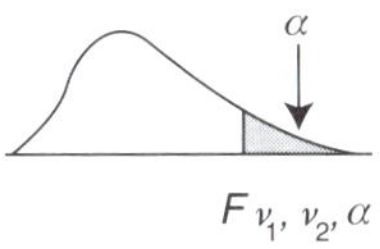

ν_2 \ ν_1	11	12	13	14	15	20	25	30	40	50	75	100	∞
1	60.47	60.71	60.90	61.07	61.22	61.74	62.05	62.26	62.53	62.69	62.90	63.01	63.33
2	9.40	9.41	9.41	9.42	9.42	9.44	9.45	9.46	9.47	9.47	9.48	9.48	9.49
3	5.22	5.22	5.21	5.20	5.20	5.18	5.17	5.17	5.16	5.15	5.15	5.14	5.13
4	3.91	3.90	3.89	3.88	3.87	3.84	3.83	3.82	3.80	3.80	3.78	3.78	3.76
5	3.28	3.27	3.26	3.25	3.24	3.21	3.19	3.17	3.16	3.15	3.13	3.13	3.11
6	2.92	2.90	2.89	2.88	2.87	2.84	2.81	2.80	2.78	2.77	2.75	2.75	2.72
7	2.68	2.67	2.65	2.64	2.63	2.59	2.57	2.56	2.54	2.52	2.51	2.50	2.47
8	2.52	2.50	2.49	2.48	2.46	2.42	2.40	2.38	2.36	2.35	2.33	2.32	2.30
9	2.40	2.38	2.36	2.35	2.34	2.30	2.27	2.25	2.23	2.22	2.20	2.19	2.16
10	2.30	2.28	2.27	2.26	2.24	2.20	2.17	2.16	2.13	2.12	2.10	2.09	2.06
11	2.23	2.21	2.19	2.18	2.17	2.12	2.10	2.08	2.05	2.04	2.02	2.01	1.97
12	2.17	2.15	2.13	2.12	2.10	2.06	2.03	2.01	1.99	1.97	1.95	1.94	1.90
13	2.12	2.10	2.08	2.07	2.05	2.01	1.98	1.96	1.93	1.92	1.89	1.88	1.85
14	2.07	2.05	2.04	2.02	2.01	1.96	1.93	1.91	1.89	1.87	1.85	1.83	1.80
15	2.04	2.02	2.00	1.99	1.97	1.92	1.89	1.87	1.85	1.83	1.80	1.79	1.76
16	2.01	1.99	1.97	1.95	1.94	1.89	1.86	1.84	1.81	1.79	1.77	1.76	1.72
17	1.98	1.96	1.94	1.93	1.91	1.86	1.83	1.81	1.78	1.76	1.74	1.73	1.69
18	1.95	1.93	1.92	1.90	1.89	1.84	1.80	1.78	1.75	1.74	1.71	1.70	1.66
19	1.93	1.91	1.89	1.88	1.86	1.81	1.78	1.76	1.73	1.71	1.69	1.67	1.63
20	1.91	1.89	1.87	1.86	1.84	1.79	1.76	1.74	1.71	1.69	1.66	1.65	1.61
25	1.84	1.82	1.80	1.79	1.77	1.72	1.68	1.66	1.63	1.61	1.58	1.56	1.52
30	1.79	1.77	1.75	1.74	1.72	1.67	1.63	1.61	1.57	1.55	1.52	1.51	1.46
35	1.76	1.74	1.72	1.70	1.69	1.63	1.60	1.57	1.53	1.51	1.48	1.47	1.41
40	1.74	1.71	1.70	1.68	1.66	1.61	1.57	1.54	1.51	1.48	1.45	1.43	1.38
45	1.72	1.70	1.68	1.66	1.64	1.58	1.55	1.52	1.48	1.46	1.43	1.41	1.35
50	1.70	1.68	1.66	1.64	1.63	1.57	1.53	1.50	1.46	1.44	1.41	1.39	1.33
60	1.68	1.66	1.64	1.62	1.60	1.54	1.50	1.48	1.44	1.41	1.38	1.36	1.29
70	1.66	1.64	1.62	1.60	1.59	1.53	1.49	1.46	1.42	1.39	1.36	1.34	1.27
80	1.65	1.63	1.61	1.59	1.57	1.51	1.47	1.44	1.40	1.38	1.34	1.32	1.24
90	1.64	1.62	1.60	1.58	1.56	1.50	1.46	1.43	1.39	1.36	1.33	1.30	1.23
100	1.64	1.61	1.59	1.57	1.56	1.49	1.45	1.42	1.38	1.35	1.32	1.29	1.21
∞	1.57	1.55	1.52	1.50	1.49	1.42	1.38	1.34	1.30	1.26	1.21	1.18	1.00

(continued)

Table A.10 Critical values of *F* with numerator and denominator degrees of freedom ν_1, ν_2, respectively (α = 0.10). *(continued)*

(α = 0.05)

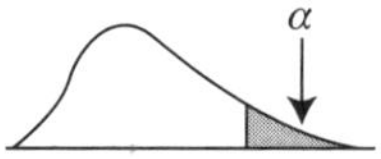

$F_{\nu_1, \nu_2, \alpha}$

ν_2 \ ν_1	1	2	3	4	5	6	7	8	9	10
1	161.45	199.50	215.71	224.58	230.16	233.99	236.77	238.88	240.54	241.88
2	18.51	19.00	19.16	19.25	19.30	19.33	19.35	19.37	19.38	19.40
3	10.13	9.55	9.28	9.12	9.01	8.94	8.89	8.85	8.81	8.79
4	7.71	6.94	6.59	6.39	6.26	6.16	6.09	6.04	6.00	5.96
5	6.61	5.79	5.41	5.19	5.05	4.95	4.88	4.82	4.77	4.74
6	5.99	5.14	4.76	4.53	4.39	4.28	4.21	4.15	4.10	4.06
7	5.59	4.74	4.35	4.12	3.97	3.87	3.79	3.73	3.68	3.64
8	5.32	4.46	4.07	3.84	3.69	3.58	3.50	3.44	3.39	3.35
9	5.12	4.26	3.86	3.63	3.48	3.37	3.29	3.23	3.18	3.14
10	4.97	4.10	3.71	3.48	3.33	3.22	3.14	3.07	3.02	2.98
11	4.84	3.98	3.59	3.36	3.20	3.09	3.01	2.95	2.90	2.85
12	4.75	3.89	3.49	3.26	3.11	3.00	2.91	2.85	2.80	2.75
13	4.67	3.81	3.41	3.18	3.03	2.92	2.83	2.77	2.71	2.67
14	4.60	3.74	3.34	3.11	2.96	2.85	2.76	2.70	2.65	2.60
15	4.54	3.68	3.29	3.06	2.90	2.79	2.71	2.64	2.59	2.54
16	4.49	3.63	3.24	3.01	2.85	2.74	2.66	2.59	2.54	2.49
17	4.45	3.59	3.20	2.96	2.81	2.70	2.61	2.55	2.49	2.45
18	4.41	3.55	3.16	2.93	2.77	2.66	2.58	2.51	2.46	2.41
19	4.38	3.52	3.13	2.90	2.74	2.63	2.54	2.48	2.42	2.38
20	4.35	3.49	3.10	2.87	2.71	2.60	2.51	2.45	2.39	2.35
25	4.24	3.39	2.99	2.76	2.60	2.49	2.40	2.34	2.28	2.24
30	4.17	3.32	2.92	2.69	2.53	2.42	2.33	2.27	2.21	2.16
35	4.12	3.27	2.87	2.64	2.49	2.37	2.29	2.22	2.16	2.11
40	4.09	3.23	2.84	2.61	2.45	2.34	2.25	2.18	2.12	2.08
45	4.06	3.20	2.81	2.58	2.42	2.31	2.22	2.15	2.10	2.05
50	4.03	3.18	2.79	2.56	2.40	2.29	2.20	2.13	2.07	2.03
60	4.00	3.15	2.76	2.53	2.37	2.25	2.17	2.10	2.04	1.99
70	3.98	3.13	2.74	2.50	2.35	2.23	2.14	2.07	2.02	1.97
80	3.96	3.11	2.72	2.49	2.33	2.21	2.13	2.06	2.00	1.95
90	3.95	3.10	2.71	2.47	2.32	2.20	2.11	2.04	1.99	1.94
100	3.94	3.09	2.70	2.46	2.31	2.19	2.10	2.03	1.97	1.93
∞	3.84	3.00	2.60	2.37	2.21	2.10	2.01	1.94	1.88	1.83

To find the critical value of *F* when α is under the lower tail denoted by $F_{\nu_1, \nu_2, 1-\alpha}$, we use the following formula:

$F_{\nu_1, \nu_2, 1-\alpha} = 1/F_{\nu_2, \nu_1, \alpha}$.

(continued)

Table A.10 Critical values of *F* with numerator and denominator degrees of freedom ν_1, ν_2, respectively ($\alpha = 0.10$). *(continued)*

(α = 0.05)

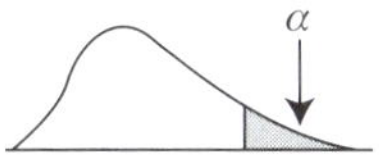

ν_2 \ ν_1	11	12	13	14	15	20	25	30	40	50	75	100	∞
1	243.0	243.9	244.7	245.4	246.0	248.0	249.3	250.1	251.1	251.8	252.6	253.0	254.3
2	19.40	19.41	19.42	19.42	19.43	19.45	19.46	19.46	19.47	19.48	19.48	19.49	19.50
3	8.76	8.74	8.73	8.71	8.70	8.66	8.63	8.62	8.59	8.58	8.56	8.55	8.53
4	5.94	5.91	5.89	5.87	5.86	5.80	5.77	5.75	5.72	5.70	5.68	5.66	5.63
5	4.70	4.68	4.66	4.64	4.62	4.56	4.52	4.50	4.46	4.44	4.42	4.41	4.37
6	4.03	4.00	3.98	3.96	3.94	3.87	3.83	3.81	3.77	3.75	3.73	3.71	3.67
7	3.60	3.57	3.55	3.53	3.51	3.44	3.40	3.38	3.34	3.32	3.29	3.27	3.23
8	3.31	3.28	3.26	3.24	3.22	3.15	3.11	3.08	3.04	3.02	2.99	2.97	2.93
9	3.10	3.07	3.05	3.03	3.01	2.94	2.89	2.86	2.83	2.80	2.77	2.76	2.71
10	2.94	2.91	2.89	2.86	2.85	2.77	2.73	2.70	2.66	2.64	2.60	2.59	2.54
11	2.82	2.79	2.76	2.74	2.72	2.65	2.60	2.57	2.53	2.51	2.47	2.46	2.40
12	2.72	2.69	2.66	2.64	2.62	2.54	2.50	2.47	2.43	2.40	2.37	2.35	2.30
13	2.63	2.60	2.58	2.55	2.53	2.46	2.41	2.38	2.34	2.31	2.28	2.26	2.21
14	2.57	2.53	2.51	2.48	2.46	2.39	2.34	2.31	2.27	2.24	2.21	2.19	2.13
15	2.51	2.48	2.45	2.42	2.40	2.33	2.28	2.25	2.20	2.18	2.14	2.12	2.07
16	2.46	2.42	2.40	2.37	2.35	2.28	2.23	2.19	2.15	2.12	2.09	2.07	2.01
17	2.41	2.38	2.35	2.33	2.31	2.23	2.18	2.15	2.10	2.08	2.04	2.02	1.96
18	2.37	2.34	2.31	2.29	2.27	2.19	2.14	2.11	2.06	2.04	2.00	1.98	1.92
19	2.34	2.31	2.28	2.26	2.23	2.16	2.11	2.07	2.03	2.00	1.96	1.94	1.88
20	2.31	2.28	2.25	2.22	2.20	2.12	2.07	2.04	1.99	1.97	1.93	1.91	1.84
25	2.20	2.16	2.14	2.11	2.09	2.01	1.96	1.92	1.87	1.84	1.80	1.78	1.71
30	2.13	2.09	2.06	2.04	2.01	1.93	1.88	1.84	1.79	1.76	1.72	1.70	1.62
35	2.07	2.01	2.01	1.99	1.96	1.88	1.82	1.79	1.74	1.70	1.66	1.63	1.56
40	2.04	2.00	1.97	1.95	1.92	1.84	1.78	1.74	1.69	1.66	1.61	1.59	1.51
45	2.01	1.97	1.94	1.92	1.89	1.81	1.75	1.71	1.66	1.63	1.58	1.55	1.47
50	1.99	1.95	1.92	1.89	1.87	1.78	1.73	1.69	1.63	1.60	1.55	1.52	1.44
60	1.95	1.92	1.89	1.86	1.84	1.75	1.69	1.65	1.59	1.56	1.51	1.48	1.39
70	1.93	1.89	1.86	1.84	1.81	1.72	1.66	1.62	1.57	1.53	1.48	1.45	1.35
80	1.91	1.88	1.84	1.82	1.79	1.70	1.64	1.60	1.54	1.51	1.45	1.43	1.32
90	1.90	1.86	1.83	1.80	1.78	1.69	1.63	1.59	1.53	1.49	1.44	1.41	1.30
100	1.89	1.85	1.82	1.79	1.77	1.68	1.62	1.57	1.52	1.48	1.42	1.39	1.28
∞	1.79	1.75	1.72	1.69	1.67	1.57	1.51	1.46	1.39	1.35	1.28	1.24	1.00

(continued)

Table A.10 Critical values of F with numerator and denominator degrees of freedom ν_1, ν_2, respectively ($\alpha = 0.10$). *(continued)*

($\alpha = 0.025$)

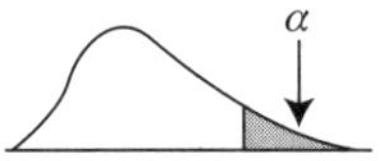

$F\nu_1, \nu_2, \alpha$

ν_2 \ ν_1	1	2	3	4	5	6	7	8	9	10
1	647.79	799.50	864.16	899.58	921.85	937.11	948.22	956.66	963.28	968.63
2	38.51	39.00	39.17	39.25	39.30	39.33	39.36	39.37	39.39	39.40
3	17.44	16.04	15.44	15.10	14.88	14.73	14.62	14.54	14.47	14.42
4	12.22	10.65	9.98	9.60	9.36	9.20	9.07	8.98	8.90	8.84
5	10.01	8.43	7.76	7.39	7.15	6.98	6.85	6.76	6.68	6.62
6	8.81	7.26	6.60	6.23	5.99	5.82	5.70	5.60	5.52	5.46
7	8.07	6.54	5.89	5.52	5.29	5.12	4.99	4.90	4.82	4.76
8	7.57	6.06	5.42	5.05	4.82	4.65	4.53	4.43	4.36	4.30
9	7.21	5.71	5.08	4.72	4.48	4.32	4.20	4.10	4.03	3.96
10	6.94	5.46	4.83	4.47	4.24	4.07	3.95	3.85	3.78	3.72
11	6.72	5.26	4.63	4.28	4.04	3.88	3.76	3.66	3.59	3.53
12	6.55	5.10	4.47	4.12	3.89	3.73	3.61	3.51	3.44	3.37
13	6.41	4.97	4.35	4.00	3.77	3.60	3.48	3.39	3.31	3.25
14	6.30	4.86	4.24	3.89	3.66	3.50	3.38	3.29	3.21	3.15
15	6.20	4.77	4.15	3.80	3.58	3.41	3.29	3.20	3.12	3.06
16	6.12	4.69	4.08	3.73	3.50	3.34	3.22	3.12	3.05	2.99
17	6.04	4.62	4.01	3.66	3.44	3.28	3.16	3.06	2.98	2.92
18	5.98	4.56	3.95	3.61	3.38	3.22	3.10	3.01	2.93	2.87
19	5.92	4.51	3.90	3.56	3.33	3.17	3.05	2.96	2.88	2.82
20	5.87	4.46	3.86	3.51	3.29	3.13	3.01	2.91	2.84	2.77
25	5.69	4.29	3.69	3.35	3.13	2.97	2.85	2.75	2.68	2.61
30	5.57	4.18	3.59	3.25	3.03	2.87	2.75	2.65	2.57	2.51
35	5.49	4.11	3.52	3.18	2.96	2.80	2.68	2.58	2.50	2.44
40	5.42	4.05	3.46	3.13	2.90	2.74	2.62	2.53	2.45	2.39
45	5.38	4.01	3.42	3.09	2.86	2.70	2.58	2.49	2.41	2.35
50	5.34	3.97	3.39	3.05	2.83	2.67	2.55	2.46	2.38	2.32
60	5.29	3.93	3.34	3.01	2.79	2.63	2.51	2.41	2.33	2.27
70	5.25	3.89	3.31	2.97	2.75	2.59	2.47	2.38	2.30	2.24
80	5.22	3.86	3.28	2.95	2.73	2.57	2.45	2.35	2.28	2.21
90	5.20	3.84	3.26	2.93	2.71	2.55	2.43	2.34	2.26	2.19
100	5.18	3.83	3.25	2.92	2.70	2.54	2.42	2.32	2.24	2.18
∞	5.02	3.69	3.12	2.79	2.57	2.41	2.29	2.19	2.11	2.05

To find the critical value of F when α is under the lower tail denoted by $F_{\nu_1,\nu_2,1-\alpha}$, we use the following formula:

$F_{\nu_1,\nu_2,1-\alpha} = 1/F_{\nu_2,\nu_1,\alpha}$.

(continued)

Table A.10 Critical values of *F* with numerator and denominator degrees of freedom ν_1, ν_2, respectively ($\alpha = 0.10$). *(continued)*

(α = 0.025)

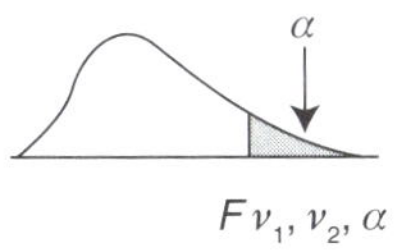

ν_2 \ ν_1	11	12	13	14	15	20	25	30	40	50	75	100
1	973.0	976.7	979.8	982.5	984.9	993.1	998.1	1001.4	1005.6	1008.1	1011.5	1013.2
2	39.41	39.41	39.42	39.43	39.43	39.45	39.46	39.46	39.47	39.48	39.48	39.49
3	14.37	14.34	14.30	14.28	14.25	14.17	14.12	14.08	14.04	14.01	13.97	13.96
4	8.79	8.75	8.71	8.68	8.66	8.56	8.50	8.46	8.41	8.38	8.34	8.32
5	6.57	6.52	6.49	6.46	6.43	6.33	6.27	6.23	6.18	6.14	6.10	6.08
6	5.41	5.37	5.33	5.30	5.27	5.17	5.11	5.07	5.01	4.98	4.94	4.92
7	4.71	4.67	4.63	4.60	4.57	4.47	4.40	4.36	4.31	4.28	4.23	4.21
8	4.24	4.20	4.16	4.13	4.10	4.00	3.94	3.89	3.84	3.81	3.76	3.74
9	3.91	3.87	3.83	3.80	3.77	3.67	3.60	3.56	3.51	3.47	3.43	3.40
10	3.66	3.62	3.58	3.55	3.52	3.42	3.35	3.31	3.26	3.22	3.18	3.15
11	3.47	3.43	3.39	3.36	3.33	3.23	3.16	3.12	3.06	3.03	2.98	2.96
12	3.32	3.28	3.24	3.21	3.18	3.07	3.01	2.96	2.91	2.87	2.82	2.80
13	3.20	3.15	3.12	3.08	3.05	2.95	2.88	2.84	2.78	2.74	2.70	2.67
14	3.09	3.05	3.01	2.98	2.95	2.84	2.78	2.73	2.67	2.64	2.59	2.56
15	3.01	2.96	2.92	2.89	2.86	2.76	2.69	2.64	2.59	2.55	2.50	2.47
16	2.93	2.89	2.85	2.82	2.79	2.68	2.61	2.57	2.51	2.47	2.42	2.40
17	2.87	2.82	2.79	2.75	2.72	2.62	2.55	2.50	2.44	2.41	2.35	2.33
18	2.81	2.77	2.73	2.70	2.67	2.56	2.49	2.44	2.38	2.35	2.30	2.27
19	2.76	2.72	2.68	2.65	2.62	2.51	2.44	2.39	2.33	2.30	2.24	2.22
20	2.72	2.68	2.64	2.60	2.57	2.46	2.40	2.35	2.29	2.25	2.20	2.17
25	2.56	2.51	2.48	2.44	2.41	2.30	2.23	2.18	2.12	2.08	2.02	2.00
30	2.46	2.41	2.37	2.34	2.31	2.20	2.12	2.07	2.01	1.97	1.91	1.88
35	2.39	2.34	2.30	2.27	2.23	2.12	2.05	2.00	1.93	1.89	1.83	1.80
40	2.33	2.29	2.25	2.21	2.18	2.07	1.99	1.94	1.88	1.83	1.77	1.74
45	2.29	2.25	2.21	2.17	2.14	2.03	1.95	1.90	1.83	1.79	1.73	1.69
50	2.26	2.22	2.18	2.14	2.11	1.99	1.92	1.87	1.80	1.75	1.69	1.66
60	2.22	2.17	2.13	2.09	2.06	1.94	1.87	1.82	1.74	1.70	1.63	1.60
70	2.18	2.14	2.10	2.06	2.03	1.91	1.83	1.78	1.71	1.66	1.59	1.56
80	2.16	2.11	2.07	2.03	2.00	1.88	1.81	1.75	1.68	1.63	1.56	1.53
90	2.14	2.09	2.05	2.02	1.98	1.86	1.79	1.73	1.66	1.61	1.54	1.50
100	2.12	2.08	2.04	2.00	1.97	1.85	1.77	1.71	1.64	1.59	1.52	1.48
∞	1.99	1.94	1.90	1.87	1.83	1.71	1.63	1.57	1.48	1.43	1.34	1.30

(continued)

Table A.10 Critical values of *F* with numerator and denominator degrees of freedom ν_1,ν_2, respectively (α = 0.10). *(continued)*

(α = 0.01)

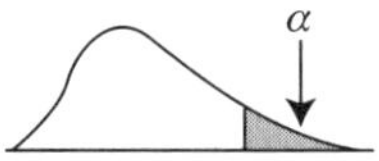

$F\nu_1, \nu_2, \alpha$

ν_2 \ ν_1	1	2	3	4	5	6	7	8	9	10
1	4052	5000	5403	5625	5764	5859	5928	5981	6022	6056
2	98.50	99.00	99.17	99.25	99.30	99.33	99.36	99.37	99.39	99.40
3	34.12	30.82	29.46	28.71	28.24	27.91	27.67	27.49	27.35	27.23
4	21.20	18.00	16.69	15.98	15.52	15.21	14.98	14.80	14.66	14.55
5	16.26	13.27	12.06	11.39	10.97	10.67	10.46	10.29	10.16	10.05
6	13.75	10.92	9.78	9.15	8.75	8.47	8.26	8.10	7.98	7.87
7	12.25	9.55	8.45	7.85	7.46	7.19	6.99	6.84	6.72	6.62
8	11.26	8.65	7.59	7.01	6.63	6.37	6.18	6.03	5.91	5.81
9	10.56	8.02	6.99	6.42	6.06	5.80	5.61	5.47	5.35	5.26
10	10.04	7.56	6.55	5.99	5.64	5.39	5.20	5.06	4.94	4.85
11	9.65	7.21	6.22	5.67	5.32	5.07	4.89	4.74	4.63	4.54
12	9.33	6.93	5.95	5.41	5.06	4.82	4.64	4.50	4.39	4.30
13	9.07	6.70	5.74	5.21	4.86	4.62	4.44	4.30	4.19	4.10
14	8.86	6.51	5.56	5.04	4.69	4.46	4.28	4.14	4.03	3.94
15	8.68	6.36	5.42	4.89	4.56	4.32	4.14	4.00	3.89	3.80
16	8.53	6.23	5.29	4.77	4.44	4.20	4.03	3.89	3.78	3.69
17	8.40	6.11	5.18	4.67	4.34	4.10	3.93	3.79	3.68	3.59
18	8.29	6.01	5.09	4.58	4.25	4.01	3.84	3.71	3.60	3.51
19	8.18	5.93	5.01	4.50	4.17	3.94	3.77	3.63	3.52	3.43
20	8.10	5.85	4.94	4.43	4.10	3.87	3.70	3.56	3.46	3.37
25	7.77	5.57	4.68	4.18	3.85	3.63	3.46	3.32	3.22	3.13
30	7.56	5.39	4.51	4.02	3.70	3.47	3.30	3.17	3.07	2.98
35	7.42	5.27	4.40	3.91	3.59	3.37	3.20	3.07	2.96	2.88
40	7.31	5.18	4.31	3.83	3.51	3.29	3.12	2.99	2.89	2.80
45	7.23	5.11	4.25	3.77	3.45	3.23	3.07	2.94	2.83	2.74
50	7.17	5.06	4.20	3.72	3.41	3.19	3.02	2.89	2.78	2.70
60	7.08	4.98	4.13	3.65	3.34	3.12	2.95	2.82	2.72	2.63
70	7.01	4.92	4.07	3.60	3.29	3.07	2.91	2.78	2.67	2.59
80	6.96	4.88	4.04	3.56	3.26	3.04	2.87	2.74	2.64	2.55
90	6.93	4.85	4.01	3.53	3.23	3.01	2.84	2.72	2.61	2.52
100	6.90	4.82	3.98	3.51	3.21	2.99	2.82	2.69	2.59	2.50
∞	6.63	4.61	3.78	3.32	3.02	2.80	2.64	2.51	2.41	2.32

To find the critical value of *F* when α is under the lower tail denoted by $F_{\nu_1,\nu_2,1-\alpha}$, we use the following formula:

$F_{\nu_1,\nu_2,1-\alpha} = 1/F_{\nu_2,\nu_1,\alpha}$.

(continued)

Table A.10 Critical values of *F* with numerator and denominator degrees of freedom ν_1, ν_2, respectively ($\alpha = 0.10$). *(continued)*

(α = 0.01)

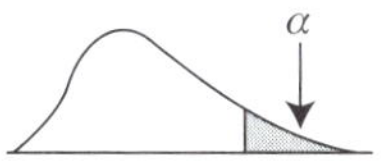

$F\nu_1, \nu_2, \alpha$

ν_2 \ ν_1	11	12	13	14	15	20	25	30	40	50	75	100
1	6056	6106	6130	6140	6157	6209	6240	6261	6287	6303	6320	6334
2	99.41	99.42	99.42	99.43	99.43	99.45	99.46	99.47	99.47	99.48	99.49	99.49
3	27.13	27.05	26.98	26.92	26.87	26.69	2658	26.50	26.41	26.35	26.28	26.24
4	14.45	14.37	14.31	14.25	14.20	14.02	13.91	13.84	13.75	13.69	13.61	13.58
5	9.96	9.89	9.82	9.77	9.72	9.55	9.45	9.38	9.29	9.24	9.17	9.13
6	7.79	7.72	7.66	7.61	7.56	7.40	7.30	7.23	7.14	7.09	7.02	6.99
7	6.54	6.47	6.41	6.36	6.31	6.16	6.06	5.99	5.91	5.86	5.79	5.75
8	5.73	5.67	5.61	5.56	5.52	5.36	5.26	5.20	5.12	5.07	5.00	4.96
9	5.18	5.11	5.05	5.01	4.96	4.81	4.71	4.65	4.57	4.52	4.45	4.41
10	4.77	4.71	4.65	4.60	4.56	4.41	4.31	4.25	4.17	4.12	4.05	4.01
11	4.46	4.40	4.34	4.29	4.25	4.10	4.01	3.94	3.86	3.81	3.74	3.71
12	4.22	4.16	4.10	4.05	4.01	3.86	3.76	3.70	3.62	3.57	3.50	3.47
13	4.02	3.96	3.91	3.86	3.82	3.66	3.57	3.51	3.43	3.38	3.31	3.27
14	3.86	3.80	3.75	3.70	3.66	3.51	3.41	3.35	3.27	3.22	3.15	3.11
15	3.73	3.67	3.61	3.56	3.52	3.37	3.28	3.21	3.13	3.08	3.01	2.98
16	3.62	3.55	3.50	3.45	3.41	3.26	3.16	3.10	3.02	2.97	2.90	2.86
17	3.52	3.46	3.40	3.35	3.31	3.16	3.07	3.00	2.92	2.87	2.80	2.76
18	3.43	3.37	3.32	3.27	3.23	3.08	2.98	2.92	2.84	2.78	2.71	2.68
19	3.36	3.30	3.24	3.19	3.15	3.00	2.91	2.84	2.76	2.71	2.64	2.60
20	3.29	3.23	3.18	3.13	3.09	2.94	2.84	2.78	2.69	2.64	2.57	2.54
25	3.06	2.99	2.94	2.89	2.85	2.70	2.60	2.54	2.45	2.40	2.33	2.29
30	2.91	2.84	2.79	2.74	2.70	2.55	2.45	2.39	2.30	2.25	2.17	2.13
35	2.80	2.74	2.69	2.64	2.60	2.44	2.35	2.28	2.19	2.13	2.06	2.02
40	2.73	2.66	2.61	2.56	2.52	2.3 7	2.27	2.20	2.11	2.06	1.98	1.94
45	2.67	2.61	2.55	2.51	2.46	2.31	2.21	2.14	2.05	2.00	1.92	1.88
50	2.63	2.56	2.51	2.46	2.42	2.27	2.17	2.10	2.01	1.95	1.87	1.82
60	2.56	2.34	2.44	2.39	2.19	2.03	2.10	1.86	1.76	1.88	1.79	1.75
70	2.51	2.45	2.40	2.35	2.31	2.15	2.05	1.98	1.87	1.83	1.74	1.70
80	2.48	2.42	2.36	2.31	2.27	2.12	2.01	1.94	1.85	1.79	1.70	1.65
90	2.45	2.39	2.33	2.27	2.24	2.09	1.99	1.92	1.82	1.76	1.67	1.62
100	2.43	2.37	2.31	2.27	2.22	2.07	1.97	1.89	1.80	1.74	1.65	1.60
∞	2.25	2.18	2.12	2.08	2.04	1.88	1.77	1.70	1.59	1.52	1.42	1.36

(continued)

Bibliography

ANSI/ASQ. 2003. *ANSI/ASQ Z1.4-2003: Sampling Procedures and Tables for Inspection by Attributes.* Milwaukee, WI: ASQ Quality Press.

———. 2003. *ANSI/ASQ Z1.9-2003: Sampling Procedures and Tables for Inspection by Variables for Percent Nonconforming.* Milwaukee, WI: ASQ Quality Press.

Automotive Industry Action Group (AIAG) and Measurement Systems Analysis (MSA) Work Group. 2002. *Measurement Systems Analysis Reference Manual.* 3rd ed. Dearborn, MI: Automotive Industry Action Group Press.

Barrentine, L. 2003. *Concepts for R&R Studies.* 2nd ed. Milwaukee, WI: ASQ Quality Press.

Berger, R., D. Benbow, A. Elshennawy, and H. F. Walker. 2007. *The Certified Quality Engineer Handbook.* 2nd ed. Milwaukee, WI: ASQ Quality Press.

Bothe, D. R. 2002. Discussion paper. *Journal of Quality Technology* 34 (1): 32–37.

Boyles, R. A. 1991. "The Taguchi Capability Index." *Journal of Quality Technology* 23 (1): 17–26.

Brown, N. 1966. "Zero Defects the Easy Way with Target Area Control." *Modern Machine Shop*, 96–100.

Champ, C. M., and W. H. Woodall. 1987. "Exact Results for Shewhart Control Charts with Supplementary Run Rules." *Technometrics* 29 (4): 393–399.

Chan, L. K., S. W. Cheng, and F. A. Spring. 1988. "A New Measure of Process Capability: C_{pm}." *Journal of Quality Technology* 20:162–175.

Chen, S. M., and N. F. Hsu. 1995. "The Asymptotic Distribution of the Process Capability Index C_{pmk}." *Commun. Statist.-Theory and Method* 24 (5): 1279–1291.

Cochran, W. G. 1977. *Sampling Techniques.* 3rd ed. New York: John Wiley & Sons.

Crowder, S. V. 1987. "Computation of ARL for Combined Individual Measurements and Moving Range Charts." *Journal of Quality Technology* 19 (1): 98–102.

———. 1989. "Design of Exponentially Weighted Moving Average Schemes." *Journal of Quality Technology* 21 (2): 155–162.

Deleryd, M. 1996. "Process Capability Studies in Theory and Practice." Licentiate thesis, Lulea University of Technology, Lulea, Sweden.

Deming, W. E. 1950. *Some Theory of Sampling.* New York: John Wiley & Sons.

———. 1951. *Elementary Principles of the Statistical Control of Quality.* 2nd ed. Tokyo: Nippon Kagaku Gijutsu Remmei.

———. 1975. "On Some Statistical Aids toward Economic Production." *Interfaces* 5 (4): 5.

———. 1982. *Quality, Productivity, and Competitive Position.* Cambridge, MA: MIT, Center for Advanced Engineering Study.

———. 1986. *Out of the Crisis.* Boston, MA: MIT, Center for Advanced Engineering Study.

Duncan, A. J. 1986. *Quality Control and Industrial Statistics.* 5th ed. Homewood, IL: Irwin.

Ford Motor Company. 1984. *Continuing Process Control and Process Capability Improvement*, Dearborn, MI.

Govindarajulu, Z. 1999. *Elements of Sampling Theory and Methods.* Upper Saddle River, NJ: Prentice Hall.

Gryna, F. M., R.C.H. Chua, and J. A. DeFeo. 2007. *Jurans Quality Planning & Analysis for Enterprise Quality.* 5th ed. New York: McGraw-Hill Publishing.

Gupta, B. C. 2005. "A New Process Capability Index C_{pnst}." *Journal of Combinatorics, Information & System Sciences* 30:67–79.

Gupta, B. C., and C. Peng. 2004. "On the Distributional and Inferential Characterization of the Process Capability Index C_{pnst}." *Journal of Statistics and Applications* 1 (1): 63–72.

Gupta, B. C., and F. H. Walker. 2005. *Applied Statistics for the Six Sigma Green Belt.* Milwaukee, WI: ASQ Quality Press.

Hawkins, D. M. 1981. "A CUSUM for a Scale Parameter." *Journal of Quality Technology* 13 (4): 228–231.

———. 1993. "Cumulative Sum Control Charting, an Underutilized SPC Tool." *Quality Engineering* 5 (3): 463–477.

Hawkins, D. M., and D. H. Olwell. 1998. *Cumulative Sum Charts and Charting for Quality Improvement.* New York: Springer-Verlag.

Hsiang, T. C., and G. Taguchi. 1985. "A Tutorial on Quality Control and Assurance—The Taguchi Methods." ASA annual meeting, Las Vegas, NV.

IBM (International Business Machines Corporation). 1984. *Process Control, Capability and Improvement.* Thornwood, NY: The Quality Institute.

Juran, J., and A. B. Godfrey. 1999. *Juran's Quality Handbook.* 5th ed. New York: McGraw-Hill Publishing.

Juran, J. M., F. M. Gryna, and R. S. Bingham Jr. 1974. *Quality Control Handbook.* New York: McGraw-Hill.

Kane, V. E. 1986. "Process Capability Indices." *Journal of Quality Technology* 18:41–52.

Kotz, S., and C. R. Lovelace. 1998. *Process Capability Indices in Theory and Practice*. London and New York: Arnold.

Ledolter, J., and A. Swersey. 1997. "An Evaluation of PRE-Control." *Journal of Quality Technology* 29 (2): 163–171.

Lohr, S. L. 1999. *Sampling: Design and Analysis*. Pacific Grove, CA: Duxbury Press.

Lucas, J. M. 1982. "Combined Shewhart-CUSUM Quality Control Schemes." *Journal of Quality Technology* 14 (2): 51–59.

Lucas, J. M., and R. B. Crosier. 1982. "Fast Initial Response for CUSUM Quality Control Schemes." *Technometrics* 24 (3): 199–205.

Lucas, J. M., and M. S. Saccucci. 1990. "Exponentially Weighted Moving Average Control Schemes: Properties and Enhancements." *Technometrics* 32 (1): 1–29.

Montgomery, D. C. 2005a. *Design and Analysis of Experiments*. 6th ed. New York: John Wiley & Sons.

———. 2005b. *Introduction to Statistical Quality Control*. 5th ed. New York: John Wiley & Sons.

Ott, E., E. Schilling, and D. Neubauer. 2005. *Process Quality Control: Troubleshooting and Interpretation of Data*. 4th ed. Milwaukee, WI: ASQ Quality Press.

Pearn, W. L., and S. Kotz. 1994. "Application Element's Method for Calculating Second and Third Generation Process Capability Indices for Nonnormal Pearsonian Populations." *Quality Engineering* 7 (1): 139–145.

Pearn, W. L., S. Kotz, and N. L. Johnson. 1992. "Distributional and Inferential Properties of Process Capability Indices." *Journal of Quality Technology* 24:216–231.

Quesenberry, C. P. 1997. *SPC Methods for Quality Improvement*. New York: John Wiley and Sons.

Roberts, S. W. 1959. "Control Chart Tests Based on Geometric Moving Averages." *Technometrics* 1 (3): 239–250.

Ryan, T. P. 2000. *Statistical Methods for Quality Improvement*. 2nd ed. New York: John Wiley & Sons.

Scheaffer, R. L., et al. 2006. *Elementary Survey Sampling*. 6th ed. Belmont, CA: Duxbury Press.

Schilling, E. G. 1982. *Acceptance Sampling in Quality Control*. New York: Marcel Dekker.

Shainin, D. 1984. "Better Than Good Old X-Bar and R Charts." In *ASQC Quality Congress Transactions*, 302–307. Milwaukee, WI: ASQC Quality Press.

Shewhart, W. A. 1980. *Economic Control of Quality of Manufactured Product*. New York: D. Van Nostrand Company.

Smith, G. 1991. *Statistical Process Control and Quality Improvement*. New York: Macmillan Publishing.

Spiring, F. A. 1997. "A Unifying Approach to Process Capability Indices." *Journal of Quality Technology* 29 (1): 49–58.

Stephens, K. S. 2001. *The Handbook of Applied Acceptance Sampling Plans, Procedures and Principles*. Milwaukee, WI: ASQ Quality Press.

Taguchi, G. 1986. *Introduction to Quality Engineering*. Tokyo: Asian Productivity Organization.

Traver, R. 1985. "Pre-Control: A Good Alternative to X-Bar–R Charts." ASQC *Quality Progress*, September, 11–14.

Urdhwareshee, H. 2006. "The Power of Pre-Control." http://www.symphonytech.com/articles/precontrol.htm.

Van Dobben de Bruyn, C. S. 1968. "Cumulative Sum Tests." In *Theory and Practice.* London: Griffin.

Vännman, K. 1995. "A Unified Approach to Capability Indices." *Statistica Sinica* 5:805–820.

Wallgren, E. 1996. "Properties of the Taguchi Capability Index for Markov Dependent Quality Characteristic." University of Oreboro, Sweden.

Wescott, R. 2007. *The Certified Manager of Quality/Organizational Excellence Handbook.* 3rd ed. Milwaukee, WI: ASQ Quality Press.

Western Electric. 1956. *Statistical Quality Control Handbook.* Indianapolis, IN: Western Electric Corporation.

Wheeler, D., and D. Chambers. 1992. *Understanding Statistical Process Control.* 2nd ed. Knoxville, TN: SPC Press.

Wheeler, D., and R. Lyday. 1989. *Evaluating the Measurement Process.* 2nd ed. Knoxville, TN: SPC Press.

Index

Page numbers followed by *f* or *t* refer to figures or tables, respectively.

A

acceptable quality limit (AQL), 178, 194
acceptance number, sampling plans and, 180–182
acceptance sampling, 2. *See also* sampling
  by attributes, 177
  double sampling plans, 184
  intent of, 173–174
  multiple sampling plans, 186
  standards, 188–193
  switching procedures, 190–191, 190*f*
  by variables, 193–194
accuracy, vs. precision, 151, 151*f*
accuracy of measurement system, defined, 151
action on output, 51–52
action on process, 51
actions on system, for variation, 53
alpha (α) risk, 7–9
ANOVA, MSA based on, 156–162
ANSI/ASQ Z1.4-2003, 188–189, 205*f*, 206*f*, 207*f*, 208*f*, 209–210*f*
  levels of inspection in, 189–191
  types of sampling and, 191–193
ANSI/ASQ Z1.9-2003, 194–198, 211*f*, 212*f*, 213–221*f*, 222*f*
  AQL levels in, 195
  Form 1 for, 195
  Form 2 for, 195
  structure and organization of, 195*f*
AOQ. *See* average outgoing quality (AOQ)
AOQL. *See* average outgoing quality limit (AOQL)
applied statistics, SQC and, 2–3, 3*f*
AQL. *See* acceptable quality limit (AQL)
ARL. *See* average run length (ARL)
ASN. *See* average sample number (ASN)
assignable causes, of variation. *See* special causes, of variation
asymptotically normal, 139
attributes
  acceptance sampling by, 177
  control charts for, 83–84, 85*t*
    c charts, 93–96
    np charts, 92–93
    p charts, 85–90
    u charts, 96–100
  defined, 83
attribute sampling plans. *See also* sampling plans
  ANSI/ASQ Z1.4-2003 and, 189
  double, 184–185
  multiple, 186
  single, 182–184
  vs. variables sampling plans, 193–194

average outgoing quality (AOQ), 178–179
for double/multiple sampling plans, 186
average outgoing quality limit (AOQL), 179–180
for double/multiple sampling plans, 186
average quality protection, 175
average run length (ARL), 57–58
of two-sided control chart, 106
average sample number (ASN), 186–188

B

bad decisions, risk associated with making, 7–9
beta (β) risk, 7–9
binomial distribution, 85, 86, 175, 176

C

calibration, 45, 60
capability analysis, 2
cause-and-effect diagram, 43, 47–48, 48*f*
c control charts, 93–96
JMP for creating, 282–283
MINITAB for, 240
center line (CL), for control charts, 54
central limit theorem (CLT), 148, 148*f*
check sheets, 43–45, 44*f*
cluster random sampling, 15, 32–37. *See also* sampling
advantages of, 33
confidence interval for population mean for, 34–37
confidence interval for population total for, 34–37
determination of sample size for, 37
estimation of population mean for, 33–34
estimation of population total for, 33–34
one-stage, 33
two-stage, 33
combined Shewhart-CUSUM control charts, 115–116
common causes, of variation, 52
confidence coefficients, 15
confidence intervals, 15
conforming, use of term, 83
consumer risk, 178
defined, 8
continuous sampling plans, 201
types of, 201–203
control charts, 43, 54*f*
action on output for, 51–52
action on process for, 51
for attributes, 83–84, 85*t*
c charts, 93–96
np charts, 92–93
p charts, 85–90
u charts, 96–100
benefits of, 56
center line for, 54
exponentially weighted moving average (*see* exponentially weighted moving average (EWMA) control charts)
lower control limit for, 54
moving average (*see* moving average (MA) control charts)
preparation for use of, 55–56
process evaluation for, 51
rational samples for, 57
for separating separate causes from common causes, 53
Shewhart (*see* Shewhart control charts)
upper control limit for, 54
uses of, 54
variation and, 52–53
control limits (CL)
calculation of, for Shewhart X bar and *R* control charts, 61–64
calculation of, for Shewhart X bar and *S* control charts, 73–75
for *np* control charts, 92–93
correlation between characteristics, determining, 55
critical defects, 189

cumulative sum (CUSUM) control charts, 101–102. *See also* combined Shewhart-CUSUM control charts
basic assumptions of, 102
for controlling process variability, 116–117
designing, 104–106
detecting small shifts and, 101
FIR feature for, 112–115, 245
JMP for creating, 286–288
MINITAB for, 243–245
one-sided, 104–106, 115
two-sided, 104–106
two-sided, using numerical procedure, 106–112
vs. Shewhart X bar-*R* control charts, 102–104, 105*f*
CUSUM control charts. *See* cumulative sum (CUSUM) control charts

D

decision making, on quantitative data, 5
defect concentration diagram, 43, 48–49, 49*f*
defect rate, 167
defects
critical, 189
major, 189
minor, 189
Deming, W. Edwards, 39–40
design of experiments (DOE), SQC and, 2–3
distinct categories, determining number of, 158–159
Dodge-Romig tables, 193
Dodge's continuous sampling plans, 201–202
double sampling, 191–192, 193*f*
double sampling plans
AOQ curve for, 186
AOQL for, 186
double, 184
OC curve for, 184–185
downward shift, 102, 106, 115, 243, 286

E

Economic Control of Quality of Manufactured Product (Shewhart), 39
environment
as a category in a cause-and-effect diagram, 48, 48*f*, 49*f*
as cause of part-to-part variation, 149
as part of a process, 41, 55, 127
in preparing control charts, 55
error of estimation, 15
estimate, 15
estimator, 15
EWMA control charts. *See* exponentially weighted moving average (EWMA) control charts
exponentially weighted moving average (EWMA) control charts, 101–102, 120–125
JMP for creating, 290–292
MINITAB for, 247–249

F

fast initial response (FIR) feature, for CUSUM control charts, 112–115, 245
fieldworkers, 13
finite populations, 12
FIR feature. *See* fast initial response (FIR) feature, for CUSUM control charts
fishbone. *See* cause-and-effect diagram
Form 1, for ANSI/ASQ Z1.9-2003, 195
Form 2, for ANSI/ASQ Z1.9-2003, 195

G

Gage repeatability and reproducibility (Gage R&R) study, 147. *See also* measurement system analysis (MSA); measurement system performance
- ANOVA method for, 156–159
- graphical representation of, 159–162, 256–259
- JMP for, 293–298, 295*f*, 296*f*, 297*f*, 298*f*
- MINITAB for, 250–259
- total, 152

geometric series, 121–122

H

histograms, 43

I

individual observations, Shewhart control charts for, 69

infinite populations, 12

inspection
- levels of, 189–191
- sampling vs. 100 percent, 174–175

interaction between instruments and operators, 149, 152

Ishikawa diagram. *See* cause-and-effect diagram

J

JMP software package
- for capability analysis, 275–277
- for creating *c* control charts, 282–283, 282*f*, 283*f*
- for creating CUSUM control charts, 286–288, 287*f*, 288*f*
- for creating EWMA control charts, 290–292, 291*f*, 292*f*
- creating new data table for, 264–265
- for creating *p* control charts, 277–281, 280*f*
- for creating *u* control charts, 284–286, 284*f*, 285*f*
- for creating UWMA chart, 288–290, 289*f*, 290*f*
- for Gage R&R study, 293–298
- getting started with, 263–264
- for measurement system capability analysis, 292–298, 295*f*, 296*f*, 297*f*, 298*f*
- normal quantile plot, 279*f*
- opening existing files, 265
- print options, 266
- for process capability analysis, 275–277, 278*f*, 279*f*
- saving files, 265–266
- Starter, 261–262
- for Shewhart control chart for individual observations, 273–275
- for Shewhart Xbar and *R* control charts, 268–270
- for Shewhart Xbar and *S* control charts
  - with equal sample size, 270–272
  - with sample size variable, 272–273
- using, 261–263
- using images for reporting, 267–268

L

linearity, 151, 151*f*

line graphs. *See* run charts

local actions, for variation, 53

lot-by-lot sampling, 175

lot size, sampling plans and, 180–182

lot tolerance percent defective (LTPD), 178

lower control limit (LCL), for control charts, 54

LTPD. *See* lot tolerance percent defective (LTPD)

M

MA control charts. *See* moving average (MA) control charts

major defects, 189

margin of error, 15

MCI. *See* measurement capability index (MCI)
measurement
  defined, 147
  volume of operations and, 7
measurement capability index (MCI), 150, 162
  as percentage of process specification, 163
  as percentage of process variation, 162–163
measurement system, defined, 147
measurement system analysis (MSA), 147
  based on ANOVA, 156–162
  based on range, 150–156
measurement system capability analysis
  computer resources for, 249–259
  JMP for, 292–298, 295*f*, 296*f*, 297*f*, 298*f*
  MINITAB for, 249–259
measurement system performance, evaluating, 149–162. *See also* Gage repeatability and reproducibility (Gage R&R) study
measurement system variation, 249, 292–293
MIL-STD-1235B, 202–203
MINITAB
  for *c* control charts, 240
  creating new worksheet, 226–227
  for CUSUM control charts, 243–245
  for EWMA control charts, 247–249
  getting starting with, 226
  for MA control charts, 245–247
  for measurement system capability analysis, 249–259
  for *np* control charts, 239
  for *p* control charts, 238–239
  print options for, 228
  for process capability analysis, 235–237
  retrieving saved MINITAB data file, 227
  saving data file, 227
  saving project, 227–228
  for Shewhart control chart for individual observations, 230–231
  for Shewhart Xbar and *R* control charts, 228–229
  for Shewhart Xbar and *S* control charts
    equal sample size, 231–233
    sample size variable, 233–235
  for *u* control charts, 241–243
  using, 225–226
minor defects, 189
moving average (MA) control charts, 101–102, 117–120
  MINITAB for, 245–247
moving range (MR), 69
MSA. *See* measurement system analysis (MSA)
multiple sampling, 191–192, 193*f*
multiple sampling plans, 186
  AOQ curve for, 186
  AOQL for, 186

N

near zero, 167
nonconforming, use of term, 83
normal inspection to reduced inspection, 190–191
normal inspection to tightened inspection, 190
np control charts, 92–93
  JMP for creating, 281
  MINITAB for, 239

O

OC curve. *See* operating characteristic (OC) curve
100 percent inspection, 174–175
one-sided CUSUM control charts, 104–106, 115
one-stage cluster random sampling, 33
operating characteristic (OC) curve, 57, 59–60, 175–176
  for double sampling plans, 184–185
  plotting, 176–177

P

Pareto charts, 43, 45–46, 45*f*, 47*f*
part-to-part variation, 149, 249, 292–293
patterns
- of defects, 45, 48–49
- of nonrandomness, 64, 66
- presence of unusual, 87
- of random variation, 54, 55
- using run charts to identify, 50–51,
- Western Electric criteria, 64

p control charts, 85–90
- control chart for fraction nonconforming with variable samples, 89–90
- control limits for, 85–87
- interpreting, for fraction nonconforming, 87–89
- JMP for creating, 277–281, 280*f*
- MINITAB for, 238–239

point estimate. *See* estimate
Poisson distribution, 94, 175, 176
population, sampled, 13
population mean, confidence interval for, 20
- for cluster random sampling, 34–37
- for simple random sampling, 20
- for systematic random sampling, 30

population mean, estimation of, 16–19
- for cluster random sampling, 33–34
- for simple random sampling, 16–19
- for stratified random sampling, 22–24
- for systematic random sampling, 28–30

populations
- defined, 12
- finite, 12
- infinite, 12
- target, 12

population total
- confidence interval for, 20
  - for cluster random sampling, 34–37
  - for simple random sampling, 20
  - for systematic random sampling, 30
- estimation of, 16–19
  - for cluster random sampling, 33–34
  - for simple random sampling, 16–19
  - for stratified random sampling, 22–24
  - for systematic random sampling, 28–30

practical versus theoretical difference, 5–6
precision, vs. accuracy, 151, 151*f*
PRE-control, 2
- advantages of, 170–171
- background of, 165–166
- color-coding scheme for, 167–168
- disadvantages of, 171–172
- goals of, 166
- mechanics of, 168–169
- necessary conditions for valid, 166–167
- statistical basis for, 170

pretests, 13
probability, defined, 8
process
- defined, 1, 41
- flowchart of, 41*f*
- variation and, 52

process capability, 79–81, 80*f*
process capability analysis, 128–129
- implementing, 129
- JMP for creating, 275–277
- MINITAB for, 235–237
- ways of using results of, 129

process capability indices (PCIs), 127–145, 166
- C_p, 130–134
- C_{pk}, 135–136
- C_{pm}, 136–138
- C_{pmk}, 138–139
- C_{pnst}, 139–144
- defined, 128
- development of, 127–130
- first-generation, 130
- flowchart of, 128*f*
- P_p and P_{pk}, 144–145

process evaluation, 1
process Six Sigma, order of topics in, 3–4, 4*f*

process variability, CUSUM control charts for controlling, 116–117
producer risk, 178
  defined, 8

Q

qualitative data, defined, 5
quality
  benefits of better, 40–41
  defined, 40
quality characteristics, 7, 56, 79, 83
  behavior of, 42
  examples of attributes, 84
  reducing variation of, 43
  using a *p* chart to study, 85
quality control charts, 39, 42
  categories of, 42
quantitative data, decision-making and, 5

R

random causes. *See* common causes, of variation
range method, 150
rational samples, for control charts, 57
reduced inspection to normal inspection, 191
repeatability, 149
  defined, 150–151, 152–153
reproducibility, 149
  defined, 151, 153
risks
  bad decisions and, 7–9
  consumer, 8, 178
  producer, 8, 178
run, defined, 57
run charts, 43, 49*f*, 50–51

S

sample, defined, 12
sample designs, 11
  cluster random sampling, 15
  simple random sampling, 13
  stratified random sampling, 13, 14
  systematic random sampling, 13, 14
sampled population, defined, 13
sample mean, defined, 17
samples, 5*f*, 7
  determining size of, 57–60
sample size
  average run length and, 57–58
  determination of, 20–21
    average run length for, 57–58
    for cluster random sampling, 37
    operating characteristic curve for, 57, 59–60
    for simple random sampling, 20–21
    for stratified random sampling, 26–27
    for systematic random sampling, 30–32
  operating characteristic curve and, 57, 59–60
  sampling plans and, 180–182
  variable, for Shewhart X bar and *S* control charts, 76–79
sample statistics, calculation of, for Shewhart X bar and *R* control charts, 60–61
sample variance, defined, 17
sampling
  acceptance (*see* acceptance sampling)
  advantages of, 174
  basic concepts of, 11–15
  cluster random (*see* cluster random sampling)
  concepts of, 175–182
  double, 191–192, 193*f*
  multiple, 191–192, 193*f*
  simple random (*see* simple random sampling)
  single, 191–192, 193*f*
  standards, 188–193
  stratified random (*see* stratified random sampling)
  systematic random (*see* systematic random sampling)
  types of, ASI/ASQ Z1.4-2003 and, 191–193

sampling frame, defined, 13
sampling inspection, 174–175
sampling plans. *See also* attribute sampling plans
  acceptance number and, 180–182
  continuous, 201–203
  lot size and, 180–182
  sample size and, 180–182
  sequential, 199–201
  standards for, 188–193
  variables, 193–198
scatter diagram, 43
sequential sampling plans, 199–201
  decision areas for, 199*f*
Shainin, Dorian, 165
Shewhart, Walter A., 39, 42
Shewhart control charts. *See also* combined Shewhart-CUSUM control charts
  for individual observations, MINITAB for, 230–231
  individual observations for, 69–72
Shewhart Xbar and *R* control charts
  calculation of control limits for, 61–64
  calculation of sample statistics for, 60–61
  constructing, with known process mean and process standard deviation, 230
  constructing, with MINITAB, 228–229
  extending current control limits for future control for, 66–68
  interpretation of, 64–66
  JMP software package for, 268–270
  rules for preparing, 60
  vs. CUSUM control charts, 102–104
  when process mean and process standard deviation are known, 68–69
Shewhart Xbar and *S* control charts
  calculation of control limits for, 73–75
  constructing, with MINITAB
    for equal sample size, 231–233
    for variable sample size, 233–235
  vs. *R* charts, 72–73
  when sample size is variable, 76–79
simple random sample, defined, 15–16
simple random sampling, 13, 14, 15–21. *See also* sampling
  confidence interval for population mean for, 20
  confidence interval for population total for, 20
  determination of sample size for, 20–21
  estimation of population mean for, 16–19
  estimation of population total for, 16–19
single sampling plans, 182–184, 191–192, 193*f*
Six Sigma
  order of topics in process of, 3
  transactional, 3–4, 4*f*
Six Sigma Green Belt, statistical quality control and, 1
SPC. *See* statistical process control (SPC)
special causes, of variation, 52
SQC. *See* statistical quality control (SQC)
stability, defined, 151
stable process, 79
standard normal distribution, 167, 170
statistical control, defined, 166
statistical process control (SPC), 1–2, 41–51
  tools of, 43–51
statistical quality control (SQC), 2
  applied statistics and, 2–4
  defined, 1
  design of experiments and, 2–4
  relationships among tools of, 165*f*
  role of statistics in, 4–5
  Six Sigma Green Belt and, 1
  tool types of, 2, 2*f*
  understanding variability with, 148–149
  use of modern, 39
statistical significance, 5–6

statistics
applied, SQC and, 2–4
role of, in SQC, 4–5
stem-and-leaf diagram, 43
stratified random sampling, 13, 14, 21–27. *See also* sampling; stratified random sampling
advantages of, 21–22
confidence interval for population mean for, 24–27
confidence interval for population total for, 24–27
determination of sample size for, 26–27
estimation of population mean for, 22–24
estimation of population total for, 22–24
process of, 22
systematic random sampling, 13, 14, 27–32
advantages of, 27–28
confidence interval for population mean for, 30
confidence interval for population total for, 30
determination of sample size for, 30–32
estimation of population mean for, 28–30
estimation of population total for, 28–30

T

target populations, 12
test significance (α), level of, 5–6
tightened inspection to normal inspection, 190
time series graphs. *See* run charts
total Gage R&R variability, 152
total process variation, 149. *See also* variation
measurement system variation, 249
part-to-part variation source, 249
total variability, components of, 151–152
transactional Six Sigma, order of topics in, 3–4, 4*f*
two-sided CUSUM control charts, 104–106
using numerical procedure, 106–112
two-stage cluster random sampling, 33
Type I error, 7–9
Type II error, 7–9

U

u control charts, 96–100
JMP for creating, 284–286
MINITAB for, 241–243
uniformly weighted moving average (UWMA) chart, JMP for creating, 288–290
upper control line (UCL), for control charts, 54
upward shift, 102, 106, 115, 243, 286
UWMA. *See* uniformly weighted moving average (UWMA) chart, JMP for creating

V

variability
in measurement process, 148–149
in production/service delivery process, 148
total, components of, 151–152
variable, defined, 42
variables sampling plans, 193–198
ANSI/ASQ Z1.9-2003 and, 194–198
benefits of, over attribute plans, 193–194
when standard deviation is known, 203–204
variation. *See also* total process variation
actions on system for, 53
causes of, 42, 127
common causes of, 52
controlling, 42
defined, 42
due to measurement instruments, 149
due to operators, 149

local actions for, 53
minimizing unnecessary, 56
part-to-part, 149
special causes of, 52
vendor certification, 174
vendor qualification, 174
V-mask, 106, 244

W

Western Electric criteria
for detecting small shifts, 101–102
for determining nonrandom patterns on control charts, 64